ASHLEY S. CRANE, Ph.D. (2007) in Theology, Murdoch University, is Principal of Harvest West Bible College in Perth, Western Australia.

Israel's Restoration

Supplements

to

Vetus Testamentum

VOLUME 122

Israel's Restoration

A Textual-Comparative Exploration of

Ezekiel 36–39

By

Ashley S. Crane

BRILL

LEIDEN • BOSTON

2008

This book is printed on acid-free paper.

Library of Congress Cataloging-in-Publication Data

Crane, Ashley S.
   Israel's restoration : a textual-comparative exploration of Ezekiel 36–39 /
by Ashley S. Crane.
      p. cm. — (Supplements to Vetus Testamentum ; v. 122)
   Includes bibliographical references and index.
   ISBN 978-90-04-16962-3 (hardback : alk. paper) 1. Bible. O.T. Ezekiel
XXXVI–XXXIX—Criticism, Textual. 2. Bible. O.T. Ezekiel XXXVI–XXXIX.
Greek—Versions. 3. Bible. O.T. Ezekiel XXXVI–XXXIX—Comparative studies.
4. Bible. O.T. Ezekiel XXXVI–XXXIX—Criticism, interpretation, etc., Jewish.
I. Title. II. Series.

   BS1545.53.C73 2008
   224'.404046—dc22

                                                                        2008031298

ISSN 0083-5889
ISBN 978 90 04 16962 3

Copyright 2008 by Koninklijke Brill NV, Leiden, The Netherlands.
Koninklijke Brill NV incorporates the imprints Brill, Hotei Publishing,
IDC Publishers, Martinus Nijhoff Publishers and VSP.

PRINTED IN THE NETHERLANDS

I dedicate this book to my wife,
Debra Ann Crane

In memory of my mother,
who saw this by faith,
Eva Muriel Crane
1930–2005

CONTENTS

FOREWORD

'You will know that I am the Lord' is a frequent affirmation in the book of Ezekiel, addressed in messages not only to Israel but also to the nations. Understanding of the reasons for and the implementation of that goal comes to subsequent generations through the reading of texts, texts that have been copied in Hebrew and translated and transmitted in Greek and other languages. Yet, these texts are not identical in the meanings conveyed.

All too often the scholarly world has been interested in looking at variants mainly as a means of determining some "original" text, whose meaning is then commented on. Ashley Crane is proposing a new approach, one that treats each manuscript with integrity, exploring the nuances and emphases of each and hence seeking to understand how Ezekiel was interpreted by the tradition represented by the copyist. His text-comparative method opens up exciting possibilities for the exploration of the whole range of biblical texts, going far beyond traditional text-critical approaches.

He demonstrates this approach by meticulous examination of Ezekiel 36–39, a section on the restoration of Ezekiel that covers many topics of interest ever since the exile. Of major significance is his discussion of the major differences in this block between Papyrus 967 and other witnesses. His is the most thorough investigation to date that considers together the "missing" 36:23c–38 and the relative position of ch. 37 and chs. 38–39. Again, the importance of his research is not only a convincing argument for the priority of the tradition represented by Papyrus 967 but an examination of each tradition with respect, listening to the different voices that have contributed to the understanding of a text which is believed to speak to each new generation and setting.

For several years it has been my privilege to journey with the writer in his research, personally learning much from his discoveries. His path has not been straightforward as research has been accompanied by responsibilities as Principal of the Harvest West Bible College in Perth. Difficulties resulting from deaths and illness of staff and amongst his own relatives, as well as the kinds of pressures and pastoral concerns that belong to the position, have provided insights as he has examined texts that themselves were not penned in the calm of a researcher's study,

divorced from life settings! His perseverance, with the kind of sharp-
ening that requires time, has led to depth in his analyses. As well as
contributing fresh insights on a key block of Scripture and the manuscript traditions, he demonstrates an exciting way forward in biblical
research.

John Olley
Perth
April 2008

ACKNOWLEDGMENTS

My highest appreciation for their assistance in completing this book goes to my family, especially my wife Debbie, for your continued support and encouragement. I could not have finished this book without you taking on so much of the responsibilities running our home. You are truly a Proverbs 31 wife, and you give me purpose and focus. Special gratitude goes to our family, Nathan and Joyce, and Joel, thank you for your understanding and sacrifice of your time.

I also thank the past and current staff and faculty of Harvest West Bible College, who helped carry the administrative load enabling the hours for this work to be accomplished.

My special thanks also to Dr. John Olley and Dr. [Prof.] William (Bill) Loader. Your guidance and encouragement, pushing me to think outside the box, enabled me to read these ancient manuscripts in a new way. John, I particularly thank you for your frequent feedback, support, for being a sounding board, your amazing eye for detail, and for your hours of proof reading.

This work had its beginning as a Ph.D. thesis, *The Restoration of Israel: Ezekiel 36–39 in Early Jewish Interpretation: A Textual-Comparative Study of the Oldest Extant Hebrew and Greek Manuscripts* (Ph.D. diss.; Murdoch: Murdoch University, 2006). I have benefited from the comments of the three examiners, Professors Daniel Block, Johan Lust and Margaret Odell, and from Professor André Lemaire, then Managing Editor of this series. Revisions of the thesis for this book owe much to them, although naturally the final version has been my responsibility.

I thank Brill (Professors André Lemaire and Hans Barstad) for agreeing to publish my work, and especially thank Ms. Mattie Kuiper (Editor of Publishing Unit Religious Studies) for guiding me through the publication process with Brill; your speedy replies were always timely and informative. Thank you for the personal face you put on publishing.

Without these mentioned, and the others who encouraged along the way, this book would not have become a reality; you all share in the contributions of this work.

Ashley Crane
Perth
April 2008

ABBREVIATIONS

Full bibliographical details are given in the Bibliography.

1, 2, 3	First, second, third person
Aq.	Aquila
ANE	The Ancient Near East
Aram.	Aramaic.
BAGD	*Greek-English Lexicon of the New Testament and Other Early Christian Literature* (Bauer, Arndt, Gingrich, Danker)
BDB	Brown Driver and Briggs *Lexicon*
BHS	*Biblia Hebraica Stuttgartensia*
CEV	Contemporary English Version
Dan.	The Book of Daniel
dat.	dative
DCH	*Dictionary of Classical Hebrew*
Deut.	The Book of Deuteronomy
DSS	Dead Sea Scrolls
EV(V)	English Version(s)
Exod.	The Book of Exodus
Ezek.	The Book of Ezekiel
f	feminine
𝔊	The Greek translation of the Old Testament; the Septuagint
𝔊ᴬ	Codex Alexandrinus
𝔊ᴮ	Codex Vaticanus
𝔊⁹⁶⁷	Papyrus 967
Gen.	The Book of Genesis
GKC	*Gesenius' Hebrew Grammar* (Cowley, ed.)
HALOT	Koehler and Baumgartner, *The Hebrew and Aramaic Lexicon of the Old Testament*
hitp.	*Hitpaʿel*
hif/hiph	*Hiphʿil*
Hol.	Holladay's *A Concise Hebrew and Aramaic Lexicon of the Old Testament*
impf	imperfect
J	The Yahwist tradition of the Pentateuch
JPS	Jewish Publication Society

KJV	King James Version
LEH	Lust, Eynikel, Hauspie, *Greek-English Lexicon of the Septuagint*
Lev.	The Book of Leviticus
LS	Liddell, Scott and Jones, *A Greek English Lexicon*
LXX	Septuagint
LXX^{A}	Codex Alexandrinus
LXX^{B}	Codex Vaticanus
LXX^{967}	Papyrus 967
m	masculine
MasEzek	Masada Ezekiel fragment
MT	Masoretic Text
𝔐	Masoretic Text
MS(S)	Manuscript(s)
MT^{A}	The Aleppo Codex
MT^{C}	The Cairo Codex of the Prophets
MT^{L}	The Leningrad Codex
NASB	The New American Standard Bible
NEB	The New English Bible
n.c.	no city
n.d.	no date
Nf	Targum Neofiti 1
NIDOTTE	*New International Dictionary of Old Testament Theology and Exegesis*
ni/niph	*Niphal*
NIV	The New International Version
NJB	The New Jerusalem Bible
NRSV	The New Revised Standard Version
Num.	The Book of Numbers
OG	The Old Greek Text
OT	The Old Testament
P	The Priestly tradition/source
P^{967}	Papyrus 967
Pap	Papyrus
perf	perfect
pi.	*Pi'el*
pl.	plural
Ps. Jonathan	Targum Pseudo-Jonathan
ptc.	participle
REB	The Revised English Bible

Rev.	The Book of Revelation
s.	singular
Σ	Symmachus (Symmachus' Version)
SoS	Song of Solomon
Syr.	The Syriac Bible
Tanach	Jewish acronym for the Old Testament
Targ.	Targum
TWOT	*Theological Wordbook of the Old Testament*
v./vv.	Verse/verses
W	Codex Wirceburgensis

The Hebrew and Greek texts used have been based on that of BHS and Rahlfs, as subsequently put into electronic form and now made available in Bible Works 6 (Norfolk: 2003).

CHAPTER ONE

A TEXTUAL-COMPARATIVE METHODOLOGY

Investigation of biblical textual variants, both between Hebrew and Greek and within each language, has traditionally been done with a view to determining an 'original' Hebrew text (*Urtext*) or at least deciding on the 'better' reading. Commentators have an interest in establishing a 'critical' text as the basis for their commentaries. Yet this leaves other variants in a sense as 'incorrect', often attributed to various forms of scribal error. Our purpose, however, is to demonstrate a different approach, which aims to treat each manuscript with equal value, whether Hebrew or Greek, listening to its voice as a clue to an interpretative trajectory.

We have chosen Ezekiel 36–39 as a basis for investigation as it contains various events through which the prophet envisaged that post-exilic Israel would go, as part of her restoration to the future God had in store for them. It is transitional between the destruction of Jerusalem and exile and the new temple of chs 40–48.

1.1. Commentators and the Text of Ezekiel

Amongst commentators on Ezekiel, Cornill (1886) was one of the first to give detailed reference to the Greek text in Ezekiel, noting differences from the Hebrew. Subsequent commentators have built on his work. Cooke's (1936, pp. xli–xlvii) extensive work in the ICC series, following the textual-critical methodologies of his day, evaluated Hebrew-Greek variants primarily to determine the 'superiority' of the Masoretic Text (MT) over the Septuagint (LXX), or vice versa. He organised variants under three categories: "[1]. The superiority of LXX to MT in cases where they differ; [2]. The superiority of MT to LXX in cases where they differ; [3]. Characteristics of LXX that do not necessarily imply a different text". Other commentators have often followed these categories with their treatment of variants. This again was done to establish a critical text for the purpose of constructing a commentary. This practice can also be seen in Zimmerli's (1979, 1983) commentaries. While he details LXX variants in his annotations, providing possible reasons, he rarely refers to them in his commentary section, since they are not part of his established critical text. Allen (1990, 1994) is another modern commentator who follows this practice, yet with less detail than Zimmerli, and frequently attributes variants to 'scribal error'. Block's (1997, 1998) commentaries also consider the Hebrew-Greek variants but with less focus on the superiority of one text over the other, and he refers to variants in his commentary section when appropriate. Other modern commentators have written with little or no reference to Hebrew-Greek variants, presumably working from an existing eclectic text, either Hebrew, Greek, or a modern language, and not directly from extant manuscripts.

1.2. A Textual-Comparative Methodology

Our purpose in what follows is not focused on examining variants in an attempt to discover any Hebrew original text (*Urtext*), nor to establish which variant is 'correct'. Rather, our purpose is to treat each text as an interpretive trajectory witness from the scribe or community wherein it originated.[1] This entails comparing the oldest extant Hebrew and Greek texts intra-linguistically, and then secondly, trans-linguistically, noting any variants and exploring possible interpretive reasons for these variants. Scribal error can then be assigned to variants without discernable interpretive intent. We may call this a 'textual-comparative' methodology. The purpose of this methodology is to give each textual witness equal status, with none considered 'superior' to the others. It accords each textual witness the ability to be 'heard' in its own right (Hebrew and/or Greek).

Our textual-comparative methodology compares extant manuscripts rather than relying on modern eclectic texts (e.g., Ziegler, Rahlfs [cf. *BHS* and *HUBP*]).[2] Whilst these modern texts are invaluable tools, they

---

[1] We occasionally use the term 'community' as while it is possible that a scribe is being idiosyncratic, it is much more likely that they are part of a wider group and their work is reflective of the milieu and understanding of that group. Thus 'community' is used in a way that recognises theological and interpretive influence wider than an individual copyist; although how wide, and whether antecedent, is indeterminate. As such, 'scribe' and 'community' are used interchangeably.

[2] *BHS* and *HUBP* are diplomatic transcriptions of Leningrad and Aleppo respectively, and therefore not eclectic works, yet they both list variants in their critical apparatus.

nevertheless follow the traditional textual-critical goal of establishing 'the most likely original' text, and placing variants into their critical apparatus. Yet this causes variants to lose a degree of interpretive impact, and inadvertently permits variants to be often attributed to scribal error. These texts may also be read without any reference to the critical apparatus leaving variants unnoted. In addition, the modern eclectic texts typically do not reveal the different paragraphing found in the various manuscripts, which is another area of early Jewish interpretation that we take into account.

Our textual-comparative methodology seeks to examine each manuscript in its own individuality and setting. While textual variants may be given in Rahlfs and Ziegler's critical editions, albeit omitting sense-division variants, the natural flow found when reading extant manuscripts more readily permits the implicit interpretive aspects of variants to be observed in clearer detail.

At no point do we disagree with the goals and methodology of textual-critical practices, as we also embrace its long held purposes and accomplishments. We seek only to suggest a complementary methodology when interacting with the ancient manuscripts, which hopefully can assist when researching or writing commentaries. These modern printed editions would be adequate if our purpose was simply a comparison of reconstructed 'original texts'.

At times LXX variants may be found to reflect a Hebrew text earlier than MT, yet this is not then used to correct MT, but to acknowledge and celebrate both as interpretive viewpoints. Our textual-comparative methodology concedes that the Hebrew before the LXX translator may well be different from MT. Yet this earlier Hebrew text is not given a 'superior' status to MT; it remains a witness to the viewpoints of that earlier scribe and/or community, just as MT does to a later community. This is also the case with intra-Greek variants, and with variants between MT and LXX. We often comment: MT says 'this' and LXX says 'that' yet without discussing which text is 'correct'. Our textual-comparative methodology frequently uses 'minus' or 'plus' for a word or passage in a given manuscript rather than 'missing' or 'added' as these terms are often used to explain scribal errors.

We acknowledge and celebrate intra-linguistic variants, especially between the different Greek manuscripts, again often seeing them as interpretive viewpoints from their originating scribal communities. Reference may be made to which was likely original, but only to assist establishing how the other variant came about, and possible exegetical and/or interpretive reasons for that variant. Our discussions frequently provide suggestions how a variant may have happened, yet without discounting the validity of the other variant(s). This will be done on a micro level with our examination of chapters 36–39, and also on a macro level with our chapter dealing with Papyrus 967. Our textual-comparative methodology also does not focus on trying to establish what came from the Prophet, or his 'school', or what was added by later redactors. We recognise these different sources only when it is clear, yet again just to acknowledge a possible interpretive exegetical trajectory.

This may initially frustrate a reader used to traditional 'textual-critical' methodology, especially in LXX studies. Opinions formed under textual or literary criticism methodologies may also be questioned, especially those that have traditionally explained variants away as scribal errors. With our methodology, Hebrew and Greek variants are not textual anomalies that have to be explained away, or ascribed to some form of scribal error. Rather, variants are frequently embraced as potential insights into early Jewish exegetical interpretation, often by the LXX community, yet also by proto-MT. This does not mean that some variants are not the result of scribal error, as clearly some are. However, we will illustrate that many variants that traditionally have been treated as scribal error are actually deliberate exegetical interaction with the text before the scribe.

Our textual-comparative methodology also considers the varying paragraph structures in early manuscripts. This is a developing methodology headed up by the Pericope Project (cf. www.pericope.net). Our methodology permits us to compare the various sense divisions within our texts, and note potentially different exegetical viewpoints, without having to establish which sense division is the 'correct' or 'authentic' one.

Our methodology enables us and others following this style, to have insight into the earliest extant exegetical interpretations by the Jewish people. These texts can therefore partially take the place of non-extant commentaries from these various early Jewish communities. This methodology can also be applied to later texts, such as Targums, Vulgate and Peshitta, to determine how various Jewish and Christian communities interpreted the texts before them. To date, we have found few scholars who regard both Hebrew and Greek variants as implicit insights to exegetical traditions. Hopefully this methodology can be utilised by scholars writing future commentaries.

1.3. OUR CHAPTER PATHWAY

Our second chapter, 'MT and LXX in Comparison', identifies extant Hebrew and Greek textual witnesses that can be utilised for our methodology. This chapter will also discuss and expand on our methodology, laying the framework for gaining an understanding of how different scribes (and perhaps their communities) in the time surrounding the Second Temple period viewed the restoration of Israel in Ezekiel 36–39. It establishes that these MT and LXX variants have their genesis in the early Jewish communities around the time period of the Second Temple rather than the later Christian times. It also examines how the Hebrew text continued its dominance in Jewish life and was not replaced by the Greek text; and how the Greek text interpretively interacted with the Hebrew. This chapter also introduces the structure of sense divisions in the representative texts.

The following four chapters (chapters 3, 4, 5, 6) progressively apply our comparative methodology on a micro level to Ezekiel 36–39. Our methodology is applied to representative Hebrew and Greek manuscripts, suggesting possible exegetical interpretations for many inter and intra-textual variants. Of necessity these chapters are technical. We do not seek to write a commentary that considers whole passages and concepts, but discuss only verses with variants that we consider may contain exegetical and interpretive insights.[3] We have two Excursuses: the first in our discussions of 37:22, detailing how נָשִׂיא, מֶלֶךְ, and ἄρχων are used in Ezekiel 37:22–25; the second at the end of Ezekiel 39 covers unique plusses in the various manuscripts.

While variants in Papyrus 967 ($\mathfrak{G}^{967}$) are considered as they occur throughout chapters 3–6, chapter 7 applies our methodology at a macro level covering $\mathfrak{G}^{967}$'s long pericope 'minus' of 36:23c–38 and unique chapter order. We examine previous discussions and proposals regarding these two textual anomalies, and then demonstrate how $\mathfrak{G}^{967}$ is a viable witness of an earlier form of the Hebrew text. Our textual-comparative methodology then permits us to examine each form: the one that which we have traditionally received, and that in $\mathfrak{G}^{967}$. We then propose what possible theologies lay behind these two textual forms, and why the text of Ezekiel was adjusted to the received text.

---

[3] It is presumed that the reader will have access to the many excellent commentaries on Ezekiel.

CHAPTER TWO

MT AND LXX IN COMPARISON

2.1. Introduction: Extant Resources

It is difficult to determine early Jewish interpretation of the text of
Ezekiel owing to the scarcity of primary resources from the time of the
Second Temple. There are no writings similar to the later (Medieval)
Jewish commentaries, and citation of Ezekiel is rare.[1] Our quest relies
on extant Hebrew and Greek biblical manuscripts (MSS). We propose
that a comparison of variants amongst these MSS, including intra-
and trans-linguistic variants, should reveal theological and exegetical
insights into the early Jewish communities which produced them, and
into their interpretation of the restoration of Israel in Ezekiel 36–39.
We call this a 'textual-comparative' methodology.

2.1.1. *Extant Hebrew MSS*

Extant Hebrew MSS of Ezekiel from the time of the Second Temple are
extremely few in number. The one major Ezekiel scroll from Qumran
(11QEzekiel) remains completely fused awaiting some future technology
which may open its record[2] (Brownlee, 1963, p. 11; Lust, 1986b, p. 90;
Herbert, 1998). The only relevant recognisable fragmentary witness from

---

[1] Litwak (1998, pp. 280–281) refers to studies done by Koch who "observes that
Paul's citations are limited to those books that Pharisaic-rabbinic Judaism, after 70 CE,
recognised as definitively canonical. Paul's preference for some books, such as Psalms,
Genesis, Deuteronomy, Isaiah and the Twelve, and his 'at the same time totally ignor-
ing' other books, such as Ezekiel, Jeremiah, Daniel, agrees with contemporary Jewish
citation and exegetical technique". There are some allusions to Ezek 37:24–28 and
39:17 in the Animal Apocalypse of 1 Enoch, but scarcely commentary.

[2] Herbert (1998, p. 21) describes various attempts to open and reconstruct 11QEze-
kiel, which is dated between "*c.* 10 BCE–30 CE". Brownlee (1963, p. 28), who was
responsible for detailed research on the actual scroll, says "the scribe was probably
roughly contemporary with that of 1QIsa[b], but he may have been slightly earlier. It
is therefore of the late pre-Herodian period or of the very early Herodian period,
roughly in the period 55–25 before Christ".

Qumran is perhaps from Ezekiel 37:23.[3] The Masada Hebrew texts do contain fragments covering Ezek. 35:11–38:14 (MasEzek), and therefore are relevant for this study, particularly for comparison with the later Masoretic texts.[4] Talmon (1999, p. 60) says that MasEzek was "evidently penned by an expert scribe in an 'early Herodian bookhand'…and can be dated to the second half of the last century BCE".[5] MasEzek therefore provides us with the earliest readable Hebrew text for Ezekiel 36–39, albeit incomplete.

The oldest *complete* Hebrew texts remain the later Masoretic texts (MT).[6] The earliest extant Masoretic MS is the Cairo Codex of the Prophets (MT^C), self-dated at 896 CE, supposedly copied by Moses ben Asher,[7] and discovered in the Cairo Genizah (Lowinger, 1971). Next is the Aleppo Codex (MT^A), written around 930 CE, presumably by Aaron ben Asher[8] (Goshen-Gottstein, 1976). The third oldest is the Leningrad Codex (MT^L), dated around 1008/9 CE (Freedman, 1998).

---

[3] This is a fragmentary section of a Cave 4 Florilegium: לו]א יטמאו עור בג[ל]ל[ו] ליהמה ('They shall no longer defile themselves with their idols') (Lust, 1986b, p. 92). Speaking on the finds from Cave 4 and Ezekiel, Lust (1986d, p. 11, n.30) claims that "to a large extent, the new finds are concordant with MT". Brooke (1985, p. 1) says "4QFlor is a fragmentary text containing quotations from the Hebrew scriptures: 2 Samuel, Exodus, Amos, Psalms, Isaiah, Ezekiel, Daniel and Deuteronomy. These quotations are variously interlaced with commentary that attempts to show the inter-relationship of the various texts and their significance".

[4] Yadin (1966, p. 187) reports that the MasEzek scroll was found in a pit that was perhaps "a kind of *geniza*", under the upper floor of what he believes was a synagogue, and states that "though the parchment was badly gnawed, we could immediately identify the writing as chapters from the *Book of Ezekiel*".

[5] Elsewhere Talmon (1997, p. 318) points out that the discovery of MasEzek in a Genizah at Masada (cf. Yadin), would suggest "that because of its condition the scroll was stored there to take it out of circulation. This would imply that it had been in use for quite some time and would underpin its dating to the latter part of the first century BCE or to early in the first century CE".

[6] Tov (2001, p. 22f.) points out the inadequacy of the term *Masoretic Text*, as it "is limited to a mere segment of the representatives of the textual tradition of [MT], namely, that textual tradition which was given its final form by Aaron Ben Asher of the Tiberian group of the Masoretes…. [Also, MT] is not attested in any one single source. Rather [MT] is an abstract unit reflected in various sources which differ from each other in many details. Moreover, it is difficult to know whether there ever existed a single text which served as the archetype of [MT]".

[7] Lowinger (1971) briefly discusses the "dubious" dates and authorships surrounding such codices.

[8] In his introduction for the facsimile edition of the Aleppo Codex, Goshen-Gottstein (1976, p. 1) says that the Tiberian Masoretes laboured "to perfect the written record of the ancient tradition," and that the "acme of perfection" is what we now call the Aleppo Codex. It is believed that Maimonides relied "exclusively" upon the Aleppo Codex, and considered it "halachically authoritative" (Goshen-Gottstein, 1976, p. 2).

Whilst these later Masoretic texts are dated well after the Second Temple period, they nevertheless "may preserve the most ancient text" (Brewer, 1992, p. 178). The link with an ancient text is actually more certain for Ezekiel due to the witness from Masada, which closely matches the later MT. This indicates that the Masoretes were not innovators or editors of their Ezekiel texts, but faithfully transmitted what they had received. Specifically, Ezekiel 36–39 contains a high level of agreement among the three earliest MT MSS and with MasEzek in the consonantal text, indicating they are from a similar textual tradition.[9] Likewise these three MT MSS contain a high level of agreement in the placement of vowels and accents by the Masoretes. This strong agreement, which is not found amongst the Greek MSS, enables us to use MT as a starting point for our textual comparisons. However, this does not imply that MT is the *Vorlage* for the various Greek translations,[10] or is the equivalent of a possible *Urtext*, or that any textual variants are 'superior' to those in the Greek texts.

2.1.2. *Extant Greek MSS*

The earliest complete extant texts of Ezekiel 36–39 are in the Greek tradition (LXX or 𝕲). We will focus on the three oldest: Papyrus 967 (P^{967}, or $𝕲^{967}$), dated late 2nd to early 3rd century CE (Kenyon, 1937, p. x; Johnson *et al.*, 1938, p. 5); Codex Vaticanus ($𝕲^B$), dated *ca.* 4th century CE (Bibliotheca-Vaticana, 1907), and the post-hexaplaric Codex Alexandrinus ($𝕲^A$), dated *ca.* 5th century CE (Thompson, 1883).

There are a number of recensional variations among these three Greek texts, possibly evidencing different *Vorlagen*, just as there are many

---

Goshen-Gottstein, and others in the Hebrew University Bible Project (*HUBP*), still hold the Aleppo Codex as the authoritative text which every other text must be judged by, and it is the text they use for their project.

[9] A decision was made not to include Codex Reuchlinianus with these other MT MSS as, whilst it has pre-Masoretic Tiberian pointing, it generally agrees with the consonantal text of the other MSS. However, it is dated *ca.* 1105, which is another hundred years after MT^L (Sperber, 1969). Yeivin (1980, p. 31) may have included Reuchlinianus when defining the parameters for his book, saying "Mss written after 1100 contain, as a rule little of interest to the study of the standard tradition and its development, and for this reason this book is not concerned with them. They do, however, contain much of value to the study of the development of the tradition up to the time of printing, and also for the study of the pronunciation of Hebrew in different periods and locations".

[10] Peters (1992, p. 1100) states that "it is dangerous, dishonest, and wrong to assume that Leningradensis B 19A (MT) lay before the pre-Christian translators".

variants between these and MT. 𝔊⁹⁶⁷ witnesses two major variants in
our textual block: firstly, a different chapter order than the other representative MSS (36–38–39–37); and secondly, the absence of 36:23c–38
(see our chapter 7).

Unfortunately, Ezekiel is not extant in Codex Sinaiticus, believed to
be part of the missing 56 leaves (Milne and Skeat, 1938, p. 5). Identifi-
able material for Ezekiel 36–39 from the Greek translations of the three
early Jewish exegetes, namely Aquila, Symmachus and Theodotion, is
also minimal.[11] Origen's Hexapla does evidence a few surviving verses
in our block, but often so fragmented that we are left with a partial witness, and often from just one exegete. Relevant fragments are recorded
in Field (1964, pp. 867–873) and Ziegler (1977, pp. 260–281). As one
may expect, extant variants from Aquila, Symmachus and Theodotion
typically follow MT, and as such offer limited insights for us.[12] They
will not be noted unless relevant to our discussion.

2.2. LXX as Translation and Interpretation

It is generally accepted that one must make theological and interpretative decisions when choosing corresponding words in the receptor
language. As such, LXX is an implicit commentary on early Jewish
interpretation as much as it is a *translation*. Whilst LXX is the first known
translation of the Hebrew text, it also "provides insights into the art of
translation of a sacred text *and the subtle (and at times blatant) way in which
it was re-interpreted in the process*" [italics mine] (Peters, 1992, p. 1102).[13]

---

[11] Ezekiel 38:4 is amongst the fragments of Theodotion (Fernández Marcos, 2000,
p. 140, n. 20). It is disappointing that there is not more available, especially Aquila, as
"the passages where Jerome mentions two editions of Aquila are all from Jeremiah,
Ezekiel and a quotation from Daniel" (Fernández Marcos, 2000, pp. 119–120). However, Tov (1997, p. 45) points out that "Aquila was interested only in the linguistic
identification of the Hebrew words, and did not introduce any exegetical elements
into his translation".

[12] For further details on Hexapla and the Three, see Fernández Marcos (2000, pp.
113f., 127f., 206f.).

[13] Again, Peters (1992, p. 1100) states that "the real value of the LXX resides not
so much in its function as a corrective to some Hebrew text of which we have a copy,
but rather as a record of the way in which a group of Jews in the 3rd century [BCE]
and for some time thereafter understood their traditions". Büchner (1997, p. 250) also
points out that "in modern scholarship it has been shown again and again that the
Septuagint is full of Jewish ideas".

Similarly, Jobes & Silva (2000, p. 22) state that it is "precisely because the Septuagint reflects the theological, social, and political interests of the translator, [that] it provides valuable information about how the Hebrew Bible was understood and interpreted at the time the translators were working".[14] This is also supported by Müller (1996, p. 23) who states "a translation will always reflect the translator's grasp of the text, including the period and the cultural setting that the translator lived in; also, where biblical writings are concerned, the translator's theology".[15]

In our case, we have three Greek texts presenting three different trajectories of theological and exegetical thought from the scribal communities in which they originated. $\mathfrak{G}^{967}$'s chapter order and pericope minus (36:23c–38) reflect the theological views of a community earlier than other MSS. It is therefore likely that the LXX translation of Ezekiel that evidences variants intra-LXX, and between LXX and MT, can provide insights into early Jewish interpretative thought and theology.[16]

2.2.1. *Translation Location*

It is generally agreed that LXX grants insights into the world and early Jewish thought of both Alexandria, Egypt (where the first translation work of the Torah took place), and later Jewish communities, doing other translations and/or recensional activity. Yet the translation location of Ezekiel is largely uncertain. Alexandrian Jews may have translated LXX Ezekiel, or it may have been translated in other Jewish communities such as Jerusalem or Babylon. However, we must also consider the possibility of Greek translations taking place simultaneously

---

[14] The complexity in using LXX for textual criticism is analysed in detail by Tov (1997).

[15] Müller (1996, p. 107) also stated that "more than anything the Septuagint testifies to the fact that at that time translation meant something more than simply finding Greek equivalents for the Hebrew words".

[16] However, we do not know the extent of any Greek cultural influence or impact upon the translators of LXX Ezekiel. Olofsson (1990b, pp. 1–5) discusses the way that Alexandrian Jews partially integrated themselves into the Greek culture and religion, which had a bearing on their translation of the Torah. However, he concludes that the religious basis of Judaism "prevented them from any real assimilation or cultural syncretism" (Olofsson, 1990b, p. 3).

in different Jewish communities.[17] Fernández Marcos (2000, p. 250) points out that

> there are three Hebrew text families: one Palestinian of an expansion-
> ist nature; another Egyptian, generally but not always complete, closely
> related to the Palestinian in its oldest phase of the Pentateuch (but not in
> Jeremiah where there are appreciable differences); and another Babylonian
> with a preference for a shorter text where it is preserved (Pentateuch and
> Former Prophets).

Each scribe or community brought its own cultural and theological concerns to the translational and transmissional process, even if these translators were all using the same *Vorlage*. However, we cannot assume that
they all had the same *Vorlage*, which also has an impact on variants.

2.2.2. *The Genesis of LXX*

It is uncertain if acceptance of LXX Torah was slow or rapid, both
within Alexandria and universally. Whilst there are proponents on
both sides of the debate, it may have taken time for overall universal
acceptance. Modern scholarship does not strongly support the historical veracity of the *Letter of Aristeas*,[18] with many instead believing that
Alexandrian Jews translated the Torah in the 3rd century BCE for
their *own* use,[19] and not because of a royal decree for the Alexandrian
Library. Even if LXX Torah was written by royal decree, there is little
indication that the Prophets were written by such decree, but rather

---

[17] Muller (1996, p. 39), speaking of the Prophetic Books, points out that "some of
them may even have been translated more than once".

[18] The uncertainty over LXX Torah may have been the reason behind the *Letter of
Aristeas* (Jobes and Silva, 2000, p. 34). For an overview of the *Letter of Aristeas* see Jellicoe
(1968, pp. 29–58), Jobes and Silva (2000, pp. 33–36), and Müller (1996, pp. 46–67).

[19] Some recent writings have revisited this issue, and, whilst still finding the *Letter of
Aristeas* a pseudograph, nevertheless believe its point that the Torah was translated in
response to Ptolemy II's decree. Collins (2000c) argues against the idea that the Jews
voluntarily translated their texts, and sees them as reluctant translators who did not
want to expose Judaism to the Hellenistic world. Perhaps Collins has overstated her
point here as the Prologue to Sirach does not reflect such reluctance. On the other
hand, the reluctance to translate may have been with relation to Torah. Yet following
that event translation continued for all other books without any apparent royal decree.
Even if Collins is correct, which is a discussion outside this work, we nevertheless have
a record with LXX of how these early Jewish communities translated into the Greek,
and continued their usage of the Greek. Therefore we can still see theological and
exegetical interpretations transmitted. In fact, we could suggest that Collins' argument
helps support our proposal that the Greek text was never written to replace the Hebrew,
but was to be used in conjunction with the Hebrew text.

for Jewish use.[20] Their use covered areas of liturgy,[21] education[22] and even apologetics,[23] as seen in their word choice when translating. These specific aspects are of primary interest to us, as they provide reason for the theological and exegetical variants. The debate continues as to the genesis of LXX, but this is largely outside the scope of this work. We do not seek to determine a definitive *Urtext* or *Vorlage* for Ezekiel 36–39, particularly as many today believe that such is now beyond establishing.[24]

Instead of the two polarized positions of de Lagarde and Kahle,[25] Tov (1997, p. 11) proposed a four stage development for LXX:

1. The original translation.
2. A multitude of textual traditions resulting from the insertion of corrections (mainly towards the Hebrew) in all known individual scrolls in the pre-Christian period, and to a lesser extent in the first century CE.

---

[20] We may suggest that whilst the original translation of Torah may have faced a reluctant acceptance (whether from opposition to the royal decree or by 'purists' who wanted to remain with just a Hebrew text), that the Prophets and Writings were also translated indicates that any initial reluctance was overcome.

[21] Whilst finding areas wanting in Thackeray's proposal of liturgical origins of LXX, Fernández Marcos (2000, p. 60) says "nevertheless, it is the most ambitious hypothesis to try to incorporate in a coherent way the whole process of decanting the Bible from the Hebrew to the Greek in its different stages".

[22] Brock (1974, p. 550) claims that "the combination of these two needs, then, the liturgical and the educational, were the real incentive behind the Greek translation of the Pentateuch. Once this momentous first step had been taken, it was only natural that the other religious writings of the Jews should follow suit—that is to say, the Prophets".

[23] When speaking about the possibility of the Torah being translated for the king's library, Müller (1996, p. 60) noted that "the fact that the translation project was given royal authorization might have been for apologetic purposes".

[24] Many have sought to reconstruct a *Vorlage*, and/or conform LXX to extant Hebrew texts, but the methodology behind this is often incorrect. The most notable in antiquity was Origen with his massive Hexapla. Whilst Origen made a valiant attempt to emend the Greek text to match the Hebrew, he did not succeed. This was mainly due to his mistaken belief that the Hebrew text before him was the same as that before the LXX translators (Jobes and Silva, 2000, p. 52). This has also been the quest of some recent commentators such as Cooke (1936, p. xl), who says "our problem is to recover a text which shall be free from alterations and corruptions, and so far nearer to the original. It becomes necessary, therefore, to examine the Versions, which were translated from an earlier form of the Hebrew text than that which we have in our Bible".

[25] Tov (1997, p. 10) simplifies the debate regarding the two dominant theories: "De Lagarde assumes an Urtext (the first translation or the hypothetical archetype of all extant manuscripts of the LXX), which subsequently divided into different text forms, while P. Kahle posited multiple translations which converged into one central tradition".

Overall, we can suggest a broad translational timeframe for the original OG Ezekiel from as early as 230 BCE (cf. Thackeray, Dorival, and Siegert) through to 132 BCE (cf. Swete, Jobes and Silva), or even as late as 50 BCE (Turner). We do not seek to be more definite, beyond confirming the translational timeframe to be Jewish rather than Christian, thus determining that many of the variants between MT and LXX are clearly evidence of early Jewish interpretation. Our study in chapter 7, covering 𝔊⁹⁶⁷, also concludes that the major textual changes took place in the Hebrew text before 50 BCE as they are witnessed in MasEzek. We therefore prefer a date between 230 and 135 BCE for the OG Ezekiel. It is undeterminable when later LXX recension(s) towards the Hebrew were translated; we suggest a broad timeframe from around 50 BCE (based on MasEzek), through to sometime in the first century CE for an initial recension (most likely reflected in 𝔊ᴮ).

2.2.4. *Number of Translators*

There are several theories as to how many scribes were involved in translating Ezekiel, Thackeray's two translator proposal remaining the benchmark.[29] Following his work on Jeremiah, and building on the work of others for Ezekiel, Thackeray (1921, p. 38) determined three divisions[30] in Ezekiel: "(1) chaps. i–xxvii which I call Ez α^i, (2) chaps. xxviii–xxxix Ez. β, and (3) chaps. xl–xlviii Ez α^{ii}" [or γ].[31] Thackeray (1903a, p. 399) claims that

> [Ezekiel] appears, like Jeremiah, to have been divided, for the purposes of translation, into two nearly equal parts, but, instead of the second hand continuing to the end, as was the case in Jeremiah, the first translator resumed the task when the difficult concluding section, containing the account of the vision of the Temple, was reached.[32]

---

[29] Since Thackeray's work others have usually agreed, some with modification of chapter divisions, yet all ascribing 36–39 to the one translator. Some have argued for a single translator (Ziegler), or for three different translators (Herrmann, Turner), or single translator with later redactor(s) (Kase, Tov).

[30] These divisions were based on detailed comparison of style and vocabulary.

[31] In his earlier work Thackeray (1903a, p. 399) provided the designation of γ to the third section, and most continue using this designation. However, Thackeray still saw the same translator for γ as α, and to avoid confusion over a two or three translator theory, he later adopted the designation of α^i and α^{ii}.

[32] Thackeray (1903a, p. 410) also stated "whether the translators already found a break in the middle of the Hebrew texts, in other words, whether the Hebrew books where transcribed on two separate scrolls, must remain doubtful".

Thackeray (1921, p. 39) believed that translator β was not as profi-
cient as the first translator (α and γ), who, he claimed, was "a master
who played a prominent part in the translation of the *Nebiim* [sic]".[33]
However, unlike his opinion of inferiority for the second translator of
Jeremiah, Thackeray (1903a, p. 410) did not believe Ezekiel's translator
β was "so markedly inferior to the first, [but] it is to be noticed that the
first translator took to himself the hardest portions of the book".[34]

   This leaves us with a degree of confidence that translator β, covering chapters 36–39, knew his craft. Therefore variants between MT
and LXX may not be due to scribal incompetence, rather they may
be exegetical and interpretive viewpoints. This immediately refers to
the OG ($\mathfrak{G}^{967}$), but it also applies to later LXX recensions towards the
Hebrew (e.g., $\mathfrak{G}^{B,A}$). It is to our advantage that all scholars ascribe the
block of Ezekiel 36–39 to the one translator (Thackeray's β), since it
enables confidence in a consistency of theological interpretation found
in the translation from Hebrew to Greek.[35]

2.2.5. *Early LXX Variants*

It is apparent that LXX variants appeared very early, well before the
Christian Era. Fernández Marcos (2000, p. 21) observed that when Ben
Sira's grandson (*ca.* 135 BCE) translated *The Wisdom of ben Sira* into
Greek, he actually "apologises for the inadequacy of his translation", in
his Prologue. Of special significance to us, his apology includes reference to differences between the Hebrew and Greek for 'the Prophets',
which may have included Ezekiel (based on our translation timeframes
above). Thus we have a witness from 135 BCE that variations in wording
already existed between the Hebrew and Greek. Whilst the Prologue
refers to translational difficulties in wording, our findings in the following
chapters evidence deliberate exegetical choices in translating from the
Hebrew to Greek. Translational difficulties may have permitted scribes
to take exegetical liberties in their word choices.

   Jobes & Silva (2000, p. 97) point out that almost all extant LXX
MSS date from 4th century CE and following, and were transmitted by

---

[33] This included the first half of Jeremiah, and the twelve Minor Prophets.
[34] Thackeray (1903a, p. 410) believed that the "two translators were set on to the
work simultaneously".
[35] For a recent detailed presentation and analysis of the different theories, and for
the consensus that chapters 36–39 have a single translator, see McGregor (1985).

Christian scribes. Yet this does not mean they are now 'Christian texts' and that the variants are Christian. As Brewer (1992, p. 180) states, "the [LXX] texts which have survived appear to be Jewish translations without much Christian influence". Swete (1989, p. 494) likewise claims that "early citations from the LXX suggest a diversity of readings and possibly the existence of two or more recensions in the first century, and lead us to believe that many of the variations in our MSS have come down from sources older than the Christian era". Tov (1988, p. 163) also found that "the NT influenced the transmission of the LXX but little. Allegedly several Christian changes were inserted at one time in LXX manuscripts, but few have survived to date". Although LXX was transmitted to us by Christian hands, there is a high degree of certainty that variants originate from early Jewish interpretation.

Therefore, we have variants between MT and LXX in Ezekiel that represent the OG (*ca.* 230–135), and are clearly Jewish and pre-Christian. These variants are continued in the later LXX MSS (e.g., $\mathfrak{G}^{B,A}$). There are also a number of variants intra-LXX that, while these MSS are from Christian hands, also represent Jewish exegetical interpretation, as the major variants between $\mathfrak{G}^{967}$ and $\mathfrak{G}^{B,A}$ reflect interaction with the Hebrew text (MT and MasEzek), and other later additional variants in $\mathfrak{G}^{B,A}$ typically reflect movement towards the Hebrew of their day. Additionally, while the 'inserted' pericope of 36:23c–38 is written in a later Theodotion style in the Greek, its witness in MasEzek indicates that this pericope also belongs to early Jewish interpretation. It is also difficult to see why Christian scribes would insert their own interpretive variants when their recensions sought to match the Hebrew text.

2.2.6. *A Fixed Text*

Some variants, such as plusses, may well be accurate representations of the Hebrew text available to the scribal editor, and "represent different stages in the history of the text" (Müller, 1996, p. 42).[36] Unfortunately, we do not have these Hebrew texts before us, so we cannot determine

---

[36] Later Müller (1996, p. 113) said "the texts finds made after the Second World War reveal that the many more or less substantial discrepancies found in the Septuagint in relation to the later Masoretic text are not necessarily owing to the translator's lack of conscientiousness...[but] they may in fact signify that the Hebrew text underlying the translation was different". Of note, the text of Jeremiah is one-seventh shorter in the Greek than in the Hebrew and has a different chapter order.

this with absolute certainty. It is apparent that the Ezekiel text before the original Greek translators was of a different Hebrew recension than MT. Sometimes these differences are only slight; other times they indicate wider variance, such as in 𝕲⁹⁶⁷ that evidences a *Vorlage* of a shorter text with a different chapter order. Jobes & Silva (2000, p. 20f.) state:

> the fact remains that the Septuagint was translated from some Hebrew text that was not identical to the Hebrew text we use today. That original Greek translation, which was produced much earlier than any surviving copy of the Hebrew Bible, is an indirect witness to its *Vorlage*, that is, the Hebrew parent text from which it is translated.

It is this complexity that Peters (1992, p. 1100) refers to when he claims that all extant LXX and MT MSS contain corruptions from the original Hebrew.

Most scholars today believe LXX represents a period in the textual and literary development of the Hebrew consonantal text before it was fixed (presumably some time surrounding the destruction of the Second Temple).[37] Regardless of the exact time when the Hebrew text was fixed and accepted,[38] this still means that extant LXX MSS may provide us with implicit insights into pre- or even proto-Masoretic Hebrew text(s); and therefore interpretation and theological exegesis from that time. Likewise, MT's unique 'plusses', not evidenced in LXX, can also provide similar insights into the continued development of the Hebrew text. For this reason we should treat the variants found in each MSS with respect, and accord them equal value to what may have been original, as both provide us with interpretive insights to early Jewish theology and exegesis.

We must also consider that whilst the Hebrew text did at some point become 'standardised', this was never the case with the Greek text, as evidenced by the varying quality of each biblical book found in the

---

[37] Talmon (1999, p. 25) argues that "the Masada biblical fragments give witness to the existence of a stabilized proto-masoretic textual tradition which had taken root in 'normative Judaism' of the time." He (1999, p. 25) also points out that the "textual fluidity, which can be observed in the Qumran scrolls and fragments of biblical books and bible-related works, which stem from the last centuries BCE, proves that these manuscripts were not subjected to such a stabilizing process".

[38] In reference to Aquila's translation, Fernández Marcos (2000, p. 117) states, "there are passages where the translation must suppose a different Vorlage from the Masoretic text as an indication that the standardization of the Hebrew text supposed by the Synod of Yamnia (c. 100 CE) did not take effect immediately or in a radical way, but instead was more the expression of an ideal to be aimed for".

various Codices. Metzger (1981, p. 74) points out that different LXX MSS vary in the translational accuracy of each book, such as with Codex Vaticanus, which has "a good text in Ezekiel, and a bad one in Isaiah". Jobes & Silva (2000, p. 31) agree:

> The particular collection of Greek texts of the biblical books that comprise the earliest one volume Bibles, such as Codex Sinaiticus and Codex Vaticanus, usually came to be by the historical happen-stance of whatever texts were at hand, irrespective of their origin or character. Therefore, whatever one may say about the history and characteristics of the Greek text of one biblical book may not be true of the others, even though they are bound together in one codex.

2.2.7. *Translation Quality and Glosses*

Scholarship seems divided over the translational and textual quality of LXX Ezekiel. Following his evaluation of LXX translations, Blaiklock (1976, p. 345) notes "Ezekiel is not well done". However, Tov (1999d, p. 397) counters this, stating "this is actually an overstatement as many of the differences between the MT and LXX were created at the time of the literary growth of the book, and therefore should not be ascribed to textual factors". Tov (1997, p. 250) earlier comments that "the recensional rewriting is not extensive" and "the Greek translation of Ezekiel is relatively literal". Metzger (1981, p. 74) notes that 𝕲ᴮ Ezekiel enjoys a high level of agreement with MT. In his work examining the 'consistency of lexical equivalents', Marquis (1986a, p. 417) concludes that "LXX-Ezekiel, in all three of its supposed translation units, is very literal" when dealing with nouns and verbs, and especially with verbs in unit β.[39] Marquis's finding holds special significance for us, as noun and verbal variants in 36–39 may therefore be more 'intentional' than in books that do not enjoy such a high degree of literalness. This permits us to have a high degree of confidence that variants are not always scribal errors, and therefore we can examine these for possible theological interpretations. Perhaps one reason for the division of scholarship over the translational quality of Ezekiel is that scholars are each referring to the quality found within the actual LXX MSS /

---

[39] Marquis (1986a, p. 417) furthermore claims "LXX-Ezekiel clearly stands closer to the literalness reflected in LXX–2 Kings and at a considerable distance from LXX-Isaiah".

Codex available to them at the time they formulated their assessments (cf. Metzger, 1981, p. 74).

It is significant that LXX Ezekiel is approximately 4–5 percent shorter than MT Ezekiel,[40] and the percentage is even greater if we take $\mathfrak{G}^{967}$ into account. This has added to the debate over whether MT or LXX represents the Hebrew *Urtext*. The even shorter text of $\mathfrak{G}^{967}$ also raises debate as to which particular LXX MS may more accurately represent the *Urtext*. Tov (1997, p. 250) uses the literalness of LXX Ezekiel as the basis to argue for a shorter Hebrew parent text than that represented in MT.[41] Often the plusses of MT have been explained away as later *glosses* or *interpolations*.[42] Yet Tov (1997, p. 250) argues that this description "is less appropriate because of the large number of these elements and because of the occurrence of parallel elements and synonymous words among the pluses of MT and new material".

Tov (1999d, p. 410 n. 19) does state that "such glosses or interpolations have been detected more in Ezekiel than in any other book of the Bible, and the model of Ezekiel negatively influenced the analysis of other books". This point may have caused Cooke (1936, p. xl) to claim that "in the Hebrew Bible perhaps no book, except 1 and 2 Samuel, has suffered more injury to its text than Ezekiel".[43] In reference to glosses, Allen (1990a, p. 408) says "the Massoretic Text of Ezekiel is notoriously beset with problems".[44] After researching the glosses in Ezekiel, Dijkstra (1986, p. 76) found that "MT and in a lesser degree the LXX show a clear tendency to preserve as many readings and grammatical-exegetical clarifications as possible". Tov (2001, p. 283)

---

[40] Tov (1997, p. 250) notes the plusses found in MT are also found in the Targum, Peshitta and Vulgate.

[41] Jobes and Silva (2000, p. 176) suggest that "the evidence offered by the two Hebrew texts of Jeremiah increases the probability that other books were translated into Greek from a shorter, different Hebrew edition that is no longer extant".

[42] For more on the glosses in Ezekiel see Dijkstra (1986, pp. 55–77); also our Excursus on unique plusses at the end of our discussion on chapter 39.

[43] Cooke (1936, p. xxvii) states, "everywhere uncertainty prevails about the text, due partly to the usual accidents of translation, but even more to the extraordinary nature of the events described.... We may blame the scribes; yet the very state of the text, with all its corruptions and inaccuracies, bears witness to the eager handling of those who studied it".

[44] Allen's (1990a, p. 408) comment that is in relation to the "apparent addition of a word or two" which he explains as 'glosses'. It is interesting that Allen (1990a, p. 408) concluded "the heavy annotation that underlies the texts in question [Ezek. 32:20, 21b; 33:31b; 34:26a; 35:6a; 39:16a] appears to reflect interest in their eschatological content". Note: writers differ as to the spelling with single or double 's' (Massoretes/Masoretes etc.).

suggests that "these additions should not be viewed as individual elements, but as components of a large-scale literary layer".[45] We may therefore examine MT plusses also as exegetical representatives from some early Jewish community.

Our studies reveal four groups of plusses in Ezekiel 36–39: firstly those unique to $\mathfrak{G}^{967}$, secondly those found in both MT and $\mathfrak{G}^{A}$, thirdly those unique to $\mathfrak{G}^{A}$, and fourthly, those unique to MT (cf. chapter 6: §6.6). These plusses have their genesis in the Jewish community, and were almost certainly added to the Greek texts to bring closer conformity to the Hebrew. $\mathfrak{G}^{A}$'s plusses likely reflect Origen's desire to match LXX to the Hebrew of his day.

It is difficult to imagine that the Jewish community would embrace any Christian plusses and insert these into their Hebrew texts, particularly when the efforts of Aquila, Symmachus and Theodotion sought to make LXX more reflective of the Hebrew text before them.[46] We can therefore propose that the Christian community adjusted their Greek texts to match changes in the Hebrew, perhaps in an effort to alleviate criticism that their LXX MSS did not accurately reflect the Hebrew. We may also suggest that the addition of MT's later plusses by Christians into 'their' Greek texts is also an implicit example of theological choice by the Christian communities.

Finally, Lust (1986a, p. 221) observed that "longer plusses in [LXX] Ezekiel are rare. Three of them are to be found in Ezek α [1–27] and six in Ezek γ [40–48], whereas none of them occur in Ezek β [28–39]. Their exegetical contents are not really relevant. They have not much bearing on the theology of the book". It is significant here that no major plusses occur in LXX Ezek β, as this shows that although the translator interpretively interacted with the Hebrew before him, he did not seek to insert innovative material, and therefore revealing a degree of respect for the text.

Importantly, later LXX scribes did not amend all changes in their Greek texts, even when correcting to the Hebrew of their day. This indicates that they understood and accepted the original translator's implicit interpretive interactions. This point is frequently overlooked.

---

[45] Tov (2001, pp. 333–334) supplies a list of such glosses, but these are all from Thackeray's section α and thus do not include any from Ezek. 36–39.

[46] Swete (1989, p. 31) claims that "the purpose of [Aquila's] translation was to set aside the *interpretation* of the LXX, in so far as it appeared to support the view of the Christian Church" [italics mine].

Our textual-comparative methodology permits us to treat these variants as significant in their own right.

2.2.8. *Continued Dominance of the Hebrew*

It has become increasingly obvious that the early Jewish communities did not discard their Hebrew texts once they had been translated into Greek. Early disputes over variants and wording are "tangible proof of the increasing dominance of the Hebrew Bible text, also among Greek speaking Jews" (Müller, 1996, p. 71f.).[47] As noted above, the Prologue for Sirach appears to appeal to the reader to continue comparisons with the Hebrew. Feldman (1988, p. 455f.) observed that the later Josephus quoted from both the Hebrew and Greek texts. We suggest that the Hebrew continued in use, even alongside the Greek translations, especially in synagogue liturgical and educational applications.[48] The continued dominance of the Hebrew texts may also be seen with the later translations done by Aquila,[49] Theodotion and Symmachus, that set the Hebrew as the 'master' text, which the Greek must follow.

Swete (1989, p. 299) importantly notes that "the manner of the LXX is not Greek, and does not even aim at being so. It is that of a book written by men of Semitic descent, who have carried their habits of thought into their adopted tongue". This may also be seen in instances where LXX syntax follows the Hebrew rather than a Greek pattern. Lust (in LEH, 2003, p. xviii) brings this out, stating:

> Although it may be based on it, Septuagint Greek cannot simply be characterized as Koine Greek. It is first of all translational Greek. This is most obvious on the level of syntax and style. The order of the words

---

[47] Gruen (1998, p. 111) proposes that the various writings of that day, including LXX, "existed as accompaniments, commentaries, alternative versions, or provocative reinterpretations, inviting the reader to make comparisons or engage in reassessments of the tradition". Furthermore, Gruen (1998, p. 111) believes "the authors of these divergent treatments had no intention of challenging or replacing biblical narrative".

[48] Müller (1996, pp. 46–67) discusses this issue in his third chapter outlining how Aristeas, Aristobulus, Philo, and Josephus all saw the Greek of the Pentateuch as equally inspired as the Hebrew.

[49] Müller (1996, p. 40) points out that Aquila "distinguished himself by rendering the text almost word for word, thus making it almost unintelligible to those who did not master the Hebrew language. But exactly this may have been the point with the enterprise, because it made the Hebrew text indispensable. Theodotion...wrote in a more elegant literary style than Aquila, but it is characteristic of him that he used Greek transcriptions of Hebrew words to a great extent".

in the translation most often sticks to that of the Hebrew original. In fact, in many passages, the Hebrew and Greek can be put into parallel columns, word by word. The result is that the syntax of the Septuagint is Hebrew rather than Greek.

Lust (2001, p. 395) defends this point, clarifying that the syntax of LXX "is largely affected by the syntax of the Hebrew source text due to the literal methods of translation employed" and is thus not strictly Koine Greek syntax.[50] Significantly Ezekiel is one of the books "that are translated more literally [and] the influence of the source language on the syntax is more pronounced than in those [books] that are translated more freely" (Lust, 2001, p. 397). Johnson (in Johnson *et al.*, 1938, p. 41) also states that "it is evident from the Hebraisms that the translators were familiar with the original tongue, but while they had a fairly extensive Greek vocabulary they were not at home in writing idiomatic Greek".[51] This suggests that the LXX Ezekiel translators, including Thackeray's translator β, were perhaps more familiar with Hebrew than traditionally thought, and were not seeking to completely replace their Hebrew texts. Therefore, this indicates they did not misunderstand the Hebrew in every variant, but rather performed theological and exegetical interpretations in their translations.

2.3. Theological Interpretation in the MSS

In exploring early Jewish interpretation of the restoration of Israel in Ezekiel 36–39, we seek to provide possible interpretative reasons for variants in our representative manuscripts. As stated above, our methodology is to take MT as a starting point, then compare the three earliest LXX texts with MT, while at the same time performing an intra-LXX comparison. We will examine each variant to see if there is any evidence, implicit or explicit, of early Jewish theological interpretation.

In the following chapters, several features will be dismissed as not having any interpretative or theological intent. These include words where

---

[50] Lust (2001, p. 395) further clarified that he does not mean "LXX syntax equals Hebrew syntax...the syntax of the Septuagint, and especially its word order, comes closer to Hebrew than to Greek, or in other words, 'is Hebrew *rather* than Greek'. It leans more towards the syntax of the source language than to that of the target language".

[51] Fernández Marcos (2000, p. 10) also says "Bilingualism...is responsible both for the syntactic peculiarities of the Greek of the Old and New Testaments".

there is a clear scribal error, or where LXX smooths out the Hebrew by using two verbs for MT's one,[52] or where LXX uses a noun for an MT verb (and vice versa), with no substantive change in the meaning. We will not take the variations of the divine name into account, as, whilst evidencing theological intent, they are not directly related to just 36–39 and the restoration of Israel, but the entire book.[53] Likely Hebrew glosses will be acknowledged where they evidence theological intent, but not where the gloss has permitted a smoother reading. We will not always note differences in word order or syntax, without any discernible theological or exegetical reason. Also, we will not comment on variant LXX spelling where there is no theological influence.[54]

Frequently scholars have explained away many of the translational variants between LXX and MT as scribal errors, often suggesting the LXX translator did not fully comprehend the Hebrew. While at the beginning of the current investigation this seemed likely, detailed observation of the data as a whole, rather than as isolated instances, led to patterns that undermined the typical 'scribal error' explanations.

2.3.1. *Trans-linguistic Wordplays*

A few instances leads us to propose that at times the LXX translator of Ezekiel 36–39 deliberately interprets the Hebrew, utilising 'trans-lingual wordplays', presuming the LXX reader (or hearer) would be familiar with the Hebrew, and so catch these wordplays and their theological and exegetical points. This scenario would find its fulfilment in the synagogue liturgy where the reading of the Hebrew is followed by the common language, permitting the bilingual hearer to appreciate the wordplay.

With a bi-lingual translator, operating within community theological framework for liturgical, educational and/or apologetic reasons, trans-lingual wordplays provide creative interpretation. This is often done by making a pun with the Hebrew spelling, switching Hebrew letters within a word. Evidence of wordplay and other interpretive practices should not surprise us, as wordplay was one of their 'habits of thought'

---

[52] As Tov (1997, p. 43) puts it "the identification of Greek words with Hebrew equivalents is based on a reconstruction of the translators' intentions, so Greek-Hebrew equivalents need not be equal from a quantitative point of view".

[53] For a detailed examination of the divine name in Ezekiel see McGregor (1985).

[54] For example, 𝕲^A frequently uses αι for 𝕲^{967,B}'s ε.

(cf. Swete above). Wordplay also occurs within the Hebrew text (and in later rabbinic literature).[55]

Wordplays should be considered where a Greek variant can be observed to exegete and interpret the Hebrew by reversing letters in the Hebrew, or making interpretive interaction on the 'sound'. Such variants should not be automatically ascribed to scribal error, but rather considered as interpretation. Interestingly, commentators have largely ignored or overlooked these possible language wordplays, usually attributing such variants to 'scribal error' and/or the translator misunderstanding the Hebrew. The following detailed study of Ezekiel 36–39 will demonstrate that this is not the case in a significant number of verses.

2.3.2. *Other Observed Exegetical Practices*

There is evidence that the LXX translator(s) seeks to speak theologically to, or on behalf of, his community. Implicit theological exegesis and interpretation is also found where the LXX translator provides a reason for MT's action or event, or outlines the result and/or consequence of actions stated in MT, or at other times provides an insight into the motivation or 'heart' behind such action. When confronted with metaphors in the Hebrew, the LXX translator typically exegetes them for the reader. There is an implicit but consistent theological difference in the way MT and LXX view 'the land'. For MT, the land is an active participant in the restorative plans of God, whereas in LXX the land is more passive, even the recipient of action. Included here are instances where MT records an action or event, but LXX uses the passive to translate as an action *against* Israel, the mountains, and/or the people. This may indicate that the LXX community felt harshly or unjustly treated by events and the nations around them in their past and also present. LXX often uses the passive voice in these instances. Their word choice also suggests at times that the translator saw himself and his community as 'post' the events of 36–39, or even that they were in the historic present.[56]

---

[55] For an overall explanation of wordplay as a rabbinical exegesis see Brewer (1992), and for example of wordplay in the Hebrew text of Ezekiel 35:1–36:15 see Allen (1990b, pp. 170–171).

[56] The aspect of a translator inserting "ideological changes" to make the texts fit the translator's timeframe is covered by Tov (2001, p. 94f.). Whilst Tov is directly dealing

As noted above, that later LXX copiers or redactors did not correct these variations, and in fact continued transmitting them, suggests that these later communities recognised and accepted them as representative of their theological traditions. Thus, we have both MT and LXX as two acceptable representations of theological trajectories of early Jewish communities for Ezekiel 36–39.

2.4. Sense Divisions

Whilst textual scholars in the past have not seen significance in sense divisions in extant texts, several today are beginning to re-examine these textual markers to determine the existence of implicit exegetical thought, in particular the international team in the Pericope Project.[57] Olley (1998, p. 111) highlighted the need to acknowledge the existence of paragraphs and other sense dividers in the text, and to consider variants of these divisions in extant manuscripts.[58] The lack of significance attributed to MT sense divisions by modern scholars can be seen today where "many a Hebrew student does not even know what a *petuḥa* or *setuma* is" (Korpel and de Moor, 1998, p. 2). Today we may discuss sense definers of 'chapters and numbered verses', yet these are later additions to the Bible and may not reflect the chapter and verse structure of early Jewish or Greek scribes.[59]

Previously, emphasis in research was placed on individual words as the focus for an understanding of meaning. However, it is common in contemporary research to "include the significance of paragraphing (sense division) and even the form of the whole document" (Olley, 1998, p. 113). To understand a text one must divide it into sense divisions, or pericopes, that will reflect the central thought of a text.

---

with the Samaritan Pentateuch, there is no reason why this same timeframe adjustment would not have occurred with LXX translators.

[57] For an online view of this project: http://www.pericope.net. There is also a Pericope series being published initially by Van Gorcum (2000 onwards) and now by Brill.

[58] Olley's initial (1993) work focused on Isaiah, and made special reference to the Hebrew University Bible Project (cf. Olley, 1998). But the same principles can be applied to the book of Ezekiel (cf. Olley, 2003) and for our purposes to the passage of particular focus (Ezek. 36–39).

[59] Chapter and verse divisions numbering familiar to the modern reader were "introduced into the Latin Bible by Stephen Langton at the beginning of the thirteenth century.... [and] numbered verses were first worked out by Rabbi Isaac Nathan in about 1440" [Hebrew Bible only] (Metzger, 1981, p. 41).

Observing existing sense divisions in our representative manuscripts can highlight what was important in the text for these early scribes and their communities, revealing interpretive and exegetical insights. This can have a major impact on interpretation. As Korpel and de Moor (1998, p. 1) say, "whether some verses do belong to a unit or not can make all the difference between a prophecy of doom and a prophecy of salvation".

We agree with Tov (1998, p. 142) that "the division of the text into sense units reflects the earliest visible component of context [sic] exegesis of the written texts". This has increased significance for us as the Masoretes do not appear to be textual innovators, and therefore most likely transmitted the sense divisions they received, which may reflect some of the earliest extant Jewish exegesis. Therefore, it would be unwise for us to exegete a passage today without any regard to the sense divisions placed by these early scribes.

These early sense divisions should cause us to question why they were placed at that point in the text, and to investigate their history: were they part of previous texts or placed by later scribes who sought to put the text into interpretive sections for theological and/or liturgical use? On this, Tov (2003, p. 473) says,

> it remains difficult to know where and in which period the tradition of verse division developed, although it stands to reason that the division into small sense units originated in conjunction with the reading from Scripture in public meetings.

Sense divisions may have their genesis in the synagogue when structuring the Torah and *haftarah* reading, reflecting early Jewish interpretation.

However, we do not intend to suggest that all sense divisions (and thus exegesis) placed by the MT or LXX scribes are correct, or that we should embrace their interpretations and exegesis today. This is pointed out by Korpel and de Moor (1998, p. 11) in their examination of sense divisions in Isaiah:

> Of course we do not contend that the Masoretes were always right. On the contrary, we intend to prove that in many cases they were simply wrong. In some cases we are able to suggest that the Masoretic distinctive accents rest on rabbinic exegesis which cannot be followed by modern scholarship anymore.

Olley (1993, p. 49) also concludes that the sense divisions in 1QIsa[a] "are not definitive for modern exegesis and reading. Nevertheless there is value in taking them into account, along with the words of the text".

Having said this, we can agree with Korpel and de Moor (1998, p. 11) when they continue to say that "in the majority of cases the Masoretic delimitation of cola, verses and strophes rests on ancient, reliable tradition which should not be rejected without proper discussion". Our textual-comparative methodology allows us to compare location of sense divisions in the various MSS, to determine any interpretive insights.

2.4.1. *Hebrew Sense Division Markers*

In MT paragraph divisions, called פסקות *pisqot* or פרשיות *parashiyyot*, were marked typically with varying gaps signifying either a major division known as a *petuḥah* (open), or a minor division called a *setumah* (closed) sense division. All three representative MT MSS use these sense dividers. Yeivin (1980, p. 41) describes these in the following diagrammatic form [xx's mine]:

Sense division location	*Petuḥah* (open)	*Setumah* (closed)
(a) Paragraph ends near the beginning of a line.	xxxxxxxxxxxxxxxxxxx xxxxx xxxxxxxxxxxxxxxxxxx	xxxxxxxxxxxxxxxxxxxxx xxxxxxxx xxxxxxxx xxxxxxxxxxxxxxxxxxxxx
(b) Paragraph ends at, or near the end of, a line.	xxxxxxxxxxxxxxxxxxx xxxxxxxxxxxxxxx xxxxxxxxxxxxxxxxxxx	xxxxxxxxxxxxxxxxxxxxx xxxxxxxxxxxxxxxxx xxxxxxxxxxxxxxxxx xxxxxxxxxxxxxxxxxxxxx

It is believed that the sense division markers indicate interpretive breaks, whereby "in principle a closed section is 'thematically related to what immediately precedes it'" (Siegel cited in Tov, 1998, p. 124).[60] A *petuḥah* is where a less relational theme is found. Tov (2001, p. 51) says "the subdivision itself into open and closed sections reflects exegesis on the extent of the content units", and explains that "the subjectivity of this exegesis created the extant differences between the various sources".

Whilst acknowledging the subjectivity, we will typically follow the pericope divisions as found in MT in our attempt to hold to some form

---

[60] Tov (1998, p. 124) does state "the vagueness of this definition leads to differences of opinion with regard to the interpretation of this relation". However, whilst admittedly vague, this definition is still functional.

of continuity with early Jewish interpretation. This is not to suggest
these 'sense divisions' occurred in the *Urtext*,[61] but that MT is a starting
point due to its general consistency among the three MSS. Variants do
exist intra-MT, yet these are more often *petuḥah* and *setumah* variants
at a particular sense division break rather than in the location of such
divisions (although location variants do occasionally occur).

2.4.2. *LXX Sense Division Markers*

There is a wider variance with pericope division locations between LXX
and MT, and even intra-LXX, which indicates that "the development
of Greek paragraphing [is] independent of the Hebrew verse tradition [as] evidenced by the number of [LXX] divisions within [MT]
verses" (Olley, 2003, p. 4). Yet, significant for our study, Olley (2003,
p. 209) observed in Ezekiel "the closer matching amongst both Greek
and Hebrew codices in chs 12–39 (at least 80%) suggests either some
interaction in the development tradition, or similar criteria operating
in both traditions".[62] Intra-LXX variances also indicate some independence among these various LXX communities, although Olley (2003,
p. 209) also found that in Ezekiel "the Greek codices show higher
matching amongst themselves than that with the Hebrew, suggesting
some Greek tradition".[63] Just as a wider variance exists intra-LXX with
pericope division locations, there is also a wider variance with *styles* of
division markers, requiring us to outline each LXX MSS's style.

---

[61] However, sense divisions can be dated very early. The call for a tradition of sense
division is found in the Talmud *b. Shabb.*103b "An open section may not be written
closed, nor a closed section open (cf. *b. Ber.* 12b). Also Sof.1.15: 'If an open section
was written as closed or a closed section as open, the scroll must be stored away'"
(Tov, 1998, p. 130). There is also a Talmudic discussion regarding sense division in
the writing of the *Mezuzot*, wherein Rabbi Ḥelbo wrote the two sections closed, whilst
Rabbi Meir "wrote them as open sections" (Tov, 1998, p. 129f.). This provides evidence
that sense divisions existed at the time of Rabbi Meir, and thus the Temple period.
Metzger (1981, p. 41) also notes that "verse divisions in the Hebrew Bible by פסוקים
is witnessed to as early as the Mishnah (Megillah iv.4)". These markers do appear in
MasEzek, therefore signifying they date to at least this timeframe.

[62] For a detailed examination of how 𝔊[967,B,A] compare with the sense division units
intra-LXX and with MT see Olley (2002, pp. 210f.; and 2003).

[63] Metzger (1981, p. 70) says that "the two-stroke sign occurs in 24 of the 31 cases
where the Masoretic text has *petuḥah* (77%), and in 38 of the 62 cases where *setuma*
occurs (66%)".

Paragraphing in 𝕲[967] "is usually indicated by two short parallel lines sloping upwards to the right[64].... [and] the following line is usually slightly offset in the left margin, and the initial letter is often written in a larger script"[65] (Johnson in Johnson *et al.*, 1938, p. 15). Olley (2002, p. 204) also notes "the common scribal practice of a space, usually of one letter, [with] the script continuing on the same line". Significantly, whilst 𝕲[967] has fewer pericope divisions than our other two representative LXX MSS, it does enjoy approximately 90% agreement in Ezekiel with the MT tradition (Olley, 2002, p. 209). This suggests that these sense divisions come from an earlier existing tradition than 𝕲[967] and MT.

𝕲[B] shows evidence of both minor and major sense unit dividers; the minor division is marked often with only a one letter break, and often *paragraphos* (e.g., 36:1, 4).[66] 𝕲[B]'s major sense division breaks are often marked with the text on one line finishing part way across a column, and the next line showing *ekthesis* (e.g., 36:16; 37:1).[67]

𝕲[A] contains more sense divisions in Ezekiel than any other representative MSS. These are typically marked as follows "the first letter of each paragraph, or, if the paragraph begins in the middle of a line, the first letter of the first complete line in it...is enlarged and projects into the left-hand margin" (Metzger, 1981, p. 86).[68] If the paragraph begins in the middle of the line there is typically a 2–3 letter break. 𝕲[A] also exhibits major breaks in a similar manner to 𝕲[B], but with the first letter of the next paragraph enlarged as well as protruding into the side column.

---

[64] Olley (2003, p. 206, n. 7) has recently questioned the origins of these markers saying "it is unclear whether the original scribe was responsible for these marks.... These are probably later insertions". Regardless of their origins, we find these marks do occur in Ezek. 36–39 in the same location as any *ekthesis* marker, and hence for us identify these paragraphs.

[65] This scribal practice is called *ekthesis*.

[66] Whilst a one letter break may not seem much to the modern mind, this does occur in a text that uses *scripta continua*.

[67] This 'major' division in 𝕲[B] (also in 𝕲[A]) may reflect MT's *petuḥah* sense division.

[68] For more on the scribal practices of 𝕲[B,A] see Milne and Skeat (1938, pp. 87–93); also Swete (1989, p. 125f.).

2.5. Moving Ahead at Micro Level

In seeking insights as to how early Jewish communities interpreted the restoration of Israel in Ezekiel 36–39, our major resources are the three oldest extant Hebrew Masoretic texts, plus the MasEzek fragment, along with the three earliest Greek texts of Ezekiel. The witness of MasEzek, close to MT including chapter order, shows the major textual changes occurred before *ca.* 50 BCE and there is little evidence of Christian influence in minor variants.[69]

In the following chapters these texts will be examined at a micro level with a textual-comparative methodology, and we will find that many of the variants commentators frequently ignore or attribute to scribal error actually contain implicit interpretations. We agree with Müller (1996, p. 102) that "the Greek translation may reasonably be seen as *evidence of a process reflecting changing traditions*[70] which only gradually came to a standstill once a particular Hebrew text became normative" [italics his]. The Hebrew continued its dominance, with LXX MSS making adjustments towards the Hebrew text of their day: 𝕲[967] the *Urtext*; 𝕲[B] reflecting the initial chapter change and pericope insertion; 𝕲[A] additional Hebrew adjustments.[71] These therefore, as far as these chapters in Ezekiel are concerned, may be seen as recensions and not just 'another' translation.

Our textual-comparative methodology does not seek to discard any text or interpretive variant, but rather leave them as an exegetical trajectory from a scribe or community. We agree with Lust (1986d, p. 16) that "both the Septuagint and Massoretic text of Ezekiel may have preserved a «final form» of the Book". Whilst Hebrew and Greek variants can be compared for exegetical and theological insights, we should not seek to use one to determine the *Vorlage* of the other, nor "reduce or adjust one to the other" (Fernández Marcos, 2000, p. 77).

This equal treatment of both traditions is the same acceptance the Greek text had with the early Jewish communities, who viewed the Septuagint as a viable translation and, at least in some quarters for the Pentateuch, as inspired as the Hebrew, and equally revered. For

---

[69] We only find a couple possible 'Christian' variants in 𝕲[A] dealing with the 'Spirit/wind' in Ezek. 37.

[70] Müller (1996, p. 103f) uses the book of Daniel as an example of the way variants may indicate flux in textual and theological traditions.

[71] For a more detailed discussion, see Excursus on Unique Plusses §6.6.

variants to continue to be transmitted in LXX, after so many recensions, indicates that later LXX scribes saw these variants as part of the LXX theological and exegetical tradition, and therefore acceptable when read alongside the Hebrew. While the traditional textual-critical methodology determines the 'original' text, our textual-comparative methodology gives insight into how the various textual communities interpretively interacted with the texts before them.[72]

---

[72] Our equal treatment of texts and variants may cause some readers to feel they are left without resolve as which is the 'correct' text. Our approach may result in a degree of 'disjointedness'; it is recommended that the reader also refer to the various commentaries for the general issues surrounding a particular verse or passage.

CHAPTER THREE

THE TEXT OF EZEKIEL 36

3.1. Introduction

This chapter, and the following three, will contain a textual comparison to determine any variants that may indicate theological or exegetical activity. We will perform an intra-MT comparative study as well as an intra-LXX assessment, and also compare MT with LXX translinguistically.

In our representative manuscripts, chapter 36 appears to be thematically divided. The first section (vv. 1–15) covers the restoration of the mountains and the accusations against the mountains and land as if it was a living entity,[1] yet at the same time challenges the 'enemy' concerning their words and deeds against God's land and people. The second section (vv. 16–21), explains the people's sin as the reason for their dispersion. The third section (vv. 22–38) focuses on the restorative activity of God, announcing what he will do for Israel, and gives the reason for his actions: 'for the sake of my name' (v. 22).

3.2. Section 1: Ezek. 36:1–15

3.2.1. *36:1–4*

We will treat 36:1–4 as one paragraph. All three MT texts studied have a *petuḥah* division before 36:1. Each of the three LXX MSS also show a sense division break before 36:1: 𝔊[967] has its standard pericope division marker, 𝔊[B] its one letter break; and 𝔊[A] starts 36:1 on a new line, perhaps reflecting MT's *petuḥah* divider. All representative texts signify that they saw the start of chapter 36 as separate from chapter 35,

---

[1] For more on the land see Galambush (1999), Habel (2001), and Stevenson (2001).

perhaps to distance the destruction of Edom[2] from the restoration of
Israel. This is significant, as many scholars today tie these two chapters
together,[3] and even see the speech in 36 as being said against Edom.
Yet, for these earlier Jewish communities, the speech is against the
'enemy' (v. 2) and the 'nations around' (v. 3). This signifies a wider
group than just Edom (v. 5). This break from chapter 35, dealing with
'Edom' enables chapter 36 to have a closer thematic link to Ezek. 6,
which speaks of the judgement on the mountains of Israel.

Both MT^C and MT^L contain a *setumah* division break after 36:4.
However, MT^A and MasEzek do not witness any break. 𝕲^967 does not
have a break after v. 4. Yet 𝕲^B has its one-letter break after both v. 3
and v. 4. 𝕲^A has a small break after v. 4 (also after vv. 2, 5, 6). This
all indicates varying sense division views for these MSS. For MT^C,L
and 𝕲^B,A, vv. 1–4 with its own sense division theologically encloses:
the boast of the enemy; the LORD's response to that boast; and the
address that goes out to the mountains (vv. 1, 4) that the mountains
should receive the prophetic proclamation, even of what is stated to
the countryside (v. 4). These texts see the countryside (v. 4) as being
within the proclamation to the mountains, whereas those who do not
see a break here (MT^A, MasEzek, 𝕲^967) have the countryside as the
addressees for vv. 5, 6.

Through its interpretive translation of this pericope, we will observe
that the LXX community sees itself surrounded by nations who despise
and hate them, and who insult and trample them down, and they
exhibit signs of feeling harshly treated.[4]

36:2[5] כֹּה אָמַר אֲדֹנָי יְהוִֹה יַעַן אָמַר הָאוֹיֵב עֲלֵיכֶם הֶאָח וּבָמוֹת
עוֹלָם לְמוֹרָשָׁה הָיְתָה לָּנוּ׃

36:2 τάδε λέγει κύριος κύριος ἀνθ' ὧν (𝕲^967,A: ὧν; 𝕲^B: οὐ) εἶπεν ὁ
ἐχθρὸς ἐφ' ὑμᾶς εὖγε (𝕲^A: εὖγε εὖγε) ἔρημα αἰώνια εἰς κατάσχεσιν
ἡμῖν ἐγενήθη

---

[2] Included in Edom is Mount Seir, which the LORD is against, and its destruction
(35:2, 3, 15), as compared with the 'Mountains of Israel' which the LORD is taking
back from the 'enemy' and is restoring because he is 'for you' (36:1–9).
[3] For example, Zimmerli, Block and Allen all treat 35:1–36:15 as a theological
block.
[4] LXX's use of the passive at these points suggests they felt these things had been
done to them and they did not deserve it to that extent.
[5] As noted previously variations in the divine name are being ignored.

MT says וּבָמוֹת עוֹלָם ('ancient heights'), but LXX has ἔρημα αἰώνια ('everlasting waste places'). Scholars typically ascribe this variant to scribal error. Allen (1990b, p. 168) states that "LXX presupposes וּשְׁמֹמוֹת or וּשְׁמוֹת 'and ruins' for Heb. וּבָמוֹת 'and high places', probably by assimilation to שְׁמֹמוֹת עוֹלָם 'perpetual ruins' in 35:9". Block (1998, p. 324) says LXX "looks suspiciously harmonistic; cf. 35:9". Cooke (1936, p. 386) believes LXX "suggests a more probable reading". However, this may be the result of a trans-linguistic wordplay, an implicit interpretation of how LXX saw the effects of idolatry on the high places[6] (cf. vv. 17–18), which caused the desolation of these mountain-ous heights and the land of Israel, requiring restoration for the nation. Therefore, LXX exegetes as 'waste places' (the effect), from MT's 'high places' (the event). 𝕲^A's additional εὖγε may be to emphasise the 'snort' of the enemy against the mountains of Israel.[7]

36:3 לָכֵן הִנָּבֵא וְאָמַרְתָּ כֹּה אָמַר אֲדֹנָי יְהוִה יַעַן בְּיַעַן שַׁמּוֹת וְשָׁאֹף
אֶתְכֶם מִסָּבִיב לִהְיוֹתְכֶם מוֹרָשָׁה לִשְׁאֵרִית הַגּוֹיִם וַתֵּעֲלוּ עַל־שְׂפַת
לָשׁוֹן וְדִבַּת־עָם:

36:3 διὰ τοῦτο προφήτευσον καὶ εἰπόν τάδε λέγει κύριος κύριος ἀντὶ τοῦ ἀτιμασθῆναι ὑμᾶς καὶ μισηθῆναι ὑμᾶς (𝕲^967: – ὑμᾶς) (𝕲^A: + ἀπὸ τῶν ἐθνῶν) (𝕲^967,B: ὑπὸ) τῶν κύκλῳ ὑμῶν τοῦ εἶναι ὑμᾶς εἰς κατάσχεσιν τοῖς καταλοίποις ἔθνεσιν καὶ ἀνέβητε λάλημα γλώσσῃ (𝕲^967,A: γλώσσης) καὶ εἰς ὀνείδισμα ἔθνεσιν (𝕲^967: καὶ εἰς ὀνειδισμὸν ἐθνῶν)[8]

MT describes the action of the enemy as יַעַן בְּיַעַן שַׁמּוֹת וְשָׁאֹף אֶתְכֶם ('because [they] devastate and crush you'), yet LXX says ἀντὶ τοῦ ἀτιμασθῆναι ὑμᾶς καὶ μισηθῆναι ὑμᾶς ('because you have been dis-honoured and you have been hated'). There is difficulty in translating שַׁמּוֹת וְשָׁאֹף, and Block (1998, p. 325 n.11) provides examples of how some have emended the Hebrew; yet he concludes such are "ill advised

---

[6] בָּמוֹת in Ezekiel typically refers to the high places where idolatry took place (cf. 6:3, 5; 16:16; 20:29). Fisch (1985, p. 238) says בָּמוֹת "in the mouth of a Hebrew prophet normally denotes idolatrous altars; but as used by the *enemy* it is a designation for the Holy Land in general". Block (1998, p. 328) also believes that in this context it is used "geographically" and "is therefore a poetic designation for the mountains of Israel". Yet Cooper (1994, p. 311, n.42) points out that "although it can have a less technical sense, the use of the term in 36:2 does allow the hearer to remember the misuse of those mountain shrines". This concept appears to have been in the mind of the LXX translator, especially as these first verses of chapter 36 appear to be a reversal or a restoration from the judgement outlined in chapter 6.

[7] 𝕲^967,B only have a single εὖγε which follows MT (cf. Gehman, 1938, p. 124).

[8] Gehman (1938, p. 124) states "syntactically Sch[eide] agrees with [MT]".

given the frequency of the root *šmm* in the context".[9] Cooke (1936, p. 386) says that LXX "may be nothing more than a guess". While forms of שָׁמֵם can mean 'appalled' or 'astonished' (Ezek. 27:35; 28:19; 32:10) its primary meaning is 'devastate/desolate' or 'waste', which suits its context here (Williams, 1997, p. 168; also *HALOT*).[10] In other places where MT uses שָׁמֵם with this primary meaning, LXX embraces the sense with ἐρημόω/ἐρῆμος ('desolate/wasted' 29:12; 30:7, 12; 32:15; 35:12, 15), ἀπόλλυμι ('destroy/demolish', 30:14), ἀπώλεια ('destruction', 32:15), ἀφανίζω ('destroy/obliterate', 36:4, 34, 35, 36). Whilst LXX uses ἀτιμάζω ('dishonour') here in 36:3 for שְׁמָמוֹת, LXX uses ἀτιμάζω elsewhere in Ezekiel (28:24, 26; 36:5) for שׁוּט ('contempt/despise'). In 36:7 LXX also uses the noun form ἀτιμία ('dishonour') for MT's כְּלִמָּה ('reproach/insult/shame') (cf. Ezek. 16:52, 54, 63; 39:26; 44:13).[11] Perhaps LXX's use of 'dishonour/shame' in 36:5, 7 influenced LXX's use of ἀτιμάζω in 36:3 when translating שְׁמָמוֹת. LXX may have seen MT's 'contempt' (v. 5) and/or 'reproach/shame' (v. 7) behind the action of the nations which LXX then interprets as 'dishonouring' here in v. 3 as the reason for MT's 'devastate' (i.e., the surrounding nations devastated them because these nations dishonoured them). Overall, rather than finding an emendation here, or seeing the LXX translator as taking a guess, we can establish that the LXX translator[12] was aware of 'destroy/desolate' as a primary meaning for שְׁמָמוֹת, but made an exegetical choice here.

שָׁאַף does not occur elsewhere in Ezekiel, but it is found in Isaiah (42:14), Jeremiah (2:24; 14:6), and Psalms (119:131), where it has the contextual meaning of 'to pant after' (Fredericks, 1997, p. 11). However, both the Psalmist (56:2, 3; 57:4) and Amos (2:7; 8:4) use שָׁאַף with the meaning of 'be a nuisance, pester' [*HALOT*], and LXX embraces this

---

[9] Zimmerli (1983, p. 228) also states "it is inadvisable to depart from the root שׁמם".

[10] Cooke's (1936, p. 394) 'preferred' suggestion 'c' has שְׁמָמוֹת as the *pi'el* of שׁמת with the meaning of "*have malicious joy* in Jewish Aram.", and then says the LXX translation "suits" this suggestion. Yet Cooke's suggestion here still does not match the meaning of ἀτιμάζω as 'dishonoured'. Cooke's suggestion 'a' has שְׁמָמוֹת as 'devastated', which is our preference above.

[11] MT also uses כְּלִמָּה in 36:6, 15 but in both places LXX translates with ὀνειδισμός ('reproach'), perhaps as a continuation of the 'insult/reproach' stated in v.3 (where MT used וְדִבַּת־עָם).

[12] We note that by 'the LXX translator' we are referring to Thackeray's 'Translator β', as this person(s) is the accepted translator of Ezekiel 36–39 (see our previous chapter 2). This applies for all future references to 'the LXX translator', unless otherwise noted.

meaning, often translating with πατέω ('trample down').[13] The LXX translator(s) of Isaiah, Jeremiah, Psalms and Amos each capture the Hebrew meanings in the various contexts and translate them accordingly. Only in Ezek. 36:3 do we find LXX using μισέω 'hate'. We therefore suggest that rather than LXX 'guessing' here (so Greenberg, 1997, p. 717), LXX has theologically interpreted MT's *action* ('crush and trample') by showing the *heart* of the enemy behind that action, exegeting that this happened to them because they were 'dishonoured and hated'. Thus, MT provides an explanation for *how* they became the possession of the surrounding nations, whereas LXX gives the attitude of the enemy as the reason *why* they became a possession.

The later 𝔊^{B,A} both implicitly emphasise this interpretive 'dishonoured and hated' by their ὑμᾶς plus that is not witnessed in 𝔊^{967} or MT. This causes the phrase to read '*you* have been dishonoured and *you* have been hated', emphasising the attitude of the enemy against them.

Further, MT has two *qal* infinitive construct verbs, yet LXX uses two passive verbs to make explicit that this action is clearly done *to* the people. LXX's use of passive verbs, here and in other instances in vv. 1–15, may indicate that LXX sees the people of the land, and therefore themselves, as harshly treated, with the action being done, or having been done, *to* them. In this way the LXX personalises the text to their situation and environment. We will find as we progress through the text that the LXX scribe or even community appears to see themselves surrounded by nations who continue to oppose them (here, dishonour and hate them), especially with the later 𝔊^{A}, as shown by its various plusses.

𝔊^{A}'s plus of ἀπὸ τῶν ἐθνῶν ('from the nations [around you]') is not represented in either 𝔊^{967,B}, which both have ὑπὸ τῶν κύκλῳ ὑμῶν ('by those around you'), nor in MT (מִסָּבִיב 'from around'). 𝔊^{A}'s plus interprets the identity of 'those around' and the direction from where the hatred is coming (ἀπό): that the enemy is not just an individual, or individuals, but the *nations* surrounding them. 𝔊^{A}'s use of ἀπό here (cf. 𝔊^{967,B} ὑπό) most likely occurs because of its plus (cf. ἀπό and ὑπό in 36:13).

---

[13] Fairbairn (1969, p. 387) claims that שָׁאַף means "to snuff up, in the manner of a wild beast, which with a keen and ravenous appetite smells after its prey, in order to seize and devour it." And in Psa. 56:2 "it is used by the Psalmist...of his cruel enemies: 'Be gracious to me, O God, for there snuffs after me man [sic] etc.'"

At the end of this verse, MT just states that they were the objects of people's talk (וְדִבַּת־עָם),[14] yet 𝕲^{B,A}'s use of the dative produces a meaning that they were a 'reproach/insult *to* the nations', and 𝕲^{967}'s use of the genitive, that they were the 'reproach/insult *of* the nations'. Thus, LXX implicitly interprets what kind of talk MT refers to, that it was reproachful and/or insulting talk. The 'insulting/reproachful talk' is taken up again in v. 6, and in v. 15 where the 'insult' is identified (miscarriage/bereavement). In vv. 6, 15 MT uses כְּלִמָּה ('insult/ reproach/shame'), which LXX translates with ὀνειδισμός. This may have influenced LXX's use of ὀνειδισμός here in v. 3 rather than λόγος, as one would anticipate. It is possible that MT's use of וְדִבַּת־עָם is a reference to the דִּבָּה ('evil report') as part of the ancient charge against the land (cf. Num. 13:32; 14:36f.), and as such LXX has interpreted דִּבָּה here as not just 'evil report' but as 'insult/reproach'. This may well be the case when we consider the context of 36:12b–15, which also alludes to the 'evil' report of the spies. We also note that LXX uses ἔθνεσιν for MT's עָם, which interprets 'nations' instead of 'people'. Often עָם is used for the people of Israel, so LXX makes it clear that this talk is against them and coming from the nations. MT's attention is on the action done by the 'enemy' to the mountains by the people—they were 'a subject of talk'; yet LXX focuses on the result of that 'talk'—they were an insult/reproach to the nations. This comes from the view of those who have been spoken against (we have been reproached/insulted) and may again suggest they felt harshly treated. When we combine this point with the 'dishonoured and hated' attitude that the LXX communities indicated in their interpretation, we then have reason for the surrounding nations' insulting talk against Israel. We may also note that LXX's exegetical use of ὀνείδισμα does not give room for LXX to reflect MT's intra-Hebrew word play with the following verse (דְּבַר־אֲדֹנָי cf. v. 4 וְדִבַּת עָם).

Thus, in v. 3 MT has the action of the enemy, which is given as the reason for the word of the LORD to be spoken to the countryside in v. 4. Yet LXX has interpreted this action as the result of attitude of the nations around, who are insulting them. This is LXX's reason for the word of the LORD in v. 4.

36:4 לָכֵן הָרֵי יִשְׂרָאֵל שִׁמְעוּ דְּבַר־אֲדֹנָי יְהוִה כֹּה־אָמַר אֲדֹנָי יְהוִה
לֶהָרִים וְלַגְּבָעוֹת לָאֲפִיקִים וְלַגֵּאָיוֹת וְלֶחֳרָבוֹת הַשֹּׁמְמוֹת וְלֶעָרִים
הַנֶּעֱזָבוֹת אֲשֶׁר הָיוּ לְבַז וּלְלַעַג לִשְׁאֵרִית הַגּוֹיִם אֲשֶׁר מִסָּבִיב:

---

[14] Eisemann (1994, p. 549) says דִּבָּה "is generally used in a sense of *defamation*".

36:4 διὰ τοῦτο ὄρη (𝔊⁹⁶⁷: – ὄρη) Ισραηλ ἀκούσατε λόγον κυρίου τάδε λέγει κύριος τοῖς ὄρεσιν καὶ τοῖς βουνοῖς καὶ ταῖς φάραγξιν καὶ τοῖς χειμάρροις καὶ (𝔊ᴬ: + ταῖς νάπαις) τοῖς ἐξηρημωμένοις καὶ ἠφανισμένοις καὶ ταῖς πόλεσιν ταῖς ἐγκαταλελειμμέναις αἳ ἐγένοντο εἰς προνομὴν καὶ εἰς (𝔊⁹⁶⁷,ᴬ: – εἰς) καταπάτημα τοῖς καταλειφθεῖσιν ἔθνεσιν (𝔊⁹⁶⁷: – ἔθνεσιν) περικύκλῳ (𝔊ᴬ: + τοῖς περικύκλῳ)

𝔊⁹⁶⁷'s minus of ὄρη directs the prophecy to 'Israel' as a nation, rather than to the mountains as in the other MSS. In 36:1 𝔊⁹⁶⁷ is minus the genitive definite article before Ισραηλ, which also makes the speech appear to be directed to 'Israel' as a people rather than to the mountains of Israel. However, in v. 8 𝔊⁹⁶⁷ follows the other LXX MSS and has the speech directed to the mountains.

As one of the recipients of the LORD's word MT has וְלֶחֳרָבוֹת (noun f.pl.) and הַשְּׁמֵמוֹת (*qal* ptc.f.pl.) (lit. 'ruins of desolating'), whereas LXX has καὶ τοῖς ἐξηρημωμένοις καὶ ἠφανισμένοις (both ptc. perf. pass. dat. neut. pl.) ('and to those [places]¹⁵ which have been made desolate and destroyed'). The LXX translator has added καὶ ἠφανισμένοις ('and been destroyed'). Thus LXX emphasises the destruction, and its use of the passive emphasises that this action has been done *to* them, that they have *been made* desolate and have *been* destroyed. The action is done against the people in MT, but our suggestion is that LXX implicitly emphasises this by its use of the passive. LXX's use of the passive participle may suggest that the LXX community saw this as an ongoing action, and that they continued to suffer reproach from surrounding nations (v. 3), and continued in their desolation and destruction (v. 4). This again echoes a feeling of being harshly treated. We suggest this reflects the viewpoint of Diaspora Jews, or even those in the land during Greco-Roman rule.

Again in v. 4, MT has לְבַז וּלְלַעַג ([the cities have become] 'a spoil and *ridicule*'), and LXX says εἰς προνομὴν καὶ εἰς καταπάτημα ([the cities have become] 'a spoil and *trampled/trodden down, destroyed*' [LEH]).¹⁶ MT's 'ridicule' is in reference to the 'talk' (v. 3b), and 'insults' (v. 13). Instead of repeating 'reproach/insult' from v. 3, which would have fitted the context of 'ridicule', LXX again appears to interpret MT's action of being ridiculed, stating they are being 'trodden underfoot',

---

¹⁵ The context suggests these verbs are not referring to humans but their environment.

¹⁶ 𝔊⁹⁶⁷,ᴬ's minus of εἰς here does not change the meaning as εἰς is mentioned earlier and carries over here.

perhaps again feeling victimised, by the surrounding nations.[17] $\mathfrak{G}^{A}$'s plus of τοῖς reads '*to those* round about', specifying the proximity of these nations. Overall, LXX catches and interprets MT's concept in v. 3 of being crushed and spoken against, and here in v. 4 of being an object of ridicule. This may indicate that LXX saw their being trampled or trodden on as the result of the 'nations round about' dishonouring and ridiculing them (so MT). These surrounding nations are spoken against in v. 5.

3.2.2. *36:5–12*

As stated above, some MSS do not have a break between vv. 4–5 (MT^{A}, MasEzek, $\mathfrak{G}^{967}$), whereas the others do, affecting the identity of the addressees for v. 5–6. It is significant that all MT MSS have a break after v. 12, with MT^{C} a *petuḥah*, and MT^{A,L} and MasEzek a *setumah*.[18] LXX varies with its sense divisions, with $\mathfrak{G}^{967}$ witnessing its division marker after v. 12, yet $\mathfrak{G}^{B}$ exhibits no clear break after v. 12. This is possibly due to $\mathfrak{G}^{B}$ finishing v. 12 at the end of a line, giving no opportunity for a single letter break. $\mathfrak{G}^{B}$ does exhibit a *paragraphos* marker at the start of the following line, but we are left unsure as to whether these markers were placed by the original scribe or a later one. It is therefore possible that $\mathfrak{G}^{B}$ does exhibit a break here. However, if not, then $\mathfrak{G}^{B}$ may have seen the 'no more cause you to miscarriage' (vv. 13–15) as the ultimate overturning of the insults (vv. 5–7) and of the restoration and fruitfulness (vv. 8–12). $\mathfrak{G}^{A}$ has small breaks after vv. 5 and 6, and a larger one in v. 7b (see below), signifying vv. 5–7a and vv. 7b–12 as self-contained theological units. $\mathfrak{G}^{A}$ has a break after v. 12, with v. 13 having the first letter large and protruding into the column. Throughout Ezekiel $\mathfrak{G}^{A}$ has numerous breaks not witnessed in any other representative text, and sees vv. 7b–12 as its own theological unit.

Overall, this pericope has the tone of Israel re-entering the land, where other nations are seen as illegal occupants of the land (v. 5). These nations will be removed (vv. 6–7), and the LORD's people 'Israel' will occupy his land (cf. 'my people—my land' vv. 8–9). They will mul-

---

[17] $\mathfrak{G}^{967}$'s minus of ἔθνεσιν leaves the text saying 'those remaining round about' leaving 'nations' as only implied. This may have been a later clarifying plus by the other MSS.

[18] This part of MasEzek is 'reconstructed' and the break is proposed (Talmon, 1999, pp. 64, 73).

tiply and be established as before, thus again inheriting the land (vv. 11–12). We will again find LXX interpreting and/or intensifying MT, and reflecting a feeling of being harshly treated. LXX may indicate that they do not see the fulfilment in their generation, and therefore interprets the text with their current situation in mind. MT appears to have a couple of theological plusses in this section (cf. vv. 7, 11), and 𝔊ᴬ has a rare minus (v. 9).

36:5 לָכֵן כֹּה־אָמַר אֲדֹנָי יְהוִה אִם־לֹא בְּאֵשׁ קִנְאָתִי דִבַּרְתִּי עַל־
שְׁאֵרִית הַגּוֹיִם וְעַל־אֱדוֹם כֻּלָּא אֲשֶׁר נָתְנוּ־אֶת־אַרְצִי לָהֶם לְמוֹרָשָׁה
בְּשִׂמְחַת כָּל־לֵבָב בִּשְׁאָט נֶפֶשׁ לְמַעַן מִגְרָשָׁהּ לָבַז:

36:5 διὰ τοῦτο τάδε λέγει κύριος κύριος εἰ μὴν ἐν πυρὶ θυμοῦ μου ἐλάλησα ἐπὶ τὰ λοιπὰ ἔθνη καὶ ἐπὶ τὴν Ιδουμαίαν πᾶσαν ὅτι ἔδωκαν τὴν γῆν μου ἑαυτοῖς εἰς κατάσχεσιν μετ᾽ εὐφροσύνης ἀτιμάσαντες ψυχὰς τοῦ ἀφανίσαι ἐν προνομῇ

For the MSS without a break between vv. 4 and 5 (MTᴬ, MasEzek, 𝔊⁹⁶⁷), v. 5 completes the speech to the countryside begun in v. 4 and sees those locations as the places of plunder. The focus is the clash of attitudes between the LORD and the nations, including all of Edom.[19] Firstly, we find the LORD's attitude. Where MT says the LORD speaks against the nations and Edom בְּאֵשׁ קִנְאָתִי ('in the fire of my jealousy'), LXX says it is ἐν πυρὶ θυμοῦ μου ('in the fire of my wrath'). We ask why LXX did not use ζῆλος ('jealousy') as in v. 6 (also 16:38). We find that earlier in 5:13 LXX used ζῆλος for קנא, and there are several times in Ezekiel when θυμός and ζῆλος are used together (e.g., 5:13; 16:38, 42; 23:25; 36:6; 38:19). These may all have influenced the usage of θυμός here, as may the use of וּבַחֲמָתִי ('and in my wrath') in v. 6. Regardless, here MT gives us the basic action or attitude of God acting out of his jealousy regarding his land, whilst LXX appears to intensify by giving the result of God being jealous, he is now angry/wrathful and this wrath appears to be directed against the nations and Edom.

In the same way, in v. 5 MT has אשר ('who/which'), that refers to "the actions of Edom and the nations involved staking claims on Yahweh's land" (Block, 1998, p. 330). Yet LXX's use of ὅτι ('because') highlights the reason for the LORD's wrath. In so doing, LXX clarifies the reason for MT's action that God is burning in wrath against the

---

[19] Some, like Cooke (1936, p. 387), say that "some later hand has specified Edom in particular". Yet the context of chapter 35, and the textual evidence that does not have a MSS without 'Edom', suggests its originality.

nations and Edom *because* they have taken his land away from his people. Thus LXX's use of ὅτι here must be considered in conjunction with the interpretive θυμός, as they both show exegetical intent.

Secondly, we have the attitude of the nations. MT says it was בִּשְׁאָט נֶפֶשׁ ('with contempt of soul' cf. 25:6, 15), but LXX has ἀτιμάσαντες ψυχὰς ('having dishonoured lives'). LXX has not treated נֶפֶשׁ as a noun describing the soul/mind of the plunderers, but as the object of their plunder—the people of the land. This enables LXX's use of an aorist participle, describing the action of 'having dishonoured' the land/people. LXX may have recognised the 'contemptuous soul' but interpreted the action of 'contempt' as 'a disregard' for their lives. This again echoes the heart of those who believe they have been plundered (v. 5c), downtrodden (v. 4), and hated (v. 3), and being harshly treated. The use of the participle may suggest that LXX sees their surrounding nations continuing to 'dishonour' them. MT's plus[20] here of כָּל־לֵבָב also theologically expands the attitude of the plunderers regarding the 'contempt of soul' that it introduces.[21]

Again, MT has לְמַעַן מִגְרָשָׁה לָבַז ('in order to plunder her pasture-land'),[22] whilst LXX has τοῦ ἀφανίσαι ἐν προνομῇ ('to destroy by plunder'), which appears to interpret the result of being plundered, perhaps from the viewpoint of those who have been plundered.[23] LXX has no mention of 'pasture', thus omitting the object that was plundered. The concept of לְמַעַן as the *purpose* for the action in MT is only implicitly referred to by LXX through its use of the infinitive. LXX appears to use the infinitive to interpret the result of MT action that 'to plunder is

---

[20] It is difficult to see why LXX would have omitted this, and so we are left with it being a later MT plus.

[21] Interestingly, Greenberg (1997, p. 718) says "*wholehearted rejoicing, with wholesouled contempt*. These are examples of Ezekiel's play on the wording of his sources". Thus Greenberg also finds 'wordplay' in the Hebrew text and Deuteronomic sources.

[22] Or 'because of its pasture, to plunder it' (NRSV).

[23] LXX may have seen מִגְרָשָׁה as גרש 'to drive out' rather than open pastures, making 'in order to drive out as spoil' (Hulst, 1960, p. 213). Allen (1990b, p. 168) sees MT מִגְרָשָׁה as an early gloss. Cooke's (1936, p. 394) suggestion that "possibly למען מגרשה is a miswritten form of להם למקרשה in the line above" is speculative and without substance. The interpretation of מִגְרָשָׁה is complex and LXX could have simplified. Block (1998, p. 326) points out that "In Leviticus and Numbers *migrāš* denotes the territory adjoining the walls of a city given to the Levites as 'pastureland,' and this is how many understand it here. However, the sense of 'pastureland' derives from the contexts in which the expression occurs, not from the word itself". We suggest that LXX did understand the 'pastureland' meaning in Numbers and Leviticus, due to an evident awareness of those two books found in the way LXX interacts with them here in Ezekiel 36 (e.g., vv. 8, 13–15).

to destroy' [possessions]. Thus, the focus of LXX appears to be on the people being destroyed rather than the land. MT's use of 'pastureland' fits with the context of 'land/ground'. Even if LXX saw the meaning of מִגְרָשָׁה as 'cast out', its use of 'destroy' (ἀφανίσαι) can be seen to interpret MT's action of being cast out: the people are destroyed.

We note Symmachus says ὑπὲρ τοῦ ἀδόκιμον ποιῆσαι αὐτήν, καὶ τοῦ διαρπάσαι ('so as to make it worthless, and to plunder') (Field, 1964, p. 867). Whilst Symmachus here could still be based on MT, yet treating the noun 'pastures' as a participle, we nevertheless find his understanding is similar to that of LXX, providing an intent for the plunder—to make God's land worthless.

While we will not deal directly with v. 6, due to the absence of any apparent theological variants, we do note that it continues the running themes of 'jealousy', 'wrath', and 'insults of the nations'. These themes appear to be the influencing factor in LXX's theological interpretation in previous verses (e.g., ὀνείδισμα 'reproach' v. 3).

36:7 לָכֵן כֹּה אָמַר אֲדֹנָי יְהוִה אֲנִי נָשָׂאתִי אֶת־יָדִי אִם־לֹא הַגּוֹיִם
אֲשֶׁר לָכֶם מִסָּבִיב הֵמָּה כְּלִמָּתָם יִשָּׂאוּ:

36:7 διὰ τοῦτο (𝔊ᴬ: + ἰδού) ἐγὼ ἀρῶ τὴν χεῖρά μου ἐπὶ τὰ ἔθνη τὰ περικύκλῳ ὑμῶν οὗ τοι τὴν ἀτιμίαν αὐτῶν λήμψονται

LXX does not reflect MT's declarative formula כֹּה אָמַר אֲדֹנָי יְהוִה, and only implies it by connection to the previous verse which also contains it. Cooke (1936, p. 387) says that LXX omits this formula "perhaps rightly; the formula stands in its proper place in v. ⁴ᵇ; here it may have come in with the insertions vv. ⁵· ⁶". Yet Cooke does not offer any other support for his suggestion. Zimmerli (1983, p. 230) says "this textual lacuna is undoubtedly a result of a harmonizing of the text in 𝔊". We note that LXX does not reflect MT's oath formula of אִם־לֹא ('surely'). This needs to be considered together with its declarative formula minus, especially as LXX included the oath formula in v. 5 (cf. εἰ μήν). Zimmerli (1983, p. 230) suggests that LXX's use of ἐπί ('against') for MT's אִם־לֹא presupposes אל, which indicates this oath formula may have been in LXX's *Vorlage*. Of note, MasEzek witnesses both the declarative and oath formulas. 𝔊ᴬ's plus of ἰδού may indicate awareness of the oath, but making 'my hand against' a stronger statement. On the other hand, LXX may not have understood the declarative and oath formulae used together here in MT. However, if LXX misunderstood the oath here, then why was it understood elsewhere? The declarative formula is followed by the oath formula in Ezek. 17:19; 33:27; 34:8;

35:6; 36:5, where LXX reflects the usage of both (with εἰ μήν). While none of these passages include the further oath of אֲנִי נָשָׂאתִי אֶת־יָדִי, these passages do demonstrate LXX's awareness of the declarative and oath formulas. Leaving out the declarative and oath formula here changes the flow of this verse, and allows LXX to have the Lord's hand raised 'against (ἐπί) the nations'. LXX's minus here may well have been intentional in order to have the Lord lifting his hand *against* the nations in a punishing action, rather than lifting his hand just in an oath as in MT.

LXX turns MT's *qal* perfect into future, from 'I have' to 'I will' [lift up my hand], suggesting LXX's focus is on the future (or even their present). The focus is on what God's hand *will* do, rather than on an oath that has been made but is not yet fully realized, as suggested by MT's 'I have' and 'they will'. This also could be a subtle interpretation of the Lord's action of lifting his hand: it will be against the nations. It may indicate that the LXX scribe either does not see these events as having yet occurred, or perhaps is looking for it to happen again in his generation.[24] The context of v. 7b, when compared to v. 6b, indicates that the 'dishonour' (ἀτιμία LXX) and/or 'insults/reproach' (כְּלִמָּה MT) that Israel is experiencing will be turned back upon those nations who are currently uttering these insults (cf. ὀνειδισμός 'reproach/shame' for כְּלִמָּה in 36:6, 15; yet ἀτιμία again in 39:26). LXX may be interacting with MT's 'insults' here by its use of 'dishonour', which appears to indicate that they saw these insults as bringing dishonour to them. We have already seen (as we will again) the feeling of being 'harshly treated' in LXX. Perhaps v. 6b is how they see their situation, and v. 7b is not their reality.

𝔊ᴬ has a large gap in v. 7b, with οὗτοί beginning on a new line with an enlarged and bolded O that signifies a larger sense division break. This then attaches the last phrase of v. 7c to the beginning of v. 8, causing this section to start with the contrasting phrase '*They* shall bear their dishonour, but *you*, mountains of Israel…'. Perhaps 𝔊ᴬ saw the restoration of Israel, both land and population, as the way the nations would 'bear their dishonour'. Their attempt to trample Israel would then be ultimately defeated.

---

[24] Even today, many interpret texts in light of current situations rather than examining where fulfilment(s) may have already occurred in the past. This is particularly true in the interpretation of eschatological texts.

36:8 וְאַתֶּם הָרֵי יִשְׂרָאֵל עַנְפְּכֶם תִּתֵּנוּ וּפֶרְיְכֶם תִּשְׂאוּ לְעַמִּי
יִשְׂרָאֵל כִּי קֵרְבוּ לָבוֹא

36:8 ὑμῶν δέ ὄρη Ισραηλ τὴν σταφυλὴν καὶ τὸν καρπὸν ὑμῶν (𝕲⁹⁶⁷ᐟᴮ:
ὑμῶν; 𝕲ᴬ: –) καταφάγεται ὁ λαός μου ὅτι (𝕲⁹⁶⁷: ἐγγίζουσιν; 𝕲ᴮᐟᴬ:
ἐλπίζουσιν) τοῦ ἐλθεῖν

Modern commentators often see 'but you' of v. 8 as a sense division
marker, and place vv. 8–12 as its own thought unit. 𝕲ᴬ is the only
ancient witness for such division, although starting with the preceding
phrase in v. 7b.

The instruction to the mountains of עַנְפְּכֶם תִּתֵּנוּ וּפֶרְיְכֶם תִּשְׂאוּ לְעַמִּי
יִשְׂרָאֵל ('your branches you will give, and your fruit you will carry to
my people Israel') in MT and MasEzek is not matched by LXX, which
simply informs the mountains τὴν σταφυλὴν καὶ τὸν καρπὸν ὑμῶν
καταφάγεται ὁ λαός μου ('your grapes and fruit, my people shall eat').
It could be that LXX "misreads '*npkm*' ['branches'] as '*nbkm*' ['grapes']"
(Block, 1998, p. 331, also Zimmerli, 1983, p. 230).[25] Alternatively, this
could be another implicit LXX wordplay, interpreting what fruit will
be on the branches; especially as grapes are symbolic in Judaism for
joy. This wordplay may be a deliberate reference to the grapes that
the 'spies' brought back, carried between two men (Num. 13:23). If
so, this reinforces the idea that the LXX translator (and perhaps his
community) had the Numbers passage in mind when translating this
section (cf. Ezek. 36:3, 13), and perhaps saw their return to the land
as another re-entering and possessing the land as their forefathers did
(cf. v. 11 'as in your beginning'). It is possible that MT also had the
Numbers passage in mind, yet more implicitly than in LXX. If so,
LXX exegetes, catching MT's implicit echo, and provides the result of
MT's action. This may be seen in LXX's καταφάγεται ὁ λαός μου ('my
people shall eat'), which interprets the need for the fruit: consumption
by God's people. It is interesting that the later Symmachus[26] has τοὺς
κλάδους ὑμῶν δώσετε, which matches MT perhaps as a correction to
LXX (Field, 1964, p. 868). Greenberg (1997, p. 719) suggests that MT
had Genesis 2 and the trees in the Garden of Eden in mind. This may
also be correct as Ezekiel contains several mentions of Eden (27:23;

---

[25] Cooke (1936, p. 395) says "the parallel 17⁸ לעשות...ולשאת makes M's text
preferable".

[26] As noted in §2.2.1, the fragmentary nature of the Hexapla leaves only this one
witness, and we are without evidence for Aquila or Theodotion. This will also be the
case in following examples where we refer to the Hexapla.

28:13; 31:9, 16, 18 [2×]; and 36:35). It is possible that both the Genesis and Numbers accounts were in the mind of MT, yet LXX only had the Numbers event in mind.

For MT, the producing of branches and fruit was a future action that would be done for the returnees. Yet for LXX, the branches already exist and are fruitful. In addition, MT has the mountains as an active participant providing for the returnees, informing the mountains that they shall 'give branches and carry/bear fruit'. Yet LXX only informs the mountains what will happen to them passively when the Lord's people will return ('your grapes and fruit my people shall eat').

𝔊ᴬ is minus ὑμῶν, just reading 'the grapes and [the] fruits', which emphasizes the passive participation of the mountains, avoiding any personal message to the mountains (cf. v. 10 where 𝔊ᴬ adds ὑμῶν, to personalise it more).

MT has לְעַמִּי יִשְׂרָאֵל, whilst LXX has only ὁ λαός μου (cf. עַמִּי 37:12). This may be an MT plus, especially as Targum follows LXX, being inserted by MT to emphasise the identity of the Lord's people, perhaps to clear up any confusion in their community (or surrounding nations). However, MasEzek witnesses יִשְׂרָאֵל, so if it was a Hebrew plus it was quite early, and as such narrows the timeframe to the Greco-Roman period, even in the Maccabean time. It is surprising that the later 𝔊ᴬ did not include this plus, as it often follows MT plusses. We do not know why Targum followed LXX here, but perhaps this was not in the Hebrew MSS used by Targum.

LXX does not reflect MT's wordplay with נשׂא, where different idioms are used: you נשׂא the insults of the nations (v. 6); I נשׂא my hand (v. 7a); [the nations] shall נשׂא insults (v. 7b); [you mountains] shall נשׂא your fruit (v. 8). Similarly, the reversal where the enemy נתן themselves the land (v. 5), and then the mountains (i.e., land) נתן their fruit to the people (v. 8). These MT wordplays may be an implicit indication of how restoration would be realised, and the ruinous activity of the enemy reversed. It is curious that LXX did not capture and reflect these and other similar Hebrew wordplays.

We find a subtle yet important intra-LXX difference where 𝔊⁹⁶⁷ has ἐγγίζουσίν ('they are drawing near' [to return]) reflecting MT's קָרְבוּ, yet 𝔊ᴮ·ᴬ have ἐλπίζουσίν ('they hope to' [return]). This 'hope' shows the heart, or attitude, of the returnees rather than just the event of 'drawing near', as in MT and 𝔊⁹⁶⁷. Gehman (in Johnson *et al.*, 1938, p. 125 [cf. p. 19]) notes that 𝔊⁹⁶⁷ "is alone amongst all Greek MSS in preserving the correct rendering of the Hebrew קרבו". He believes that this, and other similar textual indicators,[27] demonstrate that 𝕲[967] was directly influenced by the Hebrew original (*Urtext*), and that "the Scheide version represents an early tradition which may be closer to the original LXX than either B or the Syro-Hexaplar" (Gehman in Johnson *et al.*, 1938, p. 76).

Cooke (1936, p. 395) suggests "ἐλπίζουσίν [is] a corruption of ἐγγίζουσίν".[28] However, this suggestion may be questioned as ἐλπίζουσίν appears nowhere else in Ezekiel (and only found in Psa. 30:20, 144:15, 146:11; Jer. 51:14), and, perhaps more relevant, ἐλπίζω is not found in any form in Ezekiel. Whilst 𝕲[967]'s use is the only occurrence of the form ἐγγίζουσίν in Ezekiel, ἐγγίζω is a common word in Ezekiel (7:4; 9:1, 6; 12:23; 22:4, 5; 23:5; 36:8; 40:46; 42:13; 43:19; 44:13; 45:4), and therefore a word with which the later scribes of 𝕲[B,A] would have been familiar. Thus we suggest that, rather than a corruption, the later 𝕲[B,A] communities deliberately used ἐλπίζουσίν to indicate that they were still awaiting the fulfilment of the promised return. Whilst our suggestion appears to be in conflict with other evidence indicating that LXX viewed the text from the attitude of those within the land, it could be that they used ἐλπίζουσίν in the sense of a hope not in the distant future, but rather, as an event about to occur. We note that the use of ἐλπίζουσίν was continued by all other Greek MSS, perhaps because they also shared this 'hope' of return, leaving 𝕲[967] as the sole Greek witness to the Hebrew.[29] We note Ziegler has ἐγγίζουσι in his text, following 𝕲[967].

36:9 כִּי הִנְנִי אֲלֵיכֶם וּפָנִיתִי אֲלֵיכֶם וְנֶעֱבַדְתֶּם וְנִזְרַעְתֶּם:

36:9 (𝕲[967,B]: ὅτι ἰδοὺ ἐγὼ ἐφ᾽ ὑμᾶς καὶ; 𝕲[A]: ἰδοὺ ἐγὼ) ἐπιβλέψω ἐφ᾽ ὑμᾶς καὶ κατεργασθήσεσθε (𝕲[967,B]: καὶ σπαρήσεσθε; 𝕲[A]: –)

---

[27] In fact, Gehman (in Johnson *et al.*, 1938, p. 74) states that "an examination of the readings which have no counterpart in the other Greek MSS shows that Sch. has 43 cases which are an exact translation of the Hebrew". These include 36:8 already mentioned, but also 37:1; 38:8, 11, 16–17; 39:4. We must note here that Scheide's text finishes at 37:4 (which follows chapter 39 in this text).

[28] Cooke's suggestion of a 'corruption' also implicitly supports ἐγγίζουσι as original.

[29] Johnson (in Johnson *et al.*, 1938, p. 19 [cf. p. 125]) does note that "it is significant however that the Old Latin follows the Scheide text in reading *appropinquat*". This again helps support 𝕲[967]'s use as the original and correct one.

𝕲⁹⁶⁷,ᴮ both follow MT by saying the Lᴏʀᴅ is 'for them',³⁰ which is most likely a reference to Lev. 26:9. 𝕲ᴬ's minuses are curious: firstly, it is minus ὅτι, which gives the reason for the promise of v. 8; secondly, it is minus ἐφ' ὑμᾶς καί; thirdly, it is minus καὶ σπαρήσεσθε. This leaves 𝕲ᴬ saying 'See, I will look upon you, and you shall be tilled/prepared'. Block (2000, p. 39 n. 59) points out that "the formula הנני אליכם, 'Behold, I am for you' followed by ופניתי אליכם, 'and I will turn towards you,' in 36:9 deliberately reverses Yahweh's disposition" (cf. 5:8; 35:3). By its minus, 𝕲ᴬ does not reflect this reversal, nor the *inclusio* of thought from v. 5, where the Lᴏʀᴅ was 'against' the nations, and now here is 'for' his people.³¹ The second minus in 𝕲ᴬ may well be a case of *homeoarchon* (ἐφ'...ἐφ'). Yet this does not explain 𝕲ᴬ's ὅτι minus, nor the inclusion of ἐπιβλέψω between the two ἐπί. Nor does it explain 𝕲ᴬ's third minus of καὶ σπαρήσεσθε (see below). We are left with uncertainty as to the reason for 𝕲ᴬ's minuses, especially since elsewhere 𝕲ᴬ's tendency is towards plusses. The first two minuses may well be scribal errors, but 𝕲ᴬ's third minus may be the result of theological choice.

For 𝕲ᴬ the land is only tilled, but not sown, and does not have people birthed on it (cf. v. 12) (cf. καὶ σπαρήσεσθε minus). The 'sowing' in the other MSS prepares the reader for the population multiplication in vv. 10–11, and even for 𝕲⁹⁶⁷,ᴮ's 'I will birth people on you', in v. 12. Either 𝕲ᴬ's *Vorlage* did not have καὶ σπαρήσεσθε, or there was a choice to omit this, perhaps because 𝕲ᴬ's scribe (or community) did not feel the Lᴏʀᴅ was 'for them' (𝕲ᴬ's second minus), or had sown them (𝕲ᴬ's third minus). The latter suggestion appears more likely. However, we should consider 𝕲ᴬ's minus here alongside its 'δώσω' variant in v. 12a (see below) that avoids 𝕲⁹⁶⁷,ᴮ's birth metaphor; together they suggest that 𝕲ᴬ was uncomfortable with the thought of the land being sown or 'impregnated', resulting in people being birthed on it (v. 12). Thus 𝕲ᴬ's minus shows evidence of theological choice. For MT and 𝕲⁹⁶⁷,ᴮ, the land is sown, even pregnant (v. 9),³² and for 𝕲⁹⁶⁷,ᴮ the land has

---

³⁰ Waltke and O'Connor (1990, p. 194) note the differing senses of אל here, "I am *concerned for* you, and will turn *to* you [with favor]" (italic theirs).

³¹ Perhaps 𝕲ᴬ did not capture this as it has vv. 5–7a as a separate 'sense division' unit to vv. 7b–12 (or 7b–15).

³² Whilst זרע means 'seed' and is generally used agriculturally, it is also used metaphorically as in Num. 5:28 where a woman is made pregnant (*niphal*); and in Lev. 12:2 'bore children' (*hiphal*), for which Hamilton (1980, p. 923) says this "denotes the Lord

people born on it (v. 12). In MT, the land also carries the charge of it miscarrying the people, yet in LXX, it is (passively) made childless (vv. 12b–15).

36:10 וְהִרְבֵּיתִי עֲלֵיכֶם אָדָם כָּל־בֵּית יִשְׂרָאֵל כֻּלֹּה וְנֹשְׁבוּ הֶעָרִים וְהֶחֳרָבוֹת תִּבָּנֶינָה:

36:10 καὶ πληθυνῶ ἐφ᾽ ὑμᾶς ἀνθρώπους (𝕲⁹⁶⁷: + καὶ κτήνη) πᾶν οἶκον Ἰσραηλ εἰς τέλος καὶ κατοικηθήσονται αἱ πόλεις (𝕲ᴬ: + ὑμῶν) καὶ ἡ ἠρημωμένη οἰκοδομηθήσεται

It is possible that 𝕲⁹⁶⁷'s 'cattle' plus comes from v. 11, as both verses start the same way, but the plus has no place here (Gehman in Johnson *et al.*, 1938, p. 126). 𝕲ᴬ's plus of ὑμῶν (your [cities]) makes the description more personalised (cf. MT, 𝕲⁹⁶⁷,ᴮ 'the cities'). This is a reversal of the previous few verses, where the 'personalised' aspect was not present in 𝕲ᴬ (cf. minus ὑμῶν in v. 8, and its other minuses in v. 9).

That both MT and LXX include 'the whole house of Israel, all of it', may be saying "the two Kingdoms will be restored to the land. The reunion is the theme of the latter part of the next chapter" (cf. 37:15–28) (Fisch, 1985, p. 240).[33] LXX may be seen to intensify with its use of εἰς τέλος for MT כֻּלֹּה, reading 'all[34] the house of Israel to the end/completion/totality' [LEH].[35] Polak (1994, p. 57) claims that typically in the Prophets, LXX uses συντέλεια for כֻּלֹּה (cf. 11:15). Only here in 36:10, and in 20:40, which is also a promise of salvation, does LXX use εἰς τέλος.[36] Polak (1994, p. 69) states that "this solution was triggered by syntactic as well as exegetical considerations. In a promise of salvation the concept of συντέλεια would be inappropriate, so the translator could not apply the traditional rendering". LXX intensifying here may have been influenced by chapter 37, both in the regathering

---

sowing Israel" into the land. We suggest that this is also the context here (vv. 8–12), particularly if we accept the metaphor of 'miscarriage' (vv. 12c–15).

[33] Eisemann (1994, p. 551) says "the phrase alludes to the return of the ten tribes". This may be too narrow a viewpoint. The context here, and in 37:16f, is the re-uniting of the Northern and Southern kingdom.

[34] Thackeray (1909, p. 175, n.4) notes that "this use of πᾶν appears clearly to go back to the translator or an early scribe of 'Ezekiel β' (πάντα acc.sing. only in xxxvii.21, xxxix.20 in all uncials)".

[35] Polak (1994, p. 68 n.18) states that "the phrase εἰς τέλος may mean 'forever'…. However, in Koine Greek this phrase regularly means 'completely'".

[36] Ezek. 20:40, as 36:10, has the phrase כָּל־בֵּית יִשְׂרָאֵל כֻּלֹּה.

and then introducing the new concept of 'childlessness/miscarriage' that will be taken up in the following pericope. This verse presents a number of complex issues.

In speaking of the restoration of the mountains, MT states וְהוֹלַכְתִּי עֲלֵיכֶם אָדָם ('and I will cause people to walk on you'), whereas 𝕲⁹⁶⁷,ᴮ say καὶ γεννήσω ἐφ᾽ ὑμᾶς ἀνθρώπους ('and I will give birth to people on you').[44] Block (1998, p. 332) says LXX is "perhaps an inadvertent mistake or reflective of a different *Vorlage*".[45] The 'different *Vorlage*' suggestion is possible, considering the number of variants in 36:12–15, showing evidence of a text in a state of flux. However, Zimmerli (1983, p. 231) dismisses this variant as a scribal error,[46] stating that LXX "seems to presuppose והולדתי" ('and I shall cause you to give birth'). He then states, "from the point of view of content, a reference to Yahweh's 'begetting' would, in view of the context, be extremely odd. Thus [MT] is to be preferred" (Zimmerli, 1983, p. 231). On the other hand, rather than a different *Vorlage* or scribal error, LXX may well be reflecting on the 'sowing' (cf. v. 9) as 'impregnating', and then on the metaphor that continues regarding childlessness/miscarriage in this and the following pericope (vv. 12b–15). This would then enable 𝕲⁹⁶⁷,ᴮ to complete another word play here on והולכתי as והולדתי (ד for כ), causing an interpretive and exegetical shift to match the context, and their theology. For 𝕲⁹⁶⁷,ᴮ, the mountains of Israel (cf. v. 8) will give birth and will not miscarry, a charge that LXX appears to want to avoid (cf. vv. 12b–15 below).

We noted in v. 9 that 𝕲ᴬ was minus the land being 'sown', and suggested this was done by theological choice, and should be considered with 𝕲ᴬ's variant here in v. 12, where it avoids 𝕲⁹⁶⁷,ᴮ's birth metaphor by using δώσω ('and I will *give* people on you'). The concept of 'giving people' may be an attempt to find middle ground between MT and other LXX MSS. This may indicate that 𝕲ᴬ was uncomfortable with the concept of the land being 'sown' (v. 9) and having people brought to birth on it (v. 12), and therefore made theological choices in both verses.

---

[44] Brenton has 'I will increase people on you' but in so doing Brenton interprets the basic meaning of γεννήσω—to beget, bring forth.

[45] Greenberg (1997, p. 721) also says "G's bizarre 'I will beget' arose from an erroneous *Vorlage* (whwldty).

[46] Cooke (1936, p. 395) says LXX "cannot be right", but does not provide explanation.

We also note in 36:12 that where MT states וְלֹא־תוֹסִף עוֹד לְשַׁכְּלָם
('and you shall never again make them childless' OR 'miscarry them'),[47]
LXX states καὶ οὐ μὴ προστεθῆτε ἔτι ἀτεκνωθῆναι ἀπ' αὐτῶν ('and
you will no longer be made childless of them'). Here we see that
MT has the mountains as an active agent (cf. v. 8) that will no longer
'bereave/make childless' the people (or nation/s; cf. גּוֹי vv. 13–15) of
their children; or a more contextual preference, that the mountains
will no longer 'miscarry' their people.[48] Hamilton (1980, p. 923; 1997,
p. 106 [also *HALOT*]) outlines the overall use of שָׁכֹל as 'to become/
make childless', and even 'to miscarry',[49] stating that "Judah[50] is accused
of 'robbing her nation of its children'". However, he (1980, p. 923)
curiously discusses whether שָׁכֹל here refers "to the practice of infant
sacrifice or cannibalism".[51] Whilst we may question this last usage,
Hamilton [also *HALOT*] has established that שָׁכֹל, whilst typically used
for childlessness (being deprived of children), also has the meaning in
the *piel* of miscarriage, which fits the context of vv. 12–15. The charge
of 'miscarry' for MT, and even 'childless/bereaved' for LXX, here
and in the following pericope, may well be the insult spoken against
the mountains back in 36:3, 6. This is most likely a reference to the
ancient charge against the land that the spies brought back, 'a land
that devours (אכל) its inhabitants' (Num. 13:32). Now their 'enemies'
are restating this charge as an insult (cf. vv. 3, 6, 13). Cooke (1936,
p. 388) claims that "the mountains....when ravaged by famine or
wild beasts, they could be said to *make* the inhabitants *childless*". Yet
this does not appear to be what MT is stating. Rather, the mountains
are the active agent. Greenberg (1997, p. 721) points out that the *pi'el*

---

[47] Duguid (1994, p. 99) notes that לֹא...עוֹד is "a characteristic idiom of the prophet's
contrast between the way things were in the past and the way they will be in the future"
(cf. vv. 14, 15, 30; 37:22, 23; 39:7, 28).

[48] Whilst directly addressing the mountains (the subject since v. 8), this may nevertheless include all the land (cf. vv. 4, 6).

[49] Hamilton (1980, p. 923) states "Finally we note those passages in which the idea
of 'miscarriage' is prominent. The reference may be to the miscarriage of (1) animals:
ewes and she-goats, Gen 31:38; sheep, Song 4:2; 6:6; calf, Job 21:10; (2) the land (non-
productive): 2Kings 2:19, 21; Mal 3:11; (3) a woman: Exo 23:26; Hos 9:14, give them
a 'miscarrying' womb". Significant for us, is the *piel* form in Gen. 31:38; Exod. 23:26;
Job 21:10; Mal. 3:11, which gives us ground to hold the *piel* in Ezek. 36:12 also refers
to 'miscarriage'.

[50] That Hamilton is exegeting may be seen in how he refers to 'Judah' and not to
the 'mountains' of the text.

[51] Hamilton brings his own interpretation to this passage, as there is nothing explicitly
in the text to indicate infant sacrifice or cannibalism.

here "signifies an active rather than a passive losing of one's children, meaning to doing away with them or killing them off". This supports our proposed meaning of 'miscarriage' here, and in vv. 13–15. Eichrodt (1970, p. 492) notes this phrase "directly express[es] a very grim view of the land, regarding it as a sort of monster which devours its own inhabitants". That the land will no longer miscarry appears to be a reversal of Ezek. 5:17 and 14:15. Overall, for MT it is the mountains that have performed this action of miscarriage to the people, but they will never do so again.

However LXX, both in translation, and by use of the passive verb (ἀτεκνωθῆναι), does not reflect 'miscarriage'. Instead, the mountains are passive, with the action of 'being made childless' done to them, but in future the mountains will be no longer be made childless of their people. LXX's use of the passive requires its ἀπό 'plus' (also in v. 13). In this, LXX appears to absolve the mountains, and therefore the people, of any wrong doing in the past, and passes the blame for barrenness onto the other nations, who are implicitly charged with removing the people. If LXX was written at a time when they saw their enemies surrounding them (Greco-Roman era), then one can understand the statement that the land will not be made childless by their removal, as happened to their forefathers. The LXX community may have seen this as something done to them, or their forefathers, again showing evidence they felt harshly treated. LXX's use of the passive appears to offer a sense of 'comfort' to the people, saying that childlessness or expulsion from the land will not happen to them again. Theologically, this ancient charge may have been a primary concern for the potential returnees, who may have been saying, 'what is the point of returning to a land that is only going to devour us?' MT answers with the LORD informing the mountains of his personal involvement, and stating that the mountains will not miscarry his people Israel again. LXX answers by informing the mountains that 'childlessness' will not happen to them again, therefore requiring the passive.

3.2.3. 36:13–15

It is significant that all representative MSS have sense division breaks before and after this pericope. MT^C has a *petuḥah* in both locations, MT^A a *setumah* before v. 13 and *petuḥah* after v. 15, and MT^L a *setumah* in both locations. Likewise, both 𝔊^{967,A} exhibit breaks either side of this pericope. As discussed above, 𝔊^B does not have a *clear* break after

v. 12 owing to this verse finishing at the end of a line, yet there is a *paragraphos* marker at the start of the following line which may be from the original scribe. We concluded that 𝔊ᴮ shows evidence of a sense division after v. 12,[52] and it exhibits a clear break after v. 15. All these MSS thus build on the childlessness/miscarriage statement at the end of v. 12, and now deal with the insults of their enemies (cf. vv. 3, 6), which may be referring to the charge of miscarriage (MT) and/or childlessness (LXX).

This pericope is quite complex, and MT appears to struggle with the concept that the mountains/land 'miscarried' or devoured its inhabitants. There is also an interchange between singular and plural forms in the ancient insult as the focus shifts from the mountains (masc. pl.) to the land (fem. s.). This can cause confusion in our understanding of who is being addressed, and may be the reason behind MT's *ketiv* and *qere* readings, and other variants. Again, there is evidence of a text in a state of flux.

36:13 כֹּה אָמַר אֲדֹנָי יְהֹוִה יַעַן אֹמְרִים לָכֶם אֹכֶלֶת אָדָם (אָתְּי=K)
[אָתְּ=Q] וּמְשַׁכֶּלֶת (גּוֹיֵךְ=K) [גּוֹיַיִךְ=Q] הָיִית:

36:13 τάδε λέγει κύριος κύριος ἀνθ᾽ ὧν εἶπάν σοι κατέσθουσα ἀνθρώπους εἶ (𝔊⁹⁶⁷: + σὺ) καὶ ἠτεκνωμένη (𝔊⁹⁶⁷: ἀπὸ; 𝔊ᴮ·ᴬ: ὑπὸ) τοῦ ἔθνους σου ἐγένου

In the previous verses there has been a growing reference to the insult given to Israel by 'the enemy' (v. 2) and 'people' (vv. 3, 4, 6). In v. 12b is the first indication as what this 'insult' was, and in v. 13 it is clarified with the actual words of the 'enemies'. We now find that "the hostile neighbours alleged that the Land of Israel destroyed its inhabitants" (Fisch, 1985, p. 241). This again is likely a continuation of the ancient charge found in Num. 13:32 (cf. v. 12 above, and vv. 14–15).

In v. 13 we suggest (as with v. 12b) LXX remains reluctant to portray the mountains as active, even as a charge from the surrounding nations. LXX again uses the passive so the mountains are *being made* childless. MT on the other hand continues the accusation that the mountains are an active participant, devouring their people and causing miscarriage. Cooke (1936, p. 388) says, "the land is now addressed as if it were a beast of prey which devoured its people, by not producing

---

[52] As also noted above, if 𝔊ᴮ does not exhibit a break here, which indicates 𝔊ᴮ viewed vv. 13–15 as continuing the motif of 'childlessness/miscarry' from v. 12b.

the necessaries of life".[53] MT uses two verbal participles for the charge against the mountains: אֹכֶלֶת and וּמְשַׁכֶּלֶת, ('devouring' and 'miscarrying').[54] LXX reflects MT's first participle in the present participle (κατέσθουσα) permitting the charge 'you are devouring'. However, LXX then uses a passive participle ἠτεκνωμένη (with ἐγένου) to say, 'you are *being made* bereaved/childless', which continues the theological thought from v. 12b (cf. vv. 14–15). LXX therefore states, as in v. 12b, that the action of bereavement or being made childless is being done to the mountains. This again could be indicative they felt harshly treated: 'we had this happen to us and we didn't deserve it'.

MT starts the pericope using אֹמְרִים (ptc.),[55] whereas LXX uses εἶπάν (aorist). MT appears to make this a present and continuous accusation, or perhaps referring to an event yet to happen, while LXX appears to be referring to a past event, or perhaps LXX sees the accusation as in the past. This may indicate LXX's theological use of the passive to imply that 'it won't happen again'. The 'speakers' are not identified, but are likely those uttering the insults in previous verses (cf. vv. 2, 3, 6, also 15). After these words, MT uses the plural לָכֶם, whereas LXX uses a dative singular σοι, perhaps to match the singular used in the accusation in both MT and LXX. MT's use of the plural continues the Lord's speech to the mountains as a plurality (cf. vv. 1, 4, 8), and has the accusers' charge being a statement to the mountains as a whole.

We may question whether MT's *ketiv* גּוֹיֵךְ and *qere* גּוֹיַיִךְ variant, and similar in vv. 14–15,[56] refers directly to the two nations of Israel and Judah (cf. 37:11, 15–28). However, it may have been intended to include

---

[53] Greenberg (1997, p. 721) points out that Ezek. 19:3–6 accuses the kings of Judah of being like young lions 'devouring people' (cf. 34:10). However, the context of Ezek. 36:12b–15 has the land/mountains as the addressees and the accusation against the land by others (v. 13). However, Greenberg does mention the ancient charge against the land in Numbers 13; this is further discussed below in vv. 14–15.

[54] Harland (1999, p. 116) suggests that in Ezekiel the people were "so evil…that they may even have indulged in cannibalism (5:10; cf. 36:13)". Whilst a possible reference to cannibalism may be found in 5:10, the context in this pericope is the land devouring (so MT) or being made childless (so LXX).

[55] Block (1998, p. 332) notes that *BHS* emends אֹמְרִים to אָמְרָם, but argues "the indefinite pl[ural] before a quotation is encountered elsewhere in 8:12; 13:7; 37:11" (cf. Zimmerli, 1983, p. 231).

[56] MT's other *ketiv* אַתִּי and *qere* אַתְּ variant here are both 2nd person feminine singular pronouns. Block (1998, p. 332) says the *ketiv* is "archaic" but the *qere* is "more conventional" (also see Yeivin, 1980, p. 56f., #100). However, there is no difference in meaning between the *ketiv* and *qere*.

not just Israel, but the various nations that had sought to inhabit the land over the years, which the land had cast out.[57]

Finally, the intra-LXX variant where 𝕲[967] has ἀπό, which continues the ἀπ' αὐτῶν from v. 12b, and the later 𝕲[B,A] have ὑπό. This change from ἀπό to ὑπό appears to be deliberate. While ἀτεκνόω passive with ἀπό is also found in Gen. 27:45, there is no instance in LXX of ἀτεκνόω passive with ὑπό other than here. 𝕲[967] has 'you[58] have been made childless *from* your nation', while 𝕲[B,A] say 'you have been made childless *by* your nation' (cf. ὑπό as genitive with τοῦ ἔθνους σου). Both prepositions are related to the Greek use of the passive, but it appears that the idea of who 'makes childless' varies. The later 𝕲[B,A] may have been making a statement that the land was made childless *by* its nation (i.e., its people). Although 'by' matches Greenberg's (1997, p. 721) suggestion of Israel's young lions devouring and causing the barrenness, and 'by' agrees with MT, it does not match LXX's implicit feeling of being harshly treated as we have previously observed. However, 𝕲[B,A] may have included the land as one of their oppressors, feeling cast out and therefore harshly treated by the land.

36:14 לָכֵן אָדָם לֹא־תֹאכְלִי עוֹד (K=וּגוֹיֵךְ) [Q=וְגוֹיַיְךְ] לֹא
(K=תְכַשְׁלִי) [Q=תְשַׁכְּלִי־] עוֹד נְאֻם אֲדֹנָי יְהוִה:

36:14 διὰ τοῦτο ἀνθρώπους (𝕲[967]: οὐ κάταφάγεσαι; 𝕲[B,A]: οὐκέτι φάγεσαι) καὶ τὸ ἔθνος σου οὐκ ἀτεκνώσεις (𝕲[B]: ἔτι; 𝕲[967,A]: οὐκέτι) λέγει κύριος κύριος

There is a significant MT variance in v. 14 between the *qere* תְשַׁכְּלִי ('miscarry'), and *ketiv* תְכַשְׁלִי ('stumble').[59] Allen (1990b, p. 169; similarly Block, 1998, p. 332) says the "K[etiv] 'you will cause to stumble' appears to be an error by metathesis for Q[ere] 'you will make childless', the verb in vv. 12, 13". Zimmerli (1983, p. 231) claims the *ketiv* "is doubtless a scribal error" (also Greenberg, 1997, p. 722). We suggest that later MT scribes, finding the error, but reluctant to adjust the written text, inserted a *qere* 'correction' in the side column to avoid confusion for both

---

[57] Cooke (1936, p. 388) notes that "the word *nation* (*gôî*) is rarely applied to Israel and Judah in exilic and post-exilic prophecy". The insult is therefore directed at the land itself rather than the people. This also strengthens our previous point against Greenberg's suggestion of the 'young lions' or leaders of Israel devouring the people.

[58] As noted above, all the 2nd person pronouns and verb forms here in LXX are singular. In MT, only the reported speech uses the singular.

[59] See v. 13 for discussion on the first *ketiv* and *qere* variant of 'nation/s'.

This may have been done at the same time as the *ketiv/qere* variants in v. 14. This is in keeping with MT's theme of the mountains causing the childlessness/miscarriage, and thus causing the people to stumble. We should also consider that LXX may have deliberately dropped this phrase, as it once again accuses the mountains of causing the people to stumble, invoking the previous references to MT's 'miscarriage' in the previous verses, which LXX has sought to avoid in vv. 12, 13. It is perhaps significant that Targum includes the phrase, as Targum often follows LXX.[67] Yet Targum follows its *qere* reading of שכל from v. 14, bringing it also into v. 15. This may have been a Targumic adjustment towards MT (in both verses), or it may suggest that שכל was originally in both vv. 14, 15. Overall, we are left here with a slight puzzle, with MT having כשל (the *ketiv* in v. 14), Targum with שכל (the *qere* in v. 14), and LXX minus both.

We also note that in v. 15 MT, the LORD as subject of the action towards the mountains ('I will never cause you to hear') is not represented in LXX, which simply has the passive ('it will not be heard'). There is no reference to the LORD doing the action, or to the mountains, only to unidentified listeners (καὶ οὐκ ἀκουσθήσεται οὐκέτι ἐφ' ὑμᾶς 'there shall no longer be heard against you'). Again, LXX's passive denotes the inactivity of the mountains, whereas MT continues its use of active verbs. 𝕲ᴬ's variant of ἐθνῶν does not follow MT's עַמִּים as does 𝕲⁹⁶⁷,ᴮ (λαῶν).

3.3. SECTION 2: EZEK. 36:16–21

3.3.1. *36:16–21*

All representative MSS, both Hebrew and Greek, show evidence of a major sense division break between vv. 15 and 16, with v. 16 starting on a new line. MTᶜ,ᴬ both have a *petuḥah*, with MTᴸ having a 'lesser' *setumah* before 16.[68]

---

[67] Again, MasEzek is not much help in v. 15 as the actual words are not extant. The reconstructed text finds room for this entire phrase, but without absolute certainty whether MasEzek actually has לא תכשלי or לא תשכלי.

[68] Yet MTᴸ shows evidence of a preference for *setumah* breaks, so there may be no 'sense' reason for its *setumah* break rather than MTᶜ,ᴬ's *petuḥah* here.

Each Hebrew MS has a division after v. 21: MasEzek and MT^{C,A} each have a *petuḥah* after v. 21, and MT^L again having a *setumah*. While each LXX MSS has a break before v. 16, there is a greater variance at the end of this pericope. The later 𝕲^A has a major division like MT^{C,A}, showing similar emphasis on this pericope. 𝕲^B has a 2 letter break after the first phrase in v. 22, which curiously places διὰ τοῦτο εἰπὸν τῷ οἴκῳ Ισραηλ as the closing statement for this pericope rather than as the opening statement for the following pericope. It is possible that 𝕲^B saw this phrase as an *inclusio* with the 'οἶκος Ισραηλ' in v. 17, and saw τάδε λέγει κύριος as the start of the next 'verse'.[69] The earlier 𝕲⁹⁶⁷ places its paragraph marker in the middle of v. 23 and then proceeds directly into chapter 38 on the same line.[70] For 𝕲⁹⁶⁷ the 'concern for my holy name' (v. 21) is given more emphasis in this pericope, as the reason for both the scattering (vv. 16–20) and the regathering (vv. 21–23b) of 'the house of Israel'.

Overall, these MSS signify that all witnessed a change of topic between vv. 15 and 16. In the previous pericopes of Section 1 (vv. 1–15) the prophecy was addressed to the mountains and land regarding: the 'insults' against them, and their destruction at the hands of the nations around them (vv. 1–12); the ancient charge against the land (vv. 12b–15); and how the LORD will restore the mountains, and bring the people back (vv. 8–12). In this pericope, the LORD is addressing the prophet, describing the sins of 'the house of Israel'. Their sins are the reason for their having been dispersed: they defiled the land (vv. 17–18), and profaned the LORD's name (vv. 20–21). This pericope gives a theological answer to the 'charge' of the land 'miscarrying' its people (so MT), or even that the land was made childless by nations around (so LXX). It shows that the LORD removed the people because of their apostasy that defiled the land (v. 19). Here, 'the house of Israel' is spoken of in the third person. We may have been curious in the first section (vv. 1–15) as to why the prophecy of restoration was addressed to the mountains, rather than to humans. In this second section (vv. 16–21) we are now given the explanation. The humans, as inhabitants of the land (both 'my people', vv. 8, 17, and 'the nations', v. 5), have defiled the LORD's

---

[69] See comments below under 36:22–32 for τάδε λέγει κύριος as a common sense division marker in LXX. Also see Olley (2003, p. 214).

[70] The uniqueness of 𝕲⁹⁶⁷ in terms of order and the 'missing' pericope of 36:23c–38 will be discussed in chapter 7.

land (cf. vv. 5, 20) by their deeds (vv. 17–19). 36:8–15 speaks about the future of the 'house of Israel', but here we find the past being discussed (vv. 17, 21, 22, 32). A major theological shift appears to happen for LXX in this pericope, as now, unlike in the previous section, there is no hint that they felt harshly treated. Also LXX tends to use the active voice here rather than, as previously, the passive. It appears that LXX readily acknowledged the sins of their ancestors, especially idolatry. This may be the consequence of a growing Torah-focused community, whether in Alexandria, Jerusalem, Babylon or elsewhere.

This pericope also shows evidence of a text in a state of flux, possibly due to the respective scribes or communities wrestling with various theological issues in the text. We will find: a syntax change and an added line (v. 17); LXX MSS wrestling with sensitive metaphors (v. 17); MT and 𝕲ᴬ with an exegetical plus (v. 18); and LXX MSS interpretively interacting with the Hebrew text.

36:17 בֶּן־אָדָם בֵּית יִשְׂרָאֵל יֹשְׁבִים עַל־אַדְמָתָם וַיְטַמְּאוּ אוֹתָהּ
בְּדַרְכָּם וּבַעֲלִילוֹתָם כְּטֻמְאַת הַנִּדָּה הָיְתָה דַרְכָּם לְפָנָי:

This verse in LXX shows evidence of a verse in a state of flux, whether different *Vorlagen*, or influenced by theological and exegetical intent. The following layout shows our three LXX MSS. The line breaks are as they appear in the codices, with abbreviations expanded, and spacing and accents added.

	𝕲⁹⁶⁷	𝕲ᴮ	𝕲ᴬ
1	υἱὲ ἀνθρώπου	υἱὲ ἀνθρώπου	υἱὲ ἀνθρώπου οἶκος Ισραηλ κατ
2	οἶκος Ισραηλ κατῴκησεν	οἶκος Ισραηλ κατῴκη	ῴκησαν ἐπὶ τῆς γῆς αὐτῶν
3	ἐπὶ τῆς γῆς αὐτῶν καὶ ἐμί	σεν ἐπὶ τῆς γῆς αὐτῶν	καὶ ἐν ταῖς ἀκαθαρσίαις αὐτῶν
4	αναν αὐτὴν ἐν τοῖς εἰδώ	καὶ ἐμίαναν αὐτὴν ἐν	ἐμίαναν αὐτὴν ἐν τῇ ὁδῷ αὐ
5	λοις αὐτῶν και ἐν τῇ ὁδῷ	τῇ ὁδῷ αὐτῶν καὶ ἐν τοῖς	τῶν καὶ ἐν τοῖς εἰδώλοις αὐτῶν
6	αὐτῶν καὶ ἐν ταῖς αμαρτι	εἰδώλοις αὐτῶν και ταῖς	καὶ ἐν ταῖς ἀκαθαρσίαις αὐτῶν
7	αις αὐτῶν κατὰ τὴν ἀκα	ἀκαθαρσίαις αὐτῶν και	κατὰ τὴν ἀκαθαρσίαν τῆς
8	θαρσίαν τῆς ἀποκαθημέ	κατὰ τὴν ἀκαθαρσίαν τῆς	αφεδρου ἐγενήθη ἡ ὁδὸς αὐτῶν
9	νης ἐγενήθη ἡ ὁδὸς αὐτῶν	ἀποκαθημένης ἐγενή	πρὸ προσώπου μου
10	πρὸ προσώπου μου	θη ἡ ὁδὸς αὐτῶν πρὸ προ	
11		σώπου μου	

We find a unique repeated line in 𝕲ᴬ wherein all the words found in 'line 6' (their correct location), are inserted as a plus forming 'line 3' (καὶ ἐν ταῖς ἀκαθαρσίαις αὐτῶν). This plus may be the result of *homoioteleuton* with the scribe's eyes skipping from καὶ ἐμίαναν . . . καὶ ἐν ταῖς. On the other hand, the scribe may be theologically restating with a doublet, strengthening the charge 'in their uncleanness', as he did not start line 4 with καὶ (just stating ἐμίαναν αὐτήν).[71] Ziegler (1977, p. 264) does note 'line 3' as a plus for 𝕲ᴬ.[72]

MT says that the house of Israel defiled their land בְּדַרְכָּם וּבַעֲלִילוֹתָם ('in their way and deeds').[73] Whilst all LXX MSS have ἐν τῇ ὁδῷ αὐτῶν ('in their way'), the second phrase differs: καὶ ἐν ταῖς ἁμαρτίαις (𝕲⁹⁶⁷)/ ἀκαθαρσίαις (𝕲ᴮ˒ᴬ) αὐτῶν ('and in their sins/uncleanness'). LXX also has a plus ἐν τοῖς εἰδώλοις αὐτῶν ('in their idols') that is not found in MT or MasEzek. In this way, LXX gives two concepts for MT's וּבַעֲלִילוֹתָם (ἁμαρτίαις/ἀκαθαρσίαις and εἰδώλοις), or, as Cooke (1936, p. 395) says, "a double rend[ering]". Zimmerli (1983, p. 241) says this is a "double translation of וּבְגִלּוּלֵיהֶם" and that it prepares "the way for v. 17b". Thus, Cooke and Zimmerli have LXX theologically modifying the text with a double translation. Block (1998, p. 343) suggests LXX translates the Hebrew with both these concepts, "probably reflecting either a different *Vorlage* or a misreading of [וּבְגִלּוּלֵיהֶם]".[74] This 'misreading' proposal is possible, as גִּלּוּלִים (idols) is found in surrounding texts (vv. 18, 25; also 30:13; 33:25; 37:23 [as בְּגִלּוּלֵיהֶם]), and has a similar 'shape' to עֲלִילָה (וּבַעֲלִילוֹתָם).[75] However, rather than a misreading or a different *Vorlage*, we may suggest that LXX has performed a deliberate 'double translation' (cf. Cooke, Zimmerli), and may be another example of LXX wordplay with the Hebrew text. LXX may have, by wordplay based on shape with עֲלִילָה and גִּלּוּלִים, theologically expanded MT's generalized deeds of 'sin/uncleanness' to the specific deed of 'idolatry'.

---

[71] Rather than saying "the house of Israel dwelt in their land, and they defiled it", 𝕲ᴬ says "the house of Israel dwelt in their land they defiled it".

[72] This is ascertained by the order in which Ziegler deals with variants in the verse.

[73] There are six occurrences in Ezekiel where דֶּרֶךְ and עֲלִילָה are found together (14:22, 23; 20:43; 24:14; 36:17, 19).

[74] As noted elsewhere, the change from Block's transliteration to Hebrew lettering is noted by the square brackets and done to assist the reader.

[75] Whilst MT has וּבְגִלּוּלֵיהֶם in v. 18, this is part of a later MT's plus and is only found in 𝕲ᴬ, not 𝕲⁹⁶⁷˒ᴮ.

We suggest LXX made another theological choice, interpreting MT's 'deeds', 𝔊⁹⁶⁷ with ἁμαρτία and 𝔊ᴮ·ᴬ with ἀκαθαρσία. LXX Ezekiel translates עֲלִילָה in various ways: ἐνθύμημα ('thought, reasoning' 14:22, 23; 24:14), ἐπιτήδευμα ('way of living' 20:43, 44), ἁμαρτία ('sins' 21:29; 36:19 [36:17 𝔊⁹⁶⁷]). Only here do we find ἀκαθαρσία used (by 𝔊ᴮ·ᴬ), which is normally used for MT's טֻמְאָה (see below). These two Hebrew words appear in the final phrase of this verse, possibly influencing LXX's word choice(s) here, as well as the theological thought that included its εἰδώλοις plus.

There is a differing word order between the LXX MSS. 𝔊⁹⁶⁷ places the εἰδώλοις plus before the following words (εἰδώλοις/ὁδῷ/ ἁμαρτιαις), whereas 𝔊ᴮ·ᴬ place this plus between these words (ὁδῷ/ εἰδώλοις/ἀκαθαρσίαις). The latter interrupts MT's syntax, yet at the same time emphasises the plus, which may be the reason for the move.

There are differences how 'their way' (דַּרְכָּם/ὁδὸς) of 'uncleanness' was seen: MT (and MasEzek) says it was כְּטֻמְאַת הַנִּדָּה⁷⁶ ('as the uncleanness of a menstruous' [woman]).⁷⁷ Cooke (1936, p. 389) states כְּטֻמְאַת is "a figure for idolatry",⁷⁸ which may have influenced LXX's εἰδώλοις plus. 𝔊⁹⁶⁷·ᴮ say it was τῆς ἀποκαθημένης ('as a set apart woman', cf. 22:10). 𝔊ᴬ plainly states it was τῆς ἀφέδρου ('menstruation', cf. 18:6). LXX

---

⁷⁶ *HALOT* points out that כְּטֻמְאַת is the 'state of ceremonial uncleanness'. Eichrodt (1970, p. 494) also notes that טמא means "'to make unclean', [and] is derived from sacral law. He thus takes a cultic term and applies it not only to cultic sins, as, for example, in 20:30f., but also in the more general sense of showing contempt for God's holiness by breaking his commandments". Thayer (1979) says "the Septuagint equivalent to טָמֵא is ἀκάθαρτος" and means "*not cleansed, unclean*; in a ceremonial sense, that which must be abstained from according to the Levitical law, lest impurity be contracted" (cf. Lev. 15: 26, 31; 25:22).

⁷⁷ Galambush (1992, 147) says "the behavior of the people was 'like the pollution of a menstruant'". Galambush (1992, p. 146) also claims that "the *nddh* of the book of Ezekiel is Jerusalem". If the LXX communities grasped this analogy, this may have influenced their apparent wrestling with how to interpret the text here.

⁷⁸ Fisch (1985, p. 241f) clarifies that "metaphorically Israel is compared with a wife and God to a husband. Therefore in the times of unfaithfulness to Him, Israel is spoken of as having the state of a woman in her impurity. She is temporarily avoided by her husband, becoming reunited with him after purification. Similarly, Israel's banishment from the soil was due to moral impurity, but restoration to his homeland will follow upon purification". Eisemann (1994, p. 554) also speaks to this point but adds "such a woman is only in a transitional state, whereas a dead body remains contaminated. Included here is how a priest can enter a home of a menstrual woman but not where there is a dead body". Galambush (1992, p. 146) claims that Jerusalem is Yahweh's wife who has defiled herself with bloodshed (especially from child sacrifices) and idolatry.

uses both ἀποκάθημαι[79] and ἄφεδρος[80] for נִדָּה, both echoing ceremonial impurity aspects in Numbers and/or Leviticus. We suggest that
the earlier 𝕲[967,B] avoided the direct language of a menstruant woman,
perhaps due to cultural sensitivity. This can also be seen through
LXX's εἰδώλοις for MT's גִּלּוּלִים (cf. v. 18). The later 𝕲[A] appears to
have strengthened the wording with ἀφέδρου, perhaps to follow MT
more closely, or to create a greater impact regarding the offence of
the idolatrous sacrifices. If so, this, and its other 'line doublet' noted
above, provide room for 𝕲[A] to follow MT's plus in v. 18, which is
not witnessed in the earlier 𝕲[967,B]. Overall, the context of MT refers
to the offence of blood sacrificed to idols, with the people defiling the
land and themselves by their idolatrous sacrifices. LXX has taken this
contextual point and theologically expanded it.

36:18 וָאֶשְׁפֹּךְ חֲמָתִי עֲלֵיהֶם עַל־הַדָּם אֲשֶׁר־שָׁפְכוּ עַל־הָאָרֶץ
וּבְגִלּוּלֵיהֶם טִמְּאוּהָ:

36:18 καὶ ἐξέχεα τὸν θυμόν μου ἐπ' αὐτοὺς (𝕲[A]: + περὶ τοῦ αἵματος οὗ
ἐξέχεαν ἐν τῇ γῇ καὶ ἐν τοῖς ἰδώλοις αὐτῶν ἐμίαναν αὐτήν)

MT and MasEzek have עַל־הַדָּם אֲשֶׁר־שָׁפְכוּ עַל־הָאָרֶץ וּבְגִלּוּלֵיהֶם טִמְּאוּהָ
('for the blood they had poured on the land, and with their dung pellets[81]

---

[79] Typically Numbers uses ἀποκάθημαι for נִדָּה in a sense of ceremonial impuity,
which is the context of Ezek. 36:17. The ceremonial impurity link with Numbers is
supported by the idea that the LXX translator had Numbers in mind, as seen above
(cf. vv. 3, 13–15), and interacted accordingly with the Hebrew text. Ezekiel also uses
נִדָּה 7:19; 18:6; 22:10.
[80] Leviticus often uses ἄφεδρος for נִדָּה when directly referring to a menstruous
woman. Cooke (1936, p. 389) claims that "the connexion between the present passage
and the Law of Holiness is noticeable".
[81] Block (1998, p. 346f.) says "cultic (idolatry)....is identified appropriately by
Ezekiel's favorite term for idols, gillûlîm, pellets of dung, for that is what idols are in
Yahweh's sight". In 38 of the 47 occurrences of גִּלּוּלִים in Ezekiel, idolatry is identified with sexual immorality and prostitution (also see Block, 1997a, p. 226f.). Kutsko
(2000b, p. 121) covers the "basic meaning 'heap of stones'", but then says "it would
be easy to emphasize the rhetorical force of a meaning associated with dung". Elsewhere Kutsko (2000a, p. 34) says Ezekiel "exploited the dual association of (idol-)stone
and excrement in order to imply that pagan gods are...'Scheissgötter'". Kutsko does
point out that this word appears in literature held as exilic and post exilic (also Kutsko,
2000a, pp. 32–35). This could signify how these communities viewed the idol worship
of the pre-exilic communities. Tuell (2000a, p. 112) says "Ezekiel vehemently rejects
idolatry, referring to divine images pejoratively as גִּלּוּלִים ('dungballs') and steadfastly
refusing even to call them gods". We may suggest that LXX's εἰδώλοις does not fully
capture this meaning and as such can be seen as a theological interpretation of MT's
'metaphor' perhaps due to cultural sensitivities.

they had defiled it').[82] This sentence is minus in both 𝕲⁹⁶⁷,ᴮ. However, it is represented in 𝕲ᴬ, translating וּבְגִלּוּלֵיהֶם (dung pellets) with ἰδώλοις.[83] Cooke (1936, p. xli) notes this as one example of "the superiority of 𝕲 to 𝔐 in cases where they differ... [as] 𝕲 implies a Hebrew text free from words and phrases which appear to be additions or glosses in 𝔐".[84] Most see this as a later MT plus that gives theological reason for God's wrath referred to in the first part of the verse. It is hard to imagine that 𝕲⁹⁶⁷,ᴮ would have deliberately omitted this sentence, due to the previous reference to idols and uncleanness in v. 17. Wevers (1982, p. 192) suggests it "may be a late expansion explaining the impurity in terms typical of Ezekiel, viz. social violence and idolatry, cf. 22:4". Eichrodt (1970, p. 493) says "this short sentence, in a bad style... gives a brief and late characterization of the besetting sins of Israel". Allen (1990b, p. 176) agrees, stating that MT

> reads awkwardly both in respect of the repetition of עַל ('upon/because of') in different senses and in the change of construction in the last clause. It appears to have originated as two explanatory comments on v 17aγ and v 17aβγ respectively. The first appears to depend on Num 35:33, 34. LXX reflects in v 17aγ a similar need to define the vague terms: 'with their idols and their defilements.' Both sets of clarifications depend on v 25.

Kutsko (2000a, p. 127, n. 112) also believes this phrase was "added on the basis of v. 25". If these 'clarifications' depend on v. 25 then one can understand why 𝕲⁹⁶⁷ doesn't have the phrase as 𝕲⁹⁶⁷ is minus 36:23c–38.[85] But this does not explain the minus here in 𝕲ᴮ. It is possible that this phrase was added to MT after the *Vorlage* of 𝕲⁹⁶⁷,ᴮ, but early enough for the later 𝕲ᴬ (or its *Vorlage*) to include it. That

---

[82] The concept of blood defiling the land is found in 16:38; 22:4, 6, 9, 12, 27; 23:45; 33:25. Lasine (1993, p. 178) notes that "Exile, bloodshed and idolatry are linked in Ezek. 36:18", and indicates that this was a reference to times like those of Manasseh. Fisch (1985, p. 242) also notes "that the sins of homicide and idolatry were among the chief causes of Israel's banishment was stressed in xvi.36, xxiii.37".

[83] Interestingly, neither Block, Allen, Zimmerli, nor any of the other major commentators, note this is extant in 𝕲ᴬ. It is also witnessed by both Aquila and Theodotion in the Hexapla (Field, 1964, p. 868).

[84] Cooke also lists Ezek. 37:7, 12, 23; 38:16; 39:11, 14, 27 under this category.

[85] Greenberg (1997, p. 728) says the phrase 'and by their idols they defiled it' "is almost identical to that in Jer. 30:14f". This may be another place where later redactors referred to the book of Jeremiah (see discussions below on 36:23c–38 being a later addition influenced by the book of Jeremiah).

MasEzek has this phrase suggests that it may have been added into the text possibly around the same time as the Hebrew plus of 'Israel' in v. 8, except here 𝕲ᴬ included the 'plus'. This may narrow down the possible timeframe of the plus. Overall, it can be seen as a theological and exegetical plus for MT and 𝕲ᴬ.

The phrase refers back to the mention of 'menstruation' in v. 17b, which permits the plus that now speaks of blood being 'poured on the ground', indicating a wasted sacrifice.[86] The plus, combined with v. 17, is a theological interpretation regarding the value that the LORD placed upon sacrifices offered to idols:[87] it is just menstrual blood that defiles the land.[88] 𝕲ᴬ also catches MT's wordplay of 'I poured out' [because] 'they poured out', which gives theological reason for their being expelled from the land. We agree with Allen and Block's suggestion that the first clause of the plus reflects back to Num. 35:33, 34. We propose that here is another example of a later scribe reflecting back to Torah and interpreting the text for his generation (cf. the 'evil report' 36:3; 'grapes' 36:8).

36:19 וָאָפִיץ אֹתָם בַּגּוֹיִם וַיִּזָּרוּ בָּאֲרָצוֹת כְּדַרְכָּם וְכַעֲלִילוֹתָם שְׁפַטְתִּים׃

36:19 καὶ διέσπειρα αὐτοὺς εἰς τὰ ἔθνη καὶ ἐλίκμησα αὐτοὺς εἰς τὰς χώρας κατὰ (𝕲⁹⁶⁷·ᴮ: τὴν ὁδὸν; 𝕲ᴬ: τὰς ὁδοὺς) αὐτῶν καὶ κατὰ (𝕲⁹⁶⁷·ᴮ: τὴν ἁμαρτίαν; 𝕲ᴬ: τὰς ἀνομίας) αὐτῶν ἔκρινα αὐτούς

---

[86] Block (1998, 346) believes this is referring to murder (cf. Num. 35:33), but the context suggests the blood sacrifice to idols. Harland (1999, p. 120) also believes the violence spoken of in Ezekiel is murder and says "What Ezekiel stresses is that murder was not just a social crime but that it separated people from God. Those who had shed blood could have no relationship with God because of their impurity". Both murder and sacrifices could be included in this context if we consider the practice of child sacrifice (cf. 20:26; 23:36). However, whilst murder may be implied here (blood on the land), child sacrifice is not explicitly stated.

[87] On the other hand, Kutsko (2000b, p. 138) suggests that here and elsewhere in Ezekiel the "frequent charge against Israel that its people shed much blood is based on the same *imago Dei* rationale as Gen. 9: the shedding of blood is prohibited because humans are the images of God". He (2000b, p. 138) does admit "this association with Ezekiel lacks direct proof". Whilst there may be a case for Kutsko's hypothesis, it is a study outside the scope of this work. We can say that there is no clear link of v. 18 (and this pericope), with the bloodshed resulting from murder mentioned in Gen. 9. The only possible, but unlikely, link is if we consider human (child) sacrifices as part of the sacrifices spoken of in v. 18.

[88] Greenberg (1997, p. 728) observes this plus "answers to and motivates the foregoing 'I poured out my fury on them,' while interpreting (as an allusion to blood) the *ndh* element of the simile *ktm't hndh* of vs. 17".

Both Hebrew and Greek MSS have the LORD causing the dispersion of Israel from the land,[89] yet again there are subtle differences. As Greenberg (1997, p. 728) points out, MT's "'*I scattered...so that they were dispersed*' [is a] typical sequence of actions (active verb)—achieved state (passive).... Ⓖ obliterate[s] the distinction by tendering both verbs as active".[90] Unlike LXX in 36:1–15, LXX here turns from a passive view of the past and makes it an aorist active, even when MT has the second verb in the *niphal*. The reason for this may be that in vv. 1–15 the action was being done by the enemy to the mountains, whereas here in v. 19 (and surrounding verses) the LORD has done the action in response to the people's 'sin'. Thus, there is no theological room here for LXX's prior feeling of being harshly treated, and its subsequent use of passive verbs.

Ⓖ^A pluralises 'ways' (τὰς ὁδούς), whereas Ⓖ^{967,B} follow MT's singular with τὴν ὁδόν. Ⓖ^A pluralises again with τὰς ἀνομίας ('lawlessnesses', cf. 36:31, 33; 37:23), whereas Ⓖ^{967,B} again have the singular τὴν ἁμαρτίαν ('guilt/sin') following MT's עֲלִילָת ('deed'), as in v. 17.[91] In this, we suggest that Ⓖ^A subtly intensifies the text over the other MSS. This may indicate a text in a state of flux. However, it is possible that Ⓖ^A's community saw the idolatrous sins of their ancestors (and perhaps their own) in a plural sense, rather than a collective occurrence, and as an act of lawlessness against the LORD. This may be the case with Ⓖ^A's (and MT's) plus in v. 18 that covers both blood sacrifices and idol worship.

36:20 וַיָּבוֹא אֶל־הַגּוֹיִם אֲשֶׁר־בָּאוּ שָׁם וַיְחַלְּלוּ אֶת־שֵׁם קָדְשִׁי
בֶּאֱמֹר לָהֶם עַם־יְהוָה אֵלֶּה וּמֵאַרְצוֹ יָצָאוּ׃

36:20 καὶ εἰσήλθοσαν εἰς τὰ ἔθνη οὗ εἰσήλθοσαν ἐκεῖ καὶ ἐβεβήλωσαν τὸ ὄνομά μου τὸ ἅγιον ἐν τῷ λέγεσθαι αὐτούς λαὸς κυρίου οὗτοι καὶ ἐκ τῆς γῆς (Ⓖ^{967,B}: αὐτοῦ ἐξεληλύθασιν; Ⓖ^A: αὐτῶν ἐξήλθοσαν)

---

[89] Maybe both communities saw the dispersion as a fitting response by God to the sins of Israel, and that it reflects the warning of Leviticus that the land would vomit out those who defiled it (Lev. 18:25, 28; 20:22).

[90] Greenberg (1997, p. 728) points out that this "levelling [is] facilitated by the fact that in all other (previous) occurrences of this verb pair both verbs are indeed in the active (12:15; 20:23; 22:15; 29:12; 30:23, 26). In this last occurrence the prophet makes a change, as it were a closure of the series". Block (1998, p. 344) sees this as LXX harmonising MT (as in 22:15; 29:12; 30:23, 26). Whilst it may well harmonise, we suggest theological intent behind any resulting harmonisation.

[91] עֲלִילָת is used six times in conjunction with דֶּרֶךְ in Ezekiel (14:22, 23; 20:43; 24:4; 36:17, 19).

This verse has a subtle difference intra-LXX. The earlier 𝕲^967,B use the perfect καὶ ἐκ τῆς γῆς αὐτοῦ ἐξεληλύθασιν ('and they have come out of his land'), whereas 𝕲^A uses the aorist καὶ ἐκ τῆς γῆς αὐτῶν ἐξήλθοσαν ('and they came out of their land'). The use of the aorist may permit 𝕲^A to say 'they came out', perhaps seeing this as an event in their distant past.

More importantly, MT and 𝕲^967,B have '*his* land' (αὐτοῦ), whereas 𝕲^A has '*their* land' (αὐτῶν).[92] This may indicate a deliberate shift to make their claim on the land more personalised, and echoes back to v. 17a. 𝕲^A may also be seeking to say that the defilement spoken of in the previous verses (vv. 17–19) caused personal defilement upon their own land. In other words, their sin defiled their land.[93] Zimmerli (1983, p. 247) believes that the translator may again have had Num. 14:16 in mind.[94] This does appear likely, and therefore 𝕲^A appears to miss the reason for their departure from the land: that the land is the Lord's, and he gifted it to them (cf. 28:25; 37:25), but they had polluted his land, and so they had to leave it (vv. 17–19). The reason for the dispersion is therefore given as theological. It was not due to any mystical fault in the land, or capricious action of the land, or because God could not protect his people; these may have been the insults previously mentioned (vv. 1–15).

36:21 וָאֶחְמֹל עַל־שֵׁם קָדְשִׁי אֲשֶׁר חִלְּלוּהוּ בֵּית יִשְׂרָאֵל בַּגּוֹיִם
אֲשֶׁר־בָּאוּ שָׁמָּה:

36:21 καὶ ἐφεισάμην αὐτῶν διὰ τὸ ὄνομά μου τὸ ἅγιον ὃ ἐβεβήλωσαν
οἶκος Ισραηλ ἐν τοῖς ἔθνεσιν οὗ εἰσήλθοσαν ἐκεῖ

When speaking of the focus of the Lord's action, MT and MasEzek say it was because וָאֶחְמֹל עַל־שֵׁם קָדְשִׁי ('and I had compassion/spared[95] on account of my holy name'), whereas LXX has καὶ ἐφεισάμην

---

[92] Only here in 36:20 does 'his land' appear in Ezekiel; 'their land' is found in 28:25, 33:29; 34:13, 27; 36:17; 37:25; 39:26; and 'my land' in 36:5; 37:22; 38:16.

[93] This may be similar to the modern English saying that "they messed in their own nest", indicating their sin directly affected their own lives.

[94] Zimmerli (1983, pp. 246–7) points out that the "The fact of the exile had now revealed to the nations the fact that Yahweh can no longer hold together the two entities, Israel and the land, on both which his name lay. What Moses, according to Nu 14:16, held up to Yahweh in prayer as a thing to be feared now became reality".

[95] *HALOT; DCH* has 'spared'. Block (1998, p. 344) has 'concerned'. Zimmerli (1983, p. 247) has 'grieved' and refers to Ezek. 5:11; 7:4, 9; 8:18; 9:5, 10. Greenberg (1997, p. 729) has 'moved'. Thayer indicates φείδομαι ('spared/pity') is commonly used for חמל (also LEH).

the 'house of Israel' (vv. 22–32). This causes a thematic change, where the people themselves are finally addressed regarding their restoration, and how their restoration will take place.

This pericope focuses on the LORD's acting on behalf of his 'holy name' as the motive for restoration (cf. vv. 20–21). It then describes what the LORD will do for his name, putting together a string of future 'I-will' actions.[99] Now the 'house of Israel' is addressed in the second person (contrast vv. 16–21). They are the recipients of the promise of restoration, that includes a Jeremianic sounding 'new heart and new spirit' motif (v. 26; cf. Jer. 31).[100] The 'sanctification' of the people is designed to remedy the problem, and the ancient charge, of the land casting out its inhabitants, even the LORD's people. Again there is an echo of their forefathers possessing the land (cf. v. 28). This further supports the thought that both the Hebrew author and the LXX translator had the 'twelve spies' narrative in mind (cf. 36:3, 8), as well as other related passages in Numbers, including the whole Exodus event and the original possessing of the land.[101] The LORD will perform all these actions for the sake of his holy name (cf. Num. 14:11–23), as "by restoring Israel to its land, God could uphold God's own dignity before the rest of the world" (Vawter and Hoppe, 1991, p. 163).

In contrast to the surrounding texts, there is a surprising level of agreement amongst MT, LXX, and intra-𝔊^{B,A} in vv. 23b–38, again lending support to the idea that this is a later inserted text. As our goal is to observe variants as possible theological interpretations, we will not discuss verses where agreement is found. Therefore, we will not touch on a number of important verses (e.g., v. 26 'new heart/spirit').

---

[99] See Cooper (1994, pp. 316–318) for a breakdown of seven "elements of the restoration" in vv. 24–32.

[100] Block (1998, p. 353) also believes that "the influence of Deut. 30:1–10 is apparent".

[101] Block (1998, p. 353) notes that "the new exodus motif occurs ten times in Ezekiel, but it gains increasing prominence in the restoration oracles", and in a footnote lists these as "11:17; 20:34–35; 20:41–42; 28:25; 29:13; 34:13; 36:24; 37:12; 37:21; 39:27". We can agree that this new exodus motif is present in Ezekiel. Yet here it appears that the writer, and translator, has the imagery of the spies in Numbers. The implied challenge to those in this new exodus is, will they be like the 'evil' spies bringing a bad report of the land, or will they be like the two good spies who were the ones to take possession of the land. In Ezekiel 36 there is a strong motif of a new entering or possessing the land, a restored land that is fruitful and ready to receive its inhabitants. It is a land that will not cast its inhabitants out again, and will never have to bear the insults of the nations.

Nor will we discuss the different Hebrew and Greek style used here in comparison with the rest of the book. Others have already examined these aspects (e.g., Thackeray, 1921, pp. 125–126; Turner, 1956, pp. 12–24; Lust, 1981a, pp. 521–525) and we will cover linguistic issues in chapter 7. Our discussion of vv. 22–38 may therefore appear disjointed owing to the omission of the majority of verses.

If we accept our later proposal that 𝕲⁹⁶⁷ represents the *Urtext* with this chapter finishing at v. 23b, then textually vv. 12–15 is central in this chapter, forming a chiastic 'answer' to the people's concerns. For 𝕲⁹⁶⁷, 36:1–12a covers the action of the enemy and their insults (vv. 1–7), and the return of 'my people Israel' to the mountains (8–12a); vv. 12b–15 answers the ancient charge and perhaps the returnees' current concern about the mountains/land; in vv. 16–19 the LORD deals directly with the people regarding their idolatry; and in vv. 20–23b the LORD outlines that the reason for his current action of restoration is for the sake of his holy name that had been profaned.

As in vv. 1–15 LXX typically translates verbs in the future active, rather than the passive. Perhaps in this pericope the person or group who translated this section believed that they would not be harshly treated in their future, in contrast to what they appeared to have felt they were in the past (cf. vv. 1–15). This may indicate a time of translating when there was a degree of hope for freedom from oppression and for the establishment of their nation as of old (cf. 37:15–28).

36:22 לָכֵן אֱמֹר לְבֵית־יִשְׂרָאֵל כֹּה אָמַר אֲדֹנָי יְהוִֹה לֹא לְמַעַנְכֶם אֲנִי עֹשֶׂה בֵּית יִשְׂרָאֵל כִּי אִם־לְשֵׁם־קָדְשִׁי אֲשֶׁר חִלַּלְתֶּם בַּגּוֹיִם אֲשֶׁר־בָּאתֶם שָׁם: (MasEzek: בית)

36:22 διὰ τοῦτο εἰπὸν τῷ οἴκῳ Ισραηλ τάδε λέγει κύριος οὐχ ὑμῖν ἐγὼ ποιῶ οἶκος Ισραηλ ἀλλ' ἢ διὰ τὸ ὄνομά μου τὸ ἅγιον ὃ ἐβεβηλώσατε ἐν τοῖς ἔθνεσιν οὗ εἰσήλθετε ἐκεῖ

This verse has a rare intra-Hebrew variance between MT and Mas-Ezek. A MasEzek scribe has inserted בית (small, almost as superscript) into the text after בגוים and before אשר. Talmon (1999, p. 68) suggests the scribe was seeking to insert בית ישראל "under the influence of ... בית ישראל ... in the preceding verse (Ezek. 36:21), either due to a *lapus calami* (vertical dittography) or on the strength of his *Vorlage* which differed from MT". It is interesting that the scribe did not finish the whole 'insert', suggesting that either the scribe did not find the required room, or decided against the insert. If the insert was completed it would have made the text read with a second vocative, making the rebuke harsher, but it stands in MasEzek now without sense.[102] That LXX follows MT questions Talmon's suggestion that בית ישראל was in MasEzek's *Vorlage*.

As noted above, $\mathfrak{G}^B$ begins this pericope with τάδε λέγει κύριος, thus not including the previous phrase, which gives reason for the following restorative words (cf. διὰ τοῦτο). $\mathfrak{G}^B$ has this phrase as the concluding statement to the previous pericope, so causing v. 22 (and this pericope) to lose some of the prophetic impact.

36:23 וְקִדַּשְׁתִּי אֶת־שְׁמִי הַגָּדוֹל הַמְחֻלָּל בַּגּוֹיִם אֲשֶׁר חִלַּלְתֶּם
בְּתוֹכָם וְיָדְעוּ הַגּוֹיִם כִּי־אֲנִי יְהוָה נְאֻם אֲדֹנָי יְהוִה
בְּהִקָּדְשִׁי בָכֶם לְעֵינֵיהֶם:

36:23 καὶ ἁγιάσω τὸ ὄνομά μου τὸ ($\mathfrak{G}^{967,B}$: μέγα; $\mathfrak{G}^A$: ἅγιον) τὸ βεβηλωθὲν ἐν τοῖς ἔθνεσιν ὃ ἐβεβηλώσατε ἐν μέσῳ αὐτῶν καὶ γνώσονται τὰ ἔθνη ὅτι ἐγώ εἰμι κύριος[103] ($\mathfrak{G}^A$: + λέγει Αδωναι κύριος) ἐν τῷ ἁγιασθῆναί με ἐν ὑμῖν κατ' ὀφθαλμοὺς αὐτῶν

Our three representative MT texts and MasEzek all witness the declarative formula (נְאֻם אֲדֹנָי יְהוִה). However, Allen (1990b, p. 176) says this is "lacking in two Heb Mss and LXX[B]", following the note in *BHS* (cf. Block, 1998, p. 349). $\mathfrak{G}^{967}$ also does not witness this declarative formula, ending immediately before its location. $\mathfrak{G}^B$ is also minus the declarative formula, yet has the subsequent verses and received chapter order. $\mathfrak{G}^A$ has this formula, the subsequent verses, and received chapter order, matching MT (and MasEzek).[104] Wevers (1969, p. 273) says $\mathfrak{G}^{967,B}$ "omit the declaration formula, which is peculiar after the recognition formula", and then asks "but why would it be added by a traditionalist?", proposing the possibility that "it was incorporated [later in MT] to make this key verse even more impressive". We find significance in $\mathfrak{G}^A$'s use of 'Αδωναι' in its declarative formula, as Αδωναι is often attributed to the later linguistic style of Theodotion. Thus we suggest that the formula was a later plus for MT and $\mathfrak{G}^A$, as part of additional editorial work seeking to weave 36:23c–38 into the text (chapter 7 we discuss distinctive features of style and language in

---

[102] This 'superscript' style insertion also occurs in MasEzek in v. 25 with the מ in טֻמְאוֹתֵיכֶם, and in v. 30 with the ו in the middle of וּתְנוּבַת.

[103] $\mathfrak{G}^{967}$ ends at this point and immediately proceeds into 38:1. We will discuss with the uniqueness of $\mathfrak{G}^{967}$ and these issues in chapter 7 (cf. §7.4.1).

[104] This again may indicate a possible time frame for textual inclusion.

both Hebrew and Greek).[105] This would have been added at a similar time to other later changes supporting the chapter reorder (e.g., the change from קָהָל to חַיִל in 37:10, and חֵמָה to רוּחַ in 39:29).

MT and 𝕲[967,B] have 'my great name' (הַגָּדוֹל/μέγα), whereas 𝕲[A] has 'holy name' (ἅγιον).[106] This may be a theological adjustment by 𝕲[A], to match the previous verses (cf. vv. 20–22), or even a theological echo or duplication based on ἁγιάσω. Yet again we see evidence of a text in a state of flux.

36:25 וְזָרַקְתִּי עֲלֵיכֶם מַיִם טְהוֹרִים וּטְהַרְתֶּם מִכֹּל טֻמְאוֹתֵיכֶם
גְמִכָּל־גִּלּוּלֵיכֶם אֲטַהֵר אֶתְכֶם:

36:25 καὶ ῥανῶ ἐφ᾽ ὑμᾶς ὕδωρ καθαρόν καὶ καθαρισθήσεσθε ἀπὸ πασῶν τῶν ἀκαθαρσιῶν ὑμῶν καὶ ἀπὸ πάντων τῶν εἰδώλων ὑμῶν καὶ καθαριῶ ὑμᾶς

The MT accents link 'from all your uncleannesses and idols' with 'I will cleanse you'. For LXX, the addition of καί means that the cleansing from their uncleannesses and idols is linked back to the sprinkling of clean water at the beginning of the verse, with the last phrase being an independent clause (Block, 1998, p. 349). Vawter and Hoppe (1991, p. 164) point out that "what Ezekiel wanted to affirm was that without God's initiative a genuine conversion on Israel's part is impossible". LXX's independent clause emphasises this point, clearly showing that it is the LORD doing the 'cleansing' with the people as the recipients of the cleansing. Greenberg (1997, p. 730) notes that this verse is a "reversal of the personal impurity ('like the impurity of a menstruous woman [hndh]') incurred by the evils of vss. 17–18". Eisemann (1994, p. 556) brings out the interpretation with a comparison to the *mikvah* which a woman enters after her monthly menstrual cycle (also those defiled from the dead or defiled objects), and says "Just as a *mikvah* cleanses those who have become defiled, so God cleanses Israel (Yoma 85b)". The LXX translator may have been reflecting on vv. 17–18 (cf. variants there), and now, perhaps with the concept of the *mikvah* and

---

[105] See McGregor (1985) for a detailed discussion on the use of single and/or double divine names in Ezekiel.

[106] Wong (2003, p. 229) suggests that "'Holy name' and 'great name' may be synonyms here. It is also possible that 'great name' is used to avoid an overloading of the קדש terminology and at the same time underlines the great power of God".

the *haftarah* reading of Num. 19:9–22 in his mind,[107] exegetes to clarify it is the LORD who cleanses Israel.

36:30 וְהִרְבֵּיתִי אֶת־פְּרִי הָעֵץ וּתְנוּבַת הַשָּׂדֶה לְמַעַן אֲשֶׁר
לֹא תִקְחוּ עוֹד חֶרְפַּת רָעָב בַּגּוֹיִם:

36:30 καὶ πληθυνῶ τὸν καρπὸν τοῦ ξύλου καὶ τὰ γενήματα τοῦ ἀγροῦ ὅπως μὴ λάβητε (𝕲ᴬ: + ἔτι) ὀνειδισμὸν (𝕲ᴮ: λιμοῦ; 𝕲ᴬ: λαοῦ) ἐν τοῖς ἔθνεσιν

Unlike 𝕲ᴬ, 𝕲ᴮ does not attest MT's עוֹד ('again'). This could be a later MT and 𝕲ᴬ plus to emphasise the hope that they will not repeat their past tragedies in the land, nor have to endure the resulting abusive insults from the nations.

In addition to this, MT and 𝕲ᴮ have 'the insult[108] of *famine* among the nations', but 𝕲ᴬ has 'the insult of *people* among the nations.' Rather than scribal error, this may be an intra-Greek word play by 𝕲ᴬ's scribe, writing λαοῦ ('people') for λιμοῦ ('famine'). Both MT and 𝕲ᴮ fit the context, and refer back to previous references to 'insults'. However, the charge now appears to be 'famine' rather than childlessness. Famine may have been one of the events that caused the 'childlessness' (so LXX) or 'miscarrying' (so MT) from the land (cf. 36:6, 12b–15). This would fit our observation that the Hebrew author and LXX translator has the Exodus event in mind, especially from Numbers. Thus they would know that the reason for their ancestors' original departure from the land was because of famine (Gen. 45:8–11).

𝕲ᴬ's use of λαός instead of λιμός (which is in the previous verse), may be because the context now refers to the insults Israel received from the surrounding nations, invoking the memory of previous verses dealing with insults of childlessness (cf. vv. 1–15). 𝕲ᴬ appears to change the reason for the insults (of famine) to focus on where the insults were coming from (the people among the nations), and inform their

---

[107] There is a strong link between this verse, and even the pericope, with Num. 19:9–22. It was one of the earliest *haftarah* readings in the Synagogue (Thackeray, 1921, p. 126). Our suggestion here presumes the early date of the *haftarah* reading as proposed by Thackeray, and early use of the *mikvah*. See chapter 7 for the use of vv. 23c–38 in the Synagogue lectionary and *haftarah* readings. For the *mikvah* see Kotlar (1972, p. 1542), who points out that in the "closing years" of the Second Temple, the *mikvah* was used by the "common people [who] were particular about the laws of cleanness".

[108] The Greek ὀνειδισμὸν means 'disgrace/insult/reproach' [LEH]. The Hebrew חֶרְפַּת means 'disgrace/shame' [*HALOT*]. The context here leans towards 'insult' due to the previous occurrences of them being insulted by the nations (cf. 36:3, 6, 15).

community that these insults will not happen again (cf. ἔτι). 𝔊ᴬ may be referring back to the 'childlessness' of 36:15, and using wordplay to state that they will not experience a 'famine' (λιμοῦ) of 'people' (λαοῦ).[109] However, the context of this verse fits the former suggestion, as 'famine' was often the reason why the inhabitants had to leave the land, and the fertility of the land is restored before the people are said to return (vv. 8–9). 𝔊ᴬ does not bring this aspect out as clearly as the other MSS.

36:31 וּזְכַרְתֶּם אֶת־דַּרְכֵיכֶם הָרָעִים וּמַעַלְלֵיכֶם אֲשֶׁר לֹא־טוֹבִים
וּנְקֹטֹתֶם בִּפְנֵיכֶם עַל עֲוֹנֹתֵיכֶם וְעַל תּוֹעֲבוֹתֵיכֶם:

36:31 καὶ μνησθήσεσθε τὰς ὁδοὺς ὑμῶν τὰς πονηρὰς καὶ τὰ ἐπιτηδεύματα ὑμῶν τὰ μὴ ἀγαθὰ καὶ προσοχθιεῖτε κατὰ πρόσωπον αὐτῶν ἐν ταῖς ἀνομίαις ὑμῶν καὶ ἐπὶ τοῖς βδελύγμασιν ὑμῶν

MT says they will קוט ('loathe') themselves for their sins. If we take αὐτῶν as a reflexive pronoun, then LXX says 'you will. προσοχθιεῖτε be angry/offended [LEH] or loathed[110] with yourselves', and the later reading of Symmachus' καὶ σμικρυνθήσεσθε ἐνώπιον αὐτῶν would read 'and you will be diminished[111] before yourselves'. However, πρόσωπον αὐτῶν is never used reflexively in LXX for non-3rd person subjects, and always has the meaning of 'their face'. Where the reflexive subject is the 2nd person, πρόσωπον ὑμῶν is used (cf. Num. 33:55; Josh. 24:8; Jer. 49:15; Ezek. 14:6). LXX twice uses ὑμῶν in a reflexive sense in this verse, and if the translator intended this sense here then he would have used ὑμῶν again. We also note the Hebrew clearly uses a *niphal*, yet the Greek uses an active verb rather than a passive.

If we apply a non-reflexive aspect of αὐτῶν here, and translate 'their', we must determine the referent. It is possibly the preceding 'your evil ways and your practices', so 'in accordance with their presence [face]', meaning in the presence of their evil ways and practices. Symmachus thus has Israel diminished in the sight of their deeds.

Alternatively, we may suggest LXX is reflecting back on the reproach by the nations mentioned in the previous verse, and elsewhere, saying

---

[109] In 36:15 the phrase is in the plural, yet here in v. 30 it is in the singular. This indicates deliberate adjustment and thus signifies exegetical intent.

[110] προσοχθίζω here means "to be angry, to be offended, to be provoked" [LEH]. Muraoka's Lexicon says 'be weary of, dislike'. We find προσοχθίζω in Psa. 95:10 as 'angry', and as 'loathed' in Lev. 26:15, 30, 43, 44; Num. 21:5; Deut. 7:26; Psa. 35:5.

[111] For σμικρύνω as 'reduced/diminished' see Jer. 29:6; Hos. 4:3; Sir. 17:25; 35:7; Bar. 2:34.

that Israel's deeds caused Israel to be loathed in the sight of the nations.
This view permits Symmachus to read 'you will be diminished before
them', reflecting a concern that the nations around would think less of
Israel. LXX appears to have translated with a non-reflexive application for αὐτῶν to give reason for the reproachful words spoken against
them by the surrounding nations. However, it is difficult to be sure
whether the translator was referring to their deeds (v. 31a), or deeds
of the nations (v. 30b).

𝔊ᴮ uses αὐτῶν in the final phrase of v. 31 as βδελύγμασιν αὐτῶν
('their abominations'), whereas 𝔊ᴬ has ὑμῶν ('your'), following MT.
This does appear to be a scribal error based upon the first occurrence
in the verse.

3.4.2. *36:33–36*

All representative MSS exhibit division breaks before v. 33 and after
v. 36, except MasEzek, which treats vv. 22–38 as one pericope. We will
discuss vv. 33–36 and vv. 37–38 as continuing sub-sections of vv. 22–38
(our Section 3). While there are several minor textual differences in
this block, 𝔊ᴬ is of key interest, showing evidence of an eschatological
slant in v. 33. There is also a variant in v. 35 regarding Eden.

36:33 כֹּה אָמַר אֲדֹנָי יְהוִֹה בְּיוֹם טַהֲרִי אֶתְכֶם מִכֹּל עֲוֹנוֹתֵיכֶם
וְהוֹשַׁבְתִּי אֶת־הֶעָרִים וְנִבְנוּ הֶחֳרָבוֹת׃

36:33 τάδε λέγει κύριος (𝔊ᴮ: ἐν ἡμέρᾳ; 𝔊ᴬ: ἐν τῇ ἡμέρᾳ ἐκείνῃ) ᾗ
καθαριῶ ὑμᾶς ἐκ πασῶν τῶν ἀνομιῶν ὑμῶν καὶ κατοικιῶ τὰς πόλεις
καὶ οἰκοδομηθήσονται αἱ ἔρημοι

There is one minor variant where 𝔊ᴬ's plus of the definite article and
ἐκείνῃ reads 'in that day' (𝔊ᴮ 'in a day'), which appears to emphasise
a specific day or time. The phrase ἐν τῇ ἡμέρᾳ ἐκείνῃ is not very common in Ezekiel (24:26, 27; 29:21; 30:9; 38:14, 19; 39:11), but in other
books, especially Isaiah, it appears to have a messianic concept. It cannot be known whether this concept was in the mind of 𝔊ᴬ's scribe, or
whether this time of cleansing was seen as a specific day in their future.
Regardless, 𝔊ᴬ's plus permits us to see an eschatological slant.

36:34 וְהָאָרֶץ הַנְּשַׁמָּה תֵּעָבֵד תַּחַת אֲשֶׁר הָיְתָה שְׁמָמָה לְעֵינֵי כָּל־עוֹבֵר׃

36:34 καὶ ἡ γῆ ἡ ἠφανισμένη ἐργασθήσεται ἀνθ᾽ ὧν ὅτι ἠφανισμένη
ἐγενήθη κατ᾽ ὀφθαλμοὺς παντὸς (𝔊ᴮ: παροδεύοντος; 𝔊ᴬ: διοδεύοντος)

𝔊ᴮ acceptably has παροδεύοντος ([those] 'passing by'), a word not
used elsewhere in Ezekiel. 𝔊ᴬ's διοδεύοντος ([those] 'passing/travel-

ling through') captures MT's wording (עוֹבֵר), and gives answer to the desolation found by those who are passing through in 5:14, and to the fear of travelling in 14:15 (both verses use διοδεύω).

36:35 וְאָמְרוּ הָאָרֶץ הַלֵּזוּ הַנְּשַׁמָּה הָיְתָה כְּגַן־עֵדֶן וְהֶעָרִים הֶחֳרֵבוֹת
וְהַנְּשַׁמּוֹת וְהַנֶּהֱרָסוֹת בְּצוּרוֹת יָשָׁבוּ׃

36:35 καὶ ἐροῦσιν ἡ γῆ ἐκείνη ἡ ἠφανισμένη ἐγενήθη ὡς κῆπος τρυφῆς καὶ αἱ πόλεις αἱ ἔρημοι καὶ ἠφανισμέναι καὶ κατεσκαμμέναι ὀχυραὶ ἐκάθισαν

MT says that the 'restored' land has become כְּגַן־עֵדֶן ('as [the] Garden of Eden'), which LXX reflects with ὡς κῆπος τρυφῆς ('as a garden of delight' [LEH]). Only here in LXX do we find 'κῆπος' being used in the context of the *garden* [of Eden]. Elsewhere in Ezekiel (and other books) LXX translates '[עֵדֶן]גַּן' with παράδεισος (cf. Ezek. 28:13; 31:9; Gen. 2:23, 24).[112]

The theology behind the use of Eden in this inserted pericope appears to reflect a view of what the 'cleansed, rebuilt, and recreated' Israel would be in its ideal state. Fishbane (1985, p. 370) suggests that

> Ezekiel (or his redactor) juxtaposed the oracle of hope that the old Eden would be restored (36:25) with the parable of dry bones, whereby he envisages the re-creation of the corporate body of Israel—much like a new Adam—with a new flesh and a new spirit (37:4–9). But with this coupling of Edenic and Adamic imagery, national nostalgia and primordial fantasies are blended.

Levenson (1986, p. 33) also points out that Eden in Ezekiel's theology, is "an ideal of pre-political existence, and [hence] redemption which ends in the Garden of Eden is deliverance from the tensions of political life". The returnees will not have to endure the tumultuous politics that they suffered before the exile (cf. Ezek. 34). In both MT and LXX this verse, along with the surrounding verses, showcases a fully restored land abundant in produce (vv. 33–36) and people (vv. 37–38).

We must keep in mind that this verse is part of the pericope not found in 𝕲⁹⁶⁷, and likely a later inserted text. The use of κῆπος is another linguistic feature pointing to the later origin of this block in LXX. Its use may indicate that the allusion here to Eden as the nostalgic Garden of Eden for the people of God should not be confused

---

[112] LXX Ezekiel, as with other books, translates עֵדֶן rather than transliterating, bringing out the meaning of 'delight/luxury' to its readers. LXX's τρυφῆς can mean 'a state of intense satisfaction, delight, luxury' [BAGD].

with the earlier more mythological references to Tyre and Assyria in 28:19 and 31:9.[113]

36:36 וְיָדְעוּ הַגּוֹיִם אֲשֶׁר יִשָּׁאֲרוּ סְבִיבוֹתֵיכֶם כִּי אֲנִי יְהוָה בָּנִיתִי הַנֶּהֱרָסוֹת נָטַעְתִּי הַנְּשַׁמָּה אֲנִי יְהוָה דִּבַּרְתִּי וְעָשִׂיתִי׃

36:36 καὶ γνώσονται τὰ ἔθνη ὅσα ἂν καταλειφθῶσιν κύκλῳ ὑμῶν ὅτι ἐγὼ (𝔊ᴬ: + εἰμι) κύριος ᾠκοδόμησα τὰς καθῃρημένας καὶ κατεφύτευσα τὰς ἠφανισμένας (𝔊ᴬ: + ὅτι) ἐγὼ (𝔊ᴮ: κύριος; 𝔊ᴬ: κύριος κύριος) ἐλάλησα καὶ ποιήσω

𝔊ᴬ has two plusses that are not found in the other MSS. The first plus εἰμι helps support "the interpretation of אֲנִי יְהוָה as a self-contained recognition formula" (Block, 1998, p. 362). This plus causes the text to read "…know that I *am* the LORD [that] has built…". It is interesting that 𝔊ᴬ did not repeat this εἰμι plus in the second occurrence of ἐγὼ κύριος in this verse, as it also has ὅτι as a plus as if copied from the first use, and a unique double divine name (see below). 𝔊ᴬ also repeats εἰμι in v. 38, but without any significant theological change other than to bring a greater emphasis (so v. 38 will not be covered separately). We speculate that the εἰμι plus by 𝔊ᴬ's Christian scribes may have been influenced by ἐγώ εἰμι used by Jesus in John's Gospel.[114] If so, this may be an indication that the early Christian communities saw Jesus as the one who will bring about the restoration of his people. Alternatively, it may have been inserted by later Jewish scribes.

𝔊ᴬ's other plus of ὅτι refers back to the new-found knowledge of the nations, and gives reason for the LORD's speaking and doing these restorative actions. However, ὅτι appears out of place, as does 𝔊ᴬ's double divine name (κύριος κύριος) that is not found in the other

---

[113] Kutsko (2000a, p. 130) notes that use of Garden of Eden here "reflects the creation tradition found in Gen. 2:15…. [and] for the exilic community the language reverberates with images from the Israelite creation traditions." Kutsko does not mention LXX's use of κῆπος.

[114] Thackeray (1909, p. 55) says that "the use of ἐγώ εἰμι *followed by a finite verb*" is a "flagrant violation of Greek syntax", and lists the occurrence here in 𝔊ᴬ as a possible example. He explains that "it is due to a desire to discriminate in the Greek between…אני and אנכי. The observation of the fact that אנכי is the form usually employed to express 'I am' led to the adoption of the rule". Furthermore, he (*ibid.*) notes that this 'rule' "may be regarded as among the latest additions to the Greek Bible", and suggests influence by Theodotion. While the Hebrew does not have אנכי in v. 36 (cf. v. 28), 𝔊ᴬ nevertheless has translated with theological intent in both cases of אֲנִי יְהוָה.

MSS. These may have been added to emphasise the LORD's action of 'built' and 'planted'.[115]

LXX's use of the future ποιήσω ('I will do it') may be seen as an interpretation of MT's וְעָשִׂיתִי (וְ + perfect), putting the action definitely into the future. This may indicate that LXX's scribe saw this building as both complete, yet with more to take place.

3.4.3. 36:37–38

All representative MSS have a break after v. 36, except MasEzek, which treats vv. 22–38 as one pericope. All the representative MSS have a major break between chapters 36 and 37. The exception is 𝕲⁹⁶⁷, which proceeds directly from 36:23b into what we know as chapter 38 on the same line. This pericope has only one minor intra-Greek variant.

36:37 כֹּה אָמַר אֲדֹנָי יְהוִה עוֹד זֹאת אִדָּרֵשׁ לְבֵית־יִשְׂרָאֵל לַעֲשׂוֹת
לָהֶם אַרְבֶּה אֹתָם כַּצֹּאן אָדָם:

36:37 τάδε λέγει κύριος ἔτι τοῦτο (𝕲ᴮ·ᴬ: ζητηθήσομαι; Α, Σ, Θ: ζήτημα θήσομαι) τῷ οἴκῳ Ισραηλ τοῦ ποιῆσαι αὐτοῖς πληθυνῶ αὐτοὺς ὡς πρόβατα ἀνθρώπους

While MT and LXX agree here, there is a small variant in the Greek between LXX and the translations of Aquila, Symmachus and Theodotion (Field, 1964, p. 868; Ziegler, 1977, p. 266). 𝕲ᴮ·ᴬ say ζητηθήσομαι τῷ οἴκῳ Ισραηλ ('I will be sought by the house of Israel'). However, these three exegetes write ζητηθήσομαι as two separate words, ζήτημα as a noun and θήσομαι as a future middle rather than future passive. This changes the sentence to 'So the LORD says: Yet for this inquiry, I will place the house of Israel, to establish them'. This may have been due to scribal error, or it may be evidence of a different theology, whereby the later 'three exegetes' saw the 'I will be sought' as something that had happened in their past intercessions. Now they look for the reality of God placing and establishing Israel again, especially as by their time they had again been dispersed, this time at the hands of the Romans in 70 CE.

---

[115] For more on God as builder see Brettler (1989, pp. 116–118).

3.5. Summary of Observations: Ezekiel 36

Our textual-comparative methodology has identified a number of textual differences in Ezekiel 36 that are typically attributed by commentators to scribal errors, but for which there are likely exegetical and theological reasons. Following the *petuḥah* sense division breaks in MT[A], Ezekiel 36 may be divided into three major thematic sections with different addressees: the mountains (vv. 1–15), the prophet (vv. 16–21), and the 'house of Israel' (vv. 22–38).

In the first section LXX's use of passive verbs suggests the scribe and/or community felt harshly treated, seeing 'dishonour' continuing from the enemy. This feeling is reflected in LXX's interpreting the enemy's attitude towards them, whereas MT just states the enemy's action (vv. 2–5), and clarifying the enemy's action of 'insult' for MT's 'dishonour' (v. 3). LXX displays a propensity towards clarifying MT, such as defining MT's דִּבַּת־עָם in v. 3 as ὀνείδισμα, and identifying the 'fruit' in v. 8 as 'grapes'. There is a degree of uneasiness within both MT and LXX communities regarding the ancient accusation against the land in vv. 12b–15. MT appears to be more willing to permit the charge of 'miscarriage' against the land to be active, as if the land itself was the one miscarrying, whereas LXX's use of the passive verb has the land being made childless, again perhaps revealing their feeling of being harshly treated.

In the first section the LXX translator, and perhaps the original author, was reflecting on the book of Numbers, particularly the 10 spies and their 'evil report' (vv. 3, 8, 13–15, cf. Num. 13:32; 14:36f.), indicating they saw the re-possessing of the land and restoration of Israel as a new exodus.[116] There is a 'new creation' motif in v. 8, describing a fruitful place, and in MT's unique plus of the priestly blessing in 36:11. This motif may be found in the textual flow that follows Genesis: first the land is prepared and vegetated (vv. 1–15), then people placed on

---

[116] Patton (1996, p. 73) also finds a clear reference to the exodus tradition in Ezek. 20 and 23, and says "these two chapters demonstrate that, although the exodus motif does not dominate the book of Ezekiel, the traditions were clearly known to the author". Patton (1996, p. 85) goes on to say that "if exodus motifs lie behind the restoration texts, they are latent and unexploited. For Ezekiel the restoration draws more clearly on royal motifs. The return is likened to the gathering of scattered Israelites by its 'shepherd', clearly a royal image. The restoration will be that of the United Monarchy, with full occupation of the land rule by a Davidide. Central to this restoration is the re-establishment of the temple".

the land with direction for living (vv. 16–23), and thirdly the people are cleansed from their sins for future living (vv. 24–38 [minus in 𝕲⁹⁶⁷]). Some commentators suggest that Ezekiel saw himself as a new Moses;[117] however, we are unable to find this motif in the variants of Ezek. 36.

The second section, vv. 16–21, addresses the prophet regarding the sin of idolatry which it gives as the reason for the dispersion into the nations. Kutsko (2000a, p. 129) says, "it appears that Ezekiel 36 begins to describe the restoration of Israel as cleansing from sin, specifically, idolatry... Israel has taken idols into its heart". The LORD's reason for the restoration is 'for the sake of my holy/great name'. LXX's use of active verbs suggests the translator(s) accepted the LORD's charge of idolatry. This acceptance is also found with LXX's exegetical expansion of 'idols' in v. 17, especially in 𝕲ᴬ. However, 𝕲⁹⁶⁷,ᴮ both show a reluctance to state that Israel's deeds were like a 'menstruating woman' (cf. MT, 𝕲ᴬ), instead preferring to say a 'set apart woman', revealing cultural sensitivity. Another cultural sensitivity adjustment is found where LXX uses εἰδώλοις for MT's גִּלּוּלִים (cf. vv. 17, 18). MT and 𝕲ᴬ have an extended unique plus in v. 18 that indicates the scribe(s) were also reflecting on the Book of Numbers (Num. 35:33).

The third section, vv. 22–38, addressing the house of Israel, covers what the LORD will do to restore Israel to her fullness. The closer agreement between our representative texts likely results from this being an inserted pericope (see chapter 7). There is a possible echo of Num. 19:17 in the 'cleanse you' passage in v. 25, especially in LXX, which treats this as an independent clause. There is again a 'new exodus'

---

[117] McKeating (1994, p. 99) argues along with Levenson (1986) that Ezek. 40f has a number of parallels with Moses, and says "Ezekiel might be seen as fulfilling the prophecy of Deuteronomy 19, that a 'prophet like Moses' would appear". McKeating (1994, p. 103f) also notes parallels between exodus and the return in Ezek. 20. He (1994, p. 107) believes that "The Moses/Ezekiel parallelism must go back at least to this primary stage of the organisation of the book", yet it is "not necessarily that he saw himself as a Moses figure, but that he believed he had a key role in the fulfilment of his own prophecies". Kohn (1999, p. 511) says "while never mentioning Moses of old, Ezekiel in fact portrays himself as a new Moses". Kohn (1999, p. 516) saw this happening as "Ezekiel modelled himself on the ancient lawgiver Moses, issuing laws in anticipation of the 'Second Exodus' and the resettlement of the land". Greenberg (1984, p. 183) points out that "Biblical tradition regards Moses as the mediator of Israel's divine constitution, the Torah; it recognizes no other legislator—excepting Ezekiel.... As Moses spelled out the meaning of a 'holy nation' to an unformed people just liberated from Egypt, so Ezekiel specified the needful changes in the vessels and symbols of God's presence in the future commonwealth of those near redemption from the Babylonian exile. Analogy of the situation produced similar prophetic roles".

motif in vv. 24, 30, and a 'new creation' motif in v. 35 with the reference to Eden. As Batto (1987, p. 189) says, "that Ezekiel patterned the restoration upon primeval motifs is confirmed by 36:35". Whilst the absence of discernible variants caused us not to refer directly to 36:36, Kutsko (2000a, p. 129) claims the concept of a new heart in v. 36 also suggests "the language of (re)creation".

Overall, in Ezekiel chapter 36, our textual-comparative methodology has allowed us to hear many interpretive and exegetical variants in their own context.

CHAPTER FOUR

THE TEXT OF EZEKIEL 37

4.1. INTRODUCTION: EZEK. 37

When seeking to determine early Jewish interpretation in Ezekiel 37, we must keep in mind the likelihood that this chapter originally came after chapter 39, as witnessed in 𝔊[967]. The placement of chapters (or a group of pericopes) in the text has definite theological and exegetical implications. While we refer to this aspect at various points below, its complexity will receive detailed consideration in chapter 7.

Chapter 37 has two discernible thematic sections: the first deals with the 'resurrection' of the dry bones (vv. 1–14), and the second with the reuniting of the two kingdoms under a Davidic leader (vv. 15–28). The chapter can be seen as the ultimate fulfilment of the restoration of Israel, in that they are back in their land with a leader like David of old. In the received chapter order, the destruction of their enemies has yet to take place, while in 𝔊[967]'s order the Gog epic has already occurred. Kutsko (2000a) finds a creation motif in Ezek. 37:1–14.[1] Duguid (1994, p. 104) points out "The re-creation and restoration of the bones serves as a guarantee of the promised ultimate restoration of Israel as a nation. Thus in a very real sense, the vision of chapter 37 provides the ultimate answer to the prophet's question in 11:13". Fishbane (1985, p. 452) finds a chiastic structure for this pericope with verse 11 as the central part, where he sees a "profound theological transformation" taking place.[2] Curiously, Fox (1995, p. 184) says that

---

[1] There are a number of good studies on the structure and rhetorical aspects of Ezek. 37:1–14, including Fox (1995) and Allen (1993). Unfortunately these, along with the plethora of 'preaching' sources on the 'dry bones' pericope, rarely comment on variances between MT and LXX. Likewise few appear concerned about what the text may have meant to the original recipients or other early Jewish communities which remains our focus.

[2] Fishbane (1985, p. 452) also says, "For if Ezekiel, an individual, was initially inspired and relocated in the exile, in the valley of dry bones the entire unit closes with the divine assertion that YHWH will inspire the entire nation (i.e., revive them to a new life) and relocate them upon their land".

resurrection of Israel's people (37:1–14), to unite under Davidic leadership (37:15–28), and then build the new Temple (40–48). Yet, with the
received chapter order, the 'slaughter' in chapters 38–39 is of Israel's
enemies. This point, along with the motif of 'spiritual renewal' from
the 'inserted' text of 36:23c–38, indicates more of a 'moral' or 'spiritual' resurrection in 37:1–14 for national Israel, rather than a physical
bodily resurrection following warfare (cf. vv. 6c, 11).[8] Thus, 𝔊[B,A] have
the interpretive or clarifying plus of 'human' bones, possibly pointing
to a physical resurrection and not only a moral/spiritual one, although,
it still includes the moral/spiritual resurrection motif.

However, we still must examine why MT does not witness this
plus. This could be an implicit representation of MT's theology that
desired to have the resurrection as a national moral and spiritual one,
as witnessed by the chapter reorder and plus of 36:23c–38. This leaves
𝔊[967] as a possible witness of the *Urtext* that originally saw a physical
resurrection. Then, while accepting MT's chapter order and plus, a
later LXX scribe made a theological decision to insert ἀνθρωπίνων to
support their theological view that the dry bones are human, and that
there will be a physical resurrection of Israel, therefore still agreeing
with the theology of the *Urtext*.[9] This may indicate a timeframe where
Israel had experienced some measure of a 'slaughter', perhaps during
Greco-Roman times. MT could indicate a timeframe before such a
'slaughter', as they sought to 'resurrect' the hearts of their nation and
unite them against a common enemy (cf. vv. 15–28), and so does not
witness the plus found in 𝔊[B,A]. This of course is speculative, but we are
seeking to propose possible reasons for textual variants. It could be as

---

expect more—that Israelites *would* rise from the dead". Block (1992a, p. 141) also argues
for a belief of resurrection in 'ancient' Israel, saying "Ezekiel offered his countrymen
powerful declarations of hope. There is life after death, and there is hope beyond the
grave. Yahweh remains the incontestable Lord, not only of the living, but also of the
dead". See Dimant (2000) regarding how *Pseudo-Ezekiel* reveals early knowledge of
individual physical eschatological resurrection that was based on the individual's own
purity. Ezek. 37:1–14 however, reveals national resurrection, without direct mention
as the result of individual purity.

[8] The issue of a 'moral/spiritual' verses a 'physical' resurrection is discussed in
chapter 7. See Lust (1981a, pp. 529–532) for his proposal regarding the moral/physi-
cal resurrection issues. Here, we only seek to raise possible reasons for the variants
intra-LXX and LXX to MT.

[9] We do not know if these later LXX scribes had access to 𝔊[967] or other MSS
that witnessed its chapter order. Their plus, however, does match the theology of
that original order.

simple as the later LXX scribes adding ἀνθρώπινος just to clarify the meaning of bones in the context.

There is one other implicit indicator that 𝕲⁹⁶⁷ follows the Hebrew, and perhaps even the *Urtext*, more closely than 𝕲ᴮ·ᴬ. 𝕲⁹⁶⁷ follows the syntax of וַיּוֹצִאֵנִי בְרוּחַ יְהוָה with καὶ ἐξήγαγέν με ἐν πνεύματι κυρίου ('and he brought me out by the Spirit of the Lord'), whereas 𝕲ᴮ·ᴬ have καὶ ἐξήγαγέν με ἐν πνεύματι κύριος ('and the Lord brought me out by the Spirit'). 𝕲ᴮ·ᴬ follow the Hebrew word order, but interpret the syntax differently. On the other hand this is more likely an interpretation of the event, as Greenberg (1997, p. 742) points out that LXX

> construe[s] the second clause of the verse thus: 'The Lord brought me out by a wind'; but if this were meant, the placement of the subject (*YHWH*) after the adverb (*brwḥ*) is awkward. This forced reading may reflect an interpretation of the event as real rather than visionary.

Therefore we propose that MT and 𝕲⁹⁶⁷ saw this as a visionary event, but the intra-LXX variant for 𝕲ᴮ·ᴬ exegetes and interprets this as a real event. If so, this theology may have influenced 𝕲ᴮ·ᴬ's ἀνθρωπίνος plus above.

Whilst πνεῦμα, like רוּחַ, may alternatively mean 'wind', 'breath' or 's/Spirit', we suggest that the various LXX MSS alternate between these meanings as is evident by their practice of abbreviating πνεῦμα as they do with κύριος and θεός.[10] Fluctuation between abbreviating and not abbreviating may be stylistic, but v. 9, which has πνεῦμα abbreviated twice and once written in full in all representative LXX MSS, suggests theological intent. Sometimes there are intra-LXX variants of this practice in 37:1–15, which may indicate the various attempts to translate and interpret the alternative nuances of רוּחַ. As all representative LXX MSS abbreviate πνεῦμα in v. 1, we suggest that the copying communities interpreted רוּחַ here as 'the Spirit' rather than 'a wind' (contra Greenberg above).

We need to be aware of the different ways in which רוּחַ is used here, and in the rest of this pericope. Lemke (1984, p. 179) outlines these ways saying,

---

[10] 𝕲⁹⁶⁷·ᴮ agree together with each occurrence of abbreviation or not for πνεῦμα, with the only non abbreviation being the third mention of πνεῦμα in v. 9. 𝕲ᴬ has the least number of abbreviations matching 𝕲⁹⁶⁷·ᴮ only in vv. 1, 8, and the second occurrence in v. 9. Thus, 𝕲ᴬ does not abbreviate πνεῦμα in vv. 5, 6, 9a, 10, 14. Also see Isaacs (1976), especially her second chapter 'ΠΝΕΥΜΑ in the Septuagint' (pp. 10–17).

rûaḥ occurs no fewer than ten times in these fourteen verses, with varying nuances which embrace virtually the whole gamut of meanings which the term has in the Hebrew Bible. In verse 1, *rûaḥ* refers to the spirit of the LORD as the source of visionary rapture and prophetic inspiration. The term *rûaḥ* may also denote the life-giving breath or spirit coming from God, which creates living beings out of inanimate matter (cf. vs. 5, 6, 8, 9, 10 and cf. Gen. 2:4b–7 or Ps. 104:29–30). In verse 9, the term *rûaḥ* occurs in the plural and refers to the four winds of heaven. Finally in verse 14 a suffixed form of *rûaḥ* clearly refers to Yahweh's spirit as the ultimate source of life in the full range of both its physical as well as its spiritual connotations.

37:2 וְהֶעֱבִירַנִי עֲלֵיהֶם סָבִיב סָבִיב וְהִנֵּה רַבּוֹת מְאֹד עַל־פְּנֵי הַבִּקְעָה וְהִנֵּה יְבֵשׁוֹת מְאֹד:

37:2 καὶ περιήγαγέν με ἐπ' αὐτὰ κυκλόθεν (𝕲^{B,A}: + κύκλῳ) καὶ ἰδοὺ πολλὰ σφόδρα ἐπὶ προσώπου τοῦ πεδίου (𝕲^A: + καὶ ἰδοὺ) ξηρὰ σφόδρα

MT has סָבִיב סָבִיב ('all around/round about'), and 𝕲^{B,A} have κυκλόθεν κύκλῳ which follows the MT doublet, yet 𝕲^{967} has only κυκλόθεν. This may be an early 'doublet plus' in MT as emphasis that the bones were everywhere, and then added to the later 𝕲^{B,A} MSS. On the other hand, it is more likely to be a 𝕲^{967} minus, seeking to smooth out MT's 'stylistic doublet'.[11] Gehman (in Johnson *et al.*, 1938, p. 75) uses this 𝕲^{967} 'minus' as one of the evidences (also 32:18), "that the text of Sch[eide] represents a translation which is based either on a faulty Hebrew text, or is due to error in reading the Hebrew... [and] the text of Sch[eide] apparently represents an attempt to restore order out of chaos of the LXX". This doublet also occurs at 8:10 where the idols and abominations of the house of Israel are סָבִיב סָבִיב (𝕲^{B,A} just κύκλῳ [NB: 8:10 is Thackeray's translator α]). The writer may be implicitly stating this is the reason for the bones of Israel now being סָבִיב סָבִיב (cf. 37:11). After the occurrence here, סָבִיב סָבִיב is frequently used in chapters 40–43 (24 times)[12] describing the Temple dimensions. In 40–43 סָבִיב סָבִיב is typically translated with κύκλῳ and occasionally with κυκλόθεν, but

---

[11] This may be the case, as Block (1998, p. 367) notes that duplication "is characteristically Ezekielian style, occurring frequently in chs. 40–41" and then says "That the duplication is stylistic rather than emphatic is confirmed by Targumic Aramaic" (Block gives a couple of examples in support).

[12] Outside of Ezekiel סָבִיב סָבִיב occurs only in 2Chron. 4:3 where LXX has κύκλῳ κυκλοῦσιν. It is undeterminable if this LXX doublet in 2Chron. 4:3 influenced Translator β here in Ezekiel 37:2.

significantly never with both.[13] Unfortunately, these other occurrences do not leave us with any clarity regarding the occurrence in 37:2. Overall, we find that 𝕲^967 follows normal LXX practice of simplifying MT doublets using a single κύκλῳ here, and that 𝕲^B,A have added a doublet to match MT, perhaps to emphasise the fact of the 'human' (cf. 37:1 𝕲^B,A) bones being all around.

We also note that MT has a second וְהִנֵּה, perhaps as an emphasising gloss, which is only witnessed by 𝕲^A (καὶ ἰδού). This is another example of how the later 𝕲^A follows MT glosses, as observed in chapter 36.

37:5 כֹּה אָמַר אֲדֹנָי יְהוִֹה לָעֲצָמוֹת הָאֵלֶּה הִנֵּה אֲנִי מֵבִיא בָכֶם
רוּחַ וִחְיִיתֶם:

37:5 τάδε λέγει κύριος τοῖς ὀστέοις τούτοις ἰδοὺ ἐγὼ (𝕲^967: ἐπάγω ἐφ';
𝕲^B,A: φέρω εἰς) ὑμᾶς πνεῦμα ζωῆς

LXX takes MT's verb 'and you shall live' (וִחְיִיתֶם) as if it was a noun, 'life'. Thus, it can be seen to interpret the kind of רוּחַ: πνεῦμα ζωῆς ('the Spirit/breath of life). We also note the intra-LXX abbreviation variant here: 𝕲^967,B abbreviate πνεῦμα, perhaps indicating they see this as the Spirit of Life, while 𝕲^A writes πνεῦμα in full, with the possible meaning of 'wind/breath of life'. Regardless of 'Spirit' or 'breath', LXX syntax does not provide MT's result of the Spirit entering them, 'and you shall live' (also witnessed in MasEzek). This is a little unusual for LXX, since in chapter 36 LXX often took MT's action and interpreted the result, but here it appears to ignore a clear result (i.e., a practical application). Perhaps LXX was stating that they will live by the 'Spirit of life', and this was a sufficient 'result'.[14] The LXX

---

[13] Thackeray (1921, p. 38) proposed both Ezek. 8:10 and chapters 40–43 were translated by the same person, but just because that translator only used a single word for the MT doublet in those locales does not mean 'translator β' used a single word in 37:2.

[14] Greenberg (1997, p. 743) says LXX "does not show this structure, since it reads the last two words of the verse as 'breath of life', reflecting a Hebrew text influenced by the language of Gen. 6:17; 7:15". This may well be the case, as Kutsko (2000b, p. 135) points out the parallel with the Priestly Flood narrative (including the Noahide covenant) and Ezekiel. Kutsko (2000a, p. 137) also finds a parallel here (and throughout Ezek. 36–37) with the creation event of Gen. 1–2, and finds that "the recreation process must continue, as it did at creation, with God's breathing life into them" (Kutsko says this in reference to 37:8). However, speaking against Ezekiel writing out of any 'creation traditions' Petersen (1999, p. 498) claims "there do appear to be allusions to creation texts, e.g., the references to a vivifying breath/spirit though the vocabulary in Ezekiel 37:5 is different than that in Genesis 2. Nonetheless, apart from these allusions, the

translator may well have been reflecting on the previous occurrences of πνεῦμα ζωῆς (1:20, 21; 10:17: the πνεῦμα ζωῆς was in the wheels), and now sees the LORD's activity fulfilled here in resurrecting the people to life.[15] Both MT and LXX may also have been alluding to Gen. 2:7, seeing this pericope as reflecting an act of recreation by God whereby the 'human' is standing but now requiring the 'Spirit/breath of life', and thus LXX exegetically clarifies this by reading 'of life'. It may be significant that Gen. 2:17 gives death as the result of disobedience/ sin (cf. 3:19), a concept which also fits here (cf. 37:23). MT's context indicates that the Spirit will be upon them so they could have life and live in the land, to enable them to live holy lives, and LXX appears to capture this as an exegetical interpretation clarifying that this recreation is the activity of the Spirit of life. Duguid (1994, p. 105) points out that here in Ezekiel "the result of Yahweh placing his *rûaḥ* upon his people was to be life in the land, not prophecy (Ezek. 37:14)".[16]

There also seems to be an implicit theological choice of words intra-LXX regarding the Spirit/breath, with 𝔊⁹⁶⁷ stating ἐγὼ ἐπαγω ἐφ' ('I bring upon [you]'), and 𝔊ᴮ·ᴬ ἐγὼ φέρω εἰς ('I bring into [you]') [the Spirit/breath]. This may indicate a subtle shift in theology for how these LXX translators saw the interaction of the Spirit with humanity, as to whether they saw the Spirit's interaction with humanity as internal leading or external directing (however, see below regarding 𝔊ᴬ in v. 6). We also ask if the scribes were reflecting back on the Spirit been taken from Moses and placed upon the leaders of Israel (Num. 11:24–30).

37:6 וְנָתַתִּי עֲלֵיכֶם גִּדִים וְהַעֲלֵתִי עֲלֵיכֶם בָּשָׂר וְקָרַמְתִּי עֲלֵיכֶם עוֹר
וְנָתַתִּי בָכֶם רוּחַ וִחְיִיתֶם וִידַעְתֶּם כִּי־אֲנִי יְהוָה:

---

larger creation traditions, along with their attending theological implications, are absent from Ezekiel". Fitzpatrick (2004, p. 179) also finds a creational aspect, stating "the point is that this national restoration will be nothing less than an act of creation".

[15] Block (1992a, 134) lists this as the third way Ezekiel perceives death and afterlife: "Third, the means whereby the corpses are revitalized is by being infused with Yahweh's own life-giving spirit. This is how the first lump of clay became a living being; this is how these dry bones will come to life".

[16] This he contrasts with the usage in Joel 3:1f. and Numbers 11 where the coming of the Spirit was for the purpose of everyone having the ability to prophesy, but here "the endowment with the *rûaḥ* of Yahweh will not result in charismatic gifts but power for right living, which is itself the prerequisite for life in the land (Ezek. 36:27f.)" (Duguid, 1994, p. 105).

37:6 καὶ δώσω ἐφ᾽ ὑμᾶς νεῦρα καὶ ἀνάξω ἐφ᾽ ὑμᾶς σάρκας καὶ ἐκτενῶ ἐφ᾽ ὑμᾶς δέρμα καὶ δώσω πνεῦμά μου (𝔊⁹⁶⁷,ᴬ: ἐφ᾽; 𝔊ᴮ: εἰς) ὑμᾶς καὶ ζήσεσθε καὶ γνώσεσθε ὅτι ἐγώ εἰμι κύριος

LXX's plus of μου following πνεῦμά seems to interpret and make plain whose Spirit the text is referring to. This could be simply making רוּחַ/πνεῦμά point more to 'Spirit' than 'breath', thus avoiding reader confusion. This may well be the case with 𝔊⁹⁶⁷,ᴮ due to their abbreviation of πνεῦμα, although 𝔊ᴬ again does not abbreviate, leaving the potential reading of 'my breath/wind'. Block (1998, p. 368) points out that both 36:27 and 37:14 may have influenced LXX's μου plus. Irrespective, we see further evidence of LXX scribes seeking to avoid theological confusion.

There may be a slight theological difference with the variant between 𝔊⁹⁶⁷,ᴬ saying the Lord's πνεῦμά will be ἐπί ('on/upon') them, and 𝔊ᴮ, which follows MT (בְּכֶם) saying εἰς ('into') them (cf. v. 5). It appears that the earlier 𝔊⁹⁶⁷ and later 𝔊ᴬ made a theological choice. Both 𝔊⁹⁶⁷ and 𝔊ᴮ are consistent in their separate terminology in vv. 5 and 6 (ἐπί/εἰς respectively), yet 𝔊ᴬ's use of ἐπί here reverses its use of εἰς in v. 5, which suggests that it saw εἰς and ἐπί as interchangeable. On the other hand, 𝔊ᴬ's scribe may have just mechanically followed the three occurrences of ἐφ᾽ ὑμᾶς preceding this last occurrence.

37:7 וְנִבֵּאתִי כַּאֲשֶׁר צֻוֵּיתִי וַיְהִי־קוֹל כְּהִנָּבְאִי וְהִנֵּה־רַעַשׁ וַתִּקְרְבוּ עֲצָמוֹת עֶצֶם אֶל־עַצְמוֹ:

37:7 καὶ ἐπροφήτευσα καθὼς ἐνετείλατό μοι καὶ ἐγένετο (𝔊ᴬ: + φωνή) ἐν τῷ ἐμὲ (𝔊⁹⁶⁷,ᴮ: προφητεῦσαι; 𝔊ᴬ: προφητεύειν) καὶ ἰδοὺ σεισμός καὶ προσήγαγε τὰ ὀστᾶ ἑκάτερον πρὸς τὴν ἁρμονίαν αὐτοῦ

𝔊ᴬ's plus of φωνή reflects MT's קוֹל. Either 𝔊⁹⁶⁷,ᴮ did not seek to reproduce קוֹל, or it is a later MT and 𝔊ᴬ plus as suggested by Allen (1990b, p. 182), who says that it "probably originated as a [MT] comparative gloss inspired by 3:12,13 where the terms [קוֹל & רעשׁ] occur together".[17] If קוֹל was a plus, then it was early, as it is attested in MasEzek. Block (1998, p. 368) says that the whole Hebrew construction is "awkward but not unintelligible, nor is the construction unprecedented".

---

[17] As in 36:18, Cooke (1936, p. xli) lists this MT as an occurrence where "𝔊 implies a Hebrew text free from words and phrases which appear to be additions or glosses in 𝔐".

LXX provides an interpretation of MT's action of וַתִּקְרְבוּ עֲצָמוֹת
עֶצֶם אֶל־עַצְמוֹ ('and the bones came together, bone to its bone'), by
indicating its result when it states καὶ προσήγαγε τὰ ὀστᾶ ἑκάτερον
πρὸς τὴν ἁρμονίαν αὐτοῦ ('and the bones approached each to its
joint').[18] LXX develops the result of the bones coming together; they
will form *joints*.[19]

There is a slight difference intra-LXX, with 𝔊[967,B] προφητεῦσαι (aorist), and 𝔊[A] προφητεύειν (present). 𝔊[A]'s variant should be considered in
conjunction with its φωνή plus, and may be seen as an emendation to
align with MT seeing כְּ as emphasising continuous action.

37:8 וְרָאִיתִי וְהִנֵּה־עֲלֵיהֶם גִּדִים וּבָשָׂר עָלָה וַיִּקְרַם עֲלֵיהֶם עוֹר
מִלְמָעְלָה וְרוּחַ אֵין בָּהֶם:

37:8 καὶ εἶδον καὶ ἰδοὺ ἐπ' αὐτὰ νεῦρα καὶ σάρκες ἐφύοντο καὶ ἀνέβαινεν
ἐπ' αὐτὰ δέρμα ἐπάνω καὶ πνεῦμα οὐκ ἦν ἐν αὐτοῖς

MT speaks of the action of the flesh coming on the bones (וּבָשָׂר עָלָה
'and flesh came up'), whereas LXX appears to translate the result to
convey *how* the flesh came up on the bones (καὶ σάρκες ἐφύοντο 'and
flesh grew up/germinated').[20]

All 3 LXX MSS abbreviate πνεῦμα here, suggesting they saw an
absence of the Spirit and not just 'breath'. This may have been influenced by their 'Spirit of life' variant in v. 5 (except there 𝔊[A] did not
abbreviate πνεῦμα as 𝔊[967,B] did).

37:9 וַיֹּאמֶר אֵלַי הִנָּבֵא אֶל־הָרוּחַ הִנָּבֵא בֶן־אָדָם וְאָמַרְתָּ אֶל־הָרוּחַ[21]
כֹּה־אָמַר אֲדֹנָי יְהוִה מֵאַרְבַּע רוּחוֹת בֹּאִי הָרוּחַ וּפְחִי בַּהֲרוּגִים
הָאֵלֶּה וְיִחְיוּ:

---

[18] Block (1998, p. 368), following *BHS*, notes that עֲצָמוֹת is minus in 2 Hebrew
MSS, but these are later texts. It is present in all representative Hebrew texts, and so
we will not treat it as a minus.

[19] Allen (1993, p. 132) finds a wordplay between ותקרבו in v. 7 and קברותיכם in
v. 12, 13 that he says "unites these parts" of the internal structure (specifically his "first
and third parts"). LXX is unable to match this wordplay due to the word differences
in Greek for 'joined' and 'graves' (cf. v. 9).

[20] Weissert (2002, p. 138) argues that וַיִּקְרַם should not be changed from the *qal* to
niphal as some would want, and concludes "that none of the ancient translations, each
following the common ways of expression in their language, asks for one".

[21] MT[A] appears to evidence a break mid verse, with אֶל־הָרוּחַ at the end of a line,
and כֹּה־אָמַר starting with a two letter indent on the following line signifying a *setumah*
break. We observe in Ezek. 36–39 that MT[A] typically does not use a *sof pasuq* when a
'verse' finishes on the end of a line, but does have a *silluq*.

𝔊⁹⁶⁷	𝔊ᴮ	𝔊ᴬ
καὶ εἶπεν πρός με προφήτευσον ἐπι το π̅ν̅α̅ προφητευσον υιε ανθρω που καὶ εἰπὸν τῷ π̅ν̅ι̅ τά δε λέγει κ̅ς̅ ο θ̅ς̅ ἐκ τῶν τεσσάρων σου πνευμάτων ἔλθε καὶ ἐμφύσησον ἐπι τοὺς νεκροὺς τούτους καὶ ζησάτωσαν	καὶ εἶ πεν πρός με προφήτευ σον επι το π̅ν̅α̅ προφη τευσον υιε ανθρωπου καὶ εἰπὸν τῷ π̅ν̅ι̅ τάδε λέγει κ̅ς̅ ἐκ τῶν τεσσά ρων πνευμάτων ἔλθε καὶ ἐμφύσησον εἰς τοὺς νεκροὺς τούτους καὶ ζησάτωσαν	καὶ εἶπεν πρός με προφήτευσον υἱὲ ἀνθρώπου προφήτευσον ἐπὶ τὸ πνεῦμα καὶ εἰπὸν τῷ π̅ν̅ι̅ τάδε λέγει κ̅ς̅ κ̅ς̅ ελθε εκ των τεσσαρων ανεμων του ουν̅ου̅ ἔλθε το πνευμα καὶ ἐμφύ σησον εἰς τοὺς νεκροὺς τού τους καὶ ζησάτωσαν

This verse exhibits a number of variants between MT and LXX, and intra-LXX, and more unusual, it exhibits an intra-MT sense division variant, all which indicates a text, and perhaps theology, in a state of flux.

MTᴬ stands alone amongst our representative MSS by having a *setumah* break in the middle of a verse, leaving the command to prophesy in v. 9, while joining the words of the prophecy for the רוּחַ to come with MTᴬ's v. 10, and thus in a separate division. This is one of five examples in Ezekiel where MTᴬ shows evidence of פיסקא אמצע פסוק ('a section division in the middle of a verse'). Here this division occurs right before the phrase כֹּה־אָמַר אֲדֹנָי יְהוִה; MTᴬ also does this in 27:3 (cf. Tov, 2001, pp. 53–55; Olley, 2003, pp. 208, 211). This phenomenon most likely preserves another old tradition of verse division that appears to be independent of the paragraph tradition.[22] Perhaps MTᴬ saw כֹּה־אָמַר אֲדֹנָי יְהוִה as a sense division phrase marker,[23] or MTᴬ theologically treated the first phrase in v. 9 as an *inclusio* to the previous verses, and set the divine speech as the beginning to the 'interpretive' section (which in MTᴬ would be vv. 9b–14). However, MTᴬ still continues the same reading tradition as found in MTᶜ·ᴸ, and as such can be seen to preserve two traditions, one of verse division and another

---

[22] Olley (2003, pp. 208, 211) notes that "as one might expect, instances of this independence are sparse. In [MTᶜ]...only one instance, in 3:16, also in [MTᴬ·ᴸ] (preceding 'and the word of the Lord came to me saying'). [MTᴬ·ᴸ] have a further division in 43:27 (before 'and it will be on the eighth day'), and [MTᴬ] a further three, in 20:31 (after 'to this day'); 27:3 and 37:9 (both before 'thus says the Lord')".

[23] Both Olley (1993, p. 29) and Tov (2000, p. 338) note that divine speech can begin new sense divisions in the Greek text.

of reading tradition.[24] LXX faithfully follows MT until the end of this phrase ($\mathfrak{G}^{967,B}$ also follow MT in syntax), but after this point LXX exhibits several variants, mostly which exhibit LXX's wrestling with the various possible meanings of רוּחַ.

$\mathfrak{G}^{967}$ has a personal plus of σου to read 'from *your* four winds/ breaths come'. This plus may have been influenced by v. 6 and v. 14, and appears to clarify that this is the work of the Spirit, especially as $\mathfrak{G}^{967}$ has twice abbreviated πνεῦμα. $\mathfrak{G}^{967,B}$ do not abbreviate πνευμάτων, as they both did in the first two occurrences of πνεῦμα for this verse, suggesting they interpreted the action of the Spirit here as 'wind' or 'breath'. This may be due to the 'four' directions from which the πνεῦμα was to come that led them to interpret 'wind' rather than 'Spirit'.[25] $\mathfrak{G}^B$'s manuscript evidences some 'tampering' here, suggesting πνευμάτων was either corrected from an abbreviation,[26] or more likely, that it was written over another word(s) now lost to us. The whole word is very spaced out in $\mathfrak{G}^B$, especially the π̇.

$\mathfrak{G}^A$ has a series of variants that must be considered together. $\mathfrak{G}^A$ does not match $\mathfrak{G}^{967,B}$'s abbreviation for the first use of πνεῦμα, yet it does for the second. In the third occurrence (for MT's רוּחוֹת) $\mathfrak{G}^A$ does not follow $\mathfrak{G}^{967,B}$'s unabbreviated πνευμάτων, but instead clearly interprets with ἀνέμων ('winds'). This suggests $\mathfrak{G}^A$ (or its exemplar) exhibits some confusion whether MT's רוּחַ is meaning 'Spirit, breath, or wind'. Certainly $\mathfrak{G}^A$'s use of ἀνέμων is an attempt to clear up any theological ambiguity, a practice we have previously seen with

---

[24] Note that MT^A has the same *geresh* accentuation evident in MT^L (cf. *BHS*) (Yeivin, 1980, p. 167, #194; p. 168, #195; and p. 172, #201). This indicates that the reading tradition observed in MT^A does not have a significant pause where the written paragraph exists.

[25] Greenberg (1997, p. 744) notes that "the concept 'four winds/directions' is found only in late books: e.g., Jer. 49:36, 'four winds, from the four extremes of heaven'; Zech 6:5 'the four winds of heaven'". Cooke (1936, p. 400) also mentions this point, but adds that the concept "goes back to an Akkadian idiom; this accounts for the use of the same word *rûaḥ* in two such different senses".

[26] The following word (ἐλθέ) does not evidence any such textual correction, which may suggest that a later scribe just rewrote πνευμάτων, or even that the original scribe made an error that he immediately corrected. It is undeterminable as to what exactly happened here, and when it happened. Swete (1989, p. 128) notes that "the MS. has been corrected more than once; besides the scribe or contemporary *diorthotes* (B^1), we may mention an early corrector to B^a, and a late *instaurator*, who has gone over the whole text, spoiling its original beauty, and preserving oftentimes the corrections of B^a rather than the original texts". This may be one such case here!

𝕲ᴬ. But 𝕲ᴬ's use of ἀνέμων must be considered in conjunction with its unique του ουνου plus, a common 𝕲ᴬ abbreviation for οὐρανοῦ (Ziegler, 1977, p. 268).[27] This causes 𝕲ᴬ's text to speak of the Spirit (πνεῦμα abbreviated) coming from 'the four winds of heaven' or 'the four heavenly winds'. 𝕲ᴬ may see these as spiritual winds coming from heaven (and even commanded to come with its additional ἐλθε, plus).[28] This may have been influenced by the contextual allusion to creation (see below). 𝕲ᴬ's scribes may also have been reflecting upon v. 5 and πνεῦμα ζωῆς, along with reflection on v. 14 where the LORD will fill them with his Spirit (Eichrodt, 1970, p. 508f.). Interestingly, the Hexapla shows support for ἀνέμων from Aquila, yet he does not witness 𝕲ᴬ's τοῦ οὐρανοῦ plus (Field, 1964, p. 869). This supports our point that this is a unique interpretative plus for 𝕲ᴬ. We may also suggest that Aquila was seeking to clarify that MT's רוחות referred to 'winds' and not to 'Spirit'.

Block (1998, p. 369) says LXX "mistakenly" omits the vocative הָרוּחַ, yet 𝕲ᴬ does include it here, stating ἐλθε το πνεῦμα (ἐλθε as an emphasising plus). As this vocative is found only in MT and 𝕲ᴬ, we suggest it is a later plus, perhaps added at a similar time to the other unique MT/ 𝕲ᴬ plusses. The vocative makes this an imperative cry for the breath to come, and even contextually for the breath of the Spirit to come and create life in the raised but not yet resuscitated Israel (especially the case in MT). This emphasises the call for the Spirit to come back to Israel, even as a creative force.

LXX follows MT's (וּפְחִי) נפח) with its use of ἐμφυσάω.[29] These words were also used by MT and LXX in Gen. 2:7, suggesting that the LXX scribe also caught this allusion for the Spirit to 'blow' as at creation.[30]

---

[27] For more on abbreviations in 𝕲ᴬ see Thompson (1883, p. 11) and Swete (1989, p. 126).

[28] The primary usage for οὐρανοῦ in Ezekiel is with the phrase τὰ πετεινὰ τοῦ οὐρανοῦ ('the birds of the sky/heaven') [οὐρανός also abbreviated in 𝕲ᴬ] (cf. Ezek. 29:5; 31:6, 13; 32:4; 38:20). The only other occurrence (other than 𝕲ᴬ here in 37:9) is in 8:3 where the Prophet is lifted up between 'earth and sky/heaven'. For more on οὐρανός see Bietenhard (1976, pp. 188–196).

[29] As in v. 7, Allen (1993, p. 132) also finds a wordplay that "bridges the second and third [structural] parts: פחי 'breathe' (v. 9) and אני פתח 'I will open' together with בפתחי 'when I open' (vv. 12, 13)". As noted in v. 7, LXX is unable to repeat this wordplay due to the different words used in Greek.

[30] Kutsko (2000a, p. 137) says "It appears that the vision in Ezekiel 37 halts (in v. 8) at a point that leaves Israel equal to its idols—and no better. Neither they nor the intermediate formation of bodies has רוּחַ. Thus the re-creation process must continue,

Likewise, συναγωγή can be associated with 'hostile intent' (cf. Psa. 21:17; cf. BAGD # 5), yet this does not *appear* to be LXX's meaning in 37:10. It is significant that LXX only uses συναγωγή elsewhere in Ezekiel in reference to the 'gathering/multitude' of the enemies against Israel, but each occurrence is for קָהָל not for חַיִל (cf. 26:7; 27:27; 34; 32:22 (2×); 38:4, 7, 13, 15). There appears to be a deliberate lessening in LXX from MT's 'a great *army*' when referring to Israel, to just a 'great *multitude/congregation*'. Therefore, we suggest that whereas MT saw the 'purpose' for the resurrection of the dry bones was for a 'great army' as the whole house of Israel (v. 11), ready to be united into one kingdom (vv. 16–21), under a Davidic 'king' (vv. 22–25), able then to go into battle (ch. 38–39),[34] LXX has a slightly different perspective.

We suggest two possible scenarios: firstly, that LXX theologically translated συναγωγή for חַיִל in 37:10 as a pointed statement against the συναγωγή of Israel's enemies in 38–39. This was perhaps to show Israel is not insignificant amongst the 'gatherings/multitudes' of the surrounding nations. At the same time it lessens any interpretation by other nations that Israel would arise to be a military threat. Intra-LXX support may be found with how the earlier 𝔊[967,B] have πολλή yet 𝔊[A] strengthens this with μεγάλη. It is perhaps indeterminable if the use of the synagogue movement as a place of prayer and spiritual activity has any bearing on this translation, but we can propose this possibility.[35]

However, preference is to be given to our second suggestion: that LXX's use of συναγωγή reflects the original chapter order witnessed in 𝔊[967]. In this chapter order the dry bones are raised to be a 'con-gregation/multitude' gathered for spiritual purposes to live out God's Torah as one nation under a 'peaceful shepherd Davidic ruler', and not for military purposes (requiring δύναμις). This David comes with his harp, not his sword (see Excursus §4.3.1 below). This also appears to be the explanation found in the following interpretive pericope (cf. 'knowledge of the Lord' and 'my Spirit', vv. 11–14). Thus, rather than LXX 'softening' the text, MT instead has performed a 'play' on the

---

[34] However, it is significant that Ezekiel does not record this 'army' as entering any battle, not even in Ezek. 38–39. There we find God as the Divine Warrior who fights for Israel (Greenspoon, 1981, pp. 290–294).

[35] For the uncertainty of the synagogue's origins see 'The Synagogue' in Cohen (1987, pp. 111–115).

Hebrew letters, strengthening from קָהָל ('assembly/congregation') to חַיִל ('army'). Therefore, we suggest that LXX's use of συναγωγή in 37:10 reflects the original Hebrew, which was later changed from קָהָל to חַיִל, as further support for the change of chapter order, and the 'call to arms' motif (cf. chapter 7). The later three exegetes' use of δύναμις also supports our conclusion that this was an MT change done after the *Vorlage* for our three representative LXX MSS. The change from קָהָל to חַיִל would likely to have been at a similar time to other such later editorial amendments (cf. MT's declarative formula in 36:23b; the change from נָשִׂיא to מֶלֶךְ in 37:22–24; and from חמה to רוח in 39:29).

𝔊ᴬ's plus of ζωῆς continues the wording, and thus theology, from v. 5 (cf. 'breath *of life*'), theologically interpreting what kind of breath entered into the slain (cf. v. 5). 𝔊⁹⁶⁷ also has a theological plus by clarifying with a proper noun (κύριος) where MT and 𝔊ᴮ·ᴬ have only a pronoun (also in v. 11).

4.2.2. *37:11–14*

This pericope appears to be an interpretation, or an exegesis, of the previous pericope (cf. 'these bones' v. 11), yet it is not a clearly defined pericope in the various MSS. As noted above, MTᴬ starts a sense division in the middle of v. 9, but does evidence a *petuḥah* with the other MT MSS at the end of v. 14. We again note that MasEzek and MTᶜ have vv. 1–14 within the one sense division. MTᴸ differs, having a *setumah* after v. 10, and also after v. 12, finishing this pericope with a *petuḥah* after v. 14. This causes vv. 11–12 to stand alone in its own sense division in MTᴸ, emphasising the explanation that the dry bones in the previous verses are the 'whole house of Israel', and indicating that MTᴸ's scribe saw the interpretive lament of hope being dried up in v. 11 as being answered by the prophecy of their graves being opened in v. 12. The result of knowledge of the LORD and indwelling of the Spirit is also given a greater emphasis. The change in metaphor from 'bones' to 'graves' in vv. 12–14 may also have influenced MTᴸ to mark this as a separate division.

𝔊⁹⁶⁷ has vv. 1–14 as one pericope, matching the two earliest MT MSS. 𝔊ᴮ has a two-letter break after v. 10, and a major break after v. 14, with v. 15 starting on a new line. 𝔊ᴬ again exhibits more sense divisions than any other representative MSS, with divisions after v. 9, 10, 11, 12a, 14. The MSS that have a division after v. 10 (MTᴸ, MTᴬ [break v. 9b], 𝔊^{B,A}) appear to recognise that vv. 11–14 is a summary, or perhaps an interpretation, of the vision in vv. 1–10.

Only two verses contain discernible variants in this pericope (vv. 12, 13).[36] While only minor plusses, they do carry theological weight regarding the dry bones as being the people of God.

37:12 לָכֵן הִנָּבֵא וְאָמַרְתָּ אֲלֵיהֶם כֹּה־אָמַר אֲדֹנָי יְהוִֹה הִנֵּה אֲנִי
פֹתֵחַ אֶת־קִבְרוֹתֵיכֶם וְהַעֲלֵיתִי אֶתְכֶם מִקִּבְרוֹתֵיכֶם עַמִּי וְהֵבֵאתִי
אֶתְכֶם אֶל־אַדְמַת יִשְׂרָאֵל:

37:12 διὰ τοῦτο προφήτευσον καὶ εἰπόν (𝔊^A: + πρὸς αὐτούς) τάδε λέγει
(𝔊^A: + Ἀδωναι) κύριος ἰδοὺ ἐγὼ ἀνοίγω ὑμῶν τὰ μνήματα καὶ ἀνάξω
ὑμᾶς ἐκ τῶν μνημάτων ὑμῶν καὶ εἰσάξω ὑμᾶς εἰς τὴν γῆν τοῦ Ισραηλ

Both Zimmerli (1983, p. 256) and Block (1998, p. 369) state that LXX does not represent MT's two plusses of אֲלֵיהֶם and אֲדֹנָי, yet the later 𝔊^A represents both (πρὸς αὐτούς and Ἀδωναι). This again may evidence a later MT plus inserted in time for the later 𝔊^A to witness it (yet early enough for MasEzek to include both).

However, no representative LXX MS witnesses MT's other plus עַמִּי ('my people'). It is strange that 𝔊^A did not follow its typical practice and include this plus, especially as it is included in MasEzek. Allen (1990b, p. 183) sees this as "a comparative gloss on לעם 'to a people' in the verbal covenant formulation of v. 27, citing עמי in the nominal clause of 34:30; it became attached to the wrong column".[37] While Allen's 'scribal' proposal has merit, there may be a deliberate theological reason for the MT plus. Zimmerli (1983, p. 256) points out that it "introduces into the text the fully theological interpretation of covenant renewal and acceptance of the people of Yahweh". We agree with Zimmerli's point, and state that it is unlikely that LXX would have deliberately omitted such an important theological statement. Therefore, we can see this as an MT (and MasEzek) plus, theologically designed to give specific identity to those in the graves (cf. 'bones' vv. 1–11): they are 'my people'. This avoids any thought of including in the restorative action the surrounding nations, or the nations amongst

---

[36] Whilst we do not cover 37:11, Olyan (2003) has examined some nuances of נִגְזַרְנוּ לָנוּ. LXX uses ἡμῶν διαπεφωνήκαμεν here, which appears to capture MT's meaning of being cut off and/or divided.

[37] When commenting on the presence of עמי in v. 13 Allen (1990b, p. 183) proposes that it was assimilated into v. 12 from v. 13.

whom God's people live in exile.[38] MT perhaps added this plus to provide a motive for the LORD's restorative actions. This brings out the theology that if the people of God are slain and are in the grave (cf. 'battlefield' vv. 1–10), then it is God's name and reputation that is at stake (cf. 36:22, 32). Block (1998, p. 382) points out that any deletion of עַמִּי "robs the promises in vv. 12–13 of a crucial theme. The exiles' despondency arose from the conviction that with the fall of Jerusalem in 586 the deity-nation-land relationship had been ruined for ever". Therefore, עַמִּי helps restore this relationship of God's people in his land (cf. 36:5; 38:16; 37:21).

37:13 וִידַעְתֶּם כִּי־אֲנִי יְהוָה בְּפִתְחִי אֶת־קִבְרוֹתֵיכֶם וּבְהַעֲלוֹתִי
אֶתְכֶם מִקִּבְרוֹתֵיכֶם עַמִּי:

37:13 καὶ γνώσεσθε ὅτι ἐγώ εἰμι κύριος ἐν τῷ ἀνοῖξαί με τοὺς τάφους ὑμῶν τοῦ ἀναγαγεῖν με (𝔊ᴬ: + ὑμᾶς) ἐκ τῶν τάφων (𝔊ᴬ: + ὑμῶν) τὸν λαόν μου

Allen (1990b, p. 183) sees MT's use of עמי as a "dittography from v. 12", yet it is represented in both MasEzek and LXX.[39] There is a intra-LXX variance where 𝔊⁹⁶⁷,ᴮ read 'and I have brought up my people from the graves',[40] whereas 𝔊ᴬ's double plus of ὑμᾶς/ὑμῶν again matches MT ('and I have brought *you* up from *your* graves, my people'). MT and 𝔊ᴬ can be seen as emphasising that God is speaking to the people (עַמִּי), whereas 𝔊⁹⁶⁷,ᴮ provide information of God's intended action.

4.3. SECTION 2: EZEK. 37:15–28

As noted above, Ezekiel 37 can be divided thematically in half. The second half speaks of a United Kingdom (vv. 15–23), that will be governed by a Davidic ruler (vv. 24–28). Kutsko (2000a, p. 139) says that 37:13–28 "expands the image of human re-creation into the restoration of the kingdom of Israel.... As section one promises re-creation, section two promises reunification. Both are restorations of a previous

---

[38] The pictures of 'dry bones' and 'grave' are most likely metaphors of exilic Israel (Eichrodt, 1970, p. 510).

[39] Allen (1990b, p. 183) previously stated that עַמִּי in v. 12 is a "comparative gloss", and then states that עַמִּי is a "dittography from v. 12". This seems to be 'double-dipping' into his frequent 'scribal-error' explanation box.

[40] Curiously LXX switches between using τὰ μνήματα in v. 12 (2x) to τοὺς τάφους in v. 13 (2x), yet MT uses קבר in all four locations.

reality". Fox (1995, p. 180 n. 7) claims that "Ezek. 37:15–28 is probably a separate oracle joined editorially to vv. 1–14 because both speak of the future restoration of Israel". However, we are without any textual evidence to support this proposal, and this last half can be seen as the ultimate fulfilment of the first.

Each representative MS evidences a major sense division before v. 15. All MT MSS have vv. 15–28 as one large sense division, as does 𝕲⁹⁶⁷. Yet 𝕲ᴮ,ᴬ show a 2–3 letter break in the middle of v. 19, after the opening phrase of καὶ ἐρεῖς πρὸς αὐτούς; with no further break until after v. 28. The break mid v. 19 may have been inserted to provide an *inclusio* reply to v. 18 'they will say to you', v. 19 starting with 'but you will say to them'. This brings emphasis to the answer of 'oneness/unity' that follows in v. 19.

This whole pericope is intertwined with the themes of a scattered nation being formed again into a united kingdom, under one king/ruler, even a Davidic one, and a careful reading is required to grasp them all. We will find that LXX typically exegetes MT's metaphors that hold the various themes together (e.g., עֵץ vv. 16–20). We will treat David as 'king/ruler/leader' in an excursus after v. 22, as this complex issue deals with more than one verse.

37:16 וְאַתָּה בֶן־אָדָם קַח־לְךָ עֵץ אֶחָד וּכְתֹב עָלָיו לִיהוּדָה וְלִבְנֵי
יִשְׂרָאֵל (K= חֲבֵרוֹ [Q= חֲבֵרָיו) וּלְקַח עֵץ אֶחָד וּכְתוֹב עָלָיו לְיוֹסֵף
עֵץ אֶפְרַיִם וְכָל־בֵּית יִשְׂרָאֵל (K= חֲבֵרוֹ [Q= חֲבֵרָיו]:

37:16 υἱὲ ἀνθρώπου λαβὲ σεαυτῷ ῥάβδον καὶ γράψον ἐπ' αὐτὴν τὸν Ιουδαν καὶ τοὺς υἱοὺς (𝕲⁹⁶⁷,ᴮ: Ισραηλ; 𝕲ᴬ: αὐτῆς) τοὺς προσκειμένους (𝕲⁹⁶⁷,ᴬ: πρὸς; 𝕲ᴮ: ἐπ') αὐτόν καὶ ῥάβδον δευτέραν λήμψη σεαυτῷ καὶ γράψεις αὐτήν τῷ Ιωσηφ ῥάβδον Εφραιμ καὶ πάντας τοὺς υἱοὺς Ισραηλ τοὺς (𝕲⁹⁶⁷,ᴮ: προστεθέντας; 𝕲ᴬ: προσκειμένους) πρὸς αὐτόν

This verse has several plusses and minuses, and an LXX interaction with MT's metaphors. Firstly, MT has וְאַתָּה that is not represented by LXX. MT Ezekiel's וְאַתָּה is typically used as a theme change indicator, or even for special emphasis. Of the 23 verses in MT Ezekiel that begin with וְאַתָּה בֶן־אָדָם, LXX translated nearly all with καὶ σύ υἱὲ ἀνθρώπου. It is only here and in 27:2 that καὶ σύ is omitted (also in 32:12 where the whole phrase is omitted), so it is curious that LXX does not represent this. וְאַתָּה could be a later Hebrew plus in 37:16, but it is witnessed in MasEzek, showing early inclusion into the Hebrew.

Secondly, LXX omits the first אֶחָד 'one' [stick], yet in the next occurrence of אֶחָד, uses δευτέραν, thus showing knowledge of the former.

This is a good rendering of Hebrew idiom 'one.…and one.…' as 'a…and the second'.

Thirdly, some suggest that 'Ephraim's stick' may be an early addition to the text (cf. 'Ephraim' in v. 19). Zimmerli (1983, p. 268) says, "in comparison with the parallel of the first inscription, [Ephraim's stick] is additional, [and] is to be judged as an explanatory interpretative element". Allen (1990b, p. 190, n. 16e) also claims this is something "MT and the ancient versions add…[and] is generally taken as an early gloss explaining the uncommon 'Joseph' as a designation of the northern tribes".[41] However, MasEzek includes 'Ephraim's stick', as do the three earliest LXX MSS, and so this 'early gloss' must have been in the *Vorlage* of the earliest extant manuscripts, and we are without witness of a text that does not represent it. That this phrase fits the context, and is found in all our representative texts, must call into question any 'gloss/plus' proposal of early Jewish interpretation.

We suggest that there is a wordplay in MT between עֶצֶם that had to 'come together' (vv. 1–2), and עֵץ that now also have to 'come together' (vv. 16, 19). However, this is not reflected in LXX.

For MT עֵץ ('wood/stick') LXX has ῥάβδον ('ruler's rod, sceptre').[42] It is significant that LXX Ezekiel only uses ῥάβδον for MT's עֵץ in 37:16, 17, 19 and 20, with ξύλον for all other occurrences. The context here, as well as in the following vv. 17–20, indicates that MT's עֵץ appears to have the metaphoric concept of a 'ruler's rod', and not just a plain 'stick' or even a 'writing board' (cf. v. 19 where the concept of sceptre is clearer).[43] Fisch (1985, p. 249) also captures MT's metaphor with the 'stick' an "emblem of the royal sceptre". Therefore, the LXX translator appears to have interacted theologically with MT's metaphor of

---

[41] Fisch (1985, p. 250) points out that "the Northern Kingdom was named after Ephraim because its first king was Jeroboam, a descendant of that tribe".

[42] In its simple meaning ῥάβδον may be translated as 'rod/stick/staff', however it is reasonably clear in this context that the LXX translator has the fuller meaning of 'ruler's rod, sceptre' in mind [LEH]. This is all part of LXX catching MT's metaphor and translating accordingly.

[43] Block (1998, pp. 397–406) and Wegner (1999, p. 93) propose that these are just 'writing boards' used for 'temporary messages', which appears to miss MT's metaphor. Even if Block and Wegner are correct, we can argue that LXX understood, or interpreted עֵץ, as royal staffs, even as a ruler's sceptre. Furthermore, Greenberg (1997, p. 753) correctly notes that "while it is easier to write on a tablet or a diptych [i.e., a hinged writing board], the former does not associate with king or kingdom, and the latter in essence (di- 'two') contradicts the emphasis on oneness in this prophecy". We can agree with Greenberg that both suggestions miss the metaphor.

עֵץ.[44] It is quite possible that Ezekiel again had his mind on the book of Numbers as we found earlier (cf. Ezek. 36:14 and Num. 14), and is here echoing the 12 rods (מַטֶּה) gathered by Moses (Num. 17:1–11),[45] now stating that the northern and southern kingdoms should be united into the one 'accepted' rod, even as Aaron's which budded showing God's support for Aaron. Aaron's rod was used to unite the 12 tribes of Israel and correct the rebellion that separated them (Num. 17:10).[46] Even if this event in Numbers was not in Ezekiel's mind, it seems to have been in the LXX translator's mind, who may have either caught the 'echo' or made the link himself, as LXX also uses ῥάβδον in Numbers 17, where it may well be referring to Aaron's rod. Here it appears to carry the fuller meaning of a symbol of authority, as a ruler's sceptre, (cf. Zimmerli, 1983, pp. 273–274; Block, 1998, p. 398). LXX may have made this connection, as this pericope deals with the uniting of Israel's divided nation, and so chose exegetically to use ῥάβδον to make the link clearer for the reader. Commentators suggest that LXX may also be reflecting back on Ezek. 19:11 "where the מטה 'rod, stem' that became a ruler's sceptre is thrice rendered" (Allen, 1990b, p. 193).[47] With either thought, or even with both in mind, LXX looked into the fuller context of this pericope dealing with 'king/kingdom' (cf. vv. 22–25), and theologically expanded upon the metaphoric thought of

---

[44] Kutsko (2000a, p. 140) argues that by using עֵץ here, and in the following verses, "Ezekiel may be associating Israel with idols" and uses Hos. 4:12 to back his point. However, Kutsko appears to be guilty of fitting his thesis into the text instead of observing that the text itself explains the meaning of עֵץ as the tribes of Israel, and not as idols (cf. vv. 18, 19). Furthermore, the text does not mention idolatry until v. 23, and then to say that the united kingdoms/tribes (עֵץ) will not defile themselves with idols. Even if Kutsko is correct that this was Ezekiel's intent, which is unlikely, this interpretation was certainly not given to the text by the LXX translator who correctly understands the עֵץ metaphor (alternatively as a 'ruler's rod', and as 'tribes') and now exegetes for his community.

[45] However, מַטֶּה is not used with this meaning in Ezekiel, except in chapter 19.

[46] The context in Numbers declares this against the rebellion of Korah, Dathan and Abiram (Num. 16:1–40), and against the murmuring of the people (Num. 16:41–50), resulting in each tribe being required to present a representative leader with a 'rod' on which his name was written, and present them along with Aaron to the LORD for his 'selection' (Num. 17:1–13). That the LORD chose Aaron's rod above the tribal representatives showed all Israel that their unity before the LORD would be with Aaron, and thus the priestly tribe of Levi. Here in Ezek. 37:16–28 the context is that both Northern and Southern tribes will only find the LORD's acceptance and selection if they unite under the one Davidic leader. Their future was as a united kingdom, not a divided one.

[47] Allen (1990b, p. 193) correctly points out "the factor of a different Greek translator [between Ezek. 19 and 37] must be borne in mind".

עֵץ to state explicitly that a ruler's staff or sceptre would be used to unite their nation (cf. v. 19). This is another case where LXX is happy to embrace and interpret metaphors for the reader.

MT וּלְבְנֵי יִשְׂרָאֵל in this verse appears as a term for the southern kingdom,[48] and is translated by 𝕲[967,B] with τοὺς υἱοὺς Ισραηλ. Yet 𝕲[A] has τοὺς υἱοὺς αὐτῆς, thus avoiding the concept of *Israel's* sons, making the context state 'the sons of Judah'. This may be 𝕲[A]'s attempt to bring out MT's Judah/Israel (southern/northern) distinction in this pericope, again seeking to bring clarity to the reader.

At the end of v. 16 MT has בֵּית יִשְׂרָאֵל, likely as a contextual term for the northern kingdom. Yet LXX translates again with τοὺς υἱοὺς Ισραηλ, instead of οἶκος Ισραηλ as in v. 11 (cf. v. 21 οἶκος for בְּנֵי). LXX may have harmonized with the beginning of the verse. However, while Ezekiel's LXX translator(s) evidence some variation when translating בֵּית and בְּנֵי (cf. 2:3; 35:5; 43:7), we may ask if there is a possible interpretative aspect, since υἱούς means also 'descendants' (cf. v. 21).[49] This could be LXX's way of including a reference to their present. The 'house' of Israel has been scattered into the Diaspora where the 'descendants' of Israel now largely exist. LXX may be attempting to capture the contextual motif of 'oneness' by using υἱούς for both designations. This may be the case, with the concern for continued unity and identification amongst the scattered tribes, and may be the genesis for LXX's interpretation of the 'tribal' metaphors in v. 19.

There is an intra-LXX and MT *ketiv/qere* variant in this verse. With the intra-LXX variant, 𝕲[967,B] state προστεθέντας ('those added to'), yet 𝕲[A] has προσκειμένους ('those attached to'), which is a closer

---

[48] Debate exists over the theological meanings and use of בֵּית יִשְׂרָאֵל (83× in Ezekiel), and בְּנֵי יִשְׂרָאֵל (11× in Ezekiel). It is generally agreed יִשְׂרָאֵל refers to the covenant nation as a whole. Zimmerli (1983, p. 565) does not believe that בֵּית יִשְׂרָאֵל is a general designation for the northern kingdom. The lack of consistency may have influenced Zimmerli's disagreement, especially since this is the predominant phrase in Ezekiel referring to both northern and southern kingdoms. Block (1998, p. 402) suggests בְּנֵי יִשְׂרָאֵל has an ethnic focus, and is used in v. 16 to refer to the southern kingdom, whilst the use of בֵּית יִשְׂרָאֵל is a reference to the tribes of the northern kingdom. Regardless of how these terms are used elsewhere in Ezekiel, we can find support for Block's suggestion of northern/southern designation here in v. 16.

[49] We may also suggest that בֵּית יִשְׂרָאֵל has had a political concept attached to it, even as a royal house, and refers to the whole nation. Thus LXX's use here of υἱούς Ισραηλ may be an interpretative shift to focus on the people of Israel, and not a political entity (cf. v. 19 where LXX's focus is on the corporate aspect of the people uniting as one).

reflection of MT's *ketiv* חֲבֵרוֹ ('attached to him'; the *qere* חֲבֵרָיו adjusts to the plural).[50]

37:17 וְקָרַב אֹתָם אֶחָד אֶל־אֶחָד לְךָ לְעֵץ אֶחָד וְהָיוּ לַאֲחָדִים בְּיָדֶךָ׃

37:17 καὶ συνάψεις αὐτὰς πρὸς ἀλλήλας σαυτῷ εἰς ῥάβδον μίαν τοῦ δῆσαι αὐτάς καὶ ἔσονται ἐν τῇ χειρί σου

MT has לַאֲחָדִים (one [pl.]),[51] and LXX has τοῦ δῆσαι αὐτάς ('to bind them').[52] Zimmerli (1983, p. 268) proposes that MT's "לאחדים has been misunderstood by [LXX] τοῦ δῆσαι αὐτάς as a verbal form, and this has consequently brought about the independence of the conclusion in the form καὶ ἔσονται ἐν τῇ χειρί σου". We do note that the Greek is ambiguous.[53] However, this may indicate exegetical thought rather than scribal error, as it may reflect the priestly view of being the spiritual caretakers for the people. This again shows the translator(s) of LXX speaking to their present times (cf. v. 16).

It is possible that MT's use of קרב was to echo the action of the bones in v. 7 as the same verb was used there. This same echo does not appear to be evident in LXX which uses συνάπτω here in v. 17 ('tie/bind together'), yet προσάγω in v. 7 ('bring forward').

37:18 וְכַאֲשֶׁר יֹאמְרוּ אֵלֶיךָ בְּנֵי עַמְּךָ לֵאמֹר הֲלוֹא־תַגִּיד לָנוּ מָה־אֵלֶּה לָּךְ׃

37:18 καὶ ἔσται ὅταν λέγωσιν πρὸς σὲ οἱ υἱοὶ τοῦ λαοῦ σου (𝔊⁹⁶⁷,ᴮ: οὐκ ἀναγγελεῖς; 𝔊ᴬ: λέγοντες οὐκ ἀπαγγελεῖς) ἡμῖν τί ἐστιν ταῦτά σοι

---

[50] Whilst חבר can have the meaning of 'companions' (KJV; NASB) or 'associates' (NIV; NRSV), in this context we find meaning of 'joining' as the reference is to the tribes of Israel joined to Judah and the tribes joined to Joseph.

[51] Whilst rare, אֲחָדִים is also found in Gen. 11:1; 27:44; 29:20; Dan. 11:20, where, as an adjective, it agrees in number with the noun.

[52] Brenton translates this verse from LXX as "And thou shalt joint [sic] them together for thyself, so as that they should bind themselves into one stick; and they shall be in thine hand". Brenton is able to do this as his text has ἑαυτάς (reflexive) rather than αὐτάς. However, to date I have been unable to locate any LXX MSS that evidences ἑαυτάς in this location; neither Swete nor Ziegler lists any such variant. Brenton's (1851) translation was based on the 'Vatican text', which probably means the Sixtine text (cf. Swete, 1989, pp. 183–184; Jobes and Silva, 2000, p. 71).

[53] There are three possible ways to translate here: 1. 'And you shall join them to one another, for yourself to bind them into one stick; and they shall be in your hand' (taken as a unit); 2. 'And you shall join them to one another for yourself, to bind them into one stick; and they shall be one in your hand' (Dative of advantage); 3. 'And you shall join them to one another for yourself into one rod to bind them; and they shall be in your hand' (infinitive as epexegeticaly; or it could express purpose as in 2).

Only 𝕲ᴬ follows MT לֵאמֹר with λέγοντες. This may be another later MT plus followed by 𝕲ᴬ. The meaning of both ἀναγγελεῖς and ἀπαγγελεῖς is 'report, declare', but ἀπαγγελεῖς also has the concept of 'explain, interpret' [LEH]. This may have been the intended meaning by 𝕲ᴬ's scribe, as it fits the context of not just telling the story, but explaining and interpreting to his community. It is significant that in this context בְּנֵי/υἱοί means 'descendants', and is contextually referring to a united kingdom (cf. vv. 16, 21).

37:19 דַּבֵּר אֲלֵהֶם כֹּה־אָמַר אֲדֹנָי יְהוִה הִנֵּה אֲנִי לֹקֵחַ אֶת־עֵץ יוֹסֵף
אֲשֶׁר בְּיַד־אֶפְרַיִם וְשִׁבְטֵי יִשְׂרָאֵל [חֲבֵרוֹ] (חֲבֵרָיו) וְנָתַתִּי אוֹתָם עָלָיו
אֶת־עֵץ יְהוּדָה וַעֲשִׂיתִם לְעֵץ אֶחָד וְהָיוּ אֶחָד בְּיָדִי:

37:19 καὶ ἐρεῖς πρὸς αὐτούς τάδε λέγει κύριος ἰδοὺ ἐγὼ λήμψομαι
τὴν φυλὴν Ιωσηφ τὴν διὰ χειρὸς Εφραιμ καὶ τὰς φυλὰς Ισραηλ τὰς
προσκειμένας πρὸς αὐτὸν καὶ δώσω αὐτοὺς ἐπὶ τὴν φυλὴν Ιουδα καὶ
ἔσονται (𝕲⁹⁶⁷: + μοι) εἰς ῥάβδον μίαν ἐν τῇ χειρὶ Ιουδα

As noted above, 𝕲ᴮ·ᴬ have a small 2–3 letter break after the first phrase, thus placing it with the preceding verse. This is possibly another example of "scribal idiosyncrasy" wherein τάδε λέγει κύριος was often treated as a divisional marker, almost in an "mechanical" way (Olley, 2003, p. 212). Yet, in so doing, 𝕲ᴮ·ᴬ highlight the speech that follows and at the same time place vv. 19–28 into its own pericope, emphasising the uniting of the kingdoms under the Davidic ruler.

Allen (1990b, p. 190) claims MT and ancient versions add אֲשֶׁר בְּיַד־אֶפְרַיִם as a 'gloss'. Yet Block (1998, p. 397) argues the MT "represents a natural explanation, given anachronistic reference to Joseph, probably added by the prophet himself". This is found in MasEzek, and all representative LXX witnesses (χειρὸς Εφραιμ), therefore if a gloss it would have been very early, making Allen's 'gloss' proposal unprovable (cf. v. 16, 'Ephraim's stick').[54]

As in v. 16, LXX interacts with MT's metaphors, exegeting and making them explicit for the reader. MT אֶת־עֵץ יוֹסֵף ('the stick of Joseph'), and אֶת־עֵץ יְהוּדָה ('the stick of Judah'), becomes in LXX τὴν φυλὴν Ιωσηφ ('the tribe of Joseph'), and τὴν φυλὴν Ιουδα ('the tribe

---

[54] Ephraim was a son of Joseph and received inheritance in the land, and as such 'Ephraim' is a reference to the Northern Kingdom, whist Judah is a clear reference to the Southern. The importance of this plays out in the following verses where two kingdoms are united as one under a Davidic ruler.

of Judah'). With these two occurrences LXX deliberately interprets MT's metaphors, twice using φυλήν for עֵץ (not ῥάβδον as in v. 16, or ξύλον elsewhere in Ezekiel). Allen (1990b, p. 190) points out that this is "due to the translator's wish to replace metaphor with reality in this statement of Yahweh's actions". Block (1998, p. 397) notes that LXX is "interpreting the expression in accordance with šēbeṭ, which also appears, rather than translating it".[55] This does not mean that the LXX translator is incorrect, but is capturing the concept that עֵץ in this pericope has the larger meaning of a 'ruler's sceptre' (cf. v. 16). LXX views this rulership as corporate within the united northern (Joseph) and southern (Judah) tribes. MT appears to focus on the concept of the 'ruler' with reference to tribes (cf. v. 16), where LXX focuses primarily on the corporate aspect of 'tribes/people' and of their uniting. MT's focus on the 'ruler' makes way for the one Davidic ruler in vv. 22, 24. At the same time, LXX's focus on the oneness of the united tribes makes way for the one kingdom in v. 22. For the last MT wording לְעֵץ אֶחָד, LXX uses εἰς ῥάβδον μίαν (as in vv. 16, 17), perhaps because there is no direct tribal name attached with which to associate φυλήν, and the context speaks of one 'rod/staff'. This metaphoric interpretation by LXX is a wider expansion from its existing use of ῥάβδον for עֵץ, which only emphasises this usage as interpretation (and again echoes v. 16 and the interaction with Num. 17). Overall, as in v. 16, LXX has captured MT's metaphor of 'ruler's sceptre', and exegeted it in the light of its community, seeing the tribes of Israel uniting together under one ruler (cf. vv. 22–25). As Greenberg (1997, p. 755) puts it, the LXX translator "reflect the views of the sticks as sceptres. They belong to the history of interpretation, anticipating in vs. 19 what is to be revealed only in vs. 22—the restored monopoly on kingship of the Judahite Davidites".

Also in v. 19, MT states וַעֲשִׂיתִם לְעֵץ אֶחָד וְהָיוּ אֶחָד בְּיָדִי ('and I will make them one stick and they will be one in my hand'), where LXX combines the first thought with the concluding phrase καὶ ἔσονται εἰς ῥάβδον μίαν ἐν τῇ χειρὶ Ιουδα ('and they will be ($\mathfrak{G}^{967}$: + μοι 'to me [as]') one rod in the hand of Judah'). Allen (1990b, p. 190) says "LXX renders בידי as if בִיד יהודה which is an interesting evidence

---

[55] In Ezekiel, שֵׁבֶט can mean either 'rod/staff' but with the concept of a 'sceptre' and LXX follows this translating with ῥάβδος (19:11, 14; 20:37; 21:10), yet other times the meaning is 'tribe' wherein LXX uses φυλή (21:18; 37:19; 40–48 *passim*).

of the practice of abbreviation in Heb. MSS". However, Block (1998, p. 397) notes that LXX

> captures the intended sense of וְנָתַתִּי אוֹתָם עָלָיו אֶת־עֵץ יְהוּדָה,[56] presumably reading עָלָיו אֶת as על (=ἐπί). *BHS* suggest deleting אוֹתָם, but this results in an unlikely reversal of roles for the respective tribes. MT is awkward but not ungrammatical if the pl. suffix on אוֹתָם is understood to refer to the tribes that the piece of wood represents, whereas the sg. suffix on עָלָיו refers to the piece of wood that represents primarily Judah. אֶת־עֵץ יְהוּדָה is then simply an appositional explanation for the suffix.[57]

Furthermore, Block (1998, p. 397) claims that "LXX ἐν τῇ χειρὶ Ιουδα reads the suffix on בְּיָדִי as an abbreviation for יְהוּדָה". Zimmerli (1983, p. 269) also had observed this point, and stated that "𝔐 speaks of the unity of the nation of Yahweh, 𝔊 accentuates Judean messianism".[58] This theological shift observed by Zimmerli suggests that the LXX translator was aware of the Hebrew, but doing another deliberate theological interpretation, as a trans-linguistic wordplay, to leave the balance of power in the hands of Judah. This may be the case with the later references in this chapter to Davidic rulership (vv. 24–25). The focus on Judah and thus Jerusalem, and the centralising of the cultus, was a priority for the exilic and postexilic communities, as was their concern to eradicate idolatrous worship, which is also evident here in the text. Thus, instead of scribal error by LXX's scribe, we suggest theological interpretation by wordplay to establish Judean priority. We further suggest that 𝔊[967]'s unique μοι plus strengthens this, indicating that this is the LORD's view. The key word and concept in this pericope is 'oneness', and this is found, especially for LXX, in the restoration of the Davidic Kingdom and rulership (vv. 22–25). This also finds support from LXX's interpretation of the Hebrew metaphors here, and in vv. 16–17. This is not to be seen as circular reasoning, but as further indication that LXX is interpreting and exegeting the Hebrew text.

We ask why Ezekiel used 'Joseph' in the metaphor (vv. 16, 19), and suggest this was a deliberate reference to the person in Patriarchal times that united his brothers together whilst in a foreign land, and brought unity and sustenance to the family. Joseph's dry bones were

---

[56] For ease of reading, I have put in the Hebrew letters rather than Block's transliterations. This change applies for the other short quote from Block following this one.

[57] We note that GKC §117m N says 'in 37[19] read with Hitzig אֶל for את'.

[58] Cooke (1936, p. 401) says that LXX's "reading looks suspiciously like *in the hand of Ephraim* above, and may also be an explanatory addition".

those brought up out of the land of Egypt, which also fits the other primary metaphor of this chapter (Exod. 13:19; cf. Gen. 50:25). Thus Joseph was a participant in the Exodus, which again echoes the 'new exodus motif' found here and elsewhere in Ezekiel.[59] Joseph is also representative of the 10 tribes of the so-called Northern Kingdom.

There is curious variant in 37:19, where Symmachus exegetes and expands on MT saying, καὶ δώσω αὐτὰς μετὰ τοῦ συνιέναι τὴν φυλὴν τὴν βασιλικὴν Ἰούδα (Field, 1964, p. 870; Ziegler, 1977, p. 270f.).[60] There are a number of difficulties in understanding Symmachus' intent here, as well as translating the words into English. Firstly, rather than using αὐτούς as other LXX MSS, he has αὐτάς (fem. pl.) which refers to the preceding 'tribes' (φυλήν), therefore focusing on the tribal identity. Secondly, he has his own unique plus of 'μετὰ τοῦ συνιέναι', which elsewhere in both Tanach and New Testament is translated as 'with understanding/wise' [LEH], but here, with another accusative following, Symmachus appears to have intended the literal meaning of נתן and thus 'bring/set/join together' [Thayer; LS]. Thirdly, Symmachus has unusually followed LXX's exegesis of עץ, writing φυλήν, breaking with his normal practice of strictly interpreting MT (Fernández Marcos, 2000, pp. 128–133). Then fourthly, his other plus of τὴν βασιλικήν ('royal') implies a king and/or a kingdom, something which LXX Ezekiel generally seeks to avoid when referring to Israel. We would expect Symmachus to avoid such terminology owing to the constant threat of Roman presence in his day, especially when there is no textual evidence for 'royal' in MT or LXX, indicating this is a unique theological plus. The accusative form of 'τὴν φυλὴν τὴν βασιλικὴν Ἰούδα', also makes it difficult to understand Symmachus. In addition δώσω already has an object, and cannot refer to this. Perhaps the clearest sense is 'I will put them [the tribes] together with the royal tribe of Judah'. With this phrase, Symmachus' focus appears to be on the joining of all the tribes of Israel (cf. v. 16 for the parallel mention of the tribes of Israel associated with Judah). He then may be seen as promoting Judean priority by his use of τὴν βασιλικήν. Yet, we can offer no rational explanation at

---

[59] Refer to my comments introducing Ezek. 36:22–32, and Block's (1998, p. 353).

[60] It should be noted that the text of Symmachus here is Field's retro-version from the Syriac into Greek (cf. Ziegler, 1977, p. 271). Therefore the following discussion is based on Field's speculation that this was in Symmachus' Greek text.

this point other than to say it is evidence of later theological expansion, perhaps resulting from internal tensions in the first centuries CE.

37:21 וְדַבֵּר אֲלֵיהֶם כֹּה־אָמַר אֲדֹנָי יְהוִֹה הִנֵּה אֲנִי לֹקֵחַ אֶת־בְּנֵי יִשְׂרָאֵל מִבֵּין הַגּוֹיִם אֲשֶׁר הָלְכוּ־שָׁם וְקִבַּצְתִּי אֹתָם מִסָּבִיב וְהֵבֵאתִי אוֹתָם אֶל־אַדְמָתָם:

37:21 καὶ ἐρεῖς αὐτοῖς τάδε λέγει κύριος κύριος ἰδοὺ ἐγὼ λαμβάνω πάντα οἶκον Ισραηλ ἐκ μέσου τῶν ἐθνῶν οὗ εἰσήλθοσαν ἐκεῖ καὶ συνάξω αὐτοὺς ἀπὸ (𝔊^{A,B}: + πάντων) τῶν περικύκλῳ αὐτῶν καὶ εἰσάξω αὐτοὺς εἰς τὴν γῆν τοῦ Ισραηλ

LXX interprets בְּנֵי יִשְׂרָאֵל with οἶκον Ισραηλ rather than υἱοὺς Ισραηλ, a reversal of v. 16. It also has πάντα as a plus. Most commentators correctly view vv. 20–22 as an interpretative section that exegetes the previous vv. 15–19 (cf. vv. 11–14). בְּנֵי יִשְׂרָאֵל in this context appears to be a reference to 'all' the descendants of their ancestor 'Israel', which includes both tribes (cf. Jacob, v. 25). On the one hand, LXX's translation may be due to its inconsistency in translating בֵּית and בְּנֵי (cf. v. 16). However, it is possible that LXX may be interacting with this interpretative section, following the contextual flow of the uniting of tribes (cf. φυλήν v. 19), and of their descendants (v. 18), which now enables LXX to see 'all' of Diaspora Israel being gathered out of the nations, and so interpret them as 'house'. LXX's important πάντα plus lends weight to this, and may be an indication LXX is reflecting on v. 11 where both MT and LXX use the 'whole house of Israel' as an implicit reference to a united Israel (cf. 𝔊^{B,A}'s other πάντα plus below). It may also be that the reversal of υἱούς and οἶκον between vv. 16 and 21 is an LXX theological *inclusio* within this pericope.

We ask why LXX uses εἰσήλθοσαν ('went into') for MT's הָלְכוּ ('walk/journey'), when LXX uses ἐπορεύθησαν ('go, journey') for all other occurrences in Ezekiel. This may be stylistic, yet it may also be a contextual statement regarding the Diaspora, to include countries the Jewish people voluntarily entered, and not just referring to the exile.

Again in this verse, MT says וְקִבַּצְתִּי אֹתָם מִסָּבִיב ('and I will gather them from all around'), where LXX says, καὶ συνάξω αὐτοὺς ἀπὸ (𝔊^{B,A}: + πάντων) τῶν περικύκλῳ αὐτῶν ('and I will gather them from (all) that are around them'). Block (1998, p. 406) believes that "LXX presupposes *mikkol sĕbîbōtām*, 'from all that surround them'". Yet, LXX could be coming from the viewpoint of one translating *in* the land, and seeing the people gathered from all countries around them (cf. Allen v. 22). 𝔊^{B,A}'s πάντων plus expands MT and 𝔊^{967} to emphasise the

hermeneutically to its reader and community. As such, we need to consider the above mentioned variant of δίδωμι along with this μου plus, and suggest that LXX viewed this as God's land gifted to his people. For the Hebrew text, these are all future projections and hope, but for the later LXX translator they appear to be present possibilities and even partial realities. Thus the use here of 'ἐν τῇ γῇ μου' may be an attempt to bring personal ownership and involvement of God in the land and people. After proposing various reasons why MT should not be emended here (בָּאָרֶץ to בְּאַרְצִי, and with אַדְמָתָם v. 21),[67] Zimmerli (1983, p. 269) states "nevertheless, it might be wondered whether the whole complex, which is decidedly superfluous in the parallel structure of v. 22a/b [nation-king & kingdoms-nations], is not a secondary theological interpretation". But Zimmerli does not state here, nor in the body of his commentary, what that secondary theological interpretation might be! At least Zimmerli is willing to face the possibility of an interpretation rather than a scribal error.

LXX has another subtle plus where the nation will be established: MT says בָּאָרֶץ בְּהָרֵי יִשְׂרָאֵל ('in the land on the mountains of Israel', cf. chapters 6, 36), whereas LXX says ἐν τῇ γῇ μου καὶ ἐν τοῖς ὄρεσιν Ισραηλ ('in my land *and in* the mountains of Israel'). LXX's καὶ ἐν plus may serve as an exegetical clarifier to say 'that is in', or it may be that LXX seeks to mention both 'land' and 'mountains' as emphasis. Either way, LXX again interacts with the text.

There is a minor MT variant, where the *qere* appears to correct the *ketiv*[68] to state וְלֹא (*ketiv* יִהְיֶה) (*qere* יִהְיוּ) עוֹד לִשְׁנֵי גוֹיִם ('and [it *ketiv*/they *qere*] shall no longer be two nations'). Zimmerli (1983, p. 270) notes that the *ketiv* "suggests a king for each nation". Greenberg (1997, p. 756) suggests the *ketiv* "looks like a scribal error influenced by *yhyh* four words before". We note that 𝔊^A's unique plus of οὐκ strengthens the point that the kingdoms will never be divided again into two kingdoms.

LXX does not reflect MT's last instance of עוֹד, perhaps because it was "either recognizing its superfluity or reflecting of a different *Vorlage*" (Block, 1998, p. 407). The number of variants in this verse may reflect a different *Vorlage*, but more likely are theological variants. This verse,

---

[67] Block (1998, p. 406) says that "LXX presupposes בְּאַרְצִי".

[68] See on 36:14 for comments on how the *qere* can correct the *ketiv*. Given the possibilities that the *ketiv*/*qere* variants *may* reflect diverse text traditions, it is a moot point for us as to which is earlier.

along with the following verse, and even the pericope, indicate a text in a state of theological flux.

We also find a subtle, yet very important, difference with the leadership of this nation. MT says וּמֶלֶךְ אֶחָד יִהְיֶה לְכֻלָּם לְמֶלֶךְ ('and one king shall be king for all of them'). LXX says καὶ ἄρχων εἷς ἔσται (𝕲ᴬ: πάντων) αὐτῶν ('and one ruler/prince shall be for (𝕲ᴬ: all) them'). LXX does not translate מֶלֶךְ with βασιλεύς, instead using ἄρχων, and does not reflect MT's double usage of מֶלֶךְ. 𝕲⁹⁶ᴵ's dative αὐτοῖς (cf: 𝕲ᴮ·ᴬ: αὐτῶν) variant may reflect awareness of MT's ל, but it still does not witness לְכֻלָּם לְמֶלֶךְ. 𝕲ᴬ's πάντων reflects MT's לְכֻלָּם, but we question why 𝕲ᴬ did not translate the second word, לְמֶלֶךְ. Wevers (1982, p. 197) suggests that LXX "rightly omit[s] the late gloss 'king' *lmlk*... [which] may be a copyist's dittography of *lklm*, 'for all of them', in scramble". A copy error may be the case here, and his 'late gloss' suggestion is also possible. Lust (1986a, p. 218) says that "in 7:27 and once in 37:22 the Greek has no equivalent for Hebrew [מֶלֶךְ]. Most likely [the translator] did not find [מֶלֶךְ] in [his] Vorlage". This is a likely possibility, but these explanations do not answer why LXX consistently translates מֶלֶךְ in this pericope with ἄρχων. A 'simple' explanation may be that LXX made these changes with theological intent, including using ἄρχων for מֶלֶךְ, due to their views on the new Davidic leadership. LXX includes the concept of a united Israel but it does not reflect a king, but rather an ἄρχων ('leader/ruler') for them. This appears to be a complex issue, theologically motivated, and affecting more than one verse, and so we will treat this issue separately.

4.3.1. *Excursus on* מֶלֶךְ, נָשִׂיא, *and* ἄρχων *in Ezek. 37:22–25*

Earlier in Ezekiel, the LORD is declared to be the one who will 'be king' over Israel (cf. 20:33 מלך/βασιλεύω).[69] Joyce (1998, p. 335) suggests that מֶלֶךְ in 37:22 may still refer to "God as king".[70] This underlying theology appears to have influenced the wording when referring to the kings of Israel. Of the 37 occurrences of מֶלֶךְ in Ezekiel, it is significant that 25 refer to kings outside Israel. מֶלֶךְ is used for Israel's

---

[69] For more on how God is King in Ezekiel, and the Hebrew Bible, see Brettler (1989).

[70] Joyce (1998, p. 335) does clarify "However, on balance, the most natural reading of 37.22 is probably as a reference to a human king". The 'humanness' is clearly seen with the use of נָשִׂיא.

kings in just five main places: 1:2 (as part of the date formula); 7:27
(מֶלֶךְ will mourn); 17:12 (מֶלֶךְ into exile); and finally that which has
specific interest to us, 37:22, 24 where it speaks of a future Davidic
king. While Ezekiel does not avoid using מֶלֶךְ for Israel's leaders, he
does show a significant preference for נָשִׂיא ('prince/ruler'; 7:27; 12:10,
12; 19:1; 21:12, 25; 22:6; 34:24; 37:25).[71] Lemke (1984, p. 174) suggests
that מֶלֶךְ "may have had misleading or even negative connotations"
in Ezekiel's day. Ezekiel's preferred title of נָשִׂיא for Israel's kings and
leaders appears to bring out the vassal aspect of Israel's kings in a world
where Babylon dominated. It also describes how Ezekiel typically sees
the future leaders (cf. נָשִׂיא v. 25). Duguid (1994, p. 32) points this out
saying, "it is reasonable to suppose that Ezekiel intended by the term
nāśî' to convey a ruler with limited authority, genuinely representative
of the people". He also states that "the distinction between *melek* and
nāśî' is not hard and fast: the great emperors of Babylon and Egypt are
always designated *melek*, but petty kings may go by either title" (Duguid,
1994, p. 20).[72] Joyce (1998, p. 330) says that נָשִׂיא is "used elsewhere
mostly within what has commonly been called 'Priestly' material....
It is the technical term of the leader of a clan, and is always used of
authorities in subordination to a greater authority (e.g. alongside Moses
in Exod. 16:22)". Bodi (2001, p. 256) says the role of this future leader
has been modified to where he only has the authority of a vassal and
so unable to exercise "repressive or coercive function". After examining its usage in other books, McKeating (1993, p. 111) concludes that
נָשִׂיא as 'leader' "certainly does not imply royal status, but does not
exclude it. That is to say, *nāśî'* was not usually a king, but it was not felt
inappropriate to apply the word to a king". Lust (2006, p. 425) agrees
with others that Ezekiel's use of נָשִׂיא is "an echo of the leadership
patterns as pictured in the book of Numbers". This is highly likely
as we have seen a common echo to Numbers during our discussion

---

[71] Some of these occurrences appear to refer to 'leaders' rather than just 'kings' (e.g.,
7:27 has both מֶלֶךְ and נָשִׂיא in the same verse, indicating נָשִׂיא there refers to a leader
under the king (cf. 32:29 of Edom). We also find in 22:6 that the נְשִׂיאֵי יִשְׂרָאֵל are guilty
of oppressing the people, which again appears to include more than just the king. This
lends support for our point that נָשִׂיא has a vassal concept to it in Ezekiel.

[72] Cross (1975, 15) also notes that "the leader of the first return [from Babylon] was
Sin-ab-aṣur, the heir to the house of David, son of Jehoiachin. He is given the title
nāśî, which Ezekiel and his circle in the Exile preferred to *melek*, 'king', in designat-
ing the new David's office" (cf. Ezra 5:14–16). This may have been part of the exilic
Jewish terminology.

of chapters 36–39. We also note that the title נָשִׂיא rather than מֶלֶךְ is used in 40–48, without any clear Davidic-messianic nature. Yet this "does not imply a denial of its Davidic-messianic nature. The נָשִׂיא is a vassal of Yahweh, a shepherd who serves under the divine shepherd" (Raurell, 1986, p. 85).[73]

Therefore, MT's use of מֶלֶךְ in 37:22, 24 is theologically important, as Block (1998, p. 414) points out: "the present choice of *melek* highlights the restoration of Israel to full nationhood. To the prophet's audience, the use of *nāśîʿ* would have signified less than complete restoration". In an earlier work Block (1995, p. 171) writes, "in several ancient texts the divine appointment of a human king represents...the climax of the normalization of the relationship between a deity and his land/people. Accordingly, Ezekiel's anticipation of a new [messianic] king over his own people would have been understood by ancient Israelite and out-sider alike". The context in v. 22 deals with a 'united kingdom' which requires a 'king', and thus MT uses מֶלֶךְ. Greenberg (1997, p. 756) says the contextual "parallelism of 'one nation—one king'/two nations—two kingdoms' supports the authenticity of the term 'king' against 𝔊's translation 'chief'". MT's use of ל implies that this מֶלֶךְ will be a real king, ruling over a sovereign united kingdom and maintaining cohesive unity. His identity is not given until v. 24, where we find he will be a king like David, indicating a renewed 'Davidic Kingdom'. Adding to Block's point above, the exiles would have seen this *Davidic* king and kingdom as the ultimate fulfilment of restoration. Unlike נָשִׂיא, the use of מֶלֶךְ identified with 'David' of antiquity, suggests more of a military leader than a peaceful shepherd.

This raises the question as to which facet Ezekiel's Davidic leader will exhibit: warrior or worshipper, or even both. The use of מֶלֶךְ shows that "Ezekiel does not discard the Judahite monarchy, he refashions it. The prophet had a place for *a monarch* but not for *the monarchy*, that is, the social, political, and economic *system* associated with the king" [italics mine] (Vawter and Hoppe, 1991, p. 204).[74] Sloan (1992, p. 150) says,

---

[73] Fisch (1985, p. 251) simplifies by saying "while *king* signifies a political ruler, *shepherd* denotes a spiritual leader". Raurell (1986, p. 89) says that for "the Greek translator...the ideal future king of 40–48 cannot be like the one of 1–39, in spite of the fact that MT always defines him as a נשיא.

[74] Levenson (1986, p. 68f.) also argues that in Ezekiel מֶלֶךְ and נָשִׂיא can appear synonymously and that Ezekiel and his school have "not discarded kingship. They have reinterpreted it.... [as they] sought to bring the institution of monarchy under the governance of the Sinaitic covenant". Lemke (1984, p. 180) concludes that "Ezekiel

"the reunion of God, land and people can only occur at the same time as a new political order does". However, he continues that Ezekiel "does not offer a new political order as the means by which the people will return to the land". Nowhere does the text explicitly indicate that this Davidic leader will be a military conqueror, it is only implied by the chapter reorder where now this pericope comes before the Gog epic. Significantly, all four occurrences of 'David' in Ezekiel are prefaced with 'my servant' (cf. 34:23, 24; 37:24, 25). Furthermore, v. 24 indicates the duties of this Davidic מֶלֶךְ will be that of a רעה (shepherd), who will enable the people to 'walk in my judgements and observe my statutes and do them'.[75] Then, in v. 25, we find a 'softening' in MT where נָשִׂיא is used in reference to David, perhaps to state implicitly that this future Davidic leader will be a vassal under God, even as the מֶלֶךְ of the united kingdom (vv. 22–24). As such, this new Davidic king/ruler in v. 25 "will have a pastoral charge, to watch over the morals and religion of his people", rather than being a military leader (Cooke, 1936, p. 402). In the same way, this נָשִׂיא "is to devote himself entirely to the liturgy, just as Deuteronomy's king is to devote himself entirely to the study of the Law (Deut. 17:18–20)" (Vawter and Hoppe, 1991, p. 204).[76] Speiser (1963, p. 111) says that "in Ezekiel's view, great temporal power does not appear conducive to spiritual excellence, hence the prophet's personal preference for a modest principality as opposed to an ambitious empire". Therefore, we find in MT Ezekiel's theology more the concept of David as 'worshipper', than David as 'warrior'.[77] Sloan (1992, p. 150) also says Ezekiel "sees both political order and return to the land as simultaneous ends towards which spiritual practice is aimed". This questions MT's use of מֶלֶךְ in vv. 22–25. Overall, we find in MT one

---

and his disciples were not necessarily looking forward to the restoration of the Davidic monarchy. David in this passage is more an ideal symbol of Israelite unity than a specific past or future historical figure".

[75] Brettler (1989, p. 36) points out that "shepherd is one of the oldest appellations for kings in the ancient Near East" and then says "it is likely that the metaphorical use of 'shepherd' of Israelite kings contributed to the literary depiction of David (and possibly Moses) as actual shepherds".

[76] Cooke (1936, p. 403) also states this future Davidic leader "is overshadowed by the ministry of worship; his function amounts to little more than providing and attending the sacrifices on Sabbaths and festivals, 44[3] 46[1–12, 16–18]".

[77] Significantly, and perhaps in support of this point, this Davidic leader is not directly mentioned in the battles against Gog and his hordes, but rather there God is the 'warrior' (cf. 38:4a, 16, 21–23; 39:1–4, 6–7, 11). However, if chapter 37 came after chapter 39 in the *Urtext*, then this could also explain the absence of David as warrior against Gog. Ezekiel, and the translators, retained the position of God as warrior.

theology that has a resurrected and restored United Kingdom requiring a king, even a Davidic 'military' king, and then another theology where this Davidic נָשִׂיא would lead the people in spiritual pursuits, and not military activities. These two theologies represent that found in the two extant chapter orders of the received text and 𝔊⁹⁶⁷.[78]

LXX has captured the sense of נָשִׂיא with its use of ἄρχων, as it "reflects adequately enough the function, if not the etymology, of *nāśî'*" (Speiser, 1963, p. 111).[79] Yet, our interest is why LXX has translated מֶלֶךְ with ἄρχων, rather than with βασιλεύς in 37:22, 24. LXX does not evidence any major hesitancy in using 'king' when referring to those outside Israel, consistently translating with βασιλεύς.

McGregor (1985) and Raurell (1986) discuss[80] in detail the terminological preferences of the various LXX translators of Ezekiel. LXX uses βασιλεύς for Israel's king only in 1:2 (cf. the date formula), and significantly in 20:33 discussing the LORD's 'kingship' (βασιλεύσω ἐφ' ὑμᾶς), thus capturing Ezekiel's theology of the LORD as Israel's king. Lust (1986a, p. 219) notes that Ezekiel's 'translator β' consistently uses ἄρχων for either מֶלֶךְ or נָשִׂיא. The exception noted by Duguid (1994, p. 23) is where "*melek* is found together with *nāśî'* or *nāgîd*... [then] LXX harmonized the two terms, understandably in the light of Ezekiel's own usages, and translated both by *archōn*". Thus, here in 37:22–24 LXX may have simply picked up on Ezekiel's preference for נָשִׂיא, and under influence from the use of נָשִׂיא for a Davidic king in v. 25 and 34:24, translated with ἄρχων here. At the same time, LXX may well have grasped the implicit Ezekielian theology that the future Davidic ruler over the United Kingdom would be a spiritual vassal under God's kingship, and so reflected this, using ἄρχων.

Block (1998, p. 407) notes that some suggest MT should be emended in vv. 22–24 from מֶלֶךְ to נָשִׂיא to follow LXX's ἄρχων, but concludes

---

[78] For a more comprehensive discussion on this, see 'Theological Significance' in chapter 7.

[79] Speiser (1963, p. 114) later says "analogously, *nāśî'* goes back to *nāśā'* 'to raise'.... the title, in short, stands for a duly elected chieftain".

[80] Raurell (1986, p. 89) argued that the varied terminology used by LXX translators was due to their theological diversity. He proposed that ἀφηγούμενος used in 40–48 is used in a positive sense "as the ideal future monarch, who never transgresses in either the ritual or social sphere" and as such "becomes the antithesis of the ἄρχων" used in 1–39. However both Lust (1986a, p. 219) and Duguid (1994, p. 22) reject this proposal, largely because of how LXX uses ἄρχων in a positive sense for a future Davidic ruler here in 37:22, 24. This ruler is still not presented as a 'king', nor is there any royal sense to this title.

Gog epic. We propose in our discussions, that this chapter reorder was motivated by a 'call to arms', which required a military Davidic leader. As additional support for this change, and to encourage the 'call to arms' and give greater status to current military leadership, we suggest the later Hebrew editor(s) 'strengthened' the wording in 37:22–24 from נָשִׂיא to מֶלֶךְ. Lust (2006, p. 430) also finds MT adjusted to מֶלֶךְ, but suggests it was to "enhance[e] the royal messianic character of the expectation". Our proposal considers the motivation behind the chapter reorder, and we find this more probable. Therefore, rather than LXX 'softening' the Hebrew, we propose that they found נָשִׂיא in their *Vorlage*, not מֶלֶךְ. This would explain why 𝕲⁹⁶⁷, which likely represents the Old Greek, and perhaps the *Urtext*, also has ἄρχων, and the later LXX MSS continued this reading. 𝕲ᴮ·ᴬ witness the chapter reorder, but these later minor editorial changes were not in their *Vorlage*.[83] This would have been done at a similar time to other changes done after, and in support of, the chapter reorder (cf. 36:23b; קָהָל to חַיִל in 37:10; חֵמָה to רוּחַ to 39:29). MasEzek witnesses these changes, showing they are early (and Jewish), but still not yet witnessed in LXX's *Vorlage*. Block (2007, p. 34) recently stated this explanation is "unnecessarily speculative" and it "overplays the militaristic nature of *melek* and underestimates the militaristic overtones of *nāśî*".[84] Whilst it may be speculative, it is not without supporting textual evidence of other changes resulting from the chapter reorder (36:23b; 37:10; 39:29). Block is correct that Deut. 17:14–20 "prohibits a militaristic stance", yet the people requested Samuel for a militaristic king (1Sam. 8:20). A נָשִׂיא does have militaristic overtones, yet a מֶלֶךְ is more explicit, and that is why we propose that the Hebrew editor(s) changed to this more explicit militaristic leader to support the reason behind their chapter change.

---

[83] Several points already discussed in this Excursus lend further support to our proposal that the original Hebrew contained נָשִׂיא. We summarise these as: this reflects the underlying Ezekielian theology of God as King; 'king' is not used in Ezekiel with a military sense for Israel's leaders; Ezekiel shows a preference for נָשִׂיא; the title of נָשִׂיא is exclusively used in the following block of 40–48; the prophet had a place for *a monarch* but not for *the monarchy*; the immediate context vv. 2–24 has no military indication, only that of shepherding the people as a spiritual leader.

[84] That נָשִׂיא appears primarily in the Priestly writings suggest a less militaristic role.

4.3.2. *37:23–28 (resumes)*

37:23 וְלֹא יִטַמְּאוּ עוֹד בְּגִלּוּלֵיהֶם וּבְשִׁקּוּצֵיהֶם וּבְכֹל פִּשְׁעֵיהֶם
וְהוֹשַׁעְתִּי אֹתָם מִכֹּל מוֹשְׁבֹתֵיהֶם אֲשֶׁר חָטְאוּ בָהֶם וְטִהַרְתִּי אוֹתָם
וְהָיוּ־לִי לְעָם וַאֲנִי אֶהְיֶה לָהֶם לֵאלֹהִים:

37:23 ἵνα μὴ μιαίνωνται ἔτι ἐν τοῖς εἰδώλοις αὐτῶν (𝕲ᴬ: + καὶ ἐν οἷς
ἡμάρτοσαν ἐν αὐτοῖς καὶ ἐν τοῖς προσοχθίσμασιν αὐτῶν καὶ ἐν πάσαις
ταῖς βασιλείαις αὐτῶν) καὶ ῥύσομαι αὐτοὺς ἀπὸ πασῶν τῶν ἀνομιῶν
αὐτῶν ὧν (𝕲⁹⁶⁷: πνομησαν; 𝕲ᴮ·ᴬ: ἡμάρτοσαν) ἐν αὐταῖς καὶ καθαριῶ
αὐτούς καὶ ἔσονταί μοι εἰς λαόν καὶ ἐγὼ κύριος ἔσομαι αὐτοῖς εἰς
θεόν

LXX begins v. 23 with ἵνα μὴ, which continues the prophecy from
v. 22. Thus v. 23 provides a theological reason for the combining of the
kingdoms into one nation. Under a Davidic ruler, and even for the dry
bones to be resurrected to life, they must no longer defile (μιαίνωνται)
themselves with idols. By this, LXX continues to interact interpretively
with the text, reflecting back on the Davidic kingdom that worshipped
God under David's rulership and his tabernacle (vv. 24–28). MT gives
a simple statement that they will not defile themselves, but this is not
given as a reason for the restorative words in v. 22. LXX's interpretation
again echoes the postexilic concern to remove idolatry from the land.

MT, MasEzek and the later 𝕲ᴬ, include three areas of uncleanness,
with the earlier 𝕲⁹⁶⁷·ᴮ only one:

1. בְּגִלּוּלֵיהֶם—in their idols (𝕲⁹⁶⁷·ᴮ·ᴬ: εἰδώλοις)
2. וּבְשִׁקּוּצֵיהֶם—in their detestable things (𝕲⁹⁶⁷·ᴮ: minus; 𝕲ᴬ: ἡμάρτοσαν,
   commit wrong)
3. פִּשְׁעֵיהֶם—rebellion (𝕲⁹⁶⁷·ᴮ: minus; 𝕲ᴬ: προσοχθίσμασιν, offence,
   idol)[85]

---

[85] We suggest that 𝕲ᴬ reversed the Hebrew word order (a not uncommon event),
and προσοχθίσμασιν actually matches וּבְשִׁקּוּצֵיהֶם. In all of the other occurrences of
שִׁקּוּץ in Ezekiel (5:11; 7:20; 11:18, 21; 20:7, 8, 30) LXX translates with βδελύγματα
(abomination, idol) rather than 𝕲ᴬ's προσοχθίσμασιν (offence, idol) here. Likewise,
whilst 𝕲ᴬ uses ἡμάρτοσαν (commit wrong, miss mark) here, other occurrences
of פֶּשַׁע are translated as παραπτώμασιν (transgression—14:11; 18:22); ἀσεβειῶν
(ungodliness—18:28, 30, 31; 20:28; 21:29; 33:12); πλάναι (error—33:10); ἀκαθαρσίας
(uncleanness—39:24).

There are differing views regarding this section: Zimmerli (1983, p. 270) believes MT is secondary;[86] Allen (1990b, p. 190) says "it is difficult to decide whether parablepsis or secondary accretion in MT is the culprit"; Block (1998, p. 407) finds support for MT from 14:11. Yet, these two extra words are likely to be another later Hebrew plus not present in 𝕲^{967,B}'s *Vorlage*, but added prior to MasEzek, and in time to be reflected in the later 𝕲^A. This MT/𝕲^A plus theologically strengthens the simple statement of being defiled by idols (גִּלּוּל), and may even be seen as an exegetical expansion. *HALOT* notes that the concept of 'horror' or even 'monster' should be considered with הַשִּׁקּוּץ, as it is a reference to the statue itself and not just to the overall concept of idolatry. This aspect may be captured with 𝕲^A's use of προσόχθισμασιν as "offence, provocation, idol" ([LEH], a neologism; cf. Deut. 7:36; 1Kgs. 11:33; 16:32). The use of these words in this context may refer to a particular event in Israel's history such as the Seleucid polluting of the temple with the image of Zeus.

𝕲^A's extensive plus, while initially following MT, also has its own additional plus: και ἐν πάσαις ταῖς βασιλείαις αὐτῶν ('and in all their kingdoms'). It is unusual that 𝕲^A uses 'βασιλείαις' here, and not ἐθνῶν or γῆν ὑμῶν, which indicates 𝕲^A is reflecting on the δύο βασιλείας (v. 22), referring to the separate northern and southern kingdoms discussed earlier (cf. vv. 16–22). Thus, 𝕲^A is stating that the new United Kingdom will not defile itself with idolatry again. It may also refer to a broader spectrum to include the Diaspora, saying wherever they are in '*all* their kingdoms'.

The first part of this verse survives in part amongst Qumran fragments (4QFlor.) stating לו[א] יטמאו עוד בג[לו]ל[ו]ליהמה ('they shall no longer defile themselves with their idols'). We do not know if the *Vorlage* for this Florilegium had the additional MT and 𝕲^A plus, as it is not represented in the fragment. Brooke (1985, pp. 115–118) points out that this line in 4QFlor is part of a Midrash for Psa. 1:1, and is used theologically by the Qumran community to show how their two groups of 'House of David' and 'Sons of Zadok' will not defile themselves by any use of idols.

MT says the LORD will save them מִכֹּל מוֹשְׁבֹתֵיהֶם אֲשֶׁר חָטְאוּ בָהֶם ('from all their dwellings where they sinned'), yet LXX ἀπὸ πασῶν τῶν

---

[86] Zimmerli (1983, p. 270) says "ובשקוציהם ובכל פשעיהם is unattested in 𝕲", but does not note that it is attested in 𝕲^A.

ἀνομιῶν αὐτῶν ὧν ἡμάρτοσαν ἐν αὐταῖς ('from all their transgressions whereby they have sinned'). Allen (1990, p. 190) says that MT

> reflects the incorrect insertion of a vowel letter into משבתיהם = משובתיהם (cf. BHS) 'their deviations,' implied by LXX Σ. MT was influenced by the triple usage of (ו)ישבו '(and) they will dwell/dwelt' in v. 25 and perhaps by the association of בכל מושבותיהם 'in all their dwelling places' in 6:14 with כל גלוליהם 'and all their idols' in 6:13.

Block (1998, p. 407) agrees with Allen that "MT represents a metathetical error involving w and $š$", and emends MT, along with Allen, so changing the meaning from 'settlements' to 'turnings', and states that "Ezekiel's usage reflects Jeremianic influence" (also Greenberg, 1997, p. 756).[87] Block (1998, p. 407) does note that "the masculine form of [מֹושְׁבֹתֵיהֶם] is attested in 34:13, ... [yet] this sense is clearly out of place here". LXX does seem to make more sense than MT. Yet the context speaks of God bringing the people back from the nations, and the idolatrous sin of Israel occurred in their homes, and thus MT's 'dwellings in which they sinned' can also be appropriate. If so, this may be another place where LXX exhibits a trans-lingual wordplay: now rather than focusing as MT on the place where the sin was done (dwelling places), LXX focuses on the action of ἀνομία, the lawlessness that was done within their dwelling places.

Finally, the plus in 𝕲^{B,A} of κύριος (in καὶ ἐγὼ κύριος) is not found in 𝕲^{967} or MT, and emphasises the referent of ἐγώ.

37:24 וְעַבְדִּי דָוִד מֶלֶךְ עֲלֵיהֶם וְרֹועֶה אֶחָד יִהְיֶה לְכֻלָּם
וּבְמִשְׁפָּטַי יֵלֵכוּ וְחֻקֹּתַי יִשְׁמְרוּ וְעָשׂוּ אֹותָם:

37:24 καὶ ὁ δοῦλός μου Δαυιδ ἄρχων ἐν μέσῳ αὐτῶν καὶ ποιμὴν εἷς ἔσται πάντων ὅτι ἐν τοῖς προστάγμασίν μου πορεύσονται καὶ τὰ κρίματά μου φυλάξονται καὶ ποιήσουσιν αὐτά

For MT's וְעַבְדִּי דָוִד מֶלֶךְ עֲלֵיהֶם ('and my servant David will be king over them'), LXX has καὶ ὁ δοῦλός μου Δαυιδ ἄρχων ἐν μέσῳ αὐτῶν ('and my servant David will be a ruler in the midst of them'). As in v. 22, LXX uses ἄρχων as if the Hebrew had נָשִׂיא (see Excursus above). We observe a theological movement in MT: in v. 22 MT's Davidic leader was a 'king' over the United Kingdom, yet now in v. 24 there is a shift to state that he will be a רעה ('shepherd') who will enable the people

---

[87] Zimmerli (1983, p. 270 [also p. 275]) is another who believes that מִכֹּל מֹושְׁבֹתֵיהֶם "belongs clearly to the language of Jeremiah".

to follow the ways of God. MT's use of רעה reflects the role of Israel's leader in 34:23.[88] Then, in v. 25, MT uses נָשִׂיא to also describe their Davidic 'king'. MT's use of רעה and נָשִׂיא supports our suggestion that מֶלֶךְ was a later editorial emendation to the text, and that LXX translator found נָשִׂיא in his *Vorlage*. Even if מֶלֶךְ was original, the presence of רעה here, and נָשִׂיא in v. 25, may have influenced LXX's use of ἄρχων here and elsewhere in this pericope.

While MT's מֶלֶךְ is עֲלֵיהֶם ('over them'), LXX's ἄρχων is ἐν μέσῳ αὐτῶν ('in their midst'), as a passive, non-threatening ruler, reflecting the use of 'shepherd' (רעה/ποιμήν). LXX may again have been influenced by Ezek. 34:24 where MT has the Davidic ruler בְּתוֹכָם (cf. 37:26, 28). Also relevant is Deut. 17:14–20, where Israel's kings were to be from their brothers (אָחִיךָ), and were not to dominate the people, but rather spiritually lead them (Deut. 17:18f.). Another possible influence is the post-exilic shift to 'priestly rulers', away from a leader who would rule over, or dominate, the people as in pre-exilic times. There is also the overall theology in Ezekiel where "Jhwh is the only king over Israel" (Lust, 1986a, p. 217), and LXX embraces that concept having their Davidic leader as only 'a ruler in their midst'. It could also be out of concern not to cause any 'threat' to an occupying force (Seleucids or Romans). Whatever the reason, LXX has theologically softened any 'dominating' role of the Davidic leader here.

LXX's ὅτι plus reflects a theological purpose for the ἄρχων: 'so that' they would follow the ways of God. MT contextually implies this, but LXX clarifies that the Davidic leader will enable them to fulfil Torah. This captures the point that the new Davidic leader will be one who unites Sinai with Zion (Levenson, 1986, pp. 57–69). Levenson (1986, p. 75) believes the use of נָשִׂיא in Ezekiel is "as an a-political Messiah". LXX's use of ἄρχων may have also increased readers' Messianic expectation, especially as the context is in reference to David and a united Israel.[89] If so, this helps explain LXX's ὅτι plus as redirecting focus.

---

[88] Whilst a common ANE image for rulers, Jonker (1997, p. 1141) correctly points out that "unlike the usage in other ANE contexts, the title *shepherd* is never used in the OT to denote a deified king or human leader".

[89] In his examination of Ezek. 17:22–24, Lust (1995a, p. 250) concluded that the Old Greek, most notably 𝔊⁹⁶⁷, "is less open to an individual messianic interpretation than MT...the translator clearly has plurality in mind". He also suggested that the changes "in the majority of the [LXX] manuscripts is probably due to a Christian reworking of the text". Yet here in Ezek. 37, the context speaks of a future individual Davidic-messianic leader.

Lust (1986a, p. 217) appears to agree with this stating that in Ezekiel often "Israel's human messianic leader of the eschatological state does not receive the title [מֶלֶךְ] but [נָשִׂיא]".[90] However we agree with Lemke (1984, p. 180), who, writing on 37:16f., claimed

> it should be noted that while a messianic motif is present in this passage, it is a rather muted one. Ezekiel and his disciples were not necessarily looking forward to the restoration of the Davidic monarchy. David in this passage is more an ideal symbol of Israelite unity than a specific past or future historical figure. The final goal of God's future activity was his tabernacling presence among his restored people.

37:25 וְיָשְׁבוּ עַל־הָאָרֶץ אֲשֶׁר נָתַתִּי לְעַבְדִּי לְיַעֲקֹב אֲשֶׁר
יָשְׁבוּ־בָהּ אֲבוֹתֵיכֶם וְיָשְׁבוּ עָלֶיהָ הֵמָּה וּבְנֵיהֶם וּבְנֵי בְנֵיהֶם
עַד־עוֹלָם וְדָוִד עַבְדִּי נָשִׂיא לָהֶם לְעוֹלָם:

37:25 καὶ κατοικήσουσιν ἐπὶ τῆς γῆς αὐτῶν ἣν (𝕲⁹⁶⁷: εδωκα; 𝕲ᴮ·ᴬ: ἐγὼ δέδωκα) τῷ δούλῳ μου Ιακωβ οὗ κατῴκησαν ἐκεῖ οἱ πατέρες αὐτῶν καὶ κατοικήσουσιν ἐπ᾽ αὐτῆς αὐτοί (𝕲ᴬ: + καὶ οἱ υἱοι, αὐτῶν καὶ οἱ υἱοί τῶν υἱῶν αὐτῶν ἕως αἰῶνος) καὶ (𝕲ᴬ: + ἰδου) Δαυιδ ὁ δοῦλός μου ἄρχων (𝕲⁹⁶⁷: + αὐτῶν; 𝕲ᴬ: αὐτῶν ἔσται) εἰς τὸν αἰῶνα

MT says they will dwell עַל־הָאָרֶץ (on *the* land), whereas LXX says ἐπὶ τῆς γῆς αὐτῶν (on *their* land). Both texts state this was the land given to Jacob (cf. 28:25), but now LXX clarifies this as 'their' land, which theologically ties the land more directly to the future generations.

Following this, MT says אֲבוֹתֵיכֶם ('your ancestors'), and LXX has οἱ πατέρες αὐτῶν ('their fathers'). Block (1998, p. 407) says that LXX "assimilates the [MT] word to the context" (cf. יָשְׁבוּ). Cooke (1936, p. 403) also says LXX is "more in accordance with the context". This appears to be another LXX clarifying adjustment to the text.

MT and 𝕲ᴬ both have a long plus: וּבְנֵיהֶם וּבְנֵי בְנֵיהֶם עַד־עוֹלָם // καὶ οἱ υἱοί αὐτῶν καὶ οἱ υἱοί τῶν υἱῶν αὐτῶν ἕως αἰῶνος ('and their children and children's children forever'). As in 36:18, Aquila and Theodotion also witness this plus (Field, 1964, p. 870). However, this is minus in both 𝕲⁹⁶⁷·ᴮ. Zimmerli (1983, p. 270) says it has 'accidentally fallen out' in the Greek. Yet, this plus, covering perpetual living in the land, could be another later MT plus inserted after 𝕲⁹⁶⁷·ᴮ's *Vorlage*, but before 𝕲ᴬ (cf. v. 23). As with other MT/𝕲ᴬ plusses, it was added early enough for MasEzek to witness it. It may have its genesis from some

---

[90] Lust (1986a, pp. 217–221) goes into detail regarding "Israel's Kings in Ezekiel's Vocabulary" finding both theological reasons for the variants, as well as the translator's "lexicographical choices".

later editor reflecting on the context of David and a united kingdom, and reflecting back to texts such as 2Sam. 7:13, 16, 24–26 and 1Chr. 28:8 (all with עַד־עוֹלָם).

𝕲ᴬ's additional following plus of ἰδού, not represented in MT or 𝕲⁹⁶⁷ᐟᴮ, introduces and gives emphasis to David.

MT and MasEzek state that David will be their נָשִׂיא (cf. מֶלֶךְ vv. 22, 24), with LXX again using ἄρχων. Zimmerli (1983, p. 276) says that "the replacement of the מלך ('king') of v. 24 (v. 22) by נשיא ('prince') (v. 25) is due to *conscious reflection*" [italics mine]. Duguid (1994, p. 25) says that "the message Ezekiel is conveying here seems not to be that the future ruler will be a *nāśî´* (as opposed to a *melek*) but rather that the future *nāśî´* will not be like the [negative] rulers of the past". This instance of נָשִׂיא "defines David's role spiritually as Yahweh's *servant* and *their* 'prince,' rather than politically as 'king over them' (v. 24)" (Block, 1998, p. 418). Interestingly, Joyce (1998, p. 331) points out that the use of נָשִׂיא "represents a deliberate archaizing, and echo of the leadership patterns of pre-monarchic Israel, as pictured in the book of Numbers".[91] This is significant due to our previous observations concerning how Ezekiel, and definitely the LXX translator, had in mind various events relating to the exodus and possessing the land as found in Numbers. Therefore, נָשִׂיא is likely to be original. Further support can be found in the statement, 'David my servant', which emphasises the vassal nature of this new Davidic leader under the LORD's 'kingship'.

In the concluding phrase 𝕲⁹⁶⁷ reflects MT syntax by reading καὶ Δαυιδ ὁ δοῦλός μου ἄρχων αὐτῶν εἰς τὸν αἰῶνα ('and David my servant, their prince forever').[92] 𝕲ᴬ has ἔσται as a plus here, perhaps seeing an implied היה, or simply smoothing the reading. 𝕲ᴮ is minus αὐτῶν, causing its phrase to read 'and David my servant, a prince forever'. This may be due to scribal oversight.

37:26 וְכָרַתִּי לָהֶם בְּרִית שָׁלוֹם בְּרִית עוֹלָם יִהְיֶה אוֹתָם וּנְתַתִּים
וְהִרְבֵּיתִי אוֹתָם וְנָתַתִּי אֶת־מִקְדָּשִׁי בְּתוֹכָם לְעוֹלָם׃

---

[91] Joyce (1998, p. 331) also adds "This appears to be so not only in the critique of past and present but also in looking ahead to the future. Moreover, this evocation of early Israel is all the more significant since Ezekiel—unlike some others—by no means idealizes the pre-monarchic period".

[92] Zimmerli (1983, p. 276) also notes the reversal from עַבְדִּי דָוִד (v. 24) to דָוִד עַבְדִּי in v. 25, which he says may be "no more than an essentially unimportant stylistic variation... [or it] could reveal the hand of a different author".

37:26 καὶ διαθήσομαι αὐτοῖς διαθήκην εἰρήνης διαθήκη αἰωνία ἔσται (𝔊^{B,A}: μετ' αὐτῶν; 𝔊^{967}: αὐτοῖς εἰς τὸν αἰῶνα) καὶ θήσω τὰ ἅγιά μου ἐν μέσῳ αὐτῶν εἰς τὸν αἰῶνα

𝔊^{B,A} say the covenant of peace ἔσται μετ' αὐτῶν ('will be with them'), where 𝔊^{967} says ἔσται αὐτοῖς εἰς τὸν αἰῶνα ('will be for them forever'), which appears to be a *homoioteleuton* with the end of the verse (αἰωνία... αἰῶνα).[93] Block (1998, p. 408) notes that MT's אוֹתָם "is difficult.... [and is] maybe a dialectical variation" (cf. 16:60). Thus, 𝔊^{B,A} may have read אוֹתָם as אִתָּם. It may be that the *Urtext* once read יִהְיֶה אוֹתָם לְעוֹלָם but then לְעוֹלָם dropped out of MT, perhaps by scribal error owing to the other occurrences of לְעוֹלָם in this and the surrounding verses, leaving 𝔊^{967} as the only witness to the *Urtext*. On the other hand, 𝔊^{967}'s scribe may have added εἰς τὸν αἰῶνα to emphasise an eternal aspect for this 'covenant of peace'.

MT and MasEzek's plus of וּנְתַתִּים וְהִרְבֵּיתִי אוֹתָם ('and I will set them, and multiply them'), is not represented by LXX, not even 𝔊^A. Zimmerli (1983, p. 270) says that MT "cannot be correct, as is clear from the perplexity of the versions".[94] Allen (1990b, p. 191) explains the minus in LXX as by "parablepsis caused by homoeoteleuton" [sic], which may be the case as each אוֹתָם is followed by ונתתי. Block (1998, p. 408) agrees, saying "the [LXX] scribe's eye probably...skipped from one [אוֹתָם] to the other".[95] It seems unusual that LXX would have deliberately left out such a strong 'priestly' statement. We suggest that this was another later MT plus, added at the same time as the other MT 'priestly blessing' in 36:11, also without LXX witness. As with the occurrence in 36:11, this occurrence is witnessed by the later three exegetes, Aquila, Symmachus and Theodotion (καὶ δώσω αὐτούς, καὶ πληθυνῶ αὐτούς). Symmachus has his own unique and expansive plus of καὶ στηρίσω αὐτούς ('and I will establish them') (Field, 1964, p. 870). Greenberg (1997, p. 757) includes a two-step

---

[93] Sloan (1992, p. 150) points out that "for the Book of Ezekiel, the presence of God must be in the land for the land to be truly the people's, and just as important, the presence of God must be with the people for the people to be truly the land's". Sloan notes that if the people are in exile then God is also in exile and thus separated from his land. For another perspective on the 'Covenant of Peace' in the ANE see Batto (1987).

[94] By 'versions', Zimmerli means LXX, Vulgate, Targum, and Peshitta.

[95] Block (1998, p. 408) also suggests that "it may be preferable to interpret the final ם on נְתַתִּים as a datival suffix...and to see here an abbreviation for the land grant formula [וְנָתַתִּי לָכֶם אֶת־אַדְמַת יִשְׂרָאֵל] (cf. 11:17)".

proposal for its inclusion by different MT scribes. Yet, it is difficult to prove these steps. Therefore, rather than the scribal error proposals given by others, we propose that here, as in 36:11, we have a deliberate MT plus that echoes the 're-creation' aspect with which the later communities appear to have viewed the restoration of Israel (cf. 36:11, 35; 37:1–14). As noted in 36:11, this re-creation aspect could have had the original creation in mind (Gen. 1–2), or the flood event (Gen. 8:17; 9:1, 7), or even both. The scribe inserting this 'priestly blessing' may also have had the Levitical Holiness code in mind, as וְהִרְבֵּיתִי is found in the concluding part of this code (Lev. 26:9; cf. Eze. 36:10, 11, 29, 30; 37:26). Overall, this appears to be a later and deliberate MT plus, exegeting the text with a re-creational view for the return of the exiles and the restoration of Israel.

37:27 וְהָיָה מִשְׁכָּנִי עֲלֵיהֶם וְהָיִיתִי לָהֶם לֵאלֹהִים וְהֵמָּה יִהְיוּ־לִי לְעָם:

37:27 καὶ ἔσται ἡ κατασκήνωσίς μου ἐν (𝕲⁹⁶⁷: μέσῳ αὐτῶν; 𝕲ᴮ·ᴬ: αὐτοῖς) καὶ ἔσομαι αὐτοῖς θεός καὶ αὐτοί μου ἔσονται λαός

LXX has a very subtle shift from MT's וְהָיָה מִשְׁכָּנִי עֲלֵיהֶם ('and my dwelling place will be *over* them') to καὶ ἔσται ἡ κατασκήνωσίς μου [𝕲⁹⁶⁷: μέσῳ αὐτῶν; 𝕲ᴮ·ᴬ: ἐν αὐτοῖς] ('and my habitation[96] will be [𝕲⁹⁶⁷: *in their midst*] [𝕲ᴮ·ᴬ: *in them*]'). LXX may have been influenced by Lev. 26:11. 𝕲ᴮ·ᴬ appear to have also been influenced by the surrounding verses (cf. μεσω vv. 26, 28) and theologically view the 'sanctuary' and the LORD's 'habitation' as usually 'the one and same'. MT's theology of the LORD's habitation being 'over' them "may have been influenced by the *kābôd* of Yahweh, which resided over...the tent of meeting (cf. Exod. 29:45–46)" (Block, 1998, p. 421).[97] Greenberg (1997, p. 757) also observes that for MT, "the tent-sanctuary of the priestly writings was closely associated with the divine cloud that covered it by day, appearing as fire by night (Exod. 40:34–38, abbreviated from Num 9:15–23)". MT may also be referring to the temple being over them, as in height (cf. 40:2) (Cooke, 1936, p. 403). Either way, LXX appears to miss MT's point of the LORD being a covering, and thus protective, presence 'over' them, but rather has his inhabiting/dwelling in their midst, or even *in them*. This may have been influenced by the earlier references to the πνεῦμα coming into them (cf. 37:8–10, 14). Cooke

---

[96] So LEH, who also note that this is used "mostly of the Lord in the temple".
[97] For more on the *kābôd* of Yahweh in Ezekiel, see Tuell (2000a, pp. 98f.).

(1936, p. 404) points out that "according to O.T. ideas of the blessed future, man [sic] is not translated to dwell with God, but God comes down to dwell with man [sic], and His Presence transforms the earth into heaven". LXX has embraced this theology, but has done so by exegeting the Hebrew.

37:28 וְיָדְעוּ הַגּוֹיִם כִּי אֲנִי יְהוָה מְקַדֵּשׁ אֶת־יִשְׂרָאֵל בִּהְיוֹת מִקְדָּשִׁי
בְּתוֹכָם לְעוֹלָם:

37:28 καὶ γνώσονται (𝔊⁹⁶⁷,ᴮ: τὰ ἔθνη; 𝔊ᴬ: –) ὅτι ἐγώ εἰμι κύριος ὁ ἁγιάζων αὐτοὺς ἐν τῷ εἶναι τὰ ἅγιά μου ἐν μέσῳ αὐτῶν εἰς τὸν αἰῶνα (𝔊ᴬ: + λεγει κυριος)

MT says כִּי אֲנִי יְהוָה מְקַדֵּשׁ אֶת־יִשְׂרָאֵל ('that I am the LORD who sanctifies *Israel*'), whereas LXX says ὅτι ἐγώ εἰμι κύριος ὁ ἁγιάζων αὐτοὺς ('that I am the Lord who sanctifies *them*'). LXX personalises the objects being sanctified. On the other hand, perhaps 'Israel' is a later MT emendation, taking the *Urtext* pronoun and clarifying their identity. 𝔊ᴬ is minus τὰ ἔθνη, which is represented in 𝔊⁹⁶⁷,ᴮ and MT, causing 𝔊ᴬ to read 'and *they* will know', leaving the context to refer back to v. 27 with 'they' as God's people. The other MSS read that the *nations* would know what the LORD has done in restoring his people, which may fit the concept of the LORD's restoration done to sanctify his name amongst the nations (cf. 36:22).

   𝔊ᴬ's clarifying plus (not represented by MT or 𝔊⁹⁶⁷,ᴮ) of λεγει κυριος states the speaker to avoid any confusion that this prophetic word came by Ezekiel.

4.4. SUMMARY OF OBSERVATIONS: EZEKIEL 37

Ezekiel 37 has two thematic divisions: vv. 1–14 (resurrection of the dry bones), and vv. 15–28 (the reestablishment of the United Kingdom under a Davidic ruler). These follow MTᴬ's *petuḥah* sense divisions, and are also seen in LXX MSS.

   LXX continues its clarifiers, such as 𝔊ᴮ,ᴬ's ἀνθρωπίνων (v. 1), and ἁρμονίαν (v. 7), and interprets the actions of MT (flesh 'germinating' v. 8). LXX MSS vary in their use of abbreviation for πνεῦμα, suggesting variation in interpretation of רוּחַ as the Spirit of God or 'wind/breath'. Likewise the LXX MSS have variants with the activity of the πνεῦμα towards humans, with the MSS alternating the usage of εἰς/ἐπί. Ezekiel likely intended a 're-creation' motif in vv. 5, 9, 10, and LXX exegetically clarifies this. There appears an echo in 37:5 of the book of Numbers with the 'S/spirit' coming on Israel's leaders (Num. 11:24f.). Some, such as McKeating (1994), find parallels with Moses in the dry bones passage, but this is not clearly observed in any variants between MT and LXX.[98] LXX's use of συναγωγή in 37:10 most likely reflects the original Hebrew, with a later Hebrew scribe changing קָהָל to חַיִל, as support for the change of chapter order (see chapter 7).

All MSS have the second thematic section (vv. 15–28) as one sense division. LXX continues its practice of interpreting MT's metaphors clarifying the text for their generation, translating עֵץ with ῥάβδον (ruler's sceptre), interpreting MT's echo of Numbers 17:1–11, and with φυλήν (v. 19). The 'new exodus' motif is found (cf. vv. 21, 25). Our Excursus covering 'נָשִׂיא/מֶלֶךְ/ἄρχων' in vv. 22–25 reveals LXX did not theologically soften מֶלֶךְ with its use of ἄρχων, instead LXX found נָשִׂיא in its *Vorlage*. A later Hebrew editor emended נָשִׂיא to מֶלֶךְ, as support for chapter reorder.

Our textual-comparative methodology enables us to observe that chapters 36 and 37 in both MT and LXX appear to have expanded the *Urtext*. These scribes, especially LXX, have reflected on Israel's past history and transmitted the text for their contemporary communities based on their socio-political-theological world view. The initial reflection on Israel's history came from the *Urtext*, but was then often clarified by later translator(s) and redactors. We agree with Ellis (1988, pp. 686–697):

> The OT displays a hermeneutical progression in which, on the one hand, sacred accounts of God's acts in the past provided models for later accounts of his present and future activity and, on the other hand, the received sacred literature was from time to time conformed to its contemporary or future application and fulfilment. The first aspect of the process is evident in the way in which the prophets 'placed the new historical acts of God…in exactly the same category as the old basic events of the canonical history': a new creation (Ezek. 36:35), a new Exodus (Ezek. 36:8), a new covenant, a new Davidic kingdom (Ezek. 37:24), a new Zion or temple (Ezek. 40–48) [verse order adjusted for relevancy].

---

[98] McKeating (1994, p. 106) says "Just as Moses, through his prophesying, and above all through his law-giving, virtually creates a people, so Ezekiel, through *his* prophesying and law-giving (for law-giving is what we largely have in chs. 40–48) *re*-creates the people after the death and dissolution of the *gôlā*".

This raises the question as what constitutes restoration. Speaking of the different approaches which Jews and Christians have towards the Bible, Müller (1996, p. 136) points that "Judaism in its various versions sees the perspective of the Law as the constituent factor, [whereas] Christian interpretation concentrates on 'the fulfilment aspect', that is, the opening towards a decisive new achievement either in or beyond history". The fulfilment of restoration for Jewish communities in Ezekiel 36 and 37 is the people being returned to the land of Israel, living together in peace under Davidic leader, with the ability to worship and obey Torah which brings recognition to the LORD. They do not necessarily look towards some eschatological future, but they see this as possible in their present, which is evident in the way LXX exegetes the text as it translated, and with MT's plusses and emendations. Our textual-comparative methodology enables us to hear these variants at this micro level.

CHAPTER FIVE

THE TEXT OF EZEKIEL 38

5.1. INTRODUCTION: EZEK. 38

Chapters 38–39 stand together as a sub-block dealing with the destruction of Israel's enemies, yet they are still related to the textual context of the Restoration of Israel. Many scholars see this unit formed by redaction rather than by the original author.[1] However, others have attributed the core of these two chapters to the prophet.[2] Interestingly, most who see these two chapters as later do not discuss the placement of these chapters in 𝔊⁹⁶⁷, which may remove many of their proposed reasons.[3] Yet commentators note their unity, including Block (1998, p. 424), who says "this text provides one of the most impressive examples of typically Ezekielian literary 'halving,' the panels consisting of 38:1–23 and [39]:1–29".[4] While some commentators focus their energies on hypothetical textual re-constructions and the evolution of chapters 38–39, we will continue to concentrate on the text as we have received it in its Hebrew and Greek forms, especially as many of these theories are largely unprovable, and are the result of conjecture and speculation.[5]

---

[1] De Vries (1995, p. 175) is one example who sees the "succession of futuristic formulas in Ezekiel 38–39 as the work of individual redactors who used these as a device for expressing proto-apocalyptic ideals of various kinds". De Vries (1995, pp. 176–177) finds nine "secondary expansions" in these two chapters. However, these proposed 'expansions' appear to form most of these two chapters!

[2] Block (1987, p. 257) says that "in recent years interpreters have become more modest in their understanding of the text, generally acknowledging at least the core of the prophecy as from the prophet himself". Recently Odell (2005, p. 552) commented that "nothing in the oracle suggests that it was composed after the exile, and in fact, the configuration of Gog's army makes good sense in the light of the political dynamics of the seventh and sixth centuries BCE".

[3] See discussions in chapter 7.

[4] Whilst Block has '29' in the body of his text, this is a typographical error for '39'; his footnote has 39 (Block, 1998, p. 424, n. 1). This also occurs in his earlier work (Block, 1997c, p. 91). See Block (1992b, p. 157) for another example of his 'two panel, four frame' breakdown of these two chapters.

[5] For some proposed reconstructions refer to Zimmerli (1983, pp. 296–299), De Vries (1995, pp. 175f.), and Fitzpatrick (2004, pp. 74–81). Also see Ahroni (1977), who argues for post-exilic interpolation.

Both these chapters cover the LORD's military conflict with Gog and his hordes, resulting in their destruction. The placement of these chapters in the block of 36–39 indicates that the destruction of Israel's enemies is part of her restoration. Odell (2005, p. 552) says that "the defeat of Gog becomes the occasion for the full revelation of Yahweh's glory to Israel and the nations. As for Israel, its time of shame and self-loathing comes to an end". It is significant in the context of the book that this conflict takes place before the rebuilding of the Temple. Equally significant is that Israel itself is but a passive observer to the LORD's destruction of Gog and his hordes: Israel does not take an active role in this part of her ultimate restoration, just as in chapters 36–37 all they had to do was 'show up' as the LORD restored them.[6] This aspect is found more so in $\mathfrak{G}^{967}$'s chapter order than in the received order. The LORD intended to restore Israel for the sake of his holy name (36:21–23), so that his name would be known throughout the nations and no longer be defiled (37:28; 38:23; 39:7).

We again find a high degree of uniformity in MT's sense divisions in chapter 38, with all three representative MT MSS agreeing at all points with *setumah* after vv. 9, 13, 16, 17, 23 (except that MT^C has a *petuḥah* after v. 23). MasEzek agrees with the vv. 9 and 13 breaks, but the extant fragment ends after v. 14. MasEzek and MT^{C,A} separate chapters 37 and 38 with a *petuḥah*, yet MT^L uses a *setumah*, suggesting that the earlier communities saw a greater 'distance' between 37 and 38.

As in the previous chapters, the Greek MSS again offer a greater variance with their divisions. $\mathfrak{G}^{967}$ continues 38:1 on the same line immediately after 36:23b, exhibiting its normal two stroke markers. The only other discernible divisions in $\mathfrak{G}^{967}$ are after vv. 16 and 23, therefore dividing chapter 38 into two sections. $\mathfrak{G}^B$ has a long gap after 37:28 with 38:1 beginning on a new line marking a major division. It then has a minor 2 letter break after v. 9; then we find *paragraphoi* at the beginning of vv. 14 and 18 evidencing a break before these verses (vv. 14, 18 start on new lines, the preceding lines being full). However it is indeterminable if these are by the original hand.[7] $\mathfrak{G}^A$ also exhibits a major break before chapter 38:1 with v. 1 starting on a new line. There is only a minor break between chapters 38 and 39. As with

---

[6] See chapter 7 for discussions how the two extant chapter orders exhibit different viewpoints of Israel's involvement.

[7] There is also a one letter space in v. 14, before τάδε λέγει κύριος.

other chapters, 𝕲ᴬ exhibits more divisions than other representative MSS, with evidence of breaks after vv. 2, 9, 13, 14a (before τάδε λέγει κύριος), 16, 21a (after λέγει κύριος).

Overall, there is commonality between MT and LXX, with most MSS representing a major break between chapter 37 and 38 (MasEzek, MTᶜ·ᴬ, 𝕲ᴮ·ᴬ), and generally smaller divisions after vv. 9, 13, 16, 17. In chapter 38 we find that each MT sense division precedes the statement 'thus says the Lᴏʀᴅ',[8] and each division contains a clear oracle from the Lᴏʀᴅ. These oracles, combined with the four in chapter 39, form a total of nine oracle divisions, indicating a clear theological thought in this early 'exegesis'. Modern scholars either add or take from the number of these oracle divisions in chapters 38–39.[9] We will follow these nine MT divisions in our examination of the text in chapters 38 and 39.

5.2. 1ꜱᴛ Oʀᴀᴄʟᴇ: Eᴢᴇᴋ. 38:1–9

As noted above, all MSS exhibit a break before 38:1, and only 𝕲⁹⁶⁷ does not witness a break after v. 9. 𝕲ᴬ has one of its frequent breaks after v. 3a, highlighting the actual speech, and placing the initial identification of Gog into its own division. This pericope establishes that the Lᴏʀᴅ is 'against' Gog (v. 3), and that Gog and his hordes will be drawn out for battle (v. 4f.) against those dwelling securely (MT) or peacefully (LXX) in the land (v. 8), and this invading army will cover the land (v. 9). This oracle has Gog being drawn out, but not with any explicit statement that this will be for Gog's destruction; that tension is left for the final oracle in this chapter (vv. 18–23). The whole mystery surrounding Gog and those with him has captured the imagination of scholars for centuries resulting in a plethora of creative opinions regarding the text and identities of Gog and his hordes. Our focus remains on textual variants in an attempt to determine how Gog was seen in early Jewish

---

[8] The occurrence of 'thus says the Lᴏʀᴅ' as a common sense division marker in the Greek has already been noted in earlier chapters. Here we find this also occurring in the Hebrew text; for further information see Olley (2003, p. 212f.).

[9] Block (1997c, p. 99, n. 58) has noted 'seven' and states this is a prominent number in the Gog oracle: "note the enemies' seven weapons (39:9), the seven years' worth of fuel these provide (39:9), the seven months needed for the burial of the enemies' remains (39:12)".

interpretation, and not on the many modern debates surrounding
Gog's 'identity'.[10] Significantly, LXX transliterates and retains 'Gog',
and, unlike its treatment of other names (cf. vv. 5, 13), does not seek to
provide a contemporary equivalent. Alexander (1974, p. 161) notes that
it is "employed , perhaps, as a general name for any of God's enemies
at the time of the composition of the Septuagint".

38:2 בֶּן־אָדָם שִׂים פָּנֶיךָ אֶל־גּוֹג אֶרֶץ הַמָּגוֹג נְשִׂיא רֹאשׁ (רֹאשׁם :MT[A])
מֶשֶׁךְ וְתֻבָל וְהִנָּבֵא עָלָיו:

38:2 υἱὲ ἀνθρώπου στήρισον τὸ πρόσωπόν σου ἐπὶ (𝕲[967]: Ωγ; 𝕲[B,A]: Γωγ)
καὶ τὴν γῆν τοῦ Μαγωγ ἄρχοντα Ρως (𝕲[967,B]: Μεσοχ; 𝕲[A]: Μοσοχ) καὶ
Θοβελ καὶ προφήτευσον ἐπ᾽ αὐτὸν

MT has אֶרֶץ הַמָּגוֹג ([to][11] the land of Magog), which Allen (1990b,
p. 199) claims is "an early gloss from 39:6". Zimmerli (1983, p. 283)
also sees "a secondary addition" due to the "strange way [it] separates
the name of Gog from his title".[12] Lust (1995c, p. 1001) says "it is
probably a note of an editor who wished to identify Gog with Magog
as one and the same nation, or as a person symbolizing that nation".
However, if this was an MT gloss, it would have been very early as
it is witnessed in MasEzek and in all three representative LXX MSS
(καὶ τὴν γῆν τοῦ Μαγωγ).[13]

---

[10] The identity of Gog and Magog remains a debate amidst the plethora of suggestions both ancient and modern. While now often identified with Neo-Assyrian
Gugu/Gyges (Zimmerli, 1983, p. 301; Allen, 1990, p. 204), there is no main scholarly
consensus, and these "may turn out to be artificial creations" (Block, 1998, p. 434). For
a good recent resource on Gog and Magog see Bøe (2001). Railton (2003) outlines a
number of Christian, Jewish and Muslim interpretations of Gog and Magog through
the centuries. Lust (1995b, pp. 708f. [Gog]; and 999f. [Magog]) also covers a number
of historical and modern suggestions for Gog and Magog's identity. Attempts to align
Gog with Russia in some modern eschatological fulfilment of these chapters is "an
association that, given the changing political climate in the past few years, demands a
careful re-evaluation" (Tanner, 1996, p. 29). Odell (2005, p. 554) suggests "the unit's
context and reworking of Israelite prophetic traditions allow for the possibility that the
name is a cryptic allusion to Nebachadnezzar". However, there is nothing in either
the Hebrew or Greek texts that explicitly support any of these suggestions, other than
that Gog comes from the north.
[11] Cooke (1936, p. 409) says this "should be read *towards the land of Magog*, if a
direction was intended". Block (1998, p. 432) uses 'of' in his translation, as a place
where Gog is from.
[12] Eichrodt (1970, p. 518) also says that it "separates the name Gog from the title
appended to it, so this further description can hardly be original".
[13] Most commentators note that this phase is omitted in the later 𝕲[62], but Block
(1998, p. 432) says that is "probably a case of homoioteleuton".

The primary difference between MT and LXX in this phrase is LXX's plus of the καί copula, which appears to treat Μαγωγ as another people group that Ezekiel is to prophesy about (Cooke, 1936, p. 409; Block, 1998, p. 432). MT appears to have אֶרֶץ הַמָּגוֹג as a place of origin for Gog, as Eichrodt (1970, p. 518) points out, "Magog could possibly mean 'land of Gog'" (also Block, 1998, p. 433).[14] Yet this is a debated point amongst scholars, with some suggesting "the earlier form of the gloss [was] ארצה מגוג 'Magog in his land'" (Allen, 1990b, p. 199). This suggestion treats מָגוֹג as a people group rather than a locale, and thus follows LXX's reading, possibly influenced by 39:6 which may treat מָגוֹג as a people group (cf. discussions on 39:6). Unpointed, ארצה could be a ה of locale, as in Cooke's translation, which would argue against a people group. Another factor is that מָגוֹג appears in Gen. 10:2 and 1Chron. 1:5 as the second son of Japheth.[15] Here it is sufficient to say that in MT's context מָגוֹג appears to indicate a land, perhaps Gog's homeland, whereas LXX's καί plus suggests Μαγωγ is another people group.[16]

There is a minor variant intra-LXX: 𝕲^{B,A} Γωγ, 𝕲^{967} Ωγ. Gehman (in Johnson *et al.*, 1938, p. 128) says 𝕲^{967}'s Ωγ "is probably due to lipography". We may question if 𝕲^{967} was reflecting back in Israel's history to the defeat of Og king of Bashan (Num. 21:33–35), but this is unlikely due to 𝕲^{967}'s use of Γωγ from this point onwards.[17]

---

[14] Kline (1996, p. 215) suggests that מִמְּקוֹמְךָ in Ezek. 38:15 (not discussed here due to absence of discernible variants) is "a substitute for the previous 'land of Magog' (Ezek. 38:2; cf. 39:6). Indeed, the term is probably an etymological play on Magog. *Māqôm* would interpret the *mā-* in Magog (explained either by the Akkadian *māt*, 'land of,' or as the Hebrew noun prefix signifying place)".

[15] Outside of MT Ezekiel, Gog is only found 1Chron. 5:4 where he is listed as a descendent of Reuben; in LXX, Gog also appears in Num. 24:7 (for MT's Agag) and Amos 7:1 where LXX appears to interpret the identity of גֹּבַי as one of MT's locust/ caterpillar. Bøe (2001, p. 89f.) says that "the fact that Magog is the name of a person in the genealogy of Gen 10 is no real objection against [Magog being a land/country], since several of the names in Genesis 10 are names of ancestors founding tribes developing into entire peoples".

[16] LXX's treatment of 'Magog' as a separate people group would most likely have influenced the writer of Revelation to do likewise; see Bøe (2001), Kline (1996), and Tanner (1996).

[17] Lust (1995b, p. 710) mentions that "in the LXX^B version of Deut. 3:1.13; 4:47, Gog stands for Hebrew Og (king of Bashan). Lust also mentions 𝕲^{967}'s reading of 'Og' here, yet without comment.

We also note a rare intra-MT variant wherein MT[A] has רֹאשׁמ [non-final מ] and MT[C,L] רֹאשׁ. This appears to be an error by MT[A]'s scribe.[18]

In vv. 2 and 3 there is a difficulty translating נְשִׂיא רֹאשׁ מֶשֶׁךְ וְתֻבָל. LXX, Symmachus and Theodotion all transliterate רֹאשׁ as Ρως.[19] Most commentators see LXX interpreting רֹאשׁ as an ethnic group against them,[20] yet others set it as as a proper noun of a person called 'Ros', who is the prince/ruler (ἄρχοντα) of Mesoch and Thobel (cf. Brenton). Cooke (1936, p. 409 [cf. p. 415]) states that MT "by its accents intends *rōsh* to be taken as=*head*, and the phrase is to be rendered *chief-head of M. and T.*". Yet Duguid (1994, p. 20) says "*rō'š* is not to be understood here as an adjective ('chief prince') but as a noun in its own right ('prince of the chiefs')". Block (1998, p. 434) points out "the [Hebrew] syntax...is problematic. The issue revolves around whether [רֹאשׁ] is the name of an ethnic group or a common noun. Both LXX ἄρχοντα Ρως and the construct pointing of the Masoretes argue for the former". Yet, after his discussion, Block (1998, p. 435) concluded that,

> if Rosh is to be read as the first in a series of names, the conjunction should precede 'Meshech'. [רֹאשׁ] therefore is best understood as a common noun, appositional to and offering a closer definition of [נְשִׂיא]. Accordingly, *the prince, chief of Meshech and Tubal....* Ezekiel's point is that Gog is not just one of many Anatolian princely figures, but the leader amongst princes and over several tribal/national groups.

In their translations, Block (1998, p. 432), Allen (1990b, p. 197), and Zimmerli (1983, p. 284) all follow MT with Gog as the leader [רֹאשׁ] of these other groups. Interestingly Syriac, Targum, Vulgate, and Aquila (κεφαλῆς), all interpret רֹאשׁ as 'chief/head'. We propose that

---

[18] רֹאשׁמ appears at the end of a line, followed by the first part of שׁ. It appears that the scribe anticipated room for the following word (מֶשֶׁךְ), but not finding sufficient room then wrote מֹשׁךְ on the following line, yet did not delete the letters on the previous line. There are no vowels under the letters remaining on the previous line.

[19] Discussions of רֹאשׁ/Ρως in v. 2 also apply to v. 3, and to 39:1.

[20] Fairbairn (1969, p. 415) suggests that 'Ros' is the name of a people group, saying "traces have been found of a northern people anciently bearing such a name...and the great probability in the opinion, that the people referred to were the Russi, from whom the modern Russians derive their name". However, it is unknown if Ezekiel knew of, or was referring to, this people group. Tanner (1996, p. 30) points out that "if 'Rosh' is not a name place then the etymological connection with Russia is eliminated". However, whilst this may be the concern of the modern eschatological exegete, we question if this was a concern of the LXX translator(s). Tanner (1996, p. 31) says that Ezekiel would "probably not [be referring to] modern Russia" as the name '*Rus*' is a Viking import in the Middle Ages.

MT intended רֹאשׁ as a proper noun, yet LXX interpreted as another
ethnic group against them, just as it did with 'Magog'.[21]

LXX transliterates the other names with slightly alternate spelling
as Μεσοχ/Μοσοχ καὶ Θοβελ. Transliterating these particular names is
a practice found elsewhere in LXX OT (Gen. 10:2, 23; 1Chron. 1:5;
Isa. 66:19: Ezek. 32:26), which may indicate that LXX scribes did not
know the contemporary identification of these countries.[22]

38:3 וְאָמַרְתָּ֗ כֹּ֤ה אָמַר֙ אֲדֹנָ֣י יְהוִ֔ה הִנְנִ֥י אֵלֶ֖יךָ גּ֑וֹג נְשִׂ֕יא רֹ֖אשׁ מֶ֥שֶׁךְ וְתֻבָֽל׃

38:3 καὶ εἰπὸν αὐτῷ τάδε λέγει κύριος κύριος ἰδοὺ ἐγὼ ἐπὶ (𝕲⁹⁶⁷: σε;
𝕲ᴮ: –; 𝕲ᴬ: σὲ Γωγ και) ἄρχοντα Ρως (𝕲⁹⁶⁷: + καὶ) (𝕲⁹⁶⁷,ᴮ: Μεσοχ; 𝕲ᴬ:
Μοσοχ) καὶ Θοβελ

MT's וְאָמַרְתָּ is reflected in LXX (εἰπόν), with a dative pronoun plus:
αὐτῷ, which appears to clarify that speech is directed to Gog as the
overall leader of this gathering.

MT's גּוֹג is minus in both 𝕲⁹⁶⁷,ᴮ (𝕲ᴮ is also minus σέ), yet is represented in 𝕲ᴬ. This may be another later MT plus inserted early
enough for 𝕲ᴬ to witness it, and added to clarify who the speech is
directed towards, as we suggested for LXX's αὐτῷ plus. Without this
plus it reads that the Lᴏʀᴅ is against 'the chief prince' (MT), or 'Ρως'
(𝕲⁹⁶⁷,ᴮ). 𝕲⁹⁶⁷,ᴮ may witness the *Urtext*, which did not explicitly state
'Gog' as the object of the prophecy, but only implied as the 'chief
prince' (cf. our discussions on v. 2). MT's inclusion explicitly states
Gog as the object of the speech. 𝕲ᴬ's σὲ Γωγ καί gives two objects:
Γωγ and ἄρχοντα Ρως. 𝕲⁹⁶⁷'s καί plus can either refer to either just a
single person, or may permit three objects ('ἐπὶ σε ἄρχοντα Ρως και
Μεσοχ καὶ Θοβελ; see v. 2 above for discussions of 'רֹאשׁ/Ρως'). The
possible absence of 'Gog' in the *Urtext* may have influenced LXX's
treatment of 'Rosh'.

38:4 וְשׁוֹבַבְתִּ֗יךָ וְנָתַתִּ֤י חַחִים֙ בִּלְחָיֶ֔יךָ וְהוֹצֵאתִ֣י אוֹתְךָ֗ וְאֶת־כָּל־חֵילֶ֔ךָ
סוּסִ֣ים וּפָרָשִׁ֔ים לְבֻשֵׁ֥י מִכְל֖וֹל כֻּלָּ֑ם קָהָ֤ל רָב֙ צִנָּ֣ה וּמָגֵ֔ן
תֹּפְשֵׂ֥י חֲרָב֖וֹת כֻּלָּֽם׃

38:4 καὶ συνάξω σε καὶ πᾶσαν τὴν δύναμίν σου ἵππους καὶ ἱππεῖς
ἐνδεδυμένους θώρακας πάντας συναγωγὴ πολλὴ πέλται καὶ περικεφαλαῖαι
καὶ μάχαιραι

---

[21] Both LXX transliterations should be considered together, as the same thought of
another ethnic group as an enemy against them appears to be the influencing factor.
[22] For discussions on the identity of possible countries and/or people groups for
these various nouns, either ancient or modern, refer to modern commentaries, and
also Bøe (2001) and Tanner (1996).

MT's וְשׁוֹבַבְתִּיךָ וְנָתַתִּי חַחִים בִּלְחָיֶיךָ ('and I will turn you back, and I will put hooks into your jaws') is minus in LXX. Block (1998, p. 437) suggests that "LXX condenses MT's three verbs…into one". We find וְשֹׁבַבְתִּיךָ again in 39:2, but there LXX translates with καὶ συνάξω σε. MT also uses שׁוּב in 39:27 where LXX has ἀποστρέψαι (ἀποστρέφω) which captures the correct sense of 'bring back', indicating that LXX is well aware of this usage of שׁוּב. Zimmerli (1983, p. 284) also notes the occurrence of καὶ συνάξω σε for וְשֹׁבַבְתִּיךָ in 39:2 and says "this raises the question whether 𝔊 in 38:4 did not also have וְשׁוֹבַבְתִּי before it, while in the original then the words וְנַתְתִּי חַחִים בלחייך…might have been missing". However, in 38:4 LXX's use of συνάξω fits better with וְהוֹצֵאתִי and not וְשֹׁבַבְתִּיךָ, indicating that the former verb may have been the beginning of v. 4 in LXX's *Vorlage*. The phrase 'hooks in your jaws' is also found in 29:4,[23] and fully translated by LXX, again raising the question as to why LXX would not translate this phrase. Thus, either this phrase was minus in 38:4 in LXX's *Vorlage*, or it was omitted on purpose or by accident. It is doubtful that LXX would purposefully leave out such a strong statement against Gog, leaving either accidental omission, or that it was minus in LXX's *Vorlage*, with the latter as the most likely occurrence.

As such, this phrase appears to be a later MT gloss. Allen (1990b, p. 200) says that it is "a gloss intended for 39:2 [but] was misplaced here because of the similarity of context". Allen (1990b, p. 200) also suggests that "at some stage in the LXX's *Vorlage* a full text like that of MT had been revised against a shorter text but carelessly a wrong run of words was struck out". This is possible, along with the other variants in vv. 2, 3. This phrase is witnessed by MasEzek, which indicates early inclusion into the Hebrew text, and raises the question as to why later LXX MSS such as 𝔊^A did not include it. This may be another MT plus added after 𝔊^A's *Vorlage*. Theodotion includes this phrase, but with a horse-riding rather than 'fishing' analogy: καὶ περιστπέψω σε, καὶ ἐγὼ δώσω παγίδας εἰς τὰς σιαγόνας σου ('and I will wheel you around, and I will put a bridle in your jaws') (Field, 1964, p. 871; Ziegler,

---

[23] The imagery of 'hooks' for captives is also found in Hab. 1:15 and Amos 4:2. Odell (2005, p. 554) states that "Yahweh's use of hooks has parallels in the Assyrian traditions for subjugating rebellious kings. Biblical references to hooks outside of Ezekiel have a similar connotation of control that stops short of destruction".

1977, p. 272).²⁴ Wevers (1982, p. 202) claims MT's analogy "is a late expansion based on the oracle against Pharaoh, 29.4". Block (1998, p. 437) appears to disagree saying this "introduce[s] a notion foreign to the present context". MT may have been influenced by 29:4 and 39:2, combining both concepts here as a gloss to interpret how they saw Gog and his forces would be 'brought out' (וְהוֹצֵאתִי): they would be turned and drawn out like a fish on a hook, perhaps going in a direction Gog did not initially intend nor, keeping in mind the oracle's context of destruction, to a place where Gog would not want to go.

LXX translates MT's וְהוֹצֵאתִי אוֹתְךָ (hiph.: 'I will lead you out', or 'I will cause you to go out'), with καὶ συνάξω σε ('and I will gather you'). We question why LXX did not use καὶ ἐξάξω ὑμᾶς as in 11:9; 20:34 (also Exod. 6:6; 7:4, 5; Isa. 65:9). This may indicate LXX's view that Gog will be 'gathered/assembled' for destruction, which interprets MT's action of 'leading out'. Equally curious is MT's use of יצא, as the *hiphil* is typically used both in Ezekiel and in Exodus in relationship to God's 'bringing' Israel out of Egypt. This may indicate that MT saw the bringing out of Israel's enemies to their destruction as part of the ultimate restoration of Israel, a point which we find with the placement of chapters 38–39 in this block.²⁵ Israel cannot be fully restored if they remain under the threat of their enemies.

MT has לְבֻשֵׁי מִכְלוֹל ('perfectly clothed' [BDB/*HALOT*], or 'those clothed in perfection' [*DCH*]), whereas LXX has ἐνδεδυμένους θώρακας πάντας ('all dressed in breastplates'). In the other occurrence of מִכְלוֹל (23:12), LXX has ἐνδεδυκότας εὐπάρυφα ('clothed with purple') which reflects MT. Yet here, LXX seems to interpret how an army would be perfectly clothed, that is, in 'breastplates'. LXX may have been guessing regarding this 'perfect clothing', or more likely, reflecting and interpreting how the soldiers were equipped in their day.

MT has this army carrying צִנָּה וּמָגֵן ('large [body shield] and small shields'), or as most EVV 'buckler and shields', whereas LXX has πέλται

---

²⁴ Block (1998, p. 442) notes the first phrase of וְשׁוֹבַבְתִּיךָ ('and I will turn you around') "suggests the image of horsemen turning their steeds around (cf. v. 4b), a metaphor well chosen for peoples who come from a region renowned in antiquity for its horses". However, the metaphor for the second phrase is that of a hook in the jaw of a fish, and it is our point that Theodotion's wording only captures the first metaphor and not the second.

²⁵ This point stands regardless of the placement as in the received chapter order, or as in 𝔊⁹⁶⁷, as both have the context of the destruction of Israel's enemies as part of their full restoration.

καὶ περικεφαλαῖαι ('shield and helmet'). Allen (1990b, p. 200) notes that 'body shield' "is not suitable for cavalry" and says in general that "the words appear to be an explanatory gloss on מכלול 'panoply'...with כלם 'all of them' functioning as a cue word". He (1990b, p. 200) also says LXX's translation "appears to presuppose מגן וכובע 'small shield and helmet' as in 5b" (also in 27:10). While this is likely the case, we question if LXX is again adjusting the meaning to match how contemporary cavalry soldiers were equipped. MT also says תֹּפְשֵׂי חֲרָבוֹת כֻּלָּם ('all of them handling/wielding swords') referring to action of the horsemen, yet LXX has only καὶ μάχαιραι ('and swords') as just part of the equipment list previously mentioned. Some commentators delete the entire line in MT saying it is "a gloss on gorgeous attire" (Cooke, 1936, p. 410). If the 'handling/wielding' swords (תֹּפְשֵׂי) was a gloss, then we may suggest it was added to emphasise Gog's strength that would soon be cut down. Yet it is represented in all LXX MSS, so if a gloss, it must have been very early. However, we are left with explicit points regarding how LXX viewed Gog's forces would be equipped.

38:5 פָּרַס כּוּשׁ וּפוּט אִתָּם כֻּלָּם מָגֵן וְכוֹבָע׃

38:5 Πέρσαι καὶ Αἰθίοπες καὶ Λίβυες πάντες περικεφαλαίαις καὶ πέλταις

LXX uses equivalent Greek names of inhabitants, where MT lists the names of countries:[26]

פָּרַס—Πέρσαι—Persians;
כּוּשׁ—Αἰθίοπες (𝔊ᴮ Αιθιοπαις)[27]—Ethiopians;
וּפוּט—Λίβυες—Libyans;
𝔊ᴬˢ plus καὶ λυδοί adds Ludians to the list of enemies, perhaps because of their previous listing as allies of Tyre and Egypt (27:10; 30:5).

LXX's use of Greek names for the inhabitants of these countries is another example of the translator interpreting the text for his community.

---

[26] Speculation continues amongst scholars regarding the identity of these people groups, yet this is outside our sphere. For possible identities see Bøe (2001, pp. 99–107).

[27] A later corrector has written ε above the αι; thus one has B* with –αις and Bᶜ –ες. In 30:4, 9 LXX lists the country (Αἰθίοπία).

LXX also reverses the order of 'shield and helmet' and makes them both plural (perhaps to match MT's collective). Many delete the reference to 'shield and helmet' believing it is carried over from v. 4 with כֻּלָּם as a "cue word" (Block, 1998, p. 437). Yet it appears in all representative MSS. It does appear confusing at times when commentators say that v. 4 evidences glosses based on v. 5, and then state the glosses in v. 5 are based on v. 4! Cooke (1936, p. 410) speculatively maintains that "the entire verse...has found its way into the text from the margin". However, there is no textual evidence for Cooke's suggestion.

38:6 גֹּמֶר וְכָל־אֲגַפֶּיהָ בֵּית תּוֹגַרְמָה יַרְכְּתֵי צָפוֹן וְאֶת־כָּל־אֲגַפָּיו עַמִּים רַבִּים אִתָּךְ

38:6 Γομερ καὶ πάντες οἱ περὶ αὐτόν οἶκος τοῦ Θεργαμα ἀπ᾽ ἐσχάτου βορρᾶ καὶ πάντες οἱ περὶ αὐτόν καὶ ἔθνη πολλὰ μετὰ σοῦ

Here, and in v. 22, MT has וְכָל־אֲגַפָּיו ('all his band/army' [BDB], or 'troops' [HALOT]), while LXX in both occurrences says καὶ πάντες οἱ περὶ αὐτόν ('and all those around him'). Theodotion has "καὶ πάντα τὰ ὑποστηρίγματα αὐτοῦ" ('and all his supporters') (Ziegler, 1977, p. 273). Block (1998, p. 437) says that אֲגַפִּים [אֲגַף] "is a genuinely Ezekielian word, occurring outside this context (cf. vv. 9, 22; 39:4) only in 12:14 and 17:21". LXX translates the same way in each occurrence in chapters 38–39. The translator of 12:14 (Thackeray's α) used καὶ πάντας τοὺς ἀντιλαμβανομένους αὐτοῦ ('and all those helping him'). In 17:21 the translator took two Hebrew words (one with a *ketiv/qere* variant), and translated with one noun (παρατάξει) and a pronoun, without giving a specific equivalence for אֲגַפָּיו. Overall, we may suggest that אֲגַפָּיו as 'his band/army' may have been unknown to the LXX translator(s) and even to Theodotion, and hence their use of οἱ περὶ αὐτον and τὰ ὑποστηρίγματα respectively. However, both these words do catch the basic meaning that all those tied to Gomer would be included.

38:7 הִכֹּן וְהָכֵן לְךָ אַתָּה וְכָל־קְהָלֶךָ הַנִּקְהָלִים עָלֶיךָ וְהָיִיתָ לָהֶם לְמִשְׁמָר:

38:7 ἑτοιμάσθητι (𝔊ᴬ: + καὶ) ἑτοίμασον σεαυτὸν σὺ καὶ πᾶσα ἡ συναγωγή σου οἱ (𝔊⁹⁶⁷: ἐπισυνηγμένοι; 𝔊ᴮ·ᴬ: συνηγμένοι) μετὰ σοῦ καὶ ἔσῃ μοι εἰς προφυλακήν

𝔊ᴬ's καί copula plus follows MT, and allows for a smoother reading. 𝔊⁹⁶⁷·ᴮ's minus of the copula brings out the 'sharpness' of the imperative clearer than MT or 𝔊ᴬ. Zimmerli (1983, p. 286) says "𝔊 makes it more concise here by omitting the copula", yet he does not note that the copula is present in 𝔊ᴬ.

MT has לָהֶם ('to *them*'), while LXX has μοι ('to/for *me*'). Block (1998, p. 437) concludes that MT is preferable. However Zimmerli (1983, p. 286) says "𝕲, which refers the משמר to submission to Yahweh (לי), has probably preserved the original reading". Zimmerli (1983, p. 286) observes that "in 𝔐 one will think rather of the function of care and protection which the commander exercises towards his troops" (cf. Block, 1998, p. 443). We must question why MT would adjust from Zimmerli's proposed לי to לָהֶם, which moves the theological focus from God as commander to Gog as leader and carer of his troops. Rather, we propose that LXX exhibits theological exegesis stating clearly that God as commander is leading Gog and his hordes: God is the one in charge of the battle and Gog is an instrument in his hand. Wevers (1982, p. 202) says that "God and his hordes are commanded to be in Yahweh's service ready for the call to action" (cf. REB: 'hold yourself at my disposal'). This theological shift from MT may have brought a sense of comfort to the LXX community, alleviating fears of an enemy about to conquer them again, whereby God is commanding and leading Gog and his hordes to their destruction. Gog's destruction is his service to God![28]

There is a small intra-LXX variance wherein 𝕲[967] says ἐπισυνηγμένοι, 𝕲[B,A] having the shorter συνηγμένοι. While both mean 'gather/bring together', the prefix ἐπί- suggests a more hostile 'against' (cf. Micah 4:11; Zech. 12:3; 1Macc. 3:58; 40:12).

38:8 מִיָּמִים רַבִּים תִּפָּקֵד בְּאַחֲרִית הַשָּׁנִים תָּבוֹא אֶל־אֶרֶץ מְשׁוֹדֶבֶת
מֵחֶרֶב מְקֻבֶּצֶת מֵעַמִּים רַבִּים עַל הָרֵי יִשְׂרָאֵל אֲשֶׁר־הָיוּ לְחָרְבָּה תָּמִיד
וְהִיא מֵעַמִּים הוּצָאָה וְיָשְׁבוּ לָבֶטַח כֻּלָּם:

38:8 ἀφ' ἡμερῶν πλειόνων ἑτοιμασθήσεται καὶ ἐπ' ἐσχάτου ἐτῶν (𝕲[B,A]: + ἐλεύσεται καὶ) ἥξει εἰς τὴν γῆν τὴν ἀπεστραμμένην ἀπὸ μαχαίρας συνηγμένων ἀπὸ ἐθνῶν πολλῶν (𝕲[967, B]: ἐπὶ γῆν Ισραηλ; 𝕲[A]: εἰς τὴν γῆν τοῦ Ισραηλ) ἣ ἐγενήθη ἔρημος δι' ὅλου καὶ (𝕲[967,A]: αὐτός; 𝕲[B]: οὗτος) ἐξ ἐθνῶν ἐξελήλυθεν καὶ κατοικήσουσιν ἐπ' εἰρήνης ἅπαντες

MT's תִּפָּקֵד *nif.* refers to being summoned militarily (cf. Jer. 15:3; 51:27; [*HALOT*]). The *pi'el* means 'muster' (cf. Isa. 13:4), which may permit the

---

[28] Zimmerli (1983, p. 286) captures this in his translation: "and you will be at <my> service". Odell (2005, p. 555) also notes that this command "establishes Gog as Yahweh's agent". In his commentary section, Zimmerli (1983, p. 306) said "if v. 7b is correctly reconstructed on the basis of 𝕲, it refers the command to be ready specifically to readiness for 'obedience' (משמר) to Yahweh".

niphal as 'mustered' (cf. NRSV).[29] However, LXX has ἑτοιμασθήσεται (3ps) with the meaning 'to cause to be ready, put/keep in readiness, prepare' [BAGD]. This follows the double use of ἑτοιμάζω in v. 7, and may be used here to maintain an ongoing theme. Yet, LXX may be seen as interpreting the intent of MT's 'summoned': he will be prepared (for destruction).

MT twice says '*you*' [will be summoned/will come], whereas LXX twice says '*he*' [will be prepared/will come]. Both refer to Gog, but MT is preferred as it still keeps the context of the oracle directly addressing Gog (cf. v. 4f.). LXX appears clumsy as it shifts from the second person in v. 7, to the third person in v. 8, then back to the second in v. 9. The third person appears as a narration rather than God's speech to Gog through the prophet, which continues from v. 4. Zimmerli (1983, p. 286) believes LXX 'misunderstands' the Hebrew 2ms as being 3fs. It is true that the 3fs "assume the lands as the subject, but the following *killām*, 'all of them,' has the people in mind" (Block, 1998, p. 438). LXX may have been influenced by the pronoun וְהִיא (3fs 'she/it') in agreement with אֶרֶץ later in the verse. Yet LXX has the masculine (𝔊[B] οὗτος, 𝔊[967,A] αὐτός);[30] possibly LXX initially reading a 2ms as 3fs, and then interpreting a 3fs pronoun as ms. LXX possibly uses its ms to refer to 'Ἰσραηλ', as it is odd saying that 'a land' is brought out as MT states (we note both MT and LXX finish with 3pl).

For MT בְּאַחֲרִית הַשָּׁנִים ('in the latter years') LXX has ἐπ' ἐσχάτου ἐτῶν ('in the last years'). Block (1997c, p. 100) points out that "although LXX renders...with ἔσχατος, it is not clear that the end of time is in mind. The reference may be simply to a later time, when the historical phase of the exile is over and the new period of settlement in the land has arrived".

MT says 'you will come to אֶל־אֶרֶץ ("to *a* land")', whereas LXX says 'he shall come εἰς τὴν γῆν ("to *the* land")'. LXX's addition of the definite article may have theological significance by establishing which land—*the* land: for them there is only one 'land', Israel. 𝔊[B,A] have καὶ

---

[29] However, Odell (2005, p. 470) argues against 'mustered' (NRSV), stating that the *niphal* and *qal* meanings cannot be interchanged; and says that this "verse thus suggests not that Gog is mustered to go up against the land of Israel, but that he has fallen away from his duty. His attack therefore constitutes a defiance of Yahweh's plan to restore the land and people of Israel (cf. 34:11–13, 25–27; 36:6–10, 24, 32; 37:13, 21–22)".

[30] The phrase following αὐτός in 𝔊[A] has the word order reversed. Normally we do not mention this practice unless it has possible theological meaning, but this is just another minor point regarding the textual anomalies in this verse.

ἐλεύσεται as a plus leading into this phrase, which creates a rather clumsy reading; 𝕲⁹⁶⁷ follows MT.

MT has הָרֵי יִשְׂרָאֵל ('the mountains of Israel'), yet LXX has γῆν Ισραηλ ('[the] land of Israel'). It is difficult to determine which is the 'correct' reading, but as much of chapters 36–39 relate to the 'mountains' of Israel, MT is preferred. This is the only occurrence of הָרֵי יִשְׂרָאֵל out of 15 in Ezekiel in which LXX uses γῆ Ισραηλ.[31] It is unclear why LXX would use γῆ, especially when these two chapters makes it clear that Gog's destruction will be upon the mountains of Israel (cf. 39:2, 4, 17). MT may have performed a later editorial work here at a similar time to 38:21 where LXX is also minus ὄρη, and in both locales MT specifies 'the mountains' as the place of the conflict between God and Gog. Cooke (1936, p. 411) notes that "the expression [upon the mountains] is inconsistent with the deliberate vagueness of the previous clause".[32] Picking up on Cooke's point, we suggest that the surrounding context refers to the entire land (cf. vv. 8, 11, 12, 16, 18), and only here specifically to the mountains of Israel, and so LXX interprets 'mountains' to refer to the whole land and translates accordingly. The use of γῆ may reflect a different *Vorlage*.

While 𝕲⁹⁶⁷,ᴮ have ἐπί for MT's עַל, 𝕲ᴬ has εἰς, and adds τοῦ before Ισραηλ, which appears to have the enemy only coming 'into' and not 'against' the land. 𝕲⁹⁶⁷ also does not represent MT's following אֲשֶׁר (𝕲ᴮ,ᴬ: ἥ).

LXX use of ὅλου for MT's תָּמִיד is rather curious, as ὅλου is normally used for כֹּל. We again find תָּמִיד in 39:14 for the 'continual' employment of those who seek out the remains of the battle (LXX διὰ παντός). תָּמִיד is typically used in Torah and elsewhere in relation to sacrifices, a context found in Ezek. 46:14, 15 (also διὰ παντός). Ezekiel may have been performing a pun stating that the desolation of the mountains was due to the unsanctioned sacrifices held there (cf. 6:2, 3). If so, this was missed by LXX's translator(s).

---

[31] הָרֵי יִשְׂרָאֵל is found in 6:2, 3; 19:9; 33:28; 34:13, 14; 35:12; 36:1 (2x), 4, 8; 38:8; 39:2, 4, 17. Block (1998, p. 444) points out that "v. 8 may be interpreted as a shorthand version of Ezekiel's salvation oracles, especially 36:1–15, addressed to the mountains of Israel and highlighting the restoration of its population".

[32] Zimmerli (1983, p. 307) says "in mysterious secrecy the 'mountains of Israel' are not instantly named as the goal of Gog's campaign, but these mountains are spoken of as a land whose population…has been brought back from having been slaughtered by the sword (37:1–14) and has been gathered together again from among the many nations (20:32ff.)".

38:9 וְעָלִיתָ כַּשֹּׁאָה תָבוֹא כֶּעָנָן לְכַסּוֹת הָאָרֶץ אַתָּה וְכָל־אֲגַפֶּיךָ
וְעַמִּים רַבִּים אוֹתָךְ

38:9 καὶ ἀναβήσῃ ὡς ὑετὸς καὶ ἥξεις (𝕲ᴮ: ἥξει) ὡς νεφέλη κατακαλύψαι
γῆν καὶ (𝕲⁹⁶⁷: ἔσῃ; 𝕲ᴮ: ἔσει; 𝕲ᴬ: πέσῃ) σὺ καὶ πάντες οἱ περὶ σὲ καὶ
ἔθνη πολλὰ μετὰ σοῦ

MT says Gog and his bands will come upon the land כַּשֹּׁאָה, which
has the basic meaning of 'as a storm/destruction/desolation', and, as
in the present context, 'a storm that breaks out violently and suddenly'
[*HALOT*]. LXX translates with ὑετός 'heavy rain' [LEH], which does
not capture the full sense of שׁוֹאָה. As שׁוֹאָה is not found elsewhere in
Ezekiel,[33] we may suggest that LXX reflected on the 'cloud' to arrive
with ὑετός. LXX may have been seeking to lessen the severity of Gog's
coming. However, Theodotion (Ziegler, 1977, p. 273) later adjusts
towards MT by using the more appropriate καταιγίς ('a sudden blast of
wind' [LS]' or 'rushing storm' [Thayer]). Symmachus goes in a different
direction by using ἐξαίφνης ('suddenly' [LS]), indicating the speed in
which he saw Gog coming against the land. Both appear to go against
any attempt of LXX to lessen the severity with its use of ὑετός.

LXX also appears to have difficulty dealing with MT's תִּהְיֶה, perhaps
viewing it as referring to the following words and so inserting καί which
Zimmerli (1983, p. 287) says "is an inelegant secondary insertion which
disrupts the syntactical context". Whilst representing תִּהְיֶה, LXX's καί
plus causes ἔσῃ/ἔσει to refer to the following phrase, reading 'and
you will be, you and all with you'. The translator may be excused, as
we may presume that the Hebrew before him did not have the *atnach*
found in MT, supplied by the later Masoretes, which places תִּהְיֶה with
the preceding phrase. On the other hand, if the Masoretes had put the
atnach under הָאָרֶץ the text could read '...the land, you will be [there],
you and your bands...', which would support LXX (not counting their
καί plus). However, more perplexing is 𝕲ᴬ which also has the καί plus,
but distinct from 𝕲⁹⁶⁷,ᴮ, has πέσῃ causing the text to read 'and it will
fall', apparently referring back to either ὑετός or νεφέλη. 𝕲ᴬ may
have been influenced by 39:4 which has the same wording, but there
in reference to Gog falling and being devoured on the mountains of
Israel (cf. 39:1). Therefore, 𝕲ᴬ may have been stating, as in 39:4, that
Gog and 'those with you' will quickly fall as rain upon the land. This

---

[33] Zimmerli (1983, p. 307) translates שׁוֹאָה as 'thunderstorm' here and says it "might
have come from Is. 10:3".

is different to the sense of both MT and $\mathfrak{G}^{967,B}$, which have Gog coming like rain and so numerous even as a cloud covering the land.[34] $\mathfrak{G}^A$
may be seeking to bring comfort to the reader by exegeting the end
result of destruction as found in 39:4, saying that when Israel sees the
enemy covering their land as rain or a cloud, they should know that
the enemy is there for the purpose of 'falling'. Ziegler (1977, p. 273)
also notes the use of πέσῃ, and the influence from 39:4.

5.3. 2ND ORACLE: EZEK. 38:10–13

As noted above, all MT MSS and $\mathfrak{G}^{B,A}$ exhibit a sense division break
after v. 9 (except $\mathfrak{G}^{967}$ which has vv. 1–16 in the one sense division).
MT's next break comes after v. 13, as in $\mathfrak{G}^A$. $\mathfrak{G}^B$ does not evidence
another break until the end of v. 17, which places three MT sense
divisions into the one.

The previous oracle (vv. 1–9) describes what God will do. In this
oracle, the LORD speaks to Gog, revealing Gog's personal reasons for
attacking Israel. God is presented as being in complete control. Gog's
reasons include the potential spoils of war (vv. 12–13) from an easy target
(v. 11). The people living in the land in v. 12 echoes the repopulation
found in chapter 36:10, 33.

38:11 וְאָמַרְתָּ אֶעֱלֶה עַל־אֶרֶץ פְּרָזוֹת אָבוֹא הַשֹּׁקְטִים יֹשְׁבֵי לָבֶטַח
כֻּלָּם יֹשְׁבִים בְּאֵין חוֹמָה וּבְרִיחַ וּדְלָתַיִם אֵין לָהֶם:

38:11 καὶ ἐρεῖς ἀναβήσομαι ἐπὶ γῆν ἀπερριμμένην ἥξω ἐπὶ ἡσυχάζον-
τας ($\mathfrak{G}^{B,A}$: ἐν ἡσυχία; $\mathfrak{G}^{967}$: -) καὶ οἰκοῦντας ἐπ' εἰρήνης πάντας κατοικοῦντας ($\mathfrak{G}^B$: γῆν; $\mathfrak{G}^A$: πολεις; $\mathfrak{G}^{967}$: -) ἐν ᾗ οὐχ ὑπάρχει τεῖχος οὐδὲ
μοχλοί καὶ ($\mathfrak{G}^{967}$: θύρεοι; $\mathfrak{G}^{B,A}$: θύραι) οὐκ εἰσὶν αὐτοῖς

MT says they will come עַל־אֶרֶץ פְּרָזוֹת ('to a land of un-walled towns'),
where LXX has ἐπὶ γῆν ἀπερριμμένην ('to a land being rejected/
discarded').[35] Whilst the context indicates that the towns are without
walls due to the people living safely and/or securely in the land (cf.
vv. 11b, 12), LXX appears to interpret this as a state of being devastated. LXX could also be giving a postexilic interpretation that the

---

[34] Block (1998, p. 444) also says the two nouns in the Hebrew are "a metaphor for
a sudden invasion by vast numbers of troops".

[35] The literal meaning of ἀπορρίπτω is "to throw away, to put away; to reject; to
abandon" [LEH]; also "to cast forth from one's country" [LS].

villages are unprotected and un-walled because God has rejected or discarded them. LXX's passive perfect participle suggests they saw this 'rejecting/discarding' still ongoing.

𝔊^{B,A} have a unique plus of ἐν ἡσυχίᾳ ('in stillness/quiet') that is not witnessed in MT or 𝔊^{967}. Johnson (in Johnson *et al.*, 1938, p. 8) says that this as minus in 𝔊^{967} "may be due to ησυχαζοντας in the preceding line, but the phrase is not in our present Hebrew text". Lust (2002a, p. 386) states this is not a case of *homoioteleuton* in 𝔊^{967}, noting it is also minus in the Vetus Latina Codex Wirceburgensis (*W*). Thus, 𝔊^{B,A} strengthen the description of those in the land living in rest and peace.

We also find an implicit LXX interpretation where MT says יֹשְׁבֵי לָבֶטַח ('those living in safety', or 'living securely'), and LXX says οἰκοῦντας ἐπ' εἰρήνης ('those living in peace'). LXX clarifies again that to live safely or securely is to live in peace. The concept of 'peaceful living' may be found in the Hebrew (הַשֹּׁקְטִים יֹשְׁבֵי לָבֶטַח 'the peaceful ones who live securely' [*HALOT*]), yet LXX makes this point explicit.

MT's כֻּלָּם יֹשְׁבִים בְּאֵין חוֹמָה ('all of them dwelling without walls') is witnessed by 𝔊^{967}. However, the other two LXX MSS have their own unique plusses, clarifying the place where they are dwelling without walls: 𝔊^{B} κατοικοῦντας γῆν ('inhabiting *a land*'), and 𝔊^{A} κατοικοῦντας πόλεις ('inhabiting *cities*'). The change from 𝔊^{B}'s *land* to 𝔊^{A}'s *cities* may indicate that in 𝔊^{A}'s time 'Israel' is not just a land, but found in whatever city the people now inhabit. Yet, more likely, 𝔊^{A} interprets where in the land that the people are now dwelling; in cities.

At the end of this verse 𝔊^{B,A}'s θύραι matches MT's דֶּלֶת, 'doors'. Yet 𝔊^{967} has an interesting variant of θύρεοι, which means an "oblong shield (shaped like a door)" [LEH], or 'a stone put against a door to keep it shut' [LS].[36] Gehman (in Johnson *et al.*, 1938, p. 129) says that "θύρεοι is never used as a rendering for דלתים, while θυρα frequently represents דלת". It is difficult to know why 𝔊^{967} used θύρεοι, other than as a word play to state they live without walls, bars or shields.

38:12 לִשְׁלֹל שָׁלָל וְלָבֹז בַּז לְהָשִׁיב יָדְךָ עַל־חֳרָבוֹת נוֹשָׁבֹת וְאֶל־עַם מְאֻסָּף מִגּוֹיִם עֹשֶׂה מִקְנֶה וְקִנְיָן יֹשְׁבֵי עַל־טַבּוּר הָאָרֶץ:

38:12 προνομεῦσαι προνομὴν καὶ σκυλεῦσαι σκῦλα αὐτῶν τοῦ ἐπιστρέψαι χεῖρά μου εἰς τὴν ἠρημωμένην ἣ κατῳκίσθη καὶ ἐπ' ἔθνος συνηγμένον

---

[36] Gehman (in Johnson *et al.*, 1938, p. 129) also says "in Classical Greek epic θυρεος is a door-stone, placed by Polyphemus at the mouth of his den".

ἀπὸ ἐθνῶν πολλῶν πεποιηκότας κτήσεις κατοικοῦντας ἐπὶ τὸν ὀμφαλὸν τῆς γῆς

MT says לְהָשִׁיב יָדְךָ ('to turn *your* hand'), yet LXX has τοῦ ἐπιστρέψαι χεῖρά μου ('to turn *my* hand').[37] Cooke (1936, p. 412) says that LXX's "*my hand*, [is] more consistent, but not necessarily right: the writer forgets for the moment that Gog is speaking". However, it is difficult to know where Gog's proposed speech from v. 11 finishes and where God resumes as the direct speaker (both MT and LXX have God as the direct speaker in v. 13). MT appears to finish Gog's speech after בָּ in the opening phrase with its use of '*your* hand'. However, LXX's '*my* hand' appears to continue Gog's monologue throughout v. 12. On the other hand it may be that LXX has the LORD as subject of the action against the desolate places. If so, this again could be LXX's view that the desolate places were the result of God having rejected them.

LXX's πολλῶν plus ('many [nations]') seems to expand the plurality of their scattering (cf. v. 16a). MT also includes מִקְנֶה וְקִנְיָן ('cattle and possessions', cf. v. 13), with LXX one embracing κτήσεις ('property'). Zimmerli (1983, p. 287) notes that the two Hebrew words "are not attested elsewhere in Ezekiel".

Some scholars suggest a similarity between טַבּוּר (lit. 'height') and Mount Tabor (cf. Zimmerli, 1983, p. 311; Cooper, 1994, p. 338). However, if this connection was intended by Ezekiel, it is not represented in LXX's ὀμφαλός ('centre/navel'). Block (1997c, p. 101, n. 66) says that "the interpretation of תַּבּוּר [sic] as 'navel' is as ancient as LXX but should be abandoned", and retains the meaning, 'top of the world'. The only other occurrence of טַבּוּר is Jud. 9:37 where it has the meaning 'centre' or 'middle' [of Israel]. Fairbairn (1989, p. 425) suggests טַבּוּר "may include the two points—of a prominent position, and of great fullness of blessing; on both accounts fitted to awaken the envy of others". Surprisingly, *HALOT* gives only the meaning 'navel' and as "the centre of the land (or of the earth)", although all its citations are late (except Jud. 9:37), and cites LXX and Vulgate in support. BDB has 'highest part, centre', covering both bases, yet in the explanation BDB also takes on LXX's meaning of 'navel'. LXX's ὀμφαλός ('navel' [LEH]; or 'anything central—like a navel' [LS]), captures MT's metaphor, and may be speaking out of the theology of early Judaism, that Israel and

---

[37] This is for 𝕲⁹⁶⁷,ᴮ,ᴬ and Ziegler, yet Ralph has σου along with later LXX (e.g., 𝕲⁶²).

Jerusalem is the 'centre' or 'navel' of the world (Cooke, 1936, p. 412f.; Zimmerli, 1983, p. 311).[38]

38:13 שְׁבָא וּדְדָן וְסֹחֲרֵי תַרְשִׁישׁ וְכָל־כְּפִרֶיהָ יֹאמְרוּ לְךָ הֲלִשְׁלֹל
שָׁלָל אַתָּה בָא הֲלָבֹז בַּז הִקְהַלְתָּ קְהָלֶךָ לָשֵׂאת כֶּסֶף וְזָהָב
לָקַחַת מִקְנֶה וְקִנְיָן לִשְׁלֹל שָׁלָל גָּדוֹל:

38:13 Σαβα καὶ Δαιδαν καὶ ἔμποροι (𝕲⁹⁶⁷: Καρχηδόνιος; 𝕲ᴮ: Καρχηδόνιοι; 𝕲ᴬ: Χαλκηδονος) καὶ πᾶσαι αἱ (𝕲⁹⁶⁷,ᴮ: κῶμαι αὐτῶν; 𝕲ᴬ: χῶμαι αὐτῆς) ἐροῦσίν σοι εἰς προνομὴν τοῦ προνομεῦσαι σὺ ἔρχῃ καὶ σκυλεῦσαι σκῦλα συνήγαγες συναγωγήν σου λαβεῖν ἀργύριον καὶ χρυσίον ἀπενέγκασθαι κτῆσιν τοῦ σκυλεῦσαι σκῦλα

MT gives 'merchants of סֹחֲרֵי תַרְשִׁישׁ' (Tarshish) as one of Gog's allies,[39] while 𝕲⁹⁶⁷ identify their origins as Καρχηδόνιος (of Carthage), 𝕲ᴮ Καρχηδόνιοι ('Carthaginian', cf. 27:12, 25), and 𝕲ᴬ as Χαλκηδόνος ('of Chalcedon'). Elsewhere in LXX only in Isaiah (23:1, 6, 10, 14) do we find Καρχηδόνος used for תַרְשִׁישׁ, elsewhere Θαρσις. These may have been the major traders of LXX's era. Thus, LXX repeats its practice of translating with contemporary people group names as in v. 5. One can only speculate whether 𝕲ᴬ's reference to Χαλκηδόνος reflected its significance in the 4th century CE and to its position in the region of Gog, Mesech and Tubal. Is this a later scribe contextualising?

MT has כְּפִרֶיהָ (lit. 'its young lions' cf. 32:2), which is understood in many EVV and elsewhere as 'its young warriors', while LXX says καὶ πᾶσαι αἱ κῶμαι αὐτῶν ('and all their villages' [cf. NIV]).[40] Zimmerli (1983, p. 287) claims that LXX "misunderstood" the Hebrew, yet he does not clarify how. Allen (1990b, p. 200) believes "LXX Θ Syr interpreted [כְּפִרֶיהָ] as כְּפִרֶיהָ [sic] 'its villages' (= RSV). An emendation

---

[38] Block (1998, p. 447) says that the meaning of טַבּוּר הָאָרֶץ "continues to engage scholars. The common rendering 'navel of the earth,' which derives from LXX ὀμφαλός, is perpetuated in the Vulg. umbilici terrae, as well as in pseudepigraphic and rabbinic writings, and is reflected in several renowned medieval maps. But many modern interpreters have abandoned the literal 'navel' explanation, preferring to see here a figure of speech for 'the centre of the earth'. By this understanding the land of Israel/Zion is viewed as a cosmic midpoint, which accords better with later Hebrew; moreover, our prophet himself declared earlier that Yahweh had placed Jerusalem in the middle of the nations (5:5)". However Block (1998, p. 448) then goes on to state "nevertheless, this interpretation suffers from several major weaknesses and should probably be abandoned". He then discusses five key points to 'abandon' the above viewpoint. Block's rejection does not explain why LXX adopted its 'navel' view.

[39] It is unclear at this point in the text if these are military allies or bystanders. Regardless of which, it is clear they are awaiting the spoil.

[40] 𝕲ᴬ's variant of χῶμαι αὐτῆς appears to be a scribal error (χ for κ) as 'and all her mounds/heaps' (χῶμα [LS]) does not make sense.

רכליה 'its traders'…is plausible, assuming an insertion of פ for sense after corruption to כריה (וכל), but a simpler suggestion would be כריה 'its traders'". The context would point to either 'young lions/warriors' or 'traders', but LXX's 'villages' seems out of place. As LXX was working from an unpointed Hebrew text, Allen's first suggestion appears the more plausible. The Hebrew may have been 'corrupted', or, developing Allen's second suggestion, it may have been a deliberate exegetical emendation by a later scribe (cf. גָּדוֹל below). Interestingly, Symmachus has καὶ πάντες ὀλέθριοι λέοντες αὐτῆς ('and all her destructive lions'), which whilst reading כְּפָרֶיהָ as 'lions' inserts 'destructive' (Ziegler, 1977, p. 274). It may be that 'traders' was original as suggested above, but an earlier Hebrew scribe changed this to read 'lions' as witnessed by Σ. This may have been to match the surrounding context of devouring plunder, and to clarify that the merchants were not coming just as bystanders to Gog for trade, but were allies with the intent of devouring Israel's resources as lions do their prey. This change was misread by the earlier LXX translators as 'villages' (cf. Allen's first suggestion above).

MT has לִשְׁלֹל שָׁלָל גָּדוֹל ('to seize great spoil'), but LXX does not reflect גָּדוֹל either from an accidental omission or, more likely, because it was not in its *Vorlage*. It is difficult to think that LXX deliberately omitted the opportunity to expand the size of the spoil. This leaves us with the possibility of גָּדוֹל as a later MT plus, to emphasise the extent of the spoil that the community believes it has suffered. Eichrodt (1970, p. 518) sees "dittography from the beginning of the verse". However, Zimmerli (1983, p. 288) maintains "the triple accentuation of the three parallel infinitive clauses suggests the originality of 𝔐". The later Symmachus and Theodotion have πολλά and μεγάλα respectively, thus both witnessing MT (Ziegler, 1977, p. 274). It is possible that a later Hebrew editor added גָּדוֹל, at the same time 'adjusting' the Hebrew to כְּפָרֶיהָ (cf. Zimmerli and Allen above).

5.4. 3rd Oracle: Ezek. 38:14–16

Again, we have a uniform sense division break before v. 14 in all MT MSS. However, 𝔊⁹⁶⁷,ᴮ do not witness this break, unlike 𝔊ᴬ which has breaks both before and within v. 14 (between Γωγ and τάδε).

This oracle now reverts back to the LORD speaking through the prophet to Gog, informing what will happen in his upcoming gathering for the intended plunder of Israel (as in the 1st oracle). It provides the reason why the LORD will allow this to happen: for universal recognition of the LORD's holiness (cf. v. 16b). While Gog may have his own plans (the spoil), the text shows that he (and his hordes) are instruments in the LORD's hands, for the purpose of manifesting the LORD's holiness and knowledge throughout all the earth. The LORD previously stated his actions will be done so Israel will know he is the LORD (36:11, 38; 37:6, 13), and even the surrounding nations would also know (36:23, 36; 37:28), but now the LORD's defeat of this 'superpower' gathering will establish this 'knowledge' throughout the nations as a world impact statement.

This pericope again uses the terms 'my people' (cf. 36:8, 12, 28; 37:12, 13, 27; 38:14, 16; 39:7), and 'my land' (cf. 36:5; 38:16). Concerning this, Block (1997c, p. 102) states that "since the normal deity-nation-land relationships are now operative, for Gog to attack this people and invade this land is to challenge their/its divine patron".[41] Thus Gog's defeat is certain.

38:14 לָכֵן הִנָּבֵא בֶן־אָדָם וְאָמַרְתָּ לְגוֹג כֹּה אָמַר אֲדֹנָי יְהוִה
הֲלוֹא בַּיּוֹם הַהוּא בְּשֶׁבֶת עַמִּי יִשְׂרָאֵל לָבֶטַח תֵּדָע:

38:14 διὰ τοῦτο προφήτευσον υἱὲ ἀνθρώπου καὶ εἰπὸν τῷ Γωγ τάδε λέγει κύριος (𝕲⁹⁶⁷: καὶ; 𝕲ᴮ: οὐκ; 𝕲ᴬ: οὐχι) ἐν τῇ ἡμέρᾳ ἐκείνῃ ἐν τῷ κατοικισθῆναι τὸν λαόν μου Ισραηλ ἐπ᾽ εἰρήνης ἐγερθήσῃ

MT has תֵּדָע ('you will know'), yet LXX has ἐγερθήσῃ ('you will be aroused'). Allen (1990b, p. 200) suggests an MT scribal "error and metathesis" of ר and ד and he emends MT to תֵּעֹר ('you will be aroused').[42] Those who hold to an MT error use LXX as support. Yet De Vries (1995, p. 177) says that "there is no good reason to follow the LXX here...because the rhetorical question [in MT] has the intent of synchronizing Gog's earliest awareness that Israel is dwelling securely in his own land (cf. v. 8) with his departure (bw') prior to his attack ('lh) (v. 16)". Block (1998, p. 449) points out that "it is equally possible the error was committed by the LXX translators", which leaves MT

---

[41] Odell (2005, p. 553) notes how "at the beginning of the oracle, the resettled people have no particular identity, at least in the eyes of the other nations. A quiet people living in a land restored from war and affiliated with neither clan nor king, they appear ripe for the plundering. It is only when Yahweh tells Ezekiel to prophesy against Gog that they are claimed as Yahweh's people (38:14, 16) and the land is defended as Yahweh's land".

[42] Allen further suggests that תֵּדָע "may have originated as a comparative gloss relating to the formula in 39:5b, with 5:13; 17:21 (cf. 6:10) in view, which subsequently displaced the similar-looking תעֹר".

as original. MasEzek also bears witness to MT.[43] The theological difference is subtle, yet needs to be taken into consideration. Based on
Block's point, we suggest that LXX may done a trans-lingual word play
(cf. Allen: ר for ד), giving an interpretation of what will happen when
Gog 'knows' about the people dwelling securely (or peacefully): Gog
will be aroused and brought to the battle (v. 15). LXX uses the passive,
perhaps continuing the implicit motif of God being in control, as the
action is done to Gog. LXX changes the context from a question of
knowledge as in MT, to a statement of action that will be done to Gog,
yet still framed as a question. This is even clearer with 𝔊⁹⁶⁷'s minus
of οὐκ and its καί plus, which turns the context from a question into
a statement (𝔊ᴮ·ᴬ are plus οὐκ/οὐχι, but minus καί). For MT, including the interrogative הֲלֹא, the context leads into the action of v. 15,
making the interrogative into a question that presumes an answer: 'will
you not know it, and you will come'. From this theological context
we suggest that MT's reading is original, and LXX is an interpretive
wordplay that takes Gog's 'knowledge' (תֵּדָע) into the action of 'being
raised up' (תֵּעֹר).

38:16 וְעָלִיתָ עַל־עַמִּי יִשְׂרָאֵל כֶּעָנָן לְכַסּוֹת הָאָרֶץ בְּאַחֲרִית
הַיָּמִים תִּהְיֶה וַהֲבִאוֹתִיךָ עַל־אַרְצִי לְמַעַן דַּעַת הַגּוֹיִם
אֹתִי בְּהִקָּדְשִׁי בְךָ לְעֵינֵיהֶם גּוֹג׃

38:16 καὶ ἀναβήσῃ ἐπὶ τὸν λαόν μου Ισραηλ ὡς νεφέλη καλύψαι γῆν
ἐπ᾽ ἐσχάτων τῶν ἡμερῶν ἔσται καὶ ἀνάξω σε ἐπὶ τὴν γῆν μου ἵνα γνῶσιν
πάντα τὰ ἔθνη ἐμὲ ἐν τῷ ἁγιασθῆναί με ἐν σοὶ ἐνώπιον αὐτῶν

LXX has a πάντα plus ('all the nations will know'). This key plus
emphasises that the LORD's actions will not just be known by the nations
in the immediate vicinity of Israel, but by all nations, even those afar
off. This plus may also be related to the πολλῶν plus in v. 12, where
Israel is gathered from many nations (also 37:21; 39:23). These plusses
indicate that LXX was concerned that Israel was gathered out of 'all'
the nations, and that 'all' nations would know this, and would know
the LORD.

MT explicitly clarifies the subject by its placement of גּוֹג as a vocative
at the end of this verse. Cooke (1936, p. 414) notes that "at the end of
the v. 𝔊...omit O Gog, which comes awkwardly where it stands". 𝔊⁹⁶⁷

---

[43] This is the last extant word in the MasEzek fragment.

places Γωγ as a vocative at the beginning of v. 17.[44] Yet 𝕲^{B,A} both place Γωγ at the end of the introductory formula in v. 17, along with a dative article (τῷ) to clarify Gog as the addressee of God's speech. While some, like Zimmerli (1983, p. 288), suspect the originality of MT, others like Block (1998, p. 449) note "the Syr. omission of the vocative and LXX attachment of [Γωγ] to v. 17 are insufficient grounds for deleting the name". The placement of Gog at the end of MT's sentence structure "provides the first concrete indication since the opening challenge that the real antagonists in this oracle are not Yahweh and Israel, but Yahweh and Gog" (Block, 1998, p. 451). MT's placement causes 'Gog' to stand as an *inclusio* identifying the object in its sense division from vv. 14–16. These points are missed by 𝕲^{B,A}'s placement of Γωγ into v. 17, which simply identifies Γωγ as the object of God's speech. The 'antagonism' against Gog may still be found in 𝕲^{967}'s placement as a vocative at the beginning of v. 17. If 𝕲^{967} were a later LXX MS, one could argue 'Gog' was a later MT placement at the end of the sentence. However, as the earliest LXX MS supports the general locale of Gog, we suggest 'Gog' was original, and at the end of v. 16 (as in MT). It was initially placed in LXX as an opening vocative for v. 17 (as in 𝕲^{967}), but later LXX editors moved it to clarify the addressee in v. 17 (𝕲^{B,A}). This evidences LXX as a text in a state of flux.

God being honoured by the defeat of Gog echoes Exod. 14:4 where God says he will also be honoured by the demise of Pharaoh. The recognition is universal, especially with LXX (cf. πάντα plus above).

5.5. 4TH ORACLE: EZEK. 38:17

Block (1992b, p. 172) argues against ascribing this verse and vv. 18–23 "to different editorial hands" as some suggest; then, based on the style and content, he says, "it must be concluded that v. 17 enjoys relative [sense] independence from the verses that follow".[45] This statement is

---

[44] Curiously, Gehman (in Johnson *et al.*, 1938, p. 74 [cf. p. 130]) attributes Γωγ to 38:16, and claims it is one of the "43 cases which are an exact translations of the Hebrew". However, Johnson (in Johnson *et al.*, 1938, p. 177) has noted 𝕲^{967}'s normal *paragraphoi* marker ('=') in the text and attributes Γωγ as a vocative at the beginning of v. 17.

[45] Block (1998, p. 453) later says that "the new citation formula signals the commencement of the fourth literary frame. This frame consists of two unequal parts, clearly distinguished in style and purpose (v. 17, vv. 18–23).

supported by MT's paragraphing where v. 17 stands alone as its own
'sense division' oracle in all representative MT MSS. It begins 𝕲⁹⁶⁷'s
second sense division (vv. 17–23); v. 17 also begins 𝕲ᴬ's next division
(vv. 17–21a). 𝕲ᴮ has v. 17 as the last verse of the previous sense division (vv. 10–17).[46]

This indicates that the scribes behind these manuscripts, especially
MT, saw this verse as a fulfilment of their prophetic history, and sought
to establish the historical aspect of Gog's animosity against God and
his people. Block (1992b, p. 157) puts a lot of stock in this verse when
he says "for the interpretation of the Gog oracle Ezek. xxxviii 17
presents a crux".

38:17 כֹּה־אָמַר אֲדֹנָי יְהוִה הַאַתָּה־הוּא אֲשֶׁר־דִּבַּרְתִּי בְּיָמִים
קַדְמוֹנִים בְּיַד עֲבָדַי נְבִיאֵי יִשְׂרָאֵל הַנִּבְּאִים בַּיָּמִים הָהֵם שָׁנִים
לְהָבִיא אֹתְךָ עֲלֵיהֶם:

38:17 (𝕲⁹⁶⁷: Γωγ) τάδε λέγει κύριος κύριος (𝕲ᴮ·ᴬ: τῷ Γωγ) σὺ εἶ περὶ οὗ
ἐλάλησα πρὸ ἡμερῶν τῶν ἔμπροσθεν (𝕲⁹⁶⁷: ἐν χειρὶ; 𝕲ᴮ·ᴬ: διὰ χειρὸς) τῶν
δούλων μου προφητῶν τοῦ Ισραηλ ἐν ταῖς ἡμέραις ἐκείναις καὶ ἔτεσιν
τοῦ ἀγαγεῖν σε ἐπ᾽ αὐτούς

As stated above, 𝕲⁹⁶⁷'s placement of 'Γωγ' as a vocative at the beginning of v. 17 echoes the 'antagonistic challenge' against Gog found
with MT's placement of Gog as a vocative at the end of v. 16. This is
not found with 𝕲ᴮ·ᴬ's placement of τῷ Γωγ ('to Gog') after the introductory formula, which just clarifies that the oracle is spoken to Gog
and not Israel.

MT (supported by Targum) asks an unexpected rhetorical question הַאַתָּה־הוּא ('are you the one who?').[47] LXX interprets this as
an affirmative statement: σὺ εἶ περὶ οὗ ('you are the one concerning
whom'). Block (1998, p. 452) notes that "many follow LXX, Syr., and
Vulg. in reading an affirmative statement, assuming the hē on ha'attâ is
a dittography".[48] Yet this change from an MT interrogative question

---

[46] 𝕲ᴮ ends v. 16 at the end of a page and starts v. 17 at the top of the next,
causing it to be very difficult, if not impossible, to determine if any division was
intended.

[47] Block (1992b, p. 157f.) notes that "the prophet raises a question concerning Gog
which not only catches the reader off guard after vv. 14–16; it seems to have little
bearing on the furious attack upon Gog by Yahweh described in vv. 18–23".

[48] In an earlier work Block (1992b, p. 170) said that LXX's affirmative answer "may
just as well be explained as a haplographic error on the part of the translators as a
dittographic mistake by the Massoretes". Zimmerli (1983, p. 288) also "supposes" MT's
interrogative "הַ is a dittograph".

to an LXX affirmative statement is in keeping with previous instances where LXX has clarified speech towards Gog (v. 3), or MT's action (v. 14). LXX may be seen making a theological statement that there is no doubt that it is Gog who has been spoken (prophesied) about by the prophets of Israel.[49] This theology may also have influenced their placement of Gog in this verse. Fishbane (1985, p. 510) says that "the earlier vague predictions [in other books] of an enemy from the north are reinterpreted by the author of Ezek. 38–39 into a vision of world significance".[50] Fairbairn (1989, p. 425) claims that the prophecy "appeared now only in a new form, but the thing itself had been many times described by God's servants", and (1985, p. 477) "clearly the prophet saw the advancing devastation as the fulfilment of ancient prophecies.... Presumably, Ezekiel (or a pseudo-Ezekiel) believed the advent of Gog to be the true fulfilment of the ancient prediction".

Block (1992b, p. 172) concludes that the answer to MT's question regarding Gog being the fulfilment of previous prophecies should be "a firm 'NO!' ", rather than the traditional affirmative answer as found in LXX. Block's (1992b, p. 172) reason is the absence of Gog as an enemy in any previous prophecies, and an affirmative answer would render the following verses as "nonsensical" saying "how could Yahweh announce in one breath that Gog is his agent, and in the next vent his wrath on him with such fury". Block (1992b, p. 171) maintains that "even if Gog would have answered this question positively, the correct answer is negative". Fitzpatrick (2004, p. 93) says "the answer demanded by the rhetorical question was negative", and says that "interpreting the verse with a negative answer, opens up the passage that follows to understand Gog in his fundamental purpose: to be an instrument which Yhwh could use in the future to unloose his anger against Israel again". Fitzpatrick (2004, p. 91) concludes "in the final analysis, against the recommendation of the *BHS*, there is no reason to depart from

---

[49] Unfortunately, neither MT nor LXX clarify who these prophets were, other than being 'prophets of Israel', nor what they said, which has opened up a plethora of speculative proposals. For a detailed discussion of various proposals regarding their identity, see Block (1992b). Whilst many scholars propose Jeremiah (Block, 1992b, p. 166; Lust, 1995b, p. 709), Cooke (1936, p. 414) argues that "it is implied that a considerable time had passed meanwhile; Ez[ekiel] himself would not have alluded to the prophecies of Jeremiah in this way". Fitzpatrick (2004, p. 91f.) also finds in favour of Jeremiah, yet also of Isaiah.

[50] Fishbane (1985, p. 523) also says the "older prophetic promises are reappropriated in the proto-apocalyptic narratives of Ezek. 38–9".

MT". Odell (2005, p. 558) covers both bases saying "the answer to the question of v. 17 is a resounding yes-and-no: yes, others have seen Gog as the fulfilment of prophecy; but no, Gog does not have an external license to wage war on Yahweh's quiet people".

There are two other rhetorical questions addressed to Gog in the previous section wherein a positive answer is implied (cf. vv. 13, 14). In the previous pericope (vv. 14–16) the prophetic speech was addressed to Gog, and in the following pericope (vv. 18–23) the LORD is informing the prophet, not Gog, what will now take place. The LORD can therefore still use Gog as his 'puppet' (cf. Block) in the previous verses, as this 'use' will lead to Gog's destruction; Israel's prophets often spoke judgement to those who came against Israel. How one interprets v. 17 may depend upon whether one sees this as an actual question directed at Gog or a rhetorical question about Gog. After all, how would Gog know what has, or has not, been prophesied about him, or other 'enemies', from Israel's prophets? Yet, if the question was directed at Gog with an expectant answer, surely Gog would answer 'yes' in an effort to bring fear and intimidation. If v. 17 is a rhetorical question about Gog as the beginning of God's speech to the prophet (cf. $\mathfrak{G}^{967,A}$ vv. 17f.), then it also anticipates a 'yes' answer as it reflects on the prophetic oracles of judgement against Israel's enemies.

Regardless how modern commentators interpret MT's question, LXX has exegetically interpreted with an affirmative answer, rather than leaving the question for the reader to debate. LXX therefore must have seen Gog as the one whom the prophets generically spoke about as the ultimate enemy. One influence could be the interpretative tradition behind LXX's use of Γωγ for אֲגַג in Num. 24:7 (also Aquila and Symmachus), and for גֵּזִי (Amos 7:1).

LXX does not include a rendering of הַנִּבְּאִים ('who prophesied'), but the sense remains unchanged, as it is implied.[51] Block (1992b, p. 162) suggests that "this looks like an haplographic error". On the other hand this could be another later MT plus not witnessed by LXX, clarifying the action of the prophets. This may be the case, as הַנִּבְּאִים is witnessed in Theodotion as τῶν προφητευσάντων (Field, 1964, p. 871; Ziegler, 1977, p. 275).

---

[51] Curiously, Zimmerli is the only major commentator who notes this point, yet without explanation.

There is a minor intra-LXX variant where 𝔊⁹⁶⁷ follows the difficult Hebrew syntax with ἐν χειρί, which is 'smoothed' out by the later 𝔊ᴮ·ᴬ using διὰ χειρός.

5.6. 5TH ORACLE: EZEK. 38:18–23

All MT MSS have 38:18–23 as the one sense division, as does 𝔊ᴮ. As noted above, 𝔊⁹⁶⁷ begin this pericope at v. 17, and concludes at the end of the chapter (v. 23). 𝔊ᴬ also begins at v. 17, but starts another division mid v. 21, most likely again influenced by λέγει κύριος (cf. 𝔊ᴬ's division v. 14b above), its next break being after v. 23.

This oracle, addressed to the prophet, focuses on what the LORD will do when Gog finally attacks, and on the three spheres of sea, air and earth that will be impacted (cf. v. 20). It also shows that the LORD will destroy Gog in his heated wrath (v. 19), an image that appears to echo epic battles of Israel's past when their enemy turned against themselves (Jud. 7:22; 2Chron. 20:23). We may also find an echo of the LORD's overthrow of Sodom (Gen. 19:24). At the end of the previous major pericope (v. 16) we find the LORD declaring that the purpose for his action against Gog is to establish his 'greatness' and 'holiness', and so that he will be 'known' before 'many nations' (v. 23).

38:18 וְהָיָה בַּיּוֹם הַהוּא בְּיוֹם בּוֹא גוֹג עַל־אַדְמַת יִשְׂרָאֵל נְאֻם
אֲדֹנָי יְהוִה תַּעֲלֶה חֲמָתִי בְּאַפִּי: (38:19) וּבְקִנְאָתִי בְאֵשׁ־עֶבְרָתִי
דִבַּרְתִּי אִם־לֹא בַּיּוֹם הַהוּא יִהְיֶה רַעַשׁ גָּדוֹל עַל אַדְמַת יִשְׂרָאֵל:

38:18 καὶ ἔσται ἐν τῇ ἡμέρᾳ ἐκείνῃ ἐν (𝔊ᴮ·ᴬ: ἡμέρᾳ; 𝔊⁹⁶⁷: –) ᾗ ἂν ἔλθῃ Γωγ ἐπὶ τὴν γῆν τοῦ Ισραηλ λέγει κύριος κύριος ἀναβήσεται ὁ θυμός μου 38:19 καὶ ὁ ζῆλός μου ἐν πυρὶ τῆς ὀργῆς μου ἐλάλησα εἰ μὴν ἐν τῇ ἡμέρᾳ ἐκείνῃ ἔσται σεισμὸς μέγας ἐπὶ γῆς Ισραηλ

Verses 18–19 need to be considered together due to the sentence division in LXX, as shown by its syntax. Most commentators propose that בְּאַפִּי at the end of v. 18 belongs better at the start of v. 19 (Zimmerli, 1983, p. 289; Block, 1998, p. 452). On one hand, בְּאַפִּי can fit at the end of v. 18 as it completes a Hebrew idiom for anger: תַּעֲלֶה חֲמָתִי בְּאַפִּי ('my heat/rage will go up in my nose/face'). On the other hand, אַף can also alone mean 'anger' [*HALOT* #3], and if placed in v. 19 as some suggest, v. 19 would read (lit.) 'in my anger and in my jealousy in the fire of my fury I have spoken'. However each representative MT MS places בְּאַפִּי in v. 18, and so we maintain that reading. Regardless of where בְּאַפִּי is placed in MT, it is not witnessed in LXX which reads, (v. 18) 'my anger/rage will go up (v. 19) and my jealousy, in the fire of my wrath I have spoken'. Thus, LXX omits the idiom 'nose/ face'. It still reflects the intent of the Hebrew, but without the explicit point that God's rage would be seen on his 'face'.[52] This may be an example of a later scribe who no longer uses a particular Hebrew idiom, and now puts it into 'plain language'. Alternatively, LXX may have sought to avoid using such an anthropomorphic term, as Cooke (1936, p. 414) notes that Targum also paraphrases here "to avoid the anthropomorphism".

We may question why Allen (1990, p. 201) says that "sentence re-division seems necessary with LXX", when LXX does not witness the 'disputed' word. Referring to ζῆλός in v. 19, Block (1998, p. 452) says "LXX interprets 'my passion' as a second subject of *ta'ăleh* in v. 18". For MT, וּבְקִנְאָתִי is able to stand alone and leads into the following statement. LXX may have been either smoothing out a Hebrew idiom, or avoiding anthropomorphism, but the result is that LXX sees both the LORD's 'anger' (v. 18) and 'jealousy' (v. 19) as arising, rather than the LORD speaking out of his jealousy, he simply speaks 'in the fire of my wrath'.

Eichrodt (1970, p. 518) claims "'in the day when Gog comes upon the land of Israel' [is] an explanatory gloss" (cf. v. 18). However, this phrase is witnessed in all representative MT and LXX MSS. 𝔊^{B,A}'s ἡμέρᾳ in v. 18 follows MT (minus in 𝔊^{967}).

38:20 וְרָעֲשׁוּ מִפָּנַי דְּגֵי הַיָּם וְעוֹף הַשָּׁמַיִם וְחַיַּת הַשָּׂדֶה וְכָל־הָרֶמֶשׂ הָרֹמֵשׂ עַל־הָאֲדָמָה וְכֹל הָאָדָם אֲשֶׁר עַל־פְּנֵי הָאֲדָמָה וְנֶהֶרְסוּ הֶהָרִים וְנָפְלוּ הַמַּדְרֵגוֹת וְכָל־חוֹמָה לָאָרֶץ תִּפּוֹל׃

38:20 καὶ σεισθήσονται ἀπὸ προσώπου κυρίου οἱ ἰχθύες τῆς θαλάσσης καὶ τὰ πετεινὰ τοῦ οὐρανοῦ καὶ τὰ θηρία τοῦ πεδίου καὶ πάντα τὰ ἑρπετὰ τὰ ἕρποντα ἐπὶ τῆς γῆς καὶ πάντες οἱ ἄνθρωποι οἱ ἐπὶ προσώπου τῆς γῆς (𝔊^{967}: + πάσης) καὶ ῥαγήσεται τὰ ὄρη καὶ πεσοῦνται αἱ φάραγγες καὶ πᾶν τεῖχος ἐπὶ τὴν γῆν πεσεῖται (𝔊^{967}: + ἵνα γνῶσιν πάντα τὰ ἔθνη ἐμὲ ἐν σοὶ ἐνώπιον αὐτῶν)

---

[52] Fitzpatrick (2004, p. 95) says LXX's minus here "is a loss. This visible rage harkens back to the rage of the holy war described by the Israelite narrators, Josh. 8:14ff.; Judg. 4:14ff.; 5:4; 20; 1 Sam. 7:7ff.; 14:15ff.; 2 Sam. 5:20ff. It dramatically heightens the sense of the profanation of the Creator's covenant people living in right order and relationship, and the anger of their defender".

LXX's κυρίου plus in the first phrase changes to the 3rd person, so making a statement rather than continued speech as in MT (מִפָּנַי 'from my face').

MT says הַמַּדְרֵגוֹת ('the *terraces* will fall' [*HALOT*], or '*steep place*' [BDB], or '*steep way*' [*NIDOTTE*]). BHS suggests emending to הַמִּגְדָּלוֹת ('the *towers*') that will fall. Differently, LXX says it will be the φάραγγες ('the valleys/ravines'; cf. 36:4, 6; 39:11). Alternatively, Symmachus says νάπαις ('forests'; cf. 6:3; 36:6) will fall, and Theodotion φρα-γμοι, ('fences/hedges/barriers' [LEH]). MT has used a relatively rare word that does not occur elsewhere in Ezekiel (cf. SoS. 2:14), and LXX appears to have referred back to Ezek. 36:4, 6 to find a possible interpretation.

𝕲⁹⁶⁷'s plus of ἵνα γνῶσιν πάντα τὰ ἔθνη ἐμὲ ἐν σοὶ ἐνώπιον αὐτῶν ('so that all the nations will know me in you [that I am in you] in their eyes'), is not present in MT, 𝕲ᴮ·ᴬ, or in any other text, and is "probably repeated from vs. 16" (Gehman in Johnson *et al.*, 1938, p. 131). This appears to be a theologically influenced 'repeat', to again emphasise the knowledge of the LORD amongst the nations. This may have support from 𝕲⁹⁶⁷'s other πάσης plus earlier in the verse, which again emphasises that 'all' on the earth (or land) will fall, demonstrating a 'universal' viewpoint of the LORD's activity.

38:21 וְקָרָאתִי עָלָיו לְכָל־הָרַי חֶרֶב נְאֻם אֲדֹנָי יְהוִה חֶרֶב אִישׁ בְּאָחִיו תִּהְיֶה:

38:21 καὶ καλέσω ἐπ' αὐτὸν πᾶν φόβον (𝕲ᴾ·ᴬ: + μαχαίρας) λέγει κύριος μάχαιρα ἀνθρώπου ἐπὶ τὸν ἀδελφὸν αὐτοῦ ἔσται

As noted above, 𝕲ᴬ exhibits a sense division in the middle of this verse after λέγει κύριος, probably due to these very words. Yet, this places the second phrase of the verse in a following division, where it seems out of place.

Different images are conveyed by MT וְקָרָאתִי עָלָיו לְכָל־הָרַי חֶרֶב (lit. 'and I will call against him to all my mountains a sword'); 𝕲ᴮ καὶ καλέσω ἐπ' αὐτὸν πᾶν φόβον ('and I will call against him all fear'); and 𝕲⁹⁶⁷·ᴬ expanding, ...πᾶν φόβον μαχαίρας ('...all fear of a sword'). Zimmerli (1983, p. 289) believes "𝕲...has preserved the original reading" of the Hebrew, yet he does not note his position only refers to 𝕲ᴮ [Cooke (1936, p. 415) does note this refers only to 𝕲ᴮ]. Allen (1990b, p. 201) suggests "that out of the sequence הרי חרב some sense was wrested by understanding as הרהב 'frightened' (cf. KB 876a)". Yet it would be a major scribal oversight to ignore the הר[י] in between the other letters, especially when 'mountains' forms a key motif in these chapters.[53] Block (1998, p. 458) also says, "it is difficult to see how [MT] scribes could have mistakenly reproduced *hāray ḥereb*. The LXX reading may itself reflect the translator's uncertainty regarding the meaning of the word". Yet, LXX was able to correctly translate חֶרֶב in other places in Ezekiel, including 38:4, 12. Allen's (1990b, p. 201) other suggestion may offer a better solution: "הרי appears to be an adapted torso, whereby רה was written for חר under the influence of ונהרסו ההרים in v. 20, then abandoned and adapted to הרי for a modicum of sense". However, neither Allen, Zimmerli, or Block note that both 𝕲⁹⁶⁷,ᴬ include μαχαίρας as the basis of the 'fear', reflecting two representative LXX understandings of חרב as 'sword' present in this location. 𝕲⁹⁶⁷,ᴬ may have added this to conform to MT, yet this does not explain why 𝕲ᴮ did not include μαχαίρας, nor why all LXX MSS omit 'my mountains'. This may indicate that 'my mountains' was a later MT plus to re-emphasise or clarify the battle's locale, conforming to the context of the surrounding chapters. If so, MT may have added this at the same time as the MT/LXX variant of הָרַי/γῆν in v. 8 where MT also clarifies the battle's locale as being the 'mountains'. However, this suggestion leaves us without answer for LXX's use of φόβον, other than to suggest that LXX exhibits a theological exegesis of the enemy's response to the sword, and that 𝕲ᴮ omitted the mention of 'sword'. Block (1997c, p. 106) suggests that MT's call for a sword is "reminiscent of Gideon's war against the Midianites (Jdg. 7:22), when Yahweh calls for the sword, the troops in the armies of God and his allies will turn their weapons on each other". If so, 𝕲ᴮ did not appear to capture this echo; 𝕲⁹⁶⁷,ᴬ may be seen to have caught it as they do have πᾶν φόβον μάχαιρας as a lead into the phrase 'every person's sword will be against his brother'.

38:22 וְנִשְׁפַּטְתִּי אִתּוֹ בְּדֶבֶר וּבְדָם וְגֶשֶׁם שׁוֹטֵף וְאַבְנֵי אֶלְגָּבִישׁ אֵשׁ
וְגָפְרִית אַמְטִיר עָלָיו וְעַל־אֲגַפָּיו וְעַל־עַמִּים רַבִּים אֲשֶׁר אִתּוֹ:

38:22 καὶ κρινῶ αὐτὸν θανάτῳ καὶ αἵματι καὶ ὑετῷ κατακλύζοντι καὶ λίθοις χαλάζης καὶ πῦρ καὶ θεῖον βρέξω ἐπ' αὐτὸν καὶ ἐπὶ πάντας τοὺς μετ' αὐτοῦ καὶ ἐπ' ἔθνη πολλὰ μετ' αὐτοῦ

---

[53] Block (1998, p. 458) curiously claims that "the designation of the target as 'my mountains' is unprecedented in Ezekiel". Yet we do find this same concept in 38:8.

MT says the LORD will judge בְּדֶ֫בֶר ('with pestilence/plague'), whereas
LXX says with θανάτῳ ('death'), which appears to interpret the result
of plagues. However, LXX elsewhere uses θανάτῳ for בְּדֶ֫בֶר (cf. Ezek.
5:12; 6:12; 33:27; also commonly used for מות).

As in v. 6, MT has וְעַל־אֲגַפָּיו ('and on his band/troops/army'), and
LXX καὶ ἐπὶ πάντας τοὺς μετ' αὐτοῦ ('and on all those with him') (cf.
discussions of v. 6).

38:23 וְהִתְגַּדִּלְתִּי֙ וְהִתְקַדִּשְׁתִּ֔י וְנ֣וֹדַעְתִּ֔י לְעֵינֵ֖י גּוֹיִ֣ם רַבִּ֑ים וְיָדְע֖וּ
כִּֽי־אֲנִ֥י יְהוָֽה׃

38:23 καὶ μεγαλυνθήσομαι καὶ ἁγιασθήσομαι καὶ ἐνδοξασθήσομαι
καὶ γνωσθήσομαι ἐναντίον ἐθνῶν πολλῶν καὶ γνώσονται ὅτι ἐγώ εἰμι
κύριος

MT uses 2 *hithpael* perfects with preceding וֹ,[54] to reflexively state 'I will
magnify myself, and sanctify myself'. Yet LXX has 3 future passives,
the first two reflecting MT, but adding ἐνδοξασθήσομαι ('I will be glorified'). In MT the LORD is the reflexive subject of the actions, while in
LXX the action is being done to the subject (passive). Perhaps LXX
saw the result of the 'battle' with Gog (and Gog's defeat), as the event
that will enable the LORD to gain such standing and status amongst the
nations, whereas MT saw the LORD's self 'magnifying and sanctifying'
as the reason for this battle. Wong (2003, p. 225) points out that "if
Yahweh allows Gog and his army to destroy Israel, then this will lead
to a profanation of his holy name. By destroying Gog and therefore
protecting Israel, Yahweh does not allow his name to be profaned…By
protecting Israel and its land, Yahweh is safeguarding the sanctity of
his name". On the other hand, this may just be a case of 'passive as
circumlocution' as in 39:7.

5.7. SUMMARY OF OBSERVATIONS: EZEKIEL 38

Our textual-comparative methodology identifies five oracles in Ezekiel
chapter 38, each following MT's sense divisions, although LXX 𝕲[967]
combines the first two and last two, and 𝕲[B] combines the third and
fourth:

---

[54] Block (1997c, p. 106) points out that these "two involve the only occurrences of
these roots in the hithpael stem in the book. These are examples *par excellence* of the
estimative-declarative reflexive use of the hithpael stem".

1st Oracle: vv. 1–9: The Lord tells Ezekiel what to say to Gog: the gathering of Gog (by the Lord, v. 4)

2nd Oracle: vv. 10–13: The Lord speaks directly to Gog: identifies Gog's scheme to plunder

3rd Oracle: vv. 14–16: The Lord tells Ezekiel what to say to Gog: the gathering of Gog (by the Lord, v. 16)

4th Oracle: v. 17: The Lord speaks directly to Gog: sets Gog's identity and gives the challenge

5th Oracle: vv. 18–23: The Lord speaks to Ezekiel: outlines the battle and destruction of Gog (so the nations will know the Lord).

While modern commentators exert their attention on Gog's identity, LXX simply transliterates MT's 'Gog', without seeking to interpret into a contemporary name. LXX treats 'Magog' and 'Ros' as a people group (or person), rather than MT's place and rank (respectively). When MT lists countries associated with Gog, LXX lists the people groups (e.g., v. 5 MT: Libya; LXX: Libyans; v. 13 MT: Tarshish; 𝔊⁹⁶⁷: of Carthage; 𝔊ᴮ: Carthaginian; 𝔊ᴬ: of Chalcedon).

There are several places where LXX seems to interpret the Hebrew underlying MT: the possible metaphor of טַבּוּר (v. 12 'top of the world') becomes ὀμφαλός ('navel'); MT's interrogative question in v. 17 is in LXX a statement, answering that Gog was the one the prophets spoke about; battle clothing and equipment terms are according to their day, speaking of breastplates and gear more suited to cavalry (v. 4); and MT's 'leading out' is in LXX 'gathered', with the intent that they will be gathered for their destruction (v. 4). LXX indicates they saw the devastation of their land as God's rejection (cf. vv. 11, 12). 𝔊⁹⁶⁷,ᴬ's use of φόβον in v. 21 (𝔊ᴮ is minus), may exhibit a theological exegesis of the enemy's response to the sword. In addition, there are only a couple of examples where LXX may not have understood the Hebrew: LXX translated MT's אֲגַפֶּיהָ ('band/troop') with οἱ περὶ αὐτον (v. 6), and read MT's כְּפִרֶיהָ ('lions') to mean 'villages' (v. 13).

MT has a few minor plusses, one witnessed in 𝔊ᴬ (v. 3 'Gog'), yet others not (v. 4 'hooks'; v. 13 'great'; v. 17 'prophesied'; v. 18 'anger'; v. 21 'my mountains'). 𝔊⁹⁶⁷ has a long unique plus in v. 20 which further emphasises the knowledge of the Lord to the nations.

Therefore, while we did not find the same degree of textual variants as in chapters 36–37, we nevertheless did find interpretative interaction whereby many of the variants suggest a text in a state of flux.

CHAPTER SIX

THE TEXT OF EZEKIEL 39

6.1. Introduction: Ezek. 39

The focus in chapter 39,[1] while initially on the battle against Gog (vv. 1–6), is primarily on the extensive aftermath, and the resulting clean up by the people (vv. 9–10, 12–15), and by the birds and wild animals as a 'sacrifice' (vv. 17–20). This is followed by an explanation why God exiled Israel (vv. 21–24), and Israel's return from exile (vv. 25–29). The reasons for the defeat and slaughter of Gog and his hordes are woven throughout the chapter: that 'my name will no longer be profaned' (v. 7); so Israel will know the Lord's name (vv. 7, 22); the nations will know the Lord and the reason for his past actions with Israel (vv. 7, 23–24); and the Lord's glorification (vv. 13, 21, 27).

The unity amongst MT's sense divisions continues into chapter 39. All three representative MSS evidence a break between 38:23 and 39:1 (MT^C *petuḥah*; MT^{A,L} *setumah*). The other divisions occur after v. 10 (all *setumah*); v. 16 (MT^{C,L} *setumah*; MT^A *petuḥah*); v. 24 (all *setumah*); and after v. 29 (all *petuḥah*).[2]

We find a high degree of sense division agreement in chapter 39 between MT and LXX, with 𝔊^{B,A} both matching MT's divisions. 𝔊^A has only one additional division break, a 2 letter break after v. 8; 𝔊^A has a small break at v. 10, and then larger breaks at MT's other division locales (vv. 16, 24, 29). 𝔊^{967} has its sense division markers before 39:1, and another highly likely break after v. 16 where we find two 'dots' rather than 𝔊^{967}'s usual 'strokes'. Yet Johnson (in Johnson *et al.*, 1938, p. 15) points out that "sometimes one or both of these strokes degenerate into a dot or dots". Although there is only enough room for two 'dots' between vv. 16 and 17, the lower 'dot' extends slightly to the right of the upper one, and the following line is slightly offset into the margin, and so follows the pattern of the original scribe (Johnson

---

[1] Issues covered in our introduction to chapter 38 also apply to chapter 39.

[2] MasEzek is not extant after 38:14, and so we are left without its witness for chapter 39.

in Johnson *et al.*, 1938, p. 16). The only other sense division break in $\mathfrak{G}^{967}$ is at the end of the chapter, where there is an unusual 4 letter break after the sense division 'strokes' before moving into chapter 37.

As previously noted, these two chapters consist of nine oracles reflecting MT's sense divisions: five oracles occur in chapter 38 and four in chapter 39. To date, I have not found any modern commentator or English bible that exactly follows these nine ancient divisions. We will continue the numbering for these oracles from chapter 38.

6.2. 6TH ORACLE: EZEK. 39:1–10

As noted above, vv. 1–10 form a pericope in all MT MSS and $\mathfrak{G}^{B,A}$ ($\mathfrak{G}^{967}$ is the exception having vv. 1–16 as one pericope; $\mathfrak{G}^A$ shows in addition a small break after v. 8). This covers the LORD's action against Gog, bringing Gog to his destruction as sacrificial food for birds and wild animals upon Israel's mountains. This concept appears to be a reversal of creation order where humans were to have dominion over animals (Gen. 1:28; 9:1–3), and thus we may see here a 'de-creation' aspect for the enemies of God. Israel is passive in Gog's destruction (vv. 1–6), and only plays a role in the clean up of weapons (vv. 9–10). The LORD clearly states that he will destroy Gog to make his 'holy name' known in Israel (v. 7a), and to stop the profaning of his name (v. 7b), and so the nations would know that he is the 'Holy One in Israel' (v. 7c). In this pericope Gog is addressed in the singular, and appears to be without his 'hordes' (cf. 38:4–7).

39:1 וְאַתָּה בֶן־אָדָם הִנָּבֵא עַל־גּוֹג וְאָמַרְתָּ כֹּה אָמַר אֲדֹנָי יְהֹוָה
הִנְנִי אֵלֶיךָ גּוֹג נְשִׂיא רֹאשׁ מֶשֶׁךְ וְתֻבָל:

39:1 καὶ σὺ υἱὲ ἀνθρώπου προφήτευσον ἐπὶ Γωγ καὶ εἰπόν τάδε λέγει κύριος ἰδοὺ ἐγὼ ἐπὶ σὲ Γωγ ἄρχοντα Ρως Μοσοχ (𝔊^B: Μεσοχ) καὶ Θοβελ

As in chapter 38:2–3, LXX transliterates רֹאשׁ with Ρως as a proper noun, either as an ethnic group, or as a person. The plain reading is 'Gog, ruler of Ros, Mosoch and Thobel'. Brenton, perhaps influenced by 38:2, has Ρως as the prince/ruler (ἄρχοντα) of Mosoch and Thobel. Either way, LXX does not follow MT's Gog as the 'chief prince' of Meshech and Tubal (cf. discussions 38:2, 3).

39:2 וְשֹׁבַבְתִּיךָ וְשִׁשֵּׁאתִיךָ וְהַעֲלִיתִיךָ מִיַּרְכְּתֵי צָפוֹן וַהֲבִאוֹתִךָ
עַל־הָרֵי יִשְׂרָאֵל:

39:2 καὶ συνάξω σε καὶ καθοδηγήσω σε καὶ ἀναβιβῶ σε ἀπ᾽ ἐσχάτου τοῦ βορρᾶ καὶ (𝕲⁹⁶⁷: αξω; 𝕲ᴮ: ἀνάξω; 𝕲ᴬ: συνάξω) σε ἐπὶ τὰ ὄρη τοῦ Ισραηλ

MT has וְשֹׁבַבְתִּיךָ ('and I will return you' or 'I will turn you around'), while LXX says καὶ συνάξω σε ('and I will assemble you'). LXX appears to give purpose for MT's 'turning Gog around', that is, 'to assemble Gog and his forces for his destruction' (cf. 38:4 וְשֹׁבַבְתִּיךָ and καὶ συνάξω σε).

MT's וַהֲבֵאוֹתִיךָ ('I will bring you') is reflected by both 𝕲⁹⁶⁷ ἄξω σε ('I will lead you'), and 𝕲ᴮ ἀνάξω σε ('I will bring you up'), whereas 𝕲ᴬ again has συνάξω σε ('I will assemble/gather you'). Therefore 𝕲ᴬ interprets the intent behind 'bringing' Gog, it was to assemble Gog with a view to his destruction (cf. 38:4).

39:3 וְהִכֵּיתִי קַשְׁתְּךָ מִיַּד שְׂמֹאלֶךָ וְחִצֶּיךָ מִיַּד יְמִינְךָ אַפִּיל:

39:3 καὶ ἀπολῶ τὸ τόξον σου (𝕲⁹⁶⁷: ἐκ; 𝕲ᴮ·ᴬ: ἀπὸ) τῆς χειρός σου τῆς ἀριστερᾶς καὶ τὰ τοξεύματά σου ἀπὸ τῆς χειρός σου τῆς δεξιᾶς καὶ καταβαλῶ σε ἐπὶ τὰ ὄρη Ισραηλ

MT says וְהִכֵּיתִי ('I will strike [your bow]'), and LXX has ἀπολῶ ('I will destroy [your bow]'). LXX intensifies MT, and the force of the verb carries onto the arrows as well, whereas MT adds another verb saying God will cause their arrows to fall out of their hands. Symmachus has ἀποτινάξω ('I will shake off'), which reflects MT closer than other LXX.[3]

LXX inserts καί forming a new phrase towards the end of this verse, καὶ καταβαλῶ σε ('and I will cast you down'), which connects to v. 4. MT in v. 3 has two balanced phrases, with the common word order of verb-object followed by object-verb. Yet LXX has seen both objects as linked with the opening verb of v. 3 וְהִכֵּיתִי/καὶ ἀπολῶ, so leaving אַפִּיל to start the next phrase. This has lead to the insertion of καί and in later translations different positioning of the break between vv. 3 and 4.

39:4 עַל־הָרֵי יִשְׂרָאֵל תִּפּוֹל אַתָּה וְכָל־אֲגַפֶּיךָ וְעַמִּים אֲשֶׁר אִתָּךְ לְעֵיט צִפּוֹר כָּל־כָּנָף וְחַיַּת הַשָּׂדֶה נְתַתִּיךָ לְאָכְלָה:

---

[3] BAGD indicates 'shake off' is a stronger word than at first appears, with examples: "*shake off* τὶ, of a snake which has bitten a hand τὸ θηρίον εἰς τὸ πῦρ Ac 28:5" or to "*shake the dust fr. one's feet* Lk 9:5" and also "of St. Paul's beheading".

39:4 (𝔊⁹⁶⁷: + καὶ οὐ βεβηλωθήσεται τὸ ὄνομά τὸ ἅγιον) καὶ πεσῇ
σὺ καὶ πάντες οἱ περὶ σέ καὶ τὰ ἔθνη (𝔊⁹⁶⁷: + πολλα) τὰ μετὰ σοῦ
(𝔊ᴮ·ᴬ: δοθήσονται; 𝔊⁹⁶⁷: –) εἰς πλήθη ὀρνέων παντὶ πετεινῷ καὶ πᾶσι
τοῖς θηρίοις τοῦ (𝔊⁹⁶⁷: ἀγροῦ δέδωκά σε εἰς καταβρωμα; 𝔊ᴮ·ᴬ: πεδίου
δέδωκά σε καταβρωθῆναι)

MT starts v. 4 with עַל־הָרֵי יִשְׂרָאֵל תִּפּוֹל ('on the mountains of Israel,
you shall fall'), yet, as noted above, LXX has MT's opening phrase
in v. 3 due to its inserted copula. LXX inserts another copula in v. 4,
saying '*and* you will fall'.

𝔊⁹⁶⁷ has several variants to 𝔊ᴮ·ᴬ and MT:

1. 𝔊⁹⁶⁷ begins with a unique plus: καὶ οὐ βεβηλωθήσεται τὸ ὄνομά
   τὸ ἅγιον ('and the holy name will not be profaned'). This plus
   may have been inspired from v. 7, there as '*my* holy name' (cf. Lev.
   18:21). The use here of '*the* holy name' appears to be a narrative
   plus, outside of the LORD's speech, and gives added reason for Gog's
   pending fall on the mountains of Israel.
2. 𝔊⁹⁶⁷ has πολλα as a plus, reading 'the *many* nations' (minus in
   𝔊ᴮ·ᴬ). Gehman (in Johnson *et al.*, 1938, p. 132) says this is "based
   on a Hebrew reading וְעַמִּים רבים, which is found in a number of
   MSS…(cf. Ez. xxxviii.6)". Zimmerli (1983, p. 290) says Targum and
   Syriac also include 'many', stating this "strongly suggest the addition
   of רבים". As such, רבים may have been in the *Urtext*, but omitted
   very early, most likely by scribal error, and so not present in 𝔊ᴮ·ᴬ's
   Vorlage. However, it is difficult to see why following MT scribes did
   not reinsert this word back into the text.
3. 𝔊⁹⁶⁷ is minus δοθήσονται, but "it should be noted that [MT] uses
   the root נתן only once: נְתַתִּיךָ" (Gehman in Johnson *et al.*, 1938,
   p. 132). 𝔊⁹⁶⁷ therefore follows MT's syntax, causing δοθήσονται to
   be a 𝔊ᴮ·ᴬ plus.
4. Rather than 𝔊ᴮ·ᴬ's δέδωκά σε καταβρωθῆναι (pass.: 'given to be
   devoured'), 𝔊⁹⁶⁷ has δέδωκά σε εἰς καταβρωμα ('given as food') (cf.
   MT: אָכְלָה).

MT has לְעֵיט צִפּוֹר כָּל־כָּנָף ('bird of prey, bird of every wing'),[4] yet
LXX says ὀρνέων παντὶ πετεινῷ ('birds, all able to fly'). The Hebrew
construct pair (לְעֵיט צִפּוֹר) is represented by one Greek word, causing

---

[4] JPS: 'to carrion birds of every sort'.

LXX not to reflect fully MT's 'bird of prey'. Zimmerli (1983, p. 290) proposes "the versions no longer understood" MT's construct pair. In addition, 'bird' in MT is collective, represented by LXX's plural.

39:6 וְשִׁלַּחְתִּי־אֵשׁ בְּמָגוֹג וּבְיֹשְׁבֵי הָאִיִּים לָבֶטַח וְיָדְעוּ כִּי־אֲנִי יְהוָה:

39:6 καὶ ἀποστελῶ πῦρ ἐπὶ Γωγ (𝕲ᴬ: + σε) καὶ κατοικηθήσονται αἱ νῆσοι ἐπ᾽ εἰρήνης καὶ γνώσονται ὅτι ἐγώ εἰμι κύριος

MT says God's fire will come on מָגוֹג, yet LXX has Γωγ. Cooke (1936, p. 418) says "Magog here seems to be the name of a people, parallel to inhabitants of coasts-lands". Eichrodt (1970, p. 518) claims that this "whole verse…looks suspiciously like an addition", although he is without textual evidence, leaving his subjective reading based on how a modern mind can view the flow of text. Zimmerli (1983, p. 315) says that "Magog…[is] not to be replaced, as in 𝕲, by the easier reading of Gog". He points out that the context does not refer to Gog, who was dealt with in vv. 1–5, and it does not refer to "a later burning of Gog's corpse", due to v. 11 covering the burial of Gog. Zimmerli (1983, p. 315) concludes that "the aim of v. 6 [MT] is to extend the proclamation of judgment to Gog's hinterland", which covers those under Gog's rule.[5] Allen (1990b, p. 201) similarly sees LXX as "an inferior reading", holding onto MT. Block (1998, p. 463) also sees MT as original, and says that Magog is the "home territories" for Gog's armies, and is "Gog's place of origin". Differently, Lust (1995c, p. 1001) claims that the "LXX rendering…[of] Gog for MT's Magog…seems to confirm that the names Gog and Magog were interchangeable". Yet this is questionable, as 39:6 is the only occurrence where Gog is substituted for Magog, and only by LXX. Overall, LXX appears to keep God's wrath focused on Gog and not a 'hinterland'.

𝕲ᴬ has σε as plus, reading ἐπὶ Γωγ σε, emphasising the action is against Gog.

Block (1998, p. 460) points out that "LXX transforms [MT's] declaration of judgement to a promise of salvation for the coastal lands by reading וּבְיֹשְׁבֵי as וְיָשְׁבוּ ('they will return'). LXX may have been influenced by וְיָשְׁבוּ in v. 8 (also 37:25). Zimmerli (1983, p. 290) says that LXX "produced a declaration of salvation for the (hitherto

---

[5] Zimmerli goes on to propose a possible location for Magog (concluding with the 'trade list' in 27:1f. and those mentioned in 38:8, 11, 14). Block (1998, p. 463) also concludes with these lands.

unmentioned) islands". This may be another deliberate wordplay; in MT the context indicates the coast lands belong to Gog, and will suffer with Gog, yet in LXX the context implies the coastal areas of Israel, to be rescued from Gog and be 'peacefully inhabited'. This shows a difference in LXX's eschatological understanding for the 'coast lands' or 'isles' in the plan of God.

39:7 וְאֶת־שֵׁם קָדְשִׁי אוֹדִיעַ בְּתוֹךְ עַמִּי יִשְׂרָאֵל וְלֹא־אַחֵל
אֶת־שֵׁם־קָדְשִׁי עוֹד וְיָדְעוּ הַגּוֹיִם כִּי־אֲנִי יְהוָה קָדוֹשׁ בְּיִשְׂרָאֵל:

39:7 καὶ τὸ ὄνομά μου τὸ ἅγιον γνωσθήσεται ἐν μέσῳ λαοῦ μου Ισραηλ καὶ οὐ βεβηλωθήσεται τὸ ὄνομα *μου τὸ ἅγιον* οὐκέτι καὶ γνώσονται (𝔊ᴬ: + παντα) τὰ ἔθνη ὅτι ἐγώ εἰμι κύριος ἅγιος ἐν Ισραηλ (*𝔊⁹⁶⁷ reverses the syntax).

In MT's אוֹדִיעַ ('I will make known'), God causes the action. LXX does not reflect this, instead having an impersonal passive γνωσθήσεται ('it shall be [made] known'). This may be due to the practice of locution that avoids the name of God (cf. 38:23). Likewise, MT says וְלֹא־אַחֵל ('I will not let [them] profane'), while LXX uses a passive verb to say that God's name "will not be profaned".

𝔊⁹⁶⁷'s τὸ ὄνομά τὸ ἅγιον μου matches MT's syntax (אֶת־שֵׁם־קָדְשִׁי).

𝔊ᴬ's unique παντα plus states that the knowledge of the LORD as 'Holy in Israel' will be 'universal' throughout 'all nations'. This plus most likely stemmed from the thought that the LORD's name was defiled by Israel amongst all the nations they entered (cf. 36:20–22). Block (1998, p. 464) says that "this revelation was necessary because it was precisely 'in Israel' that his reputation had been defiled, leading to the nation's exile and creating impressions in the foreigners' minds concerning his character".

Finally, MT's כִּי־אֲנִי יְהוָה קָדוֹשׁ בְּיִשְׂרָאֵל ('that I am the LORD, holy in Israel'), is matched by 𝔊ᴮ. However 𝔊⁹⁶⁷,ᴬ both add the definite article ὅ to read 'the Holy One in Israel', which Cooke (1936, p. 418)[6] points out, is a "title so common in Isaiah". 𝔊⁹⁶⁷,ᴬ's plus now declares the LORD's 'title' in Israel, rather than MT and 𝔊ᴮ declaring the LORD's holy character will be known by the nations.

---

[6] Whilst Cooke notes this plus, and even that it is in 𝔊ᴬ (𝔊⁹⁶⁷ was not extant to Cooke), he does not comment on any theological shift. Contra Cooke and Zimmerli, who both correctly have 'I am Yahweh, holy in Israel' Block has 'I am Yahweh, the Holy One in Israel' (also Cooper); Allen is similar 'I am Yahweh, the one who is holy in Israel'. Curiously, Block (1998, p. 464) sees MT has stating the LORD's title rather than being a reference to his character.

39:8 הִנֵּה בָאָה וְנִהְיָתָה נְאֻם אֲדֹנָי יְהוִה הוּא הַיּוֹם אֲשֶׁר דִּבַּרְתִּי:

39:8 ἰδοὺ ἥκει καὶ (𝕲ᴮ·ᴬ: γνώσῃ ὅτι; 𝕲⁹⁶⁷: –) ἔσται λέγει κύριος κύριος
αὕτη ἐστὶν ἡ ἡμέρα ἐν ᾗ ἐλάλησα

MT says הִנֵּה בָאָה וְנִהְיָתָה ('Look! it is coming and it will be done',[7] cf.
21:12). 𝕲ᴮ·ᴬ expand MT saying, ἰδοὺ ἥκει καὶ γνώσῃ ὅτι ἔσται ('Look!
it is come and *you shall know that* it will be'). 𝕲⁹⁶⁷ is minus γνώσῃ ὅτι,
matching MT, indicating this is likely a later LXX plus. But LXX
does not make it clear who shall 'know' this coming event, as γνώσῃ is
singular and thus cannot refer back to τὰ ἔθνη (v. 7); it may therefore
refer to the prophet himself (v. 1) or to 'Israel' (vv. 7, 9), yet likely to
Gog who was previously addressed in the singular (vv. 1–5).

39:9 וְיָצְאוּ יֹשְׁבֵי עָרֵי יִשְׂרָאֵל וּבִעֲרוּ וְהִשִּׂיקוּ בְּנֶשֶׁק וּמָגֵן וְצִנָּה
בְּקֶשֶׁת וּבְחִצִּים וּבְמַקֵּל יָד וּבְרֹמַח וּבִעֲרוּ בָהֶם אֵשׁ שֶׁבַע שָׁנִים:

39:9 καὶ ἐξελεύσονται οἱ κατοικοῦντες τὰς πόλεις Ισραηλ καὶ καύσουσιν
ἐν τοῖς ὅπλοις πέλταις (𝕲⁹⁶⁷: + καὶ δόρασι) καὶ κοντοῖς καὶ τόξοις καὶ
τοξεύμασιν καὶ ῥάβδοις χειρῶν καὶ λόγχαις καὶ καύσουσιν ἐν αὐτοῖς
πῦρ ἑπτὰ ἔτη

MT uses two verbs: וּבִעֲרוּ וְהִשִּׂיקוּ ('and fire/kindle and burn') where
LXX combines as καὶ καύσουσιν ('and ignite/burn'). Cooke (1936,
p. 418) says MT's second verb "need not be struck out; for the two
are associated in Is. 44¹⁵, and there is a play on the words for *burn* and
weapons". Eichrodt (1970, p. 518) claims that "as the LXX only reads
one verb here, the first of the two expressions meaning 'to kindle'
should be deleted". Zimmerli (1983, p. 291) suggests LXX "had the
double expression in front of them and telescoped it" (also Block,
1998, p. 464). LXX apparently missed or ignored the wordplay noted
by Cooke. However the later Theodotion did capture it by including
καὶ ἐκκαύσουσιν ('and kindle').

MT has וּמָגֵן וְצִנָּה ('small shield and body shield'), and LXX has
πέλταις καὶ κοντοῖς ('small shield and spear' [LEH]; or 'and pole' [LS;
Thayer]). Allen (1990b, p. 201) claims "the lack of preposition suggests
that the phrase relating to defensive weapons is a gloss". However, Block
(1998, p. 464) observes that "the pair is attested in the versions, though
the LXX reads the second term as 'lance'". LXX may be translating
according to the equipment used by soldiers of their day (cf. 38:5). 𝕲⁹⁶⁷
also has καὶ δόρασι ('and spears') as plus before 'lance'.

---

[7] הִנֵּה conveys immediacy and imminence, thus this is not the distant future.

6.3. 7TH ORACLE: EZEK. 39:11–16

All MT MSS, and 𝕲^B,A exhibit a sense division break after v. 10 and
then again after v. 16 (𝕲^967 only exhibits a break after v. 16). MT and
𝕲^B,A view these six verses as one pericope, likely because they deal
with Gog's burial and the communal search for bones that will 'cleanse
the land' (vv. 12, 14, 16). In this pericope we will find LXX exegeting
aspects of Gog's burial place, and MT's 'the [ones] travelling'.

39:11 וְהָיָה בַיּוֹם הַהוּא אֶתֵּן לְגוֹג מְקוֹם־שָׁם קֶבֶר בְּיִשְׂרָאֵל
גֵּי הָעֹבְרִים קִדְמַת הַיָּם וְחֹסֶמֶת הִיא אֶת־הָעֹבְרִים וְקָבְרוּ
שָׁם אֶת־גּוֹג וְאֶת־כָּל־הֲמוֹנֹה וְקָרְאוּ גֵּיא הֲמוֹן גּוֹג:

39:11 καὶ ἔσται ἐν τῇ ἡμέρᾳ ἐκείνῃ δώσω τῷ Γωγ τόπον ὀνομαστόν
μνημεῖον ἐν Ισραηλ τὸ πολυάνδριον τῶν ἐπελθόντων πρὸς τῇ θαλάσσῃ καὶ
περιοικοδομήσουσιν τὸ περιστόμιον τῆς φάραγγος [12]^8 καὶ κατορύξουσιν
ἐκεῖ τὸν Γωγ καὶ πᾶν τὸ πλῆθος αὐτοῦ καὶ κληθήσεται τὸ (𝕲^967,A: γαι;
𝕲^B: τε) τὸ πολυάνδριον τοῦ Γωγ

MT has מְקוֹם־שָׁם קֶבֶר ([lit.] 'a place of there a grave'); LXX says τόπον
ὀνομαστόν ('a famous place', or 'a place of renown'). This is one of
Cooke's (1936, p. xliii) examples where "𝕲, owing to the absence of
vowel signs in the Hebrew text, confuses words written with the same
consonants, but pronounced differently". Cooke (1936, p. 419) retains
MT's reading, saying "[LXX's] change…does not suit the context so
well". Allen (1990b, p. 201) also believes that LXX appears to misread
שָׁם as שֵׁם, saying "MT is usually preferred, as a short relative clause:
'a place where there is a grave in Israel' (cf. GKC §130c, d)". Yet, this
may be another deliberate word play by LXX to state that Gog's burial
place will be well known, suggested by its use of μνημεῖον ('memorial'
[LEH]) rather than τάφος ('grave/tomb' [LEH]). This may have been
influenced by an eschatological theme regarding the destruction of Gog,
and the continued free movements of the people of the land. LXX's
reading here may also have been influenced by לְשֵׁם in v. 13. On the
other hand, the later Masoretes may have purposefully read the text
as 'there', and placed the vowels accordingly, rather than having Gog
having a 'place of renown' in Israel. However, due to the other LXX
variances in this verse, we remain with our 'wordplay' interpretive
suggestion.

---

[8] The traditional LXX divisions for vv. 12–13 differ from those in MT. This does
not affect meaning and hence for ease of reference we follow MT numbering.

MT says גֵּי הָעֹבְרִים (lit. 'the valley of the passing-through-ones' or 'the Valley of the Travellers' [cf. JPS]). Alternatively, Block (1997c, p. 109) says, "the valley of those who have passed on", which brings out the contextual aspect of death and/or burial.[9] Eichrodt (1970, p. 528) claims that "the proper reading cannot be established with any certainty, as the first name may contain some play on words referring to a legendary item in the Gog-tradition which is no longer preserved for us (its connection with the commission who 'travel' through the land is a word-play introduced at a secondary stage)". Yet his suggestion holds a lot of conjecture. Zimmerli (1983, pp. 292, 317) sees this as the name of the valley, 'Oberim Valley', transliterating the Hebrew rather than interpreting it. Allen (1990b, p. 201) claims that הָעֹבְרִים "has probably suffered assimilation to the term in v. 15 and was originally הָעֲבָרִים [sic] 'Abarim,' a mountainous district in Moab".[10] Irwin (1995, p. 98) points out that "one of the reasons that this emendation has gained such wide acceptance is the presence of the modifying phrase *qidmat hayyām*—a combination that most scholars have translated as 'east of the sea'". Irwin (1995, p. 99f.) finds in favour of the MT, but notes "in its most basic sense *qidmat* means 'opposite' or 'in front of' with the direction indicated by the perspective of the writer... [and] the phrase in question could quite easily be rendered, 'in front of/opposite the sea', a translation supported by LXX". However, Block (1998, pp. 466, 468) disagrees with the various proposals, and does not emend the text. Significantly, here LXX says τῶν ἐπελθόντων ('the coming/arriving ones'), which does not interpret הָעֹבְרִים as a place, but translates according to its form in MT. But ἐπέρχομαι can have the meaning of '*in hostile sense, to go* or *come against, to attack, assault,*' [LS] (cf. 34:4). Therefore,

---

[9] Irwin (1995, p. 110) suggests that הָעֹבְרִים recalls Molek worship practices, and says that "Ezekiel's description of the forces of Gog as 'the Ones Passing Through' [הָעֹבְרִים] suggests a connection with the actions of parents who caused the children to 'pass through/into' the fire to Molek (Lev. 18:21; 2 Kgs. 23:10; Jer. 32:35)".

[10] Cooke (1936, p. 419) also has the location as east of the Dead Sea which is "outside the Holy Land strictly so called (47[18]), and in a district which belonged to Moab; but it was sometimes held by Israel in the former days...and had Israelite connexions". Cooke also concludes the same mountain range suggested by Allen and says that the use of הָעֹבְרִים is a wordplay "on *way-farers* in the next sentence". See also Zimmerli (1983, p. 317) and Irwin (1995, p. 98f.) for discussions of possible locations, and for 'the sea'. The potential location is not part of our interest, as LXX does not translate הָעֹבְרִים as a place. Irwin correctly observes that all MT MSS witness הָעֹבְרִים, and gives several reason why this is located in Israel (Jezreel), holding that 'the sea' spoken of is the Mediterranean and not the Dead Sea (contra Cooke, 1936, p. 419).

LXX may have interpreted the 'coming ones' as Gog's hostile forces, and the ones destined to be buried in that place.

LXX does not translate literally the preceding גֵּי ('valley'), but rather exegetes it with πολυάνδριον, which, whilst literally meaning 'full of men', is often translated as 'burial place'. Bruce (1995, p. 542) proposes "communal cemetery" (cf. vv. 11, 15, 16; Jer. 19:2, 6), and so may be translated as '*mass* burial place'. LXX may have been influenced by their transliteration of 'τὸ γαι' as the burial place of Gog and his multitude (v. 11c).

LXX does not mention MT's burial location '*east of* the sea', but gives the sea itself as the destination for MT's 'travellers'.

Based on the above observations, we suggest MT's focus is on the location of Gog's burial place in Israel, גֵּי הָעֹבְרִים קִדְמַת הַיָּם ('the Valley of the Travellers east of the sea'). LXX's focus however is on interpreting those who will be buried in Gog's 'place of renown in Israel': τὸ πολυάνδριον τῶν ἐπελθόντων πρὸς τῇ θαλάσσῃ ('a mass burial place of those coming to the sea'). Thus we again find LXX exegeting and/or interpreting the Hebrew.

Following this, MT says, וְחֹסֶמֶת הִיא אֶת־הָעֹבְרִים ('and it will stop the travellers' [or 'the passing-through-ones']). LXX says, καὶ περιοικοδομήσουσιν τὸ περιστόμιον τῆς φάραγγος ([lit.] 'and they shall build up the edge of the valley' or 'dam up the valley') (so Zimmerli, 1983, p. 292). Bewer (1953, p. 165) also follows LXX, and emends MT to read וְחָסְמוּ אֶת־הַגַּיְא ('and they will dam up the valley').[11] Eichrodt (1970, pp. 517–518) suggests "and they will stop the valley", and says this is "a conjectural emendation of the impossible reading in the [MT] text". Allen (1990b, p. 201) prefers LXX and sees אֶת ־הָעֹבְרִים "as a gloss on בית ישראל 'community of Israel' in v. 12.... MT may have been corrupted after the gloss entered the text". His rationale is based on reconciling the two burial descriptions here and in v. 15. However, Block (1998, p. 467) proposes that "LXX may also have misread the Hebrew". He (1998, p. 469) also suggests that "given Ezekiel's penchant for using words with more than one sense in a given context, the second occurrence of הָעֹבְרִים could also refer to travellers who would traverse the valley but are prevented by the huge mounds of corpses blocking

---

[11] So also *BHS*. Bewer (1953, p. 165) argues that "the valley does not muzzle or stop up or dam the passers-by but it is itself muzzled or dammed up". Yet, MT may only be a figure of speech.

the valley". Following Block, we suggest that LXX, under the same interpretive thought as seen above, exegetes MT to state that the mass burial place of Gog, and 'those coming to the sea', will be to such an extent that it will 'dam up the valley', and therefore will be 'a place of renown'.

Finally, MT says וְקָרְאוּ גֵיא הֲמוֹן גּוֹג ('and they will call [it], the valley of Hamon Gog', or 'the valley of the Multitude[12] of Gog'), while LXX says καὶ κληθήσεται τὸ γαι τὸ πολυάνδριον τοῦ Γωγ ('and it will be called *the gai*, the mass burial place of Gog').[13] LXX transliterates גֵיא with a definite article, and therefore exegetes it as the name of Gog's burial place: 'the Gai [Valley]'. The LXX community may have just referred to this 'place of renown' as 'The Valley'. Odell (1994, p. 485) suggests that גֵיא הֲמוֹן גּוֹג "should be regarded as a pun on the Valley of the Son of Hinnom, the valley southwest of Jerusalem where child sacrifice and forbidden burial rites were conducted until the fall of Jerusalem" and "the Valley of the Oberim is a synonym of the Valley of Hinnom".[14] Irwin (1995, p. 96) says similarly "the prophet seems to be creating a word-play with this name and the name of the burial place of the [idolatrous] Judahites—*gê' ben-hinnōm* (Jer. 7:32)", with an MT allusion to Hinnom, and to the worship of Molek that took place there (1995, p. 102f.).[15] Kline (1996, p. 215) proposes that MT 'recalls God's wordplay interpretation of the new name, Abraham, he gave to Abram as a gift of grace: *'ab hămôn gôyîm* (Gen. 17:4–5)... In quest of such name-fame Gog mustered his multitudes, but his *hămôn*-name proclaimed his shame". It is perhaps significant that LXX again uses πολυάνδριον ('mass burial place' [see above]) here rather than Εννομ (cf. Jer. 7:32; 19:6; 32:35). We suggest that LXX captured MT's pun with the place of child sacrifices (cf. Odell, Irwin), interpreting the 'Valley of Hamon-Gog' as the place for Gog's mass burial place, known in their

---

[12] Eichrodt (1970, p. 518) puts the meaning of "*pomp* of Gog" here, but that does not appear to be correct, and it is not reflected by LXX.

[13] 𝔊ᴮ's τέ is most likely a corruption of γαι (Cooke, 1936, p. 424). Bruce (1995, p. 543) says it is "evidentially a corruption of γέ". γέ is found in 𝔊ᴮ in 39:15 (noted by Bruce), but nowhere else in LXX Ezekiel. 𝔊ᴮ appears to have been transliterating the Hebrew singular construct form of גֵיא (גֵּי).

[14] Odell (1994, p. 458) says that "Ezekiel employs this verb in its hiphil form to designate child sacrifice, one of the rites performed in the Valley of Hinnom". Block (1997c, p. 109) notes גֵיא הֲמוֹן גּוֹג "appears to play on הגּוֹם [sic] גֵּי 'the Valley of Hinnom', where the bodies of animals and criminals used to be burned" [n.b.: הִנֹּם intended].

[15] Irwin (1995, p. 101f.) believes that Ezekiel is ultimately referring to the Jezreel Valley.

time simply as 'The Gai/Valley'.[16] LXX's double use of πολυάνδριον suggests it saw both locations as the same site of Gog's mass burial place. MT seems to change the name of this valley from גֵּי to גֵּיא הֲמוֹן גּוֹג; but LXX stays with just πολυάνδριον. Symmachus (Ziegler, 1977, p. 287f.) has ἡ φάραγξ τῶν διαβάσεων ἐξ ἀνατολῆς τῆς θαλάσσης, ἡ ἐμφράσσουσα τὰς διαβάσεις ('the valley of the crossers/travellers from east of the Sea, [it] shall stop the crossers/travellers'), which appears to be an adjustment towards MT.

39:12 וּקְבָרוּם בֵּית יִשְׂרָאֵל לְמַעַן טַהֵר אֶת־הָאָרֶץ שִׁבְעָה חֳדָשִׁים:

39:12 καὶ κατορύξουσιν αὐτοὺς οἶκος Ισραηλ ἵνα καθαρισθῇ ἡ γῆ ἐν ἑπταμήνῳ

There is a subtle syntax difference between MT and LXX, with MT having an *athnach* under land (הָאָרֶץ), and then following has שִׁבְעָה חֳדָשִׁים (seven months) which is therefore linked back with the beginning verb ('to bury'). LXX has the whole phrase linked with ἵνα making the purpose as to cleanse the land *in 7 months*, whereas the purpose for MT is to just cleanse the land (cf. v. 14). This verse appears to echo priestly concerns regarding corpses defiling the land, and ritual cleansing. It may be another example where Ezekiel, and the LXX translator, are reflecting on the Book of Numbers (cf. Num. 5:2; 19:16; 35:33) (Wong, 2001, p. 136).[17]

39:13 וְקָבְרוּ כָּל־עַם הָאָרֶץ וְהָיָה לָהֶם לְשֵׁם יוֹם הִכָּבְדִי נְאֻם אֲדֹנָי יְהוִה:

39:13 καὶ κατορύξουσιν αὐτοὺς πᾶς ὁ λαὸς τῆς γῆς καὶ ἔσται αὐτοῖς εἰς ὀνομαστὸν ᾗ ἡμέρᾳ ἐδοξάσθην λέγει κύριος

LXX's αὐτούς plus provides an object (bury *them*), which is only implied by MT's context. MT says יוֹם הִכָּבְדִי ('the day I am glorified'), or as

---

[16] Bruce (1995, p. 533) points out that LXX also uses πολυάνδριος when translating 'valley' in Jer. 2:23f., and suggests that this was done because "the translator identified this 'valley' with the valley of the son(s) of Hinnom which, according to other oracles of Jeremiah, was to become a place for the disposal of corpses". We may suggest this 'identification' by LXX's translator also occurs here in Ezek. 39:11.

[17] Block (1998, p. 470) also finds a link here with Num. 19 and the concern to keep the land ceremonially clean, observing "that the process [in Ezek. 39:12] will take a full week of months, rather than the week of days prescribed in Num. 19, speaks not only of the magnitude of the task but also of the concern to render the land absolutely holy". Wong (2001, p. 136) points out that the concern here is ritual cleansing and "hence this case should not be confused with the sort of land pollution in 36:18 where moral impurity is concerned".

Block (1998, p. 467) says "on the day that I display my glory". This suggests future action, although the Hebrew infinitive is indeterminate regarding time. LXX, however, uses an aorist passive, ᾗ ἡμέρᾳ ἐδοξάσθην ('the day when I was glorified'), indicating they saw a past action. Block (1998, p. 471) also suggests that whilst MT uses the *niphal*, which "may be interpreted as a simple passive . . . it is better interpreted reflexively: Yahweh effects his own glorification, and finally receives the recognition he deserves". This is not reflected in LXX.

39:14 וְאַנְשֵׁי תָמִיד יַבְדִּילוּ עֹבְרִים בָּאָרֶץ מְקַבְּרִים אֶתהָעֹבְרִים
אֶת־הַנּוֹתָרִים עַל־פְּנֵי הָאָרֶץ לְטַהֲרָהּ מִקְצֵה שִׁבְעָה־חֳדָשִׁים יַחְקֹרוּ:

39:14 καὶ ἄνδρας διὰ παντὸς διαστελοῦσιν ἐπιπορευομένους (𝕲ᴬ: + πάντα) τὴν γῆν θάψαι τοὺς καταλελειμμένους ἐπὶ προσώπου τῆς γῆς (𝕲⁹⁶⁷: + καὶ) καθαρίσαι αὐτὴν μετὰ τὴν ἑπτάμηνον καὶ ἐκζητήσουσιν (𝕲ᴬ: + ἀκριβῶς)

The second instance of עֹבְרִים ('travellers') in MT in this verse is not witnessed by LXX. *BHS* and some EVV follow LXX. Zimmerli (1983, p. 292) suggests that this second occurrence "does not fit the context and . . . is to be regarded as an addition" (also Cooke, 1936, p. 420). Block (1998, p. 467) suggests that LXX "may have intentionally tried to smooth out an awkward reading, or omitted it by homoioteleuton. Targ.'s 'with those who pass by' changes the sense but does support MT". This may be a later MT plus, to emphasise that the burial will be done by 'travellers', and not by the people of Israel, lest they are defiled by touching the dead (cf. this 'plus' v. 15).

𝕲ᴬ has two unique plusses: 1. πάντα ('*all* [the land]'); 2. ἀκριβῶς ('[they shall search] precisely/diligently' [LEH]). Both plusses reveal the theological thought that the search will be performed intensely and extensively. This may stem from the belief that corpses and bones on the ground are a curse, and pollute the land.

As in v. 12, we find a syntactical difference between MT and LXX: in the final clause MT indicates another search was to start מִקְצֵה ('at the end of' [*HALOT*]) the seven months spoken of in v. 12, which then makes way for the action in v. 15. However, LXX takes MT's לְטַהֲרָהּ from the preceding clause and links it with 'after seven months'; this continues the previous purpose of 'cleansing' for seven months, rather than generating a new search. LXX then adds καί before the last word forming a new phrase ('and they shall seek'). Again, as in v. 12, this may result from priestly concerns over 'cleansing', and the concept of 'seven months'.

6.4. 8TH ORACLE: EZEK. 39:17–24

All representative MT and LXX MSS exhibit a break before v. 17. MT^A has a *petuḥah*, MT^{C,L} a *setumah*. $\mathfrak{G}^A$ also exhibits a major break, and $\mathfrak{G}^B$ a minor. All MSS finish this sense division after v. 24, except $\mathfrak{G}^{967}$ which continues from v. 17 until the end of the chapter (v. 29).

This pericope deals with the sacrificial meal of Gog that the LORD sets up for the birds and wild animals, which is done for the purpose of God establishing his glory among the nations (v. 21). Interestingly, this meal comes after the information regarding Gog's burial covered in the previous pericope (cf. vv. 11–16). Yet, there is a connection with v. 4 that also informs how birds and wild animals will eat the flesh of Gog and his hordes. Irwin (1995, pp. 107f.) proposes that this pericope refers to "Molek cult imagery", and is a "non-Yahwistic pattern" even if "it is Yahweh himself who brings the victim". Irwin (1995, p. 109) continues that "the picture, then, is of a sacrifice orchestrated by Yahweh, but described in decidedly non-Yahwistic terms". Yet, this is not explicitly stated in MT, and more importantly, LXX does not exegete the text in this way.

39:17 וְאַתָּה בֶן־אָדָם כֹּה־אָמַר אֲדֹנָי יְהֹוִה אֱמֹר לְצִפּוֹר כָּל־כָּנָף
וּלְכֹל חַיַּת הַשָּׂדֶה הִקָּבְצוּ וָבֹאוּ הֵאָסְפוּ מִסָּבִיב עַל־זִבְחִי אֲשֶׁר אֲנִי
זֹבֵחַ לָכֶם זֶבַח גָּדוֹל עַל הָרֵי יִשְׂרָאֵל וַאֲכַלְתֶּם בָּשָׂר וּשְׁתִיתֶם דָּם:

39:17 καὶ σύ υἱὲ ἀνθρώπου εἰπόν τάδε λέγει κύριος εἰπὸν παντὶ ὀρνέῳ
πετεινῷ καὶ πρὸς πάντα τὰ θηρία τοῦ πεδίου συνάχθητε καὶ ἔρχεσθε
(𝔊^{B,A}: συνάχθητε; 𝔊^{967}: –) ἀπὸ πάντων τῶν περικύκλῳ ἐπὶ τὴν θυσίαν
μου ἣν τέθυκα ὑμῖν θυσίαν μεγάλην ἐπὶ (𝔊^{967}: + παντα) τὰ ὄρη Ισραηλ
καὶ φάγεσθε κρέα καὶ πίεσθε αἷμα

Verse 17 enjoys a large degree of agreement between MT and LXX, which is unusual for a longer detailed verse. LXX does have a plus of 'εἰπόν' in the opening phrase (cf. 7:2). $\mathfrak{G}^{B,A}$ have συνάχθητε ('be assembled'), witnessing MT's הֵאָסְפוּ. This is minus in $\mathfrak{G}^{967}$, which perhaps saw the occurrence as a dittograph. $\mathfrak{G}^{967}$ has παντα ('all [the mountains]') as a plus, perhaps to emphasise that this sacrifice will be throughout the land.

39:18 בְּשַׂר גִּבּוֹרִים תֹּאכֵלוּ וְדַם־נְשִׂיאֵי הָאָרֶץ תִּשְׁתּוּ
אֵילִים כָּרִים וְעַתּוּדִים פָּרִים מְרִיאֵי בָשָׁן כֻּלָּם

39:18 κρέα γιγάντων φάγεσθε καὶ αἷμα ἀρχόντων τῆς γῆς πίεσθε κριοὺς
καὶ μόσχους καὶ τράγους καὶ οἱ μόσχοι ἐστεατωμένοι πάντες

MT speaks of גִּבּוֹרִים ('mighty [ones]'), and LXX of γίγαντες: (lit. 'giants'; also 'mighty one[s]' [LEH]; cf. Ezek. 32:12, 21, 27). Typically LXX uses γίγαντες for רְפָאִים, and δυνατοί for גִּבּוֹרִים, although γίγας is used for גִּבּוֹר in LXX including Ezek. 32:12, 21, 27 (2×) as well as 39:18, 20. Both these passages have mythological overtones and there are links with Gen. 6:4 and Num. 13:33. Cooke (1936, p. 421) claims "these are not members of Gog's army, who are described differently, 38³⁻⁷ 39⁴"; he then suggests they are either other enemies of Israel, "Persian forces", or those "under Antiochus III". However, this is not apparent in LXX, beyond their use of γίγας (rather than δυνατός), which still contextually refers to Gog and his hordes.

There is a difference in the sacrificial animals, where MT appears to have a full contingent with 'rams, lambs, goats, bulls', LXX only has 'rams, calves, goats' (cf. 27:21 where these are listed as trade animals). Symmachus says ταύρων μοσχων σιτιστῶν ('bulls, fatted calves'). Likewise MT declares they are all like מְרִיאֵי בָשָׁן (lit. 'fatlings of Bashan'), yet LXX interprets this as οἱ μόσχοι ἐστεατωμένοι ('the fatted calves'), and does not mention 'Bashan'.[22] Zimmerli (1983, pp. 293–294) argues for the retention of MT. Block (1998, p. 476) says that "these terms are obviously not used literally, but as animal designations for nobility".

39:19 וַאֲכַלְתֶּם־חֵלֶב לְשָׂבְעָה וּשְׁתִיתֶם דָּם לְשִׁכָּרוֹן מִזִּבְחִי
אֲשֶׁר־זָבַחְתִּי לָכֶם:

39:19 καὶ φάγεσθε στέαρ εἰς πλησμονὴν καὶ πίεσθε αἷμα εἰς μέθην ἀπὸ τῆς θυσίας μου (𝕲⁹⁶⁷: –) ἧς ἔθυσα ὑμῖν

𝕲⁹⁶⁷ is minus μου, thus it only reads 'the sacrifice', removing the personal aspect of God's sacrifice.

39:21 וְנָתַתִּי אֶת־כְּבוֹדִי בַּגּוֹיִם וְרָאוּ כָל־הַגּוֹיִם אֶת־מִשְׁפָּטִי
אֲשֶׁר עָשִׂיתִי וְאֶת־יָדִי אֲשֶׁר־שַׂמְתִּי בָהֶם:

39:21 καὶ δώσω τὴν δόξαν μου ἐν ὑμῖν καὶ ὄψονται πάντα τὰ ἔθνη τὴν κρίσιν μου ἣν ἐποίησα καὶ τὴν χεῖρά μου ἣν ἐπήγαγον ἐπ' αὐτούς

MT says that God will give his glory בַּגּוֹיִם ('among *the nations*'), whereas LXX says it will be ἐν ὑμῖν ('*in you*'). Cooke (1936, p. 424) says LXX's ἐν ὑμῖν is 'wrong[ly]'. Zimmerli (1983, p. 294) also does not agree with

---

[22] LXX shows awareness of 'Bashan' in 27:6, translating with Βασανίτιδος ('the land of Bashan'). If Thackeray is correct, then this was done via 'Translator α' rather than 'Translator β' who translated 36–39 (cf. our chapter 2).

any suggestion to emend בַּגּוֹיִם to בגוג, preferring MT. Wong (2002, p. 133) proposes that "it is possible, though not very likely that the translator wrongly read בגוים as בכם. It is more likely that the translator found the Hebrew expression uncongenial and changed it.... to ἐν ὑμῖν, referring to God's giving his glory to or among the Israelites". While we agree with Wong about the translator changing deliberately, we suggest ἐν ὑμῖν does not refer to Israel, but rather to birds and animals as the addressees in the previous verses (cf. ὑμῖν vv. 17–20). Israel has not been directly addressed in this chapter, and so cannot be the referent of ἐν ὑμῖν.[23] We agree with Wong (2002, p. 133) that "in the Hebrew, God's giving of his glory to the nations is associated with his punishment inflicted on the nations (v. 21b)". In LXX, God's glory, established in the actions of the birds and animals at the sacrificial feast, is also associated with his punishment on the nations. God's glory does not go out *for* the nations, neither in MT or LXX, but it is 'given' or 'established' in his sacrificial meal, as he punishes the nations along with Gog on the mountains of Israel (cf. vv. 17–20). These birds and animals are part of God's creation, and are acting as his agents.

39:22 וְיָדְעוּ בֵּית יִשְׂרָאֵל כִּי אֲנִי יְהוָה אֱלֹהֵיהֶם מִן־הַיּוֹם
הַהוּא וָהָלְאָה:

39:22 καὶ γνώσονται οἶκος Ισραηλ ὅτι ἐγώ εἰμι κύριος ὁ θεὸς αὐτῶν ἀπὸ τῆς ἡμέρας ταύτης καὶ ἐπέκεινα

MT says מִן־הַיּוֹם הַהוּא ('from *that* day'). LXX says ἀπὸ τῆς ἡμέρας ταύτης ('from *this* day'). LXX changes MT's eschatological 'that day' to a present reality. LXX may have interpreted their current events (the Seleucids and/or Romans) as the fulfilment of the prophet's words. After examining the occurrences of הַיּוֹם הַהוּא, and how LXX translated them, Wong observes the unique use of ταύτης here, rather than the expected ἐκείνης, and finds that the distance to this perceived event influenced LXX. Wong (2002, p. 135) says that "at the time when LXX was made, the idea of Gog had become more common.... the translator saw the Gog-event as something near to his time, and it was not longer seen as belonging to the distant indefinite future".

39:23 וְיָדְעוּ הַגּוֹיִם כִּי בַעֲוֹנָם גָּלוּ בֵית־יִשְׂרָאֵל עַל אֲשֶׁר מָעֲלוּ־בִי
וָאַסְתִּר פָּנַי מֵהֶם וָאֶתְּנֵם בְּיַד צָרֵיהֶם וַיִּפְּלוּ בַחֶרֶב כֻּלָּם:

---

[23] If Wong is correct, and ἐν ὑμῖν does refer to Israel, then we agree "the Greek rendering would also imply a change from a negative action of God with respect to the nations to a positive action of God with respect to Israel" (Wong, 2002, p. 133).

39:23 καὶ γνώσονται πάντα τὰ ἔθνη ὅτι διὰ τὰς ἁμαρτίας αὐτῶν ἠχμαλωτεύθησαν οἶκος Ισραηλ ἀνθ᾽ ὧν ἠθέτησαν εἰς ἐμέ καὶ ἀπέστρεψα τὸ πρόσωπόν μου ἀπ᾽ αὐτῶν καὶ παρέδωκα αὐτοὺς εἰς χεῖρας τῶν ἐχθρῶν αὐτῶν καὶ ἔπεσαν πάντες μαχαίρᾳ

LXX has another πάντα plus here, expanding on MT to state that 'all' the nations will know that Israel's exile was because of her sin, and not any weakness on God's part. The LORD will restore Israel to establish his reputation ('name') in Israel and in the nations (cf. v. 25–29; 36:21f.). Wong (2002, p. 136) notes the frequency of LXX's πάντα plus in this block (38:12, 16; 39:7, 23), and explains these occurrences as "an intensification or 'exaggeration' of the situation... the translator wanted to provide a more impressive picture of the battle with Gog".

MT here has גְּלוֹ ('they went into exile'; cf. v. 28), and LXX ἠχμαλωτεύθησαν ('they were led captive'). While αἰχμαλωτεύω is used for גָּלָה elsewhere (cf. Ezek. 12:3; Mic. 1:16; Lam. 2:14), LXX's use of the passive has this as an action done to Israel.

MT also says מָעֲלוּ־בִי ('they acted unfaithfully/treacherously against me' [BDB]), where LXX says ἀνθ᾽ ὧν ἠθέτησαν εἰς ἐμέ ('because they rejected me'). *TWOT* notes that "in almost all the biblical references *māʿal* is used to designate the breaking or violation of religious law as a conscious act of treachery. The victim against whom the breach is perpetrated is God".[24] *HALOT*'s 'to be untrue, violate one's legal obligations' also reflects this concept.[25] We note that ἀθετέω can mean 'to reject (the law)' [LEH; BAGD][26] and is contextually used in its other occurrence in Ezekiel (cf. 22:26, for MT's חמס 'treat violently').[27] In Ezekiel, LXX typically uses παραπίπτω 'to fall away, to commit apostasy' [LEH] for מעל (14:13; 15:8 (2×); 18:24 (2×); 20:27 (2×)). The typical context in these verses shows God speaking to Israel regarding

---

[24] Block (1998, p. 482) also gives the meaning "infidelity in covenant relationships, specifically treachery against Yahweh, the divine patron".

[25] That the context is speaking of covenantal obligations may also be found in v. 24 (not discussed here due to absence of variants), where the verb פשע ('rebellion' [*NIDOTTE*]) is used (LXX: ἀνόμημα 'lawless action' [LS]), of which Wong (2001, p. 74) says, "with Israel as the subject, it denotes a break, a completed separation from Yahweh the suzerain of Israel and therefore a breach of the covenant with Yahweh" (cf. 37:23).

[26] Thayer says "'to act toward anything as though it were annulled'; hence, to deprive a law of force by opinions or acts opposed to it, to transgress it,... Ezek. 22:26" [Thayer does not mention 39:23]; and LS has "to set aside: to deny one, refuse his request", which does not reflect the 'legal' sense the other lexicons reflect.

[27] Outside of Ezekiel, LXX uses ἀθετέω for מעל in only 1Chron. 2:7; 5:25; 2Chron. 36:14; Neh. 1:8.

their 'falling away' and/or 'committing apostasy'. However, LXX uses
ἀδικία for מעל in 39:26. We suggest that LXX used ἀθετέω here for
מעל, rather than its typical παραπίπτω, to highlight that *all* (cf. πάντα
plus) the nations will know that Israel was exiled because they rejected
God's ways.[28] Therefore, LXX use of ἀθετέω here is perhaps as an
echo back to 22:26, to imply they also rejected God's law/command-
ments. LXX may therefore be seen as interpreting MT's מעל, in a
similar way to previous chapters where we saw LXX interpreting the
heart behind MT's action.[29]

6.5. 9th Oracle: Ezek. 39:25–29

All MT MSS and 𝔊^{B,A} exhibit a sense division break before v. 25, while
𝔊^{967} has vv. 17–29 in the one long pericope. The next break for all
MSS is at the end of v. 29, which is the end of the chapter.

Whilst a number of scholars have suggested disassociating this final
pericope in chapter 39, there is no textual evidence to suggest this was
not also the work of the prophet.[30] It focuses upon the final restoration
of the nation of Israel from the exile after the defeat of Gog (vv. 25–28),
and their restored favour with God whom they will know (v. 28), and
who will no longer 'hide his face' (cf. vv. 23, 24, 29), but will pour out
his Spirit (MT), or wrath (LXX), upon them (cf. v. 29). That such a
strong statement of restoration comes at the end of the Gog account
suggests that the defeat of her enemies is a major part in the overall
restoration of Israel as a nation. In the received chapter order, they
are now free to rebuild their temple and worship the LORD (chapters

---

[28] Wong (2001, p. 105) suggests a link here to Lev. 26:40 saying "the observation
that Lev 26:40–41 seems to imply a causal link between the act of מעל (as an example
of עון) and the exile, and this link is made explicitly in Ez 39:23". However, we point
out that LXX uses ἁμαρτία 'fault/error' [LS] in Lev. 26:40 and so we question if the
LXX translator caught this link here. Curiously, in his later work, Wong (2002, p. 137)
notes LXX Ezekiel's unusual use of ἀθετέω here, but does not offer any explanation,
other than to propose מעל is a later textual addition.

[29] Cooke (1936, p. 422) claims that the phrase 'because they trespassed against me'
is in the wrong place and should be in v. 24. However all representative MSS have this
in the same location in v. 23 and so Cooke's claim is without textual witness.

[30] See Block (1987, p. 262) who says "in spite of the novel features in 21–9 caution
is advised against haste in eliminating the text as non-Ezekielian or inauthentic or
misplaced". His following pages demonstrate the cohesiveness of this final pericope
to the rest of the chapter.

40–48). However, in 𝕲[967]'s chapter order the textual flow goes into the resurrection of the Dry Bones, the establishment of the united nation under a Davidic ruler, after which they build the temple. This final pericope helps the reader understand that the Gog epic was just part of the restoration of Israel, and that God's focus was always on his people Israel, and not on her enemies who are just God's agents.[31]

39:25 לָכֵן כֹּה אָמַר אֲדֹנָי יְהוִֹה עַתָּה אָשִׁיב אֶת־(K שְׁבִית)
[Q שְׁבוּת] יַעֲקֹב וְרִחַמְתִּי כָּל־בֵּית יִשְׂרָאֵל וְקִנֵּאתִי לְשֵׁם קָדְשִׁי:

39:25 διὰ τοῦτο τάδε λέγει κύριος κύριος νῦν ἀποστρέψω τὴν αἰχμα-λωσίαν Ιακωβ καὶ ἐλεήσω τὸν οἶκον Ισραηλ καὶ ζηλώσω διὰ τὸ ὄνομα τὸ ἅγιόν μου

Unlike all the other occurrences of כָּל־בֵּית יִשְׂרָאֵל in MT, LXX does not reflect כָּל here.[32] If כָּל was in LXX's *Vorlage*, the translator perhaps did not see that God's mercy was on *all* the house of Israel, viewing their current events as judgement. This LXX minus is perhaps more noticeable due to the willingness elsewhere to insert πάντα as a plus, especially when referring to '*all* the nations' (cf. 38:12, 16, 23; 39:7, 23). After examining this frequent Ezekielian phrase, Wong (2002, p. 138) concludes that here "כל was probably first not in the Hebrew but added later. The reason for the addition is that the restoration of Israel implies the union of *all* tribes". LXX also does not witness MT's כל in the following verse (cf. '*all* their sins' v. 26), and we suggest MT added both at a later date.

For MT's וְקִנֵּאתִי לְשֵׁם קָדְשִׁי ('and I will be jealous for my holy name'), LXX says καὶ ζηλώσω διὰ τὸ ὄνομα τὸ ἅγιόν μου ('and I will be jealous on account of (or, 'for the sake of') my holy name'). Zimmerli (1983, p. 294) points out that MT's "jealousy for the name is turned by 𝕲 into 'on account of the jealousy' (διά) of the name". Wong (2002, p. 139) proposes three possibilities: "διά with the accusative here either shows that the translator understands the phrase as what it means in 36,22, or that the translator wants to harmonise the readings, or that the transla-tor attempts to emphasise the importance of the holy name of God in

---

[31] As Block (1987, p. 267) says, "with the expanded recognition formula taking up the last two verses, the text emphasizes that the covenant relationship among deity, people and land has been reinstituted. Its restoration is full and permanent. Yahweh will never leave any of them, neither will he hide is face from them again".

[32] כָּל־בֵּית יִשְׂרָאֵל occurs in 3:7; 5:4; 11:15; 12:10; 20:40; 36:10; 37:11, 16; 39:25; 45:6. LXX witnesses כל in all these places, except here.

39:27 ἐν τῷ ἀποστρέψαι με αὐτοὺς ἐκ τῶν ἐθνῶν καὶ συναγαγεῖν
(𝔊ᴮˑᴬ: με; 𝔊⁹⁶⁷: –) αὐτοὺς ἐκ τῶν χωρῶν (𝔊ᴮˑᴬ: τῶν ἐθνῶν; 𝔊⁹⁶⁷: –) καὶ
ἁγιασθήσομαι ἐν αὐτοῖς ἐνώπιον (𝔊ᴮˑᴬ: τῶν; 𝔊⁹⁶⁷: –) ἐθνῶν (𝔊⁹⁶⁷ˑᴬ: +
πολλων; 𝔊ᴮ: –)

Gehman (in Johnson *et al.*, 1938, p. 137) suggests that 𝔊⁹⁶⁷'s 'με' minus
"may be a copyist's error, but on the other hand, קבצתי אתם may
have been read by haplography as קבץ אתם, the infinitive Piel, instead
of the 1st sing. perfect".

MT says מֵאַרְצוֹת אֹיְבֵיהֶם ('from the lands of their enemies'), yet
𝔊ᴮˑᴬ say ἐκ τῶν χωρῶν τῶν ἐθνῶν ('from the countries of the nations'),
which does not reflect MT's 'enemy' (cf. 36:2 ἐχθρὸς for MT's איב).
Wong (2002, p. 141), Zimmerli (1983, p. 295), and Ziegler (1977, p. 281)
all give LXX as ἐχθρῶν ('enemy') here. Ziegler gives ἐχθρῶν as reading in V (and other Lucianic codices), then notes 𝔊⁹⁶⁷ omits, while all
others have τῶν ἐθνῶν (which includes 𝔊ᴮˑᴬ). Rahlfs' edition has ἐθνῶν.
Gehman (in Johnson *et al.*, 1938, p. 137) notes 𝔊ᴮˑᴬ's use of ἐθνῶν, but
attributes it to a "mistranslation". This is likely, yet 𝔊ᴮˑᴬ using ἐθνῶν
instead of ἐχθρῶν may reflect a situation of living in the Diaspora,
down playing possible negative terms about other nations.

Johnson (in Johnson *et al.*, 1938, p. 8 [cf. Gehman, p. 137]) also
suggests 𝔊⁹⁶⁷'s minus of τῶν ἐθνῶν (or τῶν ἐχθρῶν) is probably due to
homoeoteleuton [sic] saying it "may be due to των χωρων of proceeding
[sic] line" (similarly Ziegler). Yet Lust (2002a, p. 388) states "there is
no *homoioteleuton*", and curiously says that "here Ziegler's critical edition
has ἐχθρῶν as a plus. It is in agreement with MT and probably implies
a correction towards MT". Lust acknowledges most Greek MSS read
ἐθνῶν rather than ἐχθρῶν. Yet Lust does not clarify why 𝔊⁹⁶⁷ does not
have either word. Therefore we stand with those seeing *homoioteleuton*
for 𝔊⁹⁶⁷'s minus.

MT has הַגּוֹיִם רַבִּים ('*many* nations'). Zimmerli (1983, p. 295) believes
רַבִּים is a "secondary gloss" stating it "is not attested by 𝔊" (cf. Cooke,
1936, p. 423). However, while 𝔊ᴮ does not witness רַבִּים, scholars typically overlook that both 𝔊⁹⁶⁷ˑᴬ have πολλῶν. This demonstrates that if
רַבִּים was an MT gloss, it was early enough for even 𝔊⁹⁶⁷ to witness it,
and thus should have been in 𝔊ᴮ. Therefore, it is curious that many,
including Ziegler, omit πολλῶν from their Greek texts.

39:28 וְיָדְעוּ כִּי אֲנִי יְהוָה אֱלֹהֵיהֶם בְּהַגְלוֹתִי אֹתָם אֶל־הַגּוֹיִם
וְכִנַּסְתִּים עַל־אַדְמָתָם וְלֹא־אוֹתִיר עוֹד מֵהֶם שָׁם׃

39:28 καὶ γνώσονται ὅτι ἐγώ εἰμι κύριος ὁ θεὸς αὐτῶν ἐν τῷ ἐπιφανῆναί
με αὐτοῖς ἐν τοῖς ἔθνεσιν

MT says בְּהַגְלוֹתִי אֹתָם (hiph. infin.; 'when I led them into exile'; cf.
v. 23), whereas LXX has ἐν τῷ ἐπιφανῆναί με ('when I have been
manifest'). Block (1998, p. 478) suggests that "LXX treats the infinitive as a Niphal of גָּלָה 'to reveal'" (cf. בְּהַגְּלוֹתִי; Ezek. 21:29; 1Chr.
5:41). The context of the surrounding verses may give support to MT's
understanding as original (cf. v. 27 'in my bringing them back from the
people'; v. 28 'in my exiling them to the nations'). On the other hand,
these similarities with v. 27 could have influenced LXX to have "omitted
them as repetitions... [as] in general, the translator does not hesitate
to render 'redundancies'" (Lust, 1986c, p. 49). Lust (2002b, p. 152)
points out that "the Greek gives the verse a hopeful connotation; a
similar effect is achieved by MT through the insert of a long plus"
(see below). Zimmerli (1983, p. 295) believes LXX's use of ἐπιφαίνω
"is connected" with MT's plus not being in LXX's *Vorlage*. The LXX
translator, working with an unpointed text, and without MT's plus, may
have performed a wordplay giving a message of hope that they knew
the LORD when he manifested himself to them in the nations. LXX's
'manifest' is not required with MT's plus.

As stated above, MT exhibits a long plus from וְכִנַּסְתִּים ('and I
gathered them') to the end of the verse. This is not clearly noted by
Allen or Zimmerli. Although this plus may be a redundant repetition
from v. 27, as Lust (1986c, p. 48) states, "in general, the translator
does not hesitate to render redundancies". Therefore, LXX should
have included this if it was in their *Vorlage*. Lust (1986c, p. 51) covers
this passage in detail and concludes that this phrase "is a late [MT]
composition which was not yet attested in the *Vorlage* of the LXX". Lust
(1986c, p. 53) proposes that all the issues in v. 28 need to be considered
together, and are part of editorial work whereby "the editor added a
section, taking position in the ongoing debate concerning the question
whether everyone would be allowed to participate in the Return from
the Diaspora".[39] Lust (1986c, p. 53) concludes that "the Greek text was
probably based on a *Vorlage* differing from MT".[40] Block (1998, p. 487)
does not agree with Lust, instead suggesting "it is preferable to rec-
ognize the transitional significance of Ezekiel's style". Yet Block does
not offer any explanation for the minus in LXX. Block (1998, p. 487)

---

[39] We note Lust's (1986c, p. 53) 'disclaimer' that "this attempt towards an interpretation is hypothetic."
[40] Wong (2002, p. 142) also agrees concluding "that v. 28b is a late addition which
did not exist in the *Vorlage* of the LXX".

36,27 did not yet exist, and the promise of the spirit in 37,14 was yet
to come after 39,29".[46] Wong (2002, p. 145) then uses this observation
to propose אֲשֶׁר "has a causal meaning" ('when'), and that שפכתי
needs to be interpreted "as a prophetic past" (n.b., ἐξέχεα is aorist).
Wong (2002, p. 145) also says "this interpretation would not be possible if he had read the text in the context of the original sequence
of chapters... *and* interpreted the word as 'spirit' for the reason just
mentioned. The possible solution was to interpret רוח as θυμός". While
not agreeing with Wong's conclusion, Lust (2002b, p. 154) agrees that
"the Septuagint supports the causal interpretation". Yet, contra Wong,
Lust (2002b, p. 154) observes that "שפך רוח with the Lord as subject
is a hapax in Ezekiel....however, the reference is always to the 'spirit'
or πνεῦμά of the Lord: Joel 3,1, Zech 12,10, never to his 'anger'". We
agree with Wong that the chapter reorder must be considered, yet we
are not convinced רוח was in LXX's *Vorlage*.

Of significance, Symmachus says, καὶ ἐκχεῶ τὸ πνεῦμά μου ἐπὶ τὸν
οἶκον Ἰσραήλ ('and I will pour out my Spirit upon the house of Israel'),
which reflects a 'positive' interpretation for MT, and witnesses the
presence of רוח in his *Vorlage* (Ziegler, 1977, p. 238). Also, rather than
LXX's aorist, Symmachus uses ἐκχεῶ the 'indicative present', which
matches MT's *qal* perfect here. In addition, Symmachus translates אֲשֶׁר
with καί, making this an independent phrase.

The primary issue is whether the earlier LXX translator had רוח in
his *Vorlage*, as apparently the later Symmachus did. Lust (2002b, p. 153),
speaking against the premise that רוח was in LXX's *Vorlage* (contra Allen,
Block, Wong), states that "if in the *Vorlage* of the translator chapter 37
followed upon chapter 39, as indeed it does in p967, and given that
the donation of the רוח, meaning 'spirit, breath', plays an important
role in chapter 37, it is highly unlikely that he would have rendered
רוח by θυμός". Lust maintains רוח in 37 still had an overarching influence upon 39:29 in the original chapter order as witnessed by 𝕲⁹⁶⁷. As
an alternative proposal, Lust believes LXX's *Vorlage* had חֵמָה ('anger/
wrath'), and not רוח, and that early MT editors deliberately changed
the text from חֵמָה to רוח when chapter 39 was still followed by 37.
In an earlier work, Lust (1986c, p. 53) proposed that "in verse 29 [the

---

[46] Wong reads rather awkwardly in this last phrase, and may be best read omitting
the 'yet'. Wong intends to say that in the original (as found in 𝕲⁹⁶⁷) the promise of
the Spirit came after 39:29, and thus did not give a past context for רוח in 39:29 to
refer back to, as happens with the received chapter order.

editor] replaced God's 'wrath' by his 'spirit' as a prelude to ch. 37 where the role of the spirit was prominent".[47] Lust (2002b) still holds to this position in his later work, written in response to those interacting with his proposal (e.g., Block, Wong).

Overall, we are not convinced by the proposals that LXX used θυμός for רוּחַ, nor are we convinced רוּחַ was in LXX's *Vorlage*, otherwise surely they would have caught this message of hope, especially with their use of 'magnify' in v. 28. Whilst accepting Lust's proposal that MT emended from חֵמָה to רוּחַ, we question whether this took place *before* the chapter realignment. If before, we ask why LXX MSS witnessing MT's chapter realignment, did not also adjust their wording here to 'spirit'. We find two possibilities: firstly, LXX accepted the chapter order and just moved chapter 37 to before 38, also inserting 36:23c–38, yet without any individual word emendations made in MT, thus maintaining their traditional use of θυμός here (witnessing an early Hebrew חֵמָה). Alternatively, we propose the change in MT from חֵמָה to רוּחַ came *after* this chapter realignment, but *before* Symmachus. The chapter reorder caused 39:29 to be the final verse of the restoration block (36–39), and some later editor(s) may have decided this block should not end with the outpouring of God's 'wrath', and so changed from חֵמָה to רוּחַ to now state the LORD was pouring out his Spirit, a positive and fitting statement to end the previous chapters and begin the rebuilding of the Temple (40–48). We now have both 𝕲[967] (pre-chapter realignment), and 𝕲[B,A] (post-chapter realignment), all witnessing θυμός which evidences חֵמָ in their *Vorlage*, and then Symmachus witnessing the later editorial change to רוּחַ with πνεῦμα. Therefore, we have different Greek witnesses to the textual flux in 'proto-MT'. We also see Symmachus' use of καὶ ἐκχεω (independent phrase; indicative present) as further implicit evidence of this word change in MT. The theology of 'will pour out my Spirit' is certainly found in the 'inserted pericope' of 36:23c–38, especially in v. 27 (cf. 37:14), and MT's word change to 'my Spirit' here would act as a theological *inclusio* with the inserted text, and of their placement for chapter 37 before the Gog chapters. This change may have been done at the same time as other later MT changes (e.g., the declarative formula in 36:23b; the change from קָהָל

---

[47] Lust (1986c, p. 53) says the MT editor did this change from 'anger' to 'spirit' here, and the change from 'shame' to 'forget' (v. 26), and MT's long plus (v. 28), to bring "more hopeful connotations".

to חַיִל, in 37:10; נָשִׂיא to מֶלֶךְ 37:22–24, and the many other MT plusses not witnessed in LXX [see Excursus §6.6 below]).

Therefore we have several variances in MT and LXX in the last
pericope of chapter 39, just as we observed in the first verse of 37 in
LXX (*human* bones), and in 36:23b, all which may be seen to be due
to the change in chapter order.

This chapter finishes after v. 29, where all three MT MSS have a
petuḥah break. 𝔊[967] has its normal sense division 'strokes', but then
has an unusual 4–5 letter gap before it starts chapter 37 on the same
line. Both 𝔊[B,A] begin chapter 40:1 on a new line; 𝔊[B] leaves a 4 letter
break at the end of the previous line (a relatively extensive gap for
𝔊[B]); 𝔊[A] finishes 39:29 about two-thirds across the line. Therefore, all
representative MSS witness a major break in their own styles between
39:29 and the following chapter.

6.6. EXCURSUS: UNIQUE PLUSSES IN CHAPTERS 36–39

There are a number of plusses through chapters 36–39, either single
words or longer, which occur in only one (or two) of our representative
manuscripts. We have discussed these unique plusses as they appeared
in our examination of chapters 36–39, yet some bear further discussion
here in an attempt to determine any underlying motif. There are four
groups: firstly those unique to 𝔊[967], secondly those found in both MT
and 𝔊[A], thirdly those unique to 𝔊[A], and fourthly, those unique to MT.
These may represent stages in the development of the text. A degree
of complexity surrounds these plusses, warranting further study than the
investigation here which is concerned only with interpretive aspects.

These plusses may reveal different stages in the growth of the text.
Both 𝔊[967] and 𝔊[B] witness a *Vorlage* without the later plusses, suggesting
they reflect the original Greek more than 𝔊[A]; yet 𝔊[967] appears closer
to the Old Greek than 𝔊[B] as it does not witness the chapter order and
inserted pericope (36:23c–38). The MT plusses witnessed by 𝔊[A] show
evidence of further textual editing, but early enough for 𝔊[A] to include
them. The plusses unique to 𝔊[A], and plusses unique to MT, suggest
that both the Hebrew and Greek texts had further separate textual
development. The unique MT plusses are frequently represented in
MasEzek, creating timeline difficulties, especially considering 𝔊[A] as a
post-Hexapla MS. This may suggest that all LXX MSS, including 𝔊[A],

drew on an earlier Hebrew parent text than MasEzek. We also find
occasions where MT likely performed later interpretive word changes
as support for the chapter reorder.

6.6.1. *Plusses Unique to $\mathfrak{G}^{967}$*

$\mathfrak{G}^{967}$ typically witnesses a text with very few plusses, and may well
represent the Old Greek, and perhaps the Hebrew *Urtext*. Whilst $\mathfrak{G}^{967}$
has a few minor plusses, often one or two words, here we will focus on
its two longer unique plusses. Johnson (in Johnson *et al.*, 1938, p. 14)
claims these "are more or less stock phrases and may have been quoted
from memory".

The first is at the end of Ezek. 38:20, ἵνα γνῶσιν πάντα τὰ ἔθνη ἐμὲ
ἐν σοὶ ἐνώπιον αὐτῶν ('so that all the nations will know I am among
you before them'). This appears to be a repeat of 38:16, but it lacks
the important middle phrase (ἐν τῷ ἁγιασθῆναί 'when I am sanctified'), supporting Johnson's 'quote from memory' proposal. This plus
provides an immediate reason for God's action against Gog in the first
part of this verse.

$\mathfrak{G}^{967}$'s second unique plus is in Ezek. 39:4, οὐ μὴ βεβηλωθήσεται το
ὄνομά το ἅγιον ('will not profane the holy name'). This appears to be
another repeated phrase, this time from 39:7 (cf. 20:39; 36:20, 21, 22;
39:7, 25). It again evidences a 'quote from memory' as it is minus the
important distinction of 'my' [holy name]. The phrase comes directly
after Gog has been told he will be struck down on the mountains of
Israel, and gives immediate reason for this action. However, it interrupts the sentence flow that includes what will then happen to Gog
and his bands.

While these plusses may be 'from memory', rather than in the *Vorlage*,
their insertion reveals a 'holiness' concern, firstly that the LORD will be
known among the nations, and secondly, the protection of his name,
both common motifs in Ezekiel.

6.6.2. *Plusses Unique to MT and $\mathfrak{G}^{A}$*

Plusses unique to MT and $\mathfrak{G}^{A}$, that are not represented in $\mathfrak{G}^{967,B}$, were
apparently added to the Hebrew after $\mathfrak{G}^{967,B}$'s *Vorlage*, but in time to be
included in $\mathfrak{G}^{A}$'s *Vorlage*. MasEzek's witness to these plusses indicates
they had their genesis with early Jewish communities. Their inclusion

in 𝔊ᴬ is no doubt due to a later recension, and the hexaplaric tradition of conformity to the Hebrew.[48]

Some of these MT/𝔊ᴬ plusses have a clarifying or intensifying purpose: 'behold' 37:4; 'sound' 37:7; 'wind/breath' (as vocative) 37:9; 'in them' and 'אֲדֹנָי/ἀδωναι' in 37:12; 'saying' 37:18; 'Gog' 38:3; the declarative formula in 36:23b clarifies the LORD's involvement; 'again' 36:30 emphasises their hope they will not repeat their past tragedies in the land; and 'all' 37:22 clarifies there will be one leader for 'all'.

However, other plusses have a discernible theological purpose. In 37:23 there are two plusses enlarging their sins: firstly, 'in their detestable things (MT)/wrong' (𝔊ᴬ), and secondly, 'in their rebellion (MT)/ offence' (𝔊ᴬ). In 36:18 we find a longer plus that echoes priestly concerns, 'for the blood they had poured on the land, and with their dung pellets (MT)/idols' (𝔊ᴬ). There is also another longer plus in 37:25, 'and their children and children's children forever', which expresses their concern for longevity in the land.

6.6.3. *Plusses Unique to* 𝔊ᴬ

The few plusses unique to 𝔊ᴬ (not represented in MT nor 𝔊⁹⁶⁷,ᴮ), often expand the restorative work. 𝔊ᴬ frequently adds πάντα: 37:21 Israel's gathering will be from *all* the nations (also in 𝔊ᴮ); 37:23 'in *all* their kingdoms'; 39:7 the knowledge of the LORD in '*all* nations'; 39:14, 15 they will search *all* the land. In 36:3, 𝔊ᴬ adds '*the nations*', giving identity to 'those around', and the source of the hatred against them. There are two plusses in 𝔊ᴬ that show deeper theological thought, such as its 'repeated' line in 36:17, emphasising their uncleanliness, and its ζωῆς plus in 37:10 (breath of *life*).

6.6.4. *Plusses Unique to MT*

We also find a few plusses in MT Ezek. 36–39 that are not witnessed in any of our representative LXX MSS. It is difficult to find any reason why LXX would omit these, especially as some have solid theological

---

[48] Tov (2001, p. 139) observes that "Codex A is greatly influenced by the Hexaplaric tradition and in several books represents it faithfully. The scribe of A often adapted the text to similar verses and added harmonizing details". Talmon (1999, p. 70, n. 19) likewise observes that "where preserved, the Hexaplaric tradition is adjusted to MT".

content. This suggests they were added after the *Vorlage* for our representative LXX MSS. Significantly, where extant, we find witness for these later plusses with Aquila, Symmachus and/or Theodotion.

Some of the unique MT plusses expand, emphasise or clarify the text: in 36:5, כָּל־לֵבָב expands the attitude of the plunderers regarding their 'contempt'; in 36:7 the declarative oath and oath formula (אִם־לֹא) emphasises the Lord's action;[49] in 36:8 MT clarifies that God's people are יִשְׂרָאֵל. This clarification is also seen in 37:12 where עַמִּי gives specific identity to those whose graves are being opened; וְאַתָּה in 37:16 clarifies Ezekiel as the object of God's command; לְמֶלֶךְ in 37:22 emphasises one king for all; the phrase 'and I will turn you back, and I will put hooks into your jaws' in 38:4 clarifies how the Lord will move Gog; גָּדוֹל in 38:13 emphasises the extent the community has suffered; הַנְּבִאִים in 38:17 reinforces the action of the prophets; הָרַי in 38:21 clarifies the battle's locale; כָּל in 39:25, 26 emphasises 'all' their treachery; and 'I will gather them to their own land, not leaving any behind' in 39:28 answers concerns about being left behind in the exile.

A few unique MT plusses express priestly concerns: וְרָבוּ וּפָרוּ in 36:11, and וּנְתַתִּים וְהִרְבֵּיתִי אוֹתָם in 37:26, both echo the priestly blessing upon the restorative order; and לֹא־תַכְשִׁלִי עוֹד in 36:15 may also echo a priestly concern that the land does not cause them to stumble again; and הָעֹבְרִים in 39:14, 15 may express priestly concern that those 'travelling' through the land perform the burial so the people of Israel are not defiled by touching the remains of the dead.

While not plusses, we may also include a few places where MT most likely changed the text as a result of the chapter reorder. In these places, LXX may be found to reflect the original, leaving MT as the interpretive text. These include the later insertion of the declarative formula in 36:23b; the change from קָהָל to חַיִל in 37:10; from נָשִׂיא to מֶלֶךְ in 37:22–24; and from חֵמָה to רוּחַ in 39:29.

These plusses, along with the chapter reorder and pericope insert, permits us to agree with Tov (1986, p. 101) that MT Ezekiel reflects a redactional stage of Ezekiel rather than just being a copy.

---

[49] See our discussions for 36:7, and 37:22, where these 'plusses' may have been in the text but ignored by the translator.

6.7. Summary of Observations: Ezekiel 39

A textual-comparative methodology that examines all features of a text, including paragraphing, has shown that while 𝕲⁹⁶⁷ has only two major sections (39:1–16 and 17–29), all other manuscripts have four oracles, following on from the five oracles in chapter 38, giving a total of nine oracles tying chapters 38–39 together. The oracles in chapter 38 are detectable by the addressee of the Lord's speech, yet in chapter 39 the addressee is at times difficult to determine and the differences are thematic. This ancient division into nine oracles is often overlooked by the modern commentator:

> 6th Oracle: vv. 1–10: The Lord tells Ezekiel what to declare to Gog about his gathering and demise.
> Excursus (vv. 6–10): The Lord declares what he will do, why, and the 7 year clean up.
> 7th Oracle: vv. 11–16: The Lord declares Gog's burial place (Hamon Gog; Hamonah) and the resulting 7 month cleansing of the land.
> 8th Oracle: vv. 17–24: The Lord's declaration, through Ezekiel, of his sacrifice to the birds and animals.
> Excursus (vv. 21–24): The Lord declares Israel's sin as reason for the exile.
> 9th Oracle: vv. 25–29: The Lord declares his holy name as the reason for the restoration of Israel.

LXX maintains the transliteration of 'Gog' and therefore the ambiguity of Gog's identity; likewise 'Rhos' is kept as a proper noun of an ethnic group. As in previous chapters, LXX modifies the literal meaning of the Hebrew. In places there is smoothing: v. 4 'birds'; v. 7 𝕲ᴮ,ᴬ adjust MT's syntax; v. 9 LXX telescopes two Hebrew verbs into one; v. 4 LXX 'intensifies' the Hebrew (cf. from 'strike' to 'destroy' bows). Elsewhere there is some interpretation: in v. 4 the purpose for Gog's assembly is destruction; in v. 11 ἐπέρχομαι is likely used in a hostile sense; and in v. 21 LXX changes MT's revealing of God's glory 'in the nations' to 'in you' (i.e., in the birds and animals at the sacrificial feast). More extensive changes are evident. In v. 6 LXX transforms the declaration of judgment into a salvation message, revealing a different eschatological view for the coastlands. This eschatological shift is found again in v. 22 where LXX changes MT's 'that day' to 'this day', suggesting LXX interpreted their current events as fulfilment of the prophecy (i.e., with the Seleucids or Romans). In v. 23 LXX interprets MT's 'they acted unfaithfully' to 'they rejected me' (and his laws). Whilst some (e.g., Allen), see LXX interpreting MT's רוּחַ as 'wrath' in v. 29, LXX's *Vorlage* likely had חֵמָה and not רוּחַ; MT changing to רוּחַ after the chapter reorder to give a message of hope.

LXX interpretively interacts with the priestly concern found in Numbers over Gog's burial and cleansing of the land; in v. 11, MT focuses on the location of Gog's burial place in Israel, while LXX focuses on who will be buried; in v. 11, LXX exegetes MT to state the mass burial place of Gog will 'dam up the valley'. LXX transliterates the burial place as τὸ γαι ('the Gai'), suggesting this place was known to the reader (v. 11, 15). LXX says the burial place will be called Πολυάνδριον ('mass burial place'), for הֲמוֹנָה ('Hamonah' or 'multitude') (vv. 11, 16). In v. 11 LXX uses μνημεῖον ('memorial') rather than τάφος ('grave/tomb'), again suggesting Gog's burial place as known to the reader. MT's plus of הָעֹבְרִים (twice vv. 14, 15) may indicate priestly concern that the burial will be done by those 'travelling' through the land, and not by the people of Israel, lest they be defiled by touching the dead.

There are a number of plusses: LXX's πάντα (38:12, 16; 39:7, 14, 23) often intensifies the situation. MT's כל (vv. 25, 26) indicates the restoration of Israel implies the union of *all* tribes. 𝕲^967 has a unique plus in v. 4 'holy name'; and v. 28 MT has a long plus, 'that none would be left in the exile'. There are a number of 'adjustments' by Symmachus towards MT (vv. 11, 16, 18, 25, 26, 29). The various plusses unique to each manuscript (𝕲^967, 𝕲^A, MT and 𝕲^A and to just MT) in chapters 36–39 evidence different development stages of the text, and reveals a text in a state of flux. MasEzek's witness to MT's unique plusses show that the later Masoretes were not innovators with their Ezekiel text but faithfully transmitted what they received.

This concludes our micro-level investigations, in which our textual-comparative methodology has enabled insights into early Jewish interpretation of Ezekiel 36–39, revealing distinct theological interpretation of the text by LXX and MT, as well as intra-LXX. These early Jewish interpretations are frequently overlooked by commentators who ascribe these variants to 'scribal error', or simply include in critical apparatus, and do not discuss them in the body of their commentaries. We now will turn to an example of textual-comparative methodology at macro level.

CHAPTER SEVEN

PAPYRUS 967

7.1. Introduction: Papyrus 967

One LXX manuscript worth discussing in detail, due to its uniqueness and antiquity, is Papyrus 967 ($\mathfrak{G}^{967}$). This particular papyrus is dated from the late 2nd to early 3rd century CE, and therefore pre-hexaplaric (Johnson in Johnson *et al.*, 1938, p. 5). The main body of the papyrus was discovered in the early 1930s, and is considered Egyptian in origin; however, the origin of its parent text is uncertain. $\mathfrak{G}^{967}$ originally contained (in order) Ezekiel, Daniel, Susanna and Bel, Esther (Johnson in Johnson *et al.*, 1938, p. 3).[1]

$\mathfrak{G}^{967}$ is located today in several places. Significantly for this study, most of chapters 19–39 (on 21 leaves, i.e., 42 pages) are located in the John H. Scheide collection at Princeton University. The Scheide collection finishes at the beginning of 37:4, which follows chapter 39 in an order different from all other LXX and MT MSS.[2] The remainder of chapter 37 (37:4–28), along with other portions, is located in Madrid and Barcelona, published by Fernández Galiano (1971). Most of chapters 11:25–17:21 (on 8 leaves or 16 pages) is in the Chester Beatty collection, Dublin, and published by F.G. Kenyon (1937). Other substantial fragments (none from chapters 36–39) are located in Cologne and were published by L.G. Jahn (1972). Kenyon (1937, p. viii) says that "the Ezekiel hand is large, square in build, with well-rounded curves... It is very clear, but heavy and by no means elegant, unevenly written and spaced, and plainly not the work of a trained professional scribe". Yet Johnson (in Johnson *et al.*, 1938, p. 5) states that "the text was written by the same hand throughout in clear and carefully formed uncials".

---

[1] Johnson (in Johnson *et al.*, 1938, p. 2) notes that "the only other example of the order—Ezekiel, Daniel, Esther—is in Alexandrinus". Lust (1981a, p. 517) notes that "the text of the latter books was written by another hand".

[2] Ziegler's critical edition of Ezekiel chapters 36–39 takes $\mathfrak{G}^{967}$ into account. The first edition of the Göttingen LXX edited by Ziegler (1952) utilised the Chester Beatty and Scheide portions, while the 2nd ed (1977) now has an appendix by Fraenkel with details of the other portions.

He (in Johnson *et al.*, 1938, p. 7) also claims that "actual mistakes in copying seem to be comparatively few".[3]

Our special interest in 𝕲⁹⁶⁷ is due to its unique chapter order, where the material that is traditionally recognised as chapter 37 appears in this MS after chapter 39. In addition, 𝕲⁹⁶⁷ is minus 36:23c–38. This chapter order and significant minus are not witnessed in any other extant Hebrew or Greek MSS. The only other textual witness for this chapter order and minus is the Vetus Latina Codex Wirceburgensis (*W*) (*ca.* 6th century CE). Although Codex *W* is later, it nevertheless "represents one of the two earliest and best preserved Vetus Latina manuscripts of Ezekiel" (Block, 1998, p. 338). Lust (1981a, p. 518) observes that *W* "is not directly dependent upon the Greek papyrus" [of 𝕲⁹⁶⁷] and [n. 8] "does not follow Pap. 967 in its many omissions through *parablepsis*". Block (1998, p. 338) agrees, commenting that because Codex *W* "does not follow Papyrus 967 in many of its omissions [this] suggests it represents an independent textual witness" [to the chapter order and minus]. Kase (in Johnson *et al.*, 1938, p. 47), referring to *W*, claims that "the original translation of the Old Latin version was made from a text closely resembling that of the Scheide papyri and probably of Egyptian origin". The significance for us is that we have two different trajectory witnesses to the unique chapter order and the minus of 36:23c–38. If we follow Kase, both trajectories have similar parentage, which may be the Hebrew *Urtext*, yet certainly a parentage before the chapter reorder and insertion of 36:23c–38 found in other MSS.

Therefore, we suggest that 𝕲⁹⁶⁷ is not an innovative or maverick text, but representative of an existing textual tradition. The extent of this tradition is a matter of debate and will be discussed throughout this chapter.

Codex Vaticanus (𝕲ᴮ), which is also pre-hexaplaric in text form, does contain the 'omitted' pericope, and has the received chapter order. While the Scheide portion of 𝕲⁹⁶⁷ (chapters 19–39) shares many textual agreements with 𝕲ᴮ, "there are some 660 variants [with 𝕲ᴮ] in these 42 pages of text [which] shows that one or [the] other has diverged far from their common ancestor" (Johnson in Johnson *et al.*, 1938, p. 35). Most of these variants are minor. Interestingly, the Scheide portion has "550 variants not found in any other uncial MS.... [and]

---

[3] Johnson goes on to discuss other 'omissions'.

the new text is noteworthy for omissions, and there are *ca.* 55 examples of words or phrases found in other uncials which have been omitted in Sch[eide]" (Johnson in Johnson *et al.*, 1938, p. 18).[4] Johnson (in Johnson *et al.*, 1938, pp. 21–33) provides a list of "the readings of the Scheide text which are not found in any of the uncials" and concludes that $\mathfrak{G}^{967}$ is closer to $\mathfrak{G}^B$ than to Codex Alexandrinus ($\mathfrak{G}^A$). Johnson (in Johnson *et al.*, 1938, p. 33) notes "Variants from A only 441; agreements with A only 95; Variants from B only 129; agreements with B only 168". This suggests that the later $\mathfrak{G}^A$, which appears to have been influenced by Origen's Hexapla, is further removed from the Old Greek (OG) and Hebrew *Urtext* than the earlier $\mathfrak{G}^{967}$ and $\mathfrak{G}^B$. We also suggest that while $\mathfrak{G}^{967}$ is more closely aligned with $\mathfrak{G}^B$ than $\mathfrak{G}^A$, it nevertheless witnesses a textual trajectory and tradition different from $\mathfrak{G}^B$ and $\mathfrak{G}^A$.

It appears that $\mathfrak{G}^{967}$ represents a tradition closest to the Old Greek (OG). As Johnson (in Johnson *et al.*, 1938, p. 40) says, this MSS is "undoubtedly older than any other MS, [and] it probably represents the original LXX better than others". Lust (1981c, p. 45) agrees, saying $\mathfrak{G}^{967}$ is the "earliest witness of the prehexaplaric Septuagint of Ezekiel". Gehman (in Johnson *et al.*, 1938, p. 79) claims that

> of all our Greek MSS, the Scheide text of Ezekiel appears to be closest to the original LXX…the original LXX must have been closer to the Hebrew than [$\mathfrak{G}$]B would imply. The authority of [$\mathfrak{G}$]B as our best source for the original Septuagint must yield to this new evidence.

Gehman appears to imply that $\mathfrak{G}^{967}$ represents the Hebrew *Urtext* closer than other extant LXX MSS.[5] Following his discussion on the '*Nomen Sacrum*' in $\mathfrak{G}^{967}$, Kase (in Johnson *et al.*, 1938, p. 51) concluded that "the earliest certain evidence for the revision of the Hebrew is furnished according to the Scheide papyri and the Old Latin".[6] Lust (1981a, p. 525) also claims that $\mathfrak{G}^{967}$ represents not only the earliest LXX Ezekiel, but also the Hebrew *Vorlage*, stating that 36:23c–38 "probably was not part of his Hebrew *Vorlage*".

---

[4] See Johnson (in Johnson *et al.*, 1938, pp. 31–33) for a summary of the variants of chapters 36–39.

[5] Gehman (in Johnson *et al.*, 1938, p. 77) states that because of the various ways $\mathfrak{G}^{967}$ follows the Hebrew it "helps to confirm the authority of the Massoretic tradition".

[6] $\mathfrak{G}^{967}$ typically uses only a single Divine Name, as does the Old Latin, whereas all other extant MSS typically use a double, occasionally a triple, Divine Name.

Tov (1999d, p. 409) challenges Lust's view that $\mathfrak{G}^{967}$ reflects an accurate Hebrew *Vorlage*, stating, "This is a far reaching assumption". While $\mathfrak{G}^{967}$ may be the oldest Greek MS, and perhaps the best witness to the original LXX (OG), this does not necessarily equate to being a witness of the Hebrew *Vorlage*. Although $\mathfrak{G}^{967}$ is the earliest known extant LXX witness of Ezekiel, we must ask whether 'older' and 'shorter' always equates to 'better' or 'more accurate', as it is often easier to explain why a longer text is later. Block (1998, p. 342) comments that "a text's antiquity is not necessarily a sign of either originality or superiority". If $\mathfrak{G}^{967}$ is an accurate representation of the original LXX, we would normally expect to find other witnesses in subsequent LXX MSS. Instead $\mathfrak{G}^{967}$ stands alone amongst extant Greek texts.[7] As Block (1998, p. 340) comments, "if the absence of this section [36:23c–38] were original, it is remarkable that it is preserved in only one Greek manuscript and an obscure Latin text". Likewise, if $\mathfrak{G}^{967}$ is the best witness to the Hebrew *Vorlage*, we would expect a supporting Hebrew witness; yet MasEzek, the earliest extant Hebrew text, supports MT.

This textual evidence and the resulting problems require a detailed investigation of $\mathfrak{G}^{967}$ and its relationship with other Hebrew and Greek MSS to determine possible reasons for its unique chapter order and the significant minus of 36:23c–38. We will begin with an investigation into various proposals for this minus. Then we will examine possible reasons for $\mathfrak{G}^{967}$'s unique chapter order. Following this, we will look at other evidences that this pericope is a later insert, including its unique linguistic styles, and a possible liturgical genesis. We will also consider a possible eschatological proposal for the revised chapter order and insertion of this pericope. We then will consider other evidence external to Ezekiel including Daniel, Revelation and Targum Num. 11:26 which support the view that $\mathfrak{G}^{967}$ reflects the Old Greek and perhaps the *Urtext*. We will then consider the theological significance and timeframe for the chapter reorder and insertion of this pericope into other MSS.

---

[7] This remains the case even with the Latin witness of W to the unique chapter order and pericope minus which evidences a different parent than $\mathfrak{G}^{967}$.

7.2. $\mathfrak{G}^{967}$'s 'MISSING' PERICOPE OF 36:23C–38

One of the issues often discussed regarding $\mathfrak{G}^{967}$ is the 'missing' pericope of 36:23c–38 that deals with the gift of the new heart and new spirit. The question is whether this pericope was omitted by some form of scribal error, or if $\mathfrak{G}^{967}$ actually represents a true picture of the Greek *Vorlage*, and perhaps the Hebrew *Urtext*. If the latter is the case, then this pericope is 'plus' in all other extant Greek and Hebrew MSS and therefore must be treated as a later inserted text.

7.2.1. *Omission by* parablepsis

The occurrence of *parablepsis* in $\mathfrak{G}^{967}$ is well established. Johnson (in Johnson *et al.*, 1938, pp. 7–8) found 17 instances of possible *homoioteleuton* or *parablepsis* in the Scheide section covering chapters 19–39, including the minus of 36:23c–38.

Those proposing *parablepsis* suggest that $\mathfrak{G}^{967}$'s scribe, after finishing καὶ γνώσονται in 36:23b then transferred his eyes to the closing words καὶ γνώσονται ὅτι ἐγὼ κύριος in 36:38. The 'catch words' for the scribe would have been καὶ γνώσονται........κύριος in vv. 23 and 38. Therefore $\mathfrak{G}^{967}$ finishes this verse, and the chapter, with καὶ γνώσονται τὰ ἔθνη ὅτι ἐγώ εἰμι κύριος. The question arises as how could this have happened?

Johnson (in Johnson *et al.*, 1938, p. 8) suggests that 36:23c–38 possibly filled its own leaf, and that the scribe "overlooked an entire leaf" by *parablepsis*. While Johnson suggests that this pericope existed on its own leaf in the scribe's parent text, we propose that at some point the scribe would have realised this 'theologically rich' pericope was minus in his work and then corrected his oversight.[8]

Filson (1943) and Wevers (1969) also see *parablepsis* due to *homoioteleuton*. Like Johnson, Filson (1943, p. 28) states "the scribe was frequently guilty of skipping phrases or larger groups of words". However, he (1943, p. 31) does admit that "it is obvious that so large an omission as fifteen verses is not an ordinary scribal error", and so proposes several possibilities, including $\mathfrak{G}^{967}$'s parent text being "in the form of a scroll, [and] the scribe may have omitted several columns", but he admits this

---

[8] Our proposal assumes the scribe had read ahead at some point and was familiar with the text of Ezekiel, and was not dealing with the text for the very first time.

"is difficult to explain". Alternatively, he suggests $\mathfrak{G}^{967}$'s parent text was a codex and "the open codex presented several columns, within which the omitted section was contained, or a page was turned by error, or a sheet was lost". Filson's suggestion here reflects Johnson's. We also note Irwin's (1943, p. 63) argument against *parablepsis*: by his calculations, this pericope would have filled "the bulk of a page and three-quarters". Irwin's calculations are a bit smaller than Johnson's 'single leaf' above; if correct, this pericope would therefore have formed fewer words than an entire leaf.[9] If Irwin's 1¾ page calculation is correct, the remaining ¼ page would have included text, and would therefore have also been omitted; yet there is no witness of more than just this pericope being minus in any MS.

We may also wonder how a scribe's eyes could 'jump' such a large section covering 1,451 letters.[10] The size must be considered as an argument against *parablepsis*. Lust (1981a, p. 520) points out that "a long omission such as 36:23c–38, amounting to 1451 letters, is very unusual. The longest omission through *parablepsis* in the papyrus appears to add up to 266 letters (12:26–28), and the average is ± 20 letters". Block (1998, p. 399), agrees, saying that "an omission of 1,451 letters is too long for an accidental skip of the scribe's eye; an omission of this length is unprecedented in the papyrus".

Although it can be demonstrated that $\mathfrak{G}^{967}$ has a number of smaller minuses by *parablepsis*, Lust (1981a, p. 520) concludes that "36:23c–38 was not omitted by accident and add that even the most absent-minded scribe would not have easily overlooked a passage with such theological richness". Lust's point has further merit when we take into account that 36:23c states ἐν τῷ ἁγιασθῆναί με ἐν ὑμῖν κατ' ὀφθαλμοὺς αὐτῶν. It is difficult to imagine a scribe accidentally omitting such a strong statement about Israel's exultation before their enemies. In addition, v. 38 does not have τὰ ἔθνη . . . εἰμι, which should have indicated to the scribe that he had skipped some verses.

Therefore we should be cautious in ascribing *parablepsis* to this extended pericope, especially by the accidental turning of a leaf, when we do not know the structure of the parent text. We agree with Zimmerli (1983, p. 242) that "the omission . . . as a simple copyist's error

---

[9] Each leaf in this papyrus was written on both back and front, forming two pages of text.

[10] The letter count of 1,451 is based on this pericope as found in $\mathfrak{G}^{B}$.

due to homoioteleuton is not convincing", and therefore turn to other proposals seeking to explain the absence of this pericope in 𝕲⁹⁶⁷.

7.2.2. *Omission in* Vorlage

Another possibility is that the pericope was minus in 𝕲⁹⁶⁷'s parent text. Lust (1981a, p. 521) firmly states that "the scribe of Pap. 967 did not overlook the section in question. He simply did not find it in the MS he was copying". There are two possible explanations for this: firstly, it was originally there, but was absent for some reason at the time of copying; or secondly, the pericope was never in 𝕲⁹⁶⁷'s parent text, nor its textual history, giving us an accurate representation of LXX's *Vorlage*, and perhaps of the Hebrew *Urtext*. We must therefore investigate both possibilities covering how a pericope of this size could be minus in 𝕲⁹⁶⁷'s parent text.

Although Johnson (in Johnson *et al.*, 1938, p. 8) includes 36:23c–39 in his *parablepsis* list (suggesting the scribe overlooked an entire leaf), he alternatively suggests that "the leaf was missing" in the parent text at the time of copying. Johnson came to this conclusion by a letter-size comparison of the other leaves in this MSS, and proposed that this missing pericope would have occupied its own leaf in the parent codex covering 3 columns each page.[11] However, he (in Johnson *et al.*, 1938, p. 10) admits that this proposal is not without its problems, including "the fact that we possess no early Greek codex on papyrus with such narrow columns". This seriously undermines his proposal. Secondly, we have already noted Irwin's (1943, p. 63) different calculation of 1¾ pages for this pericope in the parent text. Thus it is unlikely that this pericope filled just the one leaf (i.e., two full pages). Therefore again this suggestion is left wanting. Yet, for the sake of a thorough investigation, we will still examine the possibility of a leaf containing this pericope being absent from 𝕲⁹⁶⁷'s *Vorlage*.

---

[11] Johnson (in Johnson *et al.*, 1938, p. 8) based this on his calculations that this pericope "would fill 6 columns of 24 lines with 10 letters to a line.… This leaf, if it existed, contained 3 columns on a page".

7.2.2.1. *Omission in* Vorlage *by Lectionary Use*

If a missing leaf in 𝕲⁹⁶⁷'s parent text is a possible option, we must ask how this could have happened. Referring to Thackeray's (1903a, p. 408) proposal that this pericope was a popular lectionary in the early church and synagogue,[12] Johnson (in Johnson *et al.*, 1938, p. 9) suggests that "possibly because the passage was a favourite [in Egypt], the leaf containing these verses had been abstracted from the original codex and had never been replaced". If this is correct, the leaf would have been absent from the parent text before the scribe at the time of copying, and therefore not transmitted into 𝕲⁹⁶⁷.

Although this suggestion has some initial appeal, it continues the presumption that this pericope existed on one leaf, a point we previously found unlikely. It also does not account for an inattentive scribe 'overlooking' that such a supposedly popular lectionary piece was missing from its original context. Furthermore, it does not consider 𝕲⁹⁶⁷'s unique chapter order. We conclude that this proposal is unlikely.

7.2.2.2. *Omission in Egyptian MSS*

It has long been noted that this pericope is written in a later proto-Theodotion style. Seeking to explain this, Johnson (in Johnson *et al.*, 1938, p. 9) suggests that "[𝕲⁹⁶⁷] or its archetype was current in Egypt in the second century, and in all these versions we may assume that chap. xxxvi. 24–38 was omitted". He then proposes that a later LXX reviser, noting the minus, "took the version of Theodotion and inserted it boldly into the text...all later texts of the LXX have evidently been derived from this revised text".[13] Significantly, he (in Johnson *et al.*, 1938, p. 10) later includes a suggestion by Kase that this passage was "lacking in the Hebrew text used by the translator, and that the earliest Greek texts circulating in Egypt did not have these verses".

This appears to be a modification of Johnson's above-mentioned *parablepsis* proposal. Here, instead of occurring in 𝕲⁹⁶⁷ (or its parent text), the *parablepsis* occurred earlier, and was followed by Egyptian LXX MSS. It is also problematic how a 'Theodotion' style pericope, replacing

---

[12] Note that Thackeray did not know this pericope was minus in 𝕲⁹⁶⁷. His lectionary proposal sought to explain the Theodotion styled Greek in this pericope. See 'Insertion by Lectionary' [§7.4.2] below for more of Thackeray's proposal.

[13] Johnson (in Johnson *et al.*, 1938, p. 9) does not believe the reviser was Origen as 𝕲ᴮ contains this passage. Furthermore, he notes that "Evidently Origen knew only this revised version, and never observed that the passage was borrowed from a source other than the original LXX" (in Johnson *et al.*, 1938, p. 11).

a (*parablepsis*) minus in an Egyptian MS, now exists in all other extant LXX MSS. While this proposal does provide a possible answer for the unique Greek in this pericope, it does not address the unique *Hebrew* vocabulary.[14] It also does not address 𝕲⁹⁶⁷'s unique chapter order, a factor that must be considered in conjunction with the minus.

Having said this, we note Kase's proposal, as presented by Johnson, that the pericope was absent from the translator's Hebrew text, as this supports the findings of others such as Lust. However, in agreement with Lust, we propose that the minus was not just confined to Egyptian MSS, but that it was never in the Hebrew *Urtext*, and therefore never in LXX's *Vorlage*. Before we investigate this proposal, there is one more suggestion from a prominent scholar that should be examined.

7.2.3. *Omission by Accident*

Rather than accepting the above proposals of omission by *parablepsis* or *Vorlage*, Block (1998, p. 340)[15] proposes that "an accidental loss of a leaf or two seems more likely". However, unlike Johnson or Irwin, Block does not state how he calculates that this pericope occupied up to 'two leafs' (or four pages). This leaves his proposal appearing rather vague, especially given Johnson's calculation of one full leaf, and Irwin's of $1\frac{3}{4}$ page (less than one leaf). Block (1998, p. 340) also does not suggest how this 'accidental' loss took place, but with regard to the linguistic style he says that "those responsible for the transmission of the LXX recognized the gap and filled it with a reading that bears remarkable resemblance to Theodotion's text-form". Interestingly, he uses 'gap/filled' to avoid any concept of 'inserted'. Block, perhaps unwittingly, places this proposed 'Theodotion-filled' LXX MS as the *Vorlage* to subsequent LXX MSS. Again this explanation does not provide an answer to the later-styled Hebrew in this pericope, a factor which must be considered together with the Theodotion-styled Greek. The different linguistic Hebrew style suggests this pericope was minus also in an earlier Hebrew text. Block's 'accidental loss' proposal also does not provide any explanation for the unique chapter order of 𝕲⁹⁶⁷, a factor that must be considered together with this pericope minus.

---

[14] See Linguistic Styles (§7.4.1) below.
[15] Block says this in response to Lust's proposal (see below).

None of these 'omission' proposals discussed so far consider how these textual differences occurred in the separate Latin witness of *W*. One may be able to present these proposals for one MS, but the likelihood of these same textual differences occurring in a separate witness seriously questions any scribal error or accidental loss. We can agree with Lust (1981a, p. 519) that "it can now be accepted as proven that the omission of 36:23c–38 was not purely a scribal error".

7.3. $\mathfrak{G}^{967}$'s Unique Chapter Order

Examination of the main omission proposals has shown them to be unsatisfactory. Further they do not consider $\mathfrak{G}^{967}$'s unique chapter order and its relevance for the status of the pericope. Both features need to be considered together, otherwise one might arrive at two separate proposals.[16] A better solution would be to search for a proposal providing a plausible answer to both textual issues.

Curiously, most scholars do not enter into detailed discussion of $\mathfrak{G}^{967}$'s unique chapter order. Some even ignore it, focusing only on possible reasons for the 'missing' pericope, and therefore arriving at the various scribal error proposals previously discussed.[17]

Spottorno ([1981] cited in McGregor, 1985, p. 19) claims "the arrangement and omission in 967 could be...easily explained on the grounds of accidental damage to the text at some early stage". However this

---

[16] This is the weakness of Patmore's recent contribution, as he quickly dismisses Lust's proposal that the chapter reorder generated the need for the pericope insertion. Patmore looks at the proposed written dates for MasEzek and $\mathfrak{G}^{967}$ concluding the earlier MasEzek must be correct, rather than carefully considering the possibility that $\mathfrak{G}^{967}$ represents the Old Greek and a Hebrew *Urtext* before a chapter reorder and pericope insertion. He concludes (2007, p. 242) that "behind the texts of Papyrus 967 and the MT lie two distinct *Vorlagen*, and unless new materials come to light, there is not credible way of establishing the historical precedence of originality of either". This point will be challenged and answered in our discussions below.

[17] One would not know of $\mathfrak{G}^{967}$'s unique chapter order from Allen's (1990) commentary. Zimmerli (1983) does not give any clear explanation for $\mathfrak{G}^{967}$'s order, other than to mention its existence. Block (1998, pp. 338–442) briefly mentions the different order but offers no explanation, other than to say "the present arrangement of 36:23c–38 and ch. 37 follows a typical Ezekielian pattern of raising a subject, only to drop it immediately, and then returning to it for fuller development in a subsequent oracle". Block defends the received order without clearly explaining the occurrence of $\mathfrak{G}^{967}$'s order.

proposal does not account for the Vetus Latina witness of W.[18] Johnson (in Johnson et al., 1938, p. 13) spends little time explaining the chapter order, referring to it as a "dislocation", but significantly suggests that this dislocation "may have been in the early Hebrew text itself".[19]

Block (1998, p. 339) says that "if this [pericope] were an accidental omission, v. 23b should be followed by 37:1, not by 38:1, with ch. 37 being inserted between chs. 39 and 40".[20] This is a major point, yet Block unfortunately does not provide us with a clear solution. This point demands that the 'minus' "has to be considered together with the transposition of chap. 37" (Lust, 1981a, p. 520).

If we suggest, as above, that it would have taken a very 'absent-minded' scribe to omit this pericope, we must now suggest that it would have taken an extremely 'incompetent' scribe to place the words for chapter 37 *after* chapter 39. For both 'errors' to occur in the one MSS would be an example of scribal incompetency of the highest order. The alternative is that $\mathfrak{G}^{967}$'s scribe accurately reflected the parent text before him. This appears to be a more plausible explanation, especially if we accept that $\mathfrak{G}^{967}$ overall reflects the OG LXX, which shows evidence of a 'pre-revised' Hebrew text. Therefore, we can set aside scribal incompetency as a valid explanation for both of these unique textual variants in $\mathfrak{G}^{967}$, and state that its scribe was diligent in transmitting the text before him. This text shows strong textual and theological continuity.

In the middle of last century, Cooke (1936, p. xxv) noted that the last two chapters in the received order (38–39) do not seem to flow smoothly with the passages that preceded them, stating that "the last two chapters appear to be a later insertion... [as] they disturb the peace which has settled down upon the restored Israel". Cooke's suggestion has some validity, as one would expect that the restored nation of Israel united under a Davidic spiritual leader (37:16–24) would proceed into

---

[18] Spottorno's work was not available for us to examine whether he considers W.

[19] Johnson (in Johnson et al., 1938, p. 13) also comments that "the displacement was corrected in B, and therefore the correction probably ante-dates Origen, who is said to have found dislocations of verses and chapters which he put into the proper position."

[20] It should be noted, that while the text in $\mathfrak{G}^{967}$ flows from 36:23c directly into chapter 38 with the common one letter spacing and // division marker, there is an unprecedented 4–5 letter gap when it flows from chapter 39 into 37, which Johnson (in Johnson et al., 1938, p. 12) says "whether this indicates that [the scribe] was aware of the dislocation, it is impossible to say".

the rebuilding of the Temple (40–48). Instead Israel finds itself facing Gog and his hordes in battle (38–39). At the time of Cooke's writing, 𝕲⁹⁶⁷ was yet to be published. 𝕲⁹⁶⁷ gives us an alternative chapter order, and allows us to compare the implicit theologies behind the two variant chapter orders. Had Cooke known of 𝕲⁹⁶⁷, it is possible he may have arrived at an alternative conclusion, one that saw 𝕲⁹⁶⁷'s chapter order, and its 'minus' pericope, as providing a more logical thematic flow, rather than seeing chapters 38–39 as a later insertion.

We need to acknowledge that 𝕲⁹⁶⁷'s chapter order makes logical, reasonable and acceptable theological sense. There is continuity with 35:1–36:23b and what follows. This order acceptably links the oracles against Edom, and other largely unspecified 'enemies', and the battle against Gog and his hordes (38–39). Lust (2002b, p. 149) points out that

> both sections open with the same formula: 'Son of man, set your face against...' (35:2; 38:2). It is perhaps even more remarkable that, in both cases, Israel's enemy is given more or less mythological features. They are not well defined historical nations, but typologically representations of 'the enemy'.... Moreover, at the end of both the Edom and the Gog sections the mythological enemy disappears from the scene, while the author focuses on the relationship between the Lord and his people (36,8–23a; 39,21–29).

Most overlook these connections as they are not clearly discernible in the received chapter order. Lust (2002b, p. 149) further observes that "chapter 37, following upon 39, forms a good continuation of this scene: it draws attention to the dry bones of the Israelites, presumably fallen in the battle against Gog.[21] They are revitalised by the spirit [sic] of the Lord". In addition, the end of chapter 37 establishes a clear path for the Temple in chapter 40 with its references to 'my sanctuary' (37:26) and 'my dwelling place/tabernacle' (v. 27). In 𝕲⁹⁶⁷'s chapter order, Israel is restored on the mountains of Israel (36:1–23b), the wars are now over with the 'enemy' destroyed (38–39), Israel is resurrected into a united Davidic kingdom (37), the Temple is built and worship restored (40–48). The received chapter order does not offer this 'flow' of thought and, in many ways, is less logical.

---

[21] Lust is referring to the battle field covered with scattered bones in chapter 39.

Yet, Zimmerli (1983, p. 245) states that "the section which ends with v 23bα gives, on its own, a fragmentary impression. The real material exposition of Yahweh's proving that his name is holy is missing from it". Lust (1981a, p. 525) summarises Zimmerli, saying that 36:16–23b "cries out for a continuation". We propose that in 𝕲⁹⁶⁷'s chapter order, chapter 38 is an acceptable 'continuation' from 36:23b, as it shows the way the LORD will vindicate his holiness: his judgement upon Gog (38–39), the raising up of his people (37:1–14), and their uniting as one nation under a Davidic shepherd-leader (37:15–28). Further evidence of continuation or fulfilment can be found in 𝕲⁹⁶⁷'s order where 36:16–23b is followed by chapter 38 with its repeated references to God showing himself 'holy' (cf. קדשׁ in 36:23b and 38:16, 23; 39:7, 27). Also, in 𝕲⁹⁶⁷'s order, fulfilment of the nations knowing the LORD and his holiness (36:23b) can immediately be found in his judgment of Gog and his hordes in chapters 38–39. This idea of fulfilment is not seen in the received order, with the 'dry bones' in 37 following 36. It is also significant that 36:23c has the same phrase 'sanctified in you before their eyes',²² as 38:16. We propose that a later editor deliberately inserted this phrase into v. 23c as part of his 'weaving' vv. 23c–38 into the existing text. If 𝕲⁹⁶⁷ reflects the OG and *Urtext*, then 36:23b originally came shortly before this phrase in 38:16. This may have 'inspired' the editor to also include it in the beginning of his newly formed inserted pericope. We also suggest that 36:23b completes the oracle starting in 36:16, as it answers the concern of why and how God's people were scattered. This was all part of a holy God's response to his people's idolatry (vv. 16–18), and their profaning his holy name (vv. 20–22). This shows that God was the one who scattered them (v. 19). Finally, 𝕲⁹⁶⁷'s context of 'dry bones' (in chapter 37), continues the context of the scattered (therefore 'dry') bones in chapter 39. In the received chapter order, there is no immediate *clear* reason for the existence of the dry bones in chapter 37.

Overall, we can see that 𝕲⁹⁶⁷ has theological and text continuity. Therefore, we should remove the various scribal error proposals for its chapter order and pericope minus. This then leaves us seeking a solution for both of these issues.

---

²² The only difference is that in 36:23c, 'in you' is plural, as it speaks of the house of Israel (cf. v. 22), and in 38:16 it is the singular, as it refers to Gog.

Lust (1981a, p. 526f.) believes 𝔊⁹⁶⁷'s pericope minus and chapter order witnesses the Hebrew *Vorlage*. He is not alone in his proposal; we noted above the suggestion of Kase and Johnson (in Johnson *et al.*, 1938, pp. 10, 13) that 𝔊⁹⁶⁷'s chapter order "may have been in the early Hebrew text itself". Yet, unlike Kase and Johnson, Lust viewed both textual issues as one, proposing that the chapter reorder placing chapter 37 before 38–39, as found in other MSS, generated the need for the insertion of 36:23c–38 (Lust, 1981a, p. 528). Lust (1981a, p. 527) finds no theological place for the 'missing' pericope in 𝔊⁹⁶⁷'s chapter order. Furthermore, Lust (1981a, p. 531f.) believes that this chapter reorder and pericope insertion was theologically motivated by eschatological concerns.

This suggestion holds more credibility than any other, as it answers both the differing chapter order, the disputed pericope, and how the former created the need for the latter. It also suggests a possible motive for both textual issues.

7.4. LATER INSERTION (AND REORDER), NOT OMISSION

The proposal we now explore is that the pericope's insertion was linked with the changed (received) chapter order, with 𝔊⁹⁶⁷ and the Old Latin *W* as the only extant witnesses to the original text. We will consider here other evidence that this pericope was a later innovation and inclusion, and then discuss the possible theological reasons for its inclusion, including lectionary and eschatological proposals.

7.4.1. *Linguistic Styles Suggesting Later Insertion*

Thackeray (1903a, p. 407) was one of the first scholars to observe that the Greek style and vocabulary of 36:23c–38 was different from the surrounding text in extant LXX MSS. This was before the discovery of 𝔊⁹⁶⁷, which makes his observations and findings all the more significant. Thackeray (1921, p. 124) says that although 36:23c–38 appears in the section of his designated 'translator β' "it has no kinship with his work". Thackeray (1921, p. 125) claims "the Greek of this passage stands out prominently from its context; it is a patch of a different texture from the surrounding fabric. The limits can be exactly defined". He suggests this pericope was the work of another hand, designated as ββ, with several Greek linguistic links to the styles of later Jewish exegetes such as Theodotion, Symmachus, and those of the 'Asiatic' Jewish exegetical school.[23] Thackeray (1921, pp. 125–126) provides a number of examples of words used in 36:23c–38 that do not occur elsewhere in LXX Ezekiel, yet are used by Theodotion:

1. ἀθροίσω for קבץ (piel) in v. 24; elsewhere in β translated by συνάγειν (7 times).
2. The plural γαιῶν in v. 24, occurring "only here in Ez. LXX, [and] was preferred by the Asiatic school and is used by 'the three' in Ez. xxix. 12" (p. 125).
3. In v. 31 προσοχθιεῖτε κατὰ πρόσωπον αὐτῶν ('you will be angry/hateful in their sight') for וּנְקֹטֹתֶם בִּפְנֵיהֶם (cf. κόψονται πρόσωπα 6:9; κόψεσθε τὰ πρόσωπα 20:43).
4. The transliteration of ἀδωναί in vv. 33, 37 as in 𝔊[B] before κύριος.[24] This "is the rendering of the Asiatic school" (p. 125).[25]
5. The use of ἀνθ' ὧν ὅτι for תחת אשר (v. 34); "ordinarily rendered in Ez. by ἀνθ' ὧν. Such combinations of particles are characteristic of the Asiatic school" (p. 125).
6. The use of παροδεύοντος for עבד; normally translator β uses διαπορεύεσθαι.
7. ὡς κῆπος τρυφῆς in v. 35; normally παράδεισος in β (28:13; 31:8 [2×]; 31:9). "Theodotion has κῆπος in those passages and in Genesis" (p. 126).
8. The absence of εἰμι in 'I am the Lord' in vv. 36, 38 (cf. εἰμι in 36:23b; 37:6 and the many other occurrences of the recognition formula in the β-section of Ezekiel).

From these examples, Thackeray (1903a, p. 408) proposes that "in this section...we appear to have a clear case of the influence for some

---

[23] Whilst Thackeray uses the phrase 'Asiatic school' in several locations, he appears to be one of the few who do so. Lust (1981a, p. 521) uses this term when referring to Thackeray's work. We will also use it only in the context of his work. It is difficult to determine his meaning exactly, but we may suggest it broadly meant 'non-Egyptian', or even 'Palestinian'. He does appear to include Theodotion in this 'Asiatic school' (Thackeray, 1921, p. 125).

[24] The use of the single and double Divine name in Ezekiel is a complex issue and beyond our scope. See Johnson (1938), Zimmerli (1983, pp. 556–562), McGregor (1985), Spottorno y Díaz-Caro (1985), Lust (1996a), Olley (2004), and other major commentators.

[25] Curiously Lust (1981a, p. 521) says this occurs in "Pap. 967". This is an obvious typographical error on his part, as he later correctly refers to 𝔊[B].

other version, resembling that of Theodotion". While P.D.M. Turner (2001, p. 281) considers that Thackeray's "schema might be considered less than watertight",[26] others have accepted his proposal of another hand exhibiting Theodotion traits. Johnson (in Johnson *et al.*, 1938, p. 9) appears to accept this pericope as 'Theodotion', without further evidence beyond Thackeray. Lust (1981a, p. 521) refers to a number of Thackeray's linguistic examples, also concluding that the Greek is a later Theodotion styled insertion. McGregor (1985, p. 190), refer-ring to the way scholars observe that this pericope shows evidence of a "different type of text", concludes that "there does not seem to be any indication that this view is incorrect".

Yet linguistic peculiarities, indicating that this pericope is a later insert, are not just found in the Greek text. Lust (1981a, p. 521) notes that "the Hebrew text itself shows quite a few peculiarities and *hapax legomena*". Zimmerli (1983, p. 245) discusses the "linguistically unusual [Hebrew] elements" contained in this pericope:[27]

> such as the unique אנכי ('I') of v. 28, the only occurrence in Ezekiel of מעלל ('deed') in v. 31, the תחת אשר ('instead') of v. 34, the הלזו ('this') of v. 35, as well as the antithesis 'build-plant,' characteristic of the language of Jeremiah but attested in Ezekiel only in the later addition in 28:26.

Lust (1981a, p. 522) claims that the Hebrew peculiarities in this pericope suggest "the redactor of Ezek 36:23c–38 leans heavily on Deutero-Jeremiah, more so than the redactors of the rest of the book".[28] Tov (1999, p. 409) covers a number of these Hebrew elements, also stat-ing that these "remind one of Jeremiah's language and not that of Ezekiel's".[29]

---

[26] Turner makes this statement regarding Thackeray's 'schema' for the whole book, including that of this pericope. Turner (2001, p. 281) also states regarding this peri-cope that "very few examples, and most of these showing variants, are given by way of support". She does not return to any direct discussion of this pericope, and these unique variants pointed out by Thackeray and others remain unexplained. Turner's (2001, p. 286) statement that "there was nothing in the language incompatible with an Egyptian origin" is a general statement covering the whole book.

[27] Also see Allen (1990b, p. 177) for a summarised list of "the non-Ezekielian nature of the Hebrew".

[28] Lust (1981a, pp. 522–533) lists several examples of links with Jeremiah's writings and thus theology, including v. 28 'the land I gave to your fathers', v. 31 'evil conduct', vv. 35, 38 'dry', v. 33 'to cleanse' with the object 'iniquities', v. 36 'build/plant'.

[29] It was commonly thought that Ezekiel 'borrowed' from Jeremiah (Zimmerli, 1979, pp. 44–46). However recent scholars have proposed a reversal of this schema. This

The 'new heart, new spirit' theme, often associated with Jeremiah, is also found in Ezek. 11:19, but not developed to the extent that it is in this pericope. We may suggest that 11:19 helped to inspire this pericope. Lust (1981a, p. 525) defends his proposed link with Jeremiah stating that "Zimmerli's objections against such a conclusion are not convincing".[30]

Although these variances may not be overwhelming in number, they nevertheless show that most verses in this pericope show different linguistic style from the surrounding texts, the LXX showing evidence of the style of Theodotion, and the Hebrew sharing similarities with Jeremiah, and/or Deutero-Jeremiah. These linguistic differences for 36:23c–38, in both the Greek and Hebrew, signify a later insertion. Yet we need more evidence that this pericope was minus in the *Urtext*, and not just a 'later insertion' replacing a pericope left out of some texts.

The existence of some minor stylistic 'stitches' in the text further support the proposal that this pericope is a later insert for other MSS, and not in the Hebrew *Urtext*. Firstly, as observed in chapter 3, the declarative formula is a 'plus' in v. 23b in both MT (נְאֻם אֲדֹנָי יְהוִה) and the later 𝕲ᴬ (λέγει Αδωναι κύριος),[31] absent from both 𝕲⁹⁶⁷ and 𝕲ᴮ (𝕲⁹⁶⁷ finishes chapter 36 right before this formula found in MT and 𝕲ᴬ). This, plus 𝕲ᴬ's use of Αδωναι, a transliteration attributed to Theodotion's style, suggests this declarative formula was a later editorial addition.[32] That it is not found in 𝕲ᴮ, which does include 36:23c–38, shows evidence of a text in a state of flux, with later editorial work continuing to weave this pericope into the text.

---

discussion is beyond the scope of this study, as we seek only to examine possibilities that 36:23c–38 is a later insert into Ezekiel. See P.D.M. Turner (2001), and Leene (2000).

[30] Whilst Zimmerli (1983, p. 245) observed the linguistic connection with Jeremiah, he goes on to discuss how 36:22–32 may be an original but later unit, and then says "the possible absence of the passage from 𝕲⁹⁶⁷ and the peculiar character of the translation of it would then be a problem for the history only of 𝕲, but not of 𝔐". In this Zimmerli reveals his reluctance to have this pericope minus in the Hebrew *Urtext*. This reluctance may well come from this uncertainty as to whether future discoveries of other 𝕲⁹⁶⁷ fragments may contain this pericope.

[31] We note again that 𝕲ᴬ is a post hexaplaric MS and therefore often, yet not always, follows MT plusses. What is unique in this case is 𝕲ᴬ's use of Αδωναι, again showing evidence of a later 'Theodotion' style.

[32] Lust (1981a, p. 525) also mentions that the "Coptic-Sahidic MS...contains three complete oracles from Ezekiel, the last of which is precisely 36:16–23b". To date we have not been able to obtain a copy of this MS to personally verify Lust. However, if Lust is correct, and we have no reason to doubt, this is a very significant completion point for this oracle. This supports our suggestion that the *Urtext* finished at 23b with 23c–38 being an inserted text.

We also present the following arguments from silence. First is the surprising level of intra-textual agreement between MT and 𝕲^{B,A} in this pericope, in comparison to surrounding pericopes (cf. chapter 3). This may suggest that both languages for this pericope were written in a similar timeframe, perhaps by similar hands. Secondly, MasEzek, as the oldest extant text, has this entire pericope (vv. 22–38) in the one sense division. 𝕲^B starts its sense division for this pericope *after* the opening phrase in v. 22 with τάδε λέγει κύιος. Although this phrase is a common and almost 'mechanical' sense division marker in LXX (Olley, 2003, p. 215), it is perhaps another implicit indicator of a text in a state of flux. Thirdly, we propose that 𝕲^{B,A}'s use of ἀνθρωπίνων in 37:1 would have been unnecessary if chapter 37 followed 39 (as in 𝕲^{967}), as it would be apparent that the 'dry bones' were human. Although this is not found in MT or 𝕲^{967}, a later LXX copyist apparently thought that clarification was required. Fourthly, there is a number of variants at the end of chapter 39 (e.g., vv. 28–29) that may have resulted from a change of chapter order.[33] Thus, we find textual activity at all junction points of the chapter reorder. This supports the proposal that chapter 37 was originally after chapter 39 but relocated to follow chapter 36; subsequently, to support the relocation, 36:23c–38 was inserted into the text. Finally, as noted above, 𝕲^{967}'s unique chapter order and pericope 'minus' shows theological and textual flow.

Of interest to us, some scholars propose that the last two micro-sections in this pericope are the product of later redactors. Zimmerli (1983, pp. 244–5) claims that vv. 33–36 and vv. 37–38 "stand apart from the main body in vv. 22–32. It is clear from their introductions[34] that both units are secondary additions". Allen (1990, p. 178) also proposes that these two passages are "a product of later redaction". It is curious that Zimmerli and Allen are willing to ascribe these two micro-sections as 'secondary additions', and yet refrain from stating that the entire pericope was a later insert.[35]

---

[33] These variants are too complex to discuss here but they are examined in detail in chapter 6, especially v. 29 with MT's move from 'wrath' to 'Spirit'.

[34] Zimmerli (1983, p. 245) notes they are introduced by "bipartite proof-saying" rather than "messenger formula".

[35] Zimmerli's reluctance may be due to his uncertainty at the time of writing his commentary as to whether this pericope was present in a yet to be discovered fragment for 𝕲^{967}. The subsequent discovery of fragments has verified that this pericope is not extant in 𝕲^{967}. Zimmerli did mention these discoveries in his introduction but unfortunately did not use this information to clarify any new stance he may have taken.

The different linguistic styles and related issues, support the proposal that 36:23c–38 was not in $\mathfrak{G}^{967}$'s *Vorlage*, or in the Hebrew *Urtext*, but was a later insert for both the Hebrew and Greek texts.[36] The question at this point is whether this pericope found its way in by either the Hebrew or Greek text. Lust (1981a, p. 528) proposes that this pericope was inserted initially into the Hebrew text to theologically support the changed chapter order, and was added into the Greek text by redactors seeking to align the Greek to the revised Hebrew. Following his discussion on Lust's proposal, Tov (1999d, pp. 409–410) cautiously states,

> this presumed late intrusion in the Hebrew book of Ezekiel was also added subsequently in the Greek textual tradition...If the evidence of P. Chester Beatty and La [*W*] can be trusted, the OG lacked a section which is secondary in the Hebrew text of Ezekiel and this information is essential for our understanding of the literary growth of the book.

Along with Lust, we suggest that changing theological climate created the decision to rearrange the chapter order. This in turn created the need[37] for the 'new' pericope, which may have been included in Hebrew and Greek texts at a similar time. This would explain the linguistic uniqueness of both the Hebrew and Greek, and the surprising lack of intra-textual variants. The theology of this pericope appears to match the theology behind the chapter reorder (see discussions below). A united effort among scribes could have resulted in the pericope's inclusion and revised chapter reorder being placed into all extant texts, with the only surviving exceptions being $\mathfrak{G}^{967}$ and the Vetus Latin *W*. We now turn to various proposals seeking to determine the theological reasons, pathways and possible source(s) for the insertion of this pericope and the chapter reorder.

7.4.2. *Insertion via Lectionary*

Following his observations on the unique linguistic styles in both the Hebrew and Greek for 36:24–38, Thackeray (1921, p. 118) provides several suggestions as to how this proto-Theodotion styled pericope came about in the Greek, and concludes that it "is an independent

---

[36] It is rather curious that Joyce (1989) never considers this option in his quest to find answers for the theology and purpose of this pericope.

[37] We agree with Lust that the theology in $\mathfrak{G}^{967}$'s chapter order does not 'need' this pericope, and as such it was produced to assist a smoother theological flow in the chapter reorder.

version made for lectionary purposes". He (1921, p. 126) asks two significant questions: "(1) Has this Greek lesson come to us from Church or Synagogue? (2) Is it earlier or later than its context?" In his earlier 1903 work, he does not appear to suggest that this pericope was secondary to the surrounding text, rather he explored possible lectionary explanations for the linguistic and stylistic differences. His questions appear to have broadened in his later *Schweich Lectures*. He (1921, p. 129) struggles to understand how it was possible that "a later version of this lectionary passage supplanted that of the original Alexandrian company in the parent MS. from which all our MSS. are descended". As 𝔊⁹⁶⁷ was discovered after Thackeray, he was not aware of its pericope minus or chapter order. Unfortunately, we will never know whether Thackeray would have supported a liturgical *genesis* for this pericope in both Hebrew and Greek had he known of 𝔊⁹⁶⁷. We, however, *are* aware of 𝔊⁹⁶⁷, and as such will use the basis of Thackeray's proposal to examine the possibility of lectionary use *creating* this pericope, which then assisted acceptance of its insertion into the text of Ezekiel following the chapter reorder.

A secondary suggestion from Thackeray (1903a, p. 408), which he himself did not find overly satisfactory, was that LXX 36:24–38 in "the version of Theodotion, or one resembling it, was used in the lessons of the *Christian* Church,[38] and that in some unexplained way the lesson for Pentecost has in this passage supplanted the older version of the translation". We agree with Thackeray that this explanation is most unlikely. Although it may provide an answer for the Theodotion styled Greek, it does not provide a satisfactory explanation for the Hebrew text. It is unimaginable that an early Jewish community would have incorporated a Christian Pentecost lectionary passage into their Hebrew texts. Thackeray (1921, p. 126) does question how a 'later' lectionary reading by the Christian church could "affect all known MSS. and to leave no trace of any earlier version." This reasoning caused Thackeray to prefer a 'Synagogue' possibility.

---

[38] Thackeray arrives at this possible explanation based on an 11th Century lectionary in the British Museum that gives Ezek. 36:24–28 (the promise of the Spirit) as the third of three readings on Pentecost. In his later work Thackeray (1921, p. 126) said "in the scheme of O. T. lessons in use in the Greek Church, preserved in LXX lectionaries, the first five verses of our passage are assigned to the vigil (παραμονή) of Pentecost".

Thackeray's primary proposal was that the linguistic uniqueness of the Greek redundant found its origin through the Synagogue *haftarah*[39] lectionary, even stating that 36:23c–38 "is an independent version made for lectionary purposes" (Thackeray, 1921, p. 118). It is generally thought that, while the basic framework of the Torah portion readings may date back to Ezra, the accompanying *haftarah* reading list "is considered by critics to have been begun in the time of the Maccabees" (Thackeray, 1903a, p. 408).[40] Jacob (1972, p. 1246) comments that "it may be assumed that the custom [of regular readings] dates from about the first half of the third century BCE, since the Septuagint was apparently compiled for the purpose of public reading in the Synagogue".[41] Rabinowitz (1972, p. 1343) claims "the origin of the custom of reading a portion of the prophets after the Torah reading is unknown. The most plausible suggestion...is that the custom was instituted during the persecutions by Antiochus Epiphanes which preceded the Hasmonean revolt". Cohen (1997, p. 248), after a review of Philo's use of the Latter Prophets that correspond with *haftarot* readings, concludes that "a strong case can be made that this reflects the existence, already in Philo's day, of the traditional string of *Haftaroth*: Admonition, Consolation, Repentance".[42] N. Turner (1956, p. 20) also argues that the initial translation of the Prophetic books occurred for lectionary purposes and states, "that may be why we have so many traces of earlier fragmentary versions".[43]

Thackeray (1903a, p. 408) asks, "is it too bold a conjecture that a very early version of this section, resembling that of Theodotion, and

---

[39] The *haftarah* is the reading from the Prophets that followed the scheduled Torah readings.

[40] Büchler (1893, p. 423) mentions that "tradition assumes three stages in the development of the custom of reading the Law; the first is connected with Moses, the second with the Prophets, and the third with Ezra".

[41] We also find support from Acts 15:21 which states that Moses is read in the Synagogues each Sabbath, showing this was common practice at the time of writing. Acts 13:15 mentions both a Torah and *haftarah* readings, and Luke 4:17 has Jesus reading from Isaiah, suggesting this was the *haftarah* reading in Nazareth at that time. This shows that *haftarah* readings were an established practice by the times of Jesus. However, we have no evidence in the New Testament that Ezekiel was used as a *haftarah* reading, nor if they kept the same cycle as later Jewish communities.

[42] Cohen (1997, p. 225) starts her discussion by clarifying that "although our knowledge of the history of Jewish liturgical practices has advanced significantly, far more remains buried in the seemingly impenetrable mists of antiquity".

[43] While Turner did not directly refer to $\mathfrak{G}^{967}$ with this statement, we nevertheless have another scholar who proposes that some textual variants generated from various lectionary readings.

used for lectionary purposes in the Jewish Synagogue, was incorporated by the translators?" He also says that the entire passage of 36:16–38 "was read at a very early time as a lesson in the Jewish Synagogue". He refines his 'Synagogue *haftarah*' proposal in his 1921 paper, pointing out that 36:16–38 was part of "the primitive *Haphtarah* for the Sabbath known as that of the 'Red Cow'" (also known as the 'Red Heifer', cf. Num. 19) (Thackeray, 1921, p. 126). Numbers 19:1–22 deals with the use of purifying waters, and he claims the primary *haftarah* verse was 36:25 וְזָרַקְתִּי עֲלֵיכֶם מַיִם טְהוֹרִים וּטְהַרְתֶּם ('I will sprinkle clean water on you, and you will be clean').[44]

Thackeray (1921, p. 127) states that this 'Red Cow' Sabbath was the *Parah* Sabbath, "one of the four 'extraordinary' sabbaths,[45] which in Talmudic times fell in the last month of the ecclesiastical year". These special readings were outside the normal Torah reading schedule and "the choice of the *haftarot* for the Four Special Sabbaths depends on the special additional portion read on these days, and not on the ordinary Sabbath portion" (Rabinowitz, 1972, p. 1343).[46]

Thackeray (1921, p. 127) claims that these four special lectionary readings predated and may have even begun the normal 'Sabbath readings'. This may be the case, as Rabinowitz (1972, p. 1343) points out that while the Talmud lists the *haftarot* readings for the four special Sabbaths, "nowhere in the Talmud are the *haftarot* given for ordinary Sabbaths, which were not fixed until after the talmudic period". Thackeray (1921, p. 128) also proposes that these four special Sabbaths and their accompanying readings[47] came about over ritual disputes,[48] and that this pericope "was a call to purification on the opening sabbath of the new year".[49]

---

[44] Lust (1981a, p. 523) notes the link between Ezek. 36 and Num. 19, without mentioning its liturgical use.

[45] The four original special Sabbaths are *Sheḳalim*, *Ẓakor* ('Remember' Amalek), *Parah*, *Haḥodesh* (the month) (Thackeray, 1921, p. 127). See Büchler (1893, p. 448–453) for more on the four special Sabbaths.

[46] Significantly, Ezek. 36:16–38 continues to this day as the corresponding *haftarah* reading for Num. 19 on the special *Parah* Sabbath (Hertz, 1960, p. 999).

[47] It is interesting to note that three of the four extraordinary Sabbath *haftarot* readings come from Ezekiel.

[48] Rabinowitz (1972, p. 1343) mentions, without comment, Büchler's proposal that the *haftarot* readings originated against the Samaritans, and then later against the Sadducees (cf. Büchler, 1893, pp. 424–425).

[49] In support of this, Thackeray (1921, p. 128) points out that both the passage of "the Temple half shekel [and] the red cow...are the subjects of special treatises in the Talmud".

The link for 36:23c–38 to the Red Cow Sabbath can also be seen in the Targum of 36:25, "and *I will forgive your sins, as though you had been purified* by the waters of sprinkling and *by the ashes of the heifer sin-offering*" (Levey, 1987, p. 101).[50] The *Parah* Sabbath is also tied into the Passover festival, as seen in the Targum of Ezek. 36:38: "Like the *holy people*, like the *people who are cleansed and come* to Jerusalem at the time of the *Passover* festivals, so the cities of the *land of Israel* which were ruined, will be filled with people, the *people of the House of Israel*, and they shall know that I am the Lord" (Levey, 1987, p. 102). Targum here may have been a later emotive call for the Diaspora Jews to attend Passover in Jerusalem, as neither MT nor LXX mention any particular festival in Ezek. 36:25, 38. The Targum may also have included these expansions in defence of this pericope's inclusion into the text of Ezekiel.

Thackeray (1921) claims this early Synagogue *haftarah* liturgical use influenced the unique Greek in this pericope. His reasoning appears to be that, according to synagogue tradition, the scheduled *haftarah* is first read in the Synagogue in Hebrew, and then verbalised into the common language (in this case, Greek). This Greek verbal translation for 36:23c–38 was then written down in a contemporary (i.e., Theodotion-like) style which later found its way into all LXX MSS. Yet, he does express perplexity as to how the Greek idiosyncrasies in 36:23–38 replaced the existing text in all known MSS, concluding that this happened "in some unexplained way" (Thackeray, 1921, p. 129).[51]

Thackeray's proposal may explain to how the Greek obtained its Theodotion style in this pericope, but it does not fully explain the unique Hebrew style. Further, if the Synagogue *haftarah* liturgical use then covered *all* of vv. 16–38 as it does now, why we do not find similar later linguistic styles in vv. 16–23b as we find in vv. 23c–38? Finally, Thackeray's Synagogue liturgical proposal does not address the important chapter reorder issue.

Thackeray may have found different and more plausible answers had he known of 𝔊⁹⁶⁷. We can propose that 36:23c–38 had its *genesis* as part of the development of these four special Sabbath *haftarot* readings,

---

[50] Levey uses italics to indicate where Targum Jonathan expanded the text (also for 36:38). Levey (1987, p. 101 n. 14) also says that "R. Akiba cites this v. in what I consider to be an assertion against Christian baptism. God Himself purifies Israel, *m.Yoma* 8:9. Cf. *S.S R.* 1:19, where Torah is the purifying element".

[51] Earlier, Thackeray (1903b, p. 585) states "the rendering given of the lessons read on the great festivals, such as Pentecost, in the synagogues in Alexandria, formed the basis on which a complete translation was afterwards engrafted".

and was initially used for this liturgical purpose. We also propose that the *haftarah* portion may have originally been 36:16–23b. The use of נִדָּה in 36:17 and the corresponding Num. 19:1–22 Torah passage may have evoked thoughts of the *mikvah*, where the woman is 'washed clean', forming the theological basis for the liturgical formation of vv. 23c–38, as a greater call to purity (especially v. 25). Alternatively, this pericope may have had a separate liturgical life, and now was included into Ezekiel due to the call to purity. The 'pouring' of God's wrath (36:18) may have inspired the response of the 'pouring of cleansing water' in this restorative new pericope (v. 25). We suggest that the text forming vv. 23c–38 was then inserted into the text of Ezekiel following the existing *haftarah* reading (36:16–23b), even as support for the chapter reorder, as it is based on a similar theology that influenced the chapter reorder. This then expanded the *haftarah* reading to its current length of 36:16–38. This would have been written first in the Hebrew, and then in Greek, both styled according to their timeframe. This proposal does provide a plausible answer for the unique Hebrew and Greek style, and for the large degree of trans-linguistic unity. We do admit this proposal is very speculative, and only presented as a possible genesis for this pericope.

However, our proposal here is still insufficient. While it may provide a possible explanation for the genesis and subsequent inclusion of 36:23c–38, even as support for the chapter reorder, it does not provide any *reason* for that chapter reorder occurring. We therefore need to find a proposal that gives plausible explanation for both issues, and especially any theology that may have generated the chapter reorder.

7.4.3. *Lust's Theological/Eschatological Proposal*

In a paper given 2001 (published 2003), Lust sought to give reason for three significant longer 'minuses' in $\mathfrak{G}^{967}$ Ezekiel, 12:26–28; 32:24b–26; 36:23c–38, that have often been explained as *parablepsis*.[52] There is a fourth minus and verse reordering in chapter 7 in $\mathfrak{G}^{B,A}$ and other

---

[52] Johnson (in Johnson *et al.*, 1938, p. 8) points out that his list of omissions in $\mathfrak{G}^{967}$, including these three, all "have one significant factor in common.... these omissions resolve themselves into units of 10 letters.... [thus] the most obvious explanation is that this MS or one of its ancestors was copied from a text which has 10 letters to a line, and that the omission was due to *parablepsis*". However, Lust (2002c, p. 22) counters that no extant "ancient papyri seem to have such short lines" and Johnson's counting "appears to be rather arbitrary".

major LXX MSS; but this section is not extant in 𝕲⁹⁶⁷. He proposes a central 'eschatological' theme, suggesting that they have actually been 'inserted' into all other LXX and MT MSS. His conclusion is that they are not 'minus' in 𝕲⁹⁶⁷ or the Hebrew *Urtext*, but rather, 'plus' in all other extant MSS. Lust proposes that they were deliberately added into the Hebrew, and subsequently into LXX, because of changing eschatological and canonical concerns. It does appear strange that a translator would omit these significant passages that all carry a similar theme, especially as the translator of Ezekiel is considered so literal.[53] This suggests that we again have evidence in Ezekiel of a text still in a state of flux, which must be understood in the light of literary criticism. Lust (2002c, p. 25) states that "in cases like the present one [i.e., 'minuses'], text-critical and literary critical issues are very much entangled". This also raises the possibility that there were two Ezekie-lian texts circulating, as with Jeremiah and Proverbs, one with these plusses and one without.

Lust (2003, p. 86) claims that "the authorities responsible for the Hebrew 'canon' appear to have been suspicious in matters of 'apoca-lyptics' ", and they seem reluctant to include apocalyptic literature into the canon. Therefore, these 'plusses' "may have been inserted in order to answer objections against the admission of the Book of Ezekiel, with its apocalyptic-coloured visions" (Lust, 2003, p. 86). These plusses appear to lessen a futuristic apocalyptic aspect in Ezekiel, and bring these events into a present context. This causes the book of Ezekiel to have a contemporary application, which Lust believes facilitated a smoother inclusion into the canon. This raises the question of what evidence exists that this was of concern to those determining the Hebrew canon, especially as Lust holds to such a position as 'fact'. We now examine Lust's argument in detail, beginning with the three significant 'minuses' in 𝕲⁹⁶⁷.

The first is 12:26–28, a passage that deals with true and false proph-ecy (cf. 12:21–25). Filson (1943, p. 28) believes this 'minus' in 𝕲⁹⁶⁷ is another example of *parablepsis* as 12:26 and 13:1 contain the same words. Yet Lust (2003, p. 85) claims it is actually a later insertion that "interrupts this connection between chapters 12 and 13. Indeed, its

---

[53] Tov (1999d, p. 400) says, "Since we rule out the possibility that the otherwise literal translator of Ezekiel was involved in shortening, MT should be considered expanded".

theme is that of Ezekiel's vision on the final days, and not that of true and false prophecy in general". The context of v. 27 is the accusation of the people: they see Ezekiel's vision(s) as having future eschatological fulfilment, but they are seeking present completion, as the lack of fulfilment causes the prophecy to appear false. Lust (2002c, p. 25) clarifies the people's complaint, that the visions spoken of in v. 27 "are for remote future times and cannot be tested". Block (1997a, p. 392) also claims that "the address appears to be directed at the exiles who have become disillusioned with Ezekiel".[54] Lust (2002c, p. 26) believes that the חָזוֹן ('vision') in v. 27 "is no longer a simply synonym of prophecy or prophetic experience. Here it stands rather for 'apocalyptic vision'. This vision is for 'many years ahead, for distant times'". Lust (2003, p. 86) says that v. 28 'historicizes' the surrounding textual content regarding God's actions, and bring the events spoken of into the present or immediate future, rather than in some eschatological future. These inserted verses therefore give answer to the attacks against Ezekiel's prophecies, a point which may be emphasised with 𝕲^{B,A}'s additional plus of παραπικραίνων ('provoking').[55] It cannot be proven, despite Lust's claims, if the motive was to ease the 'apocalyptic' concerns of those deciding the Hebrew canon. However, this pericope does stand as its own unit, with a clear message of 'present' rather than 'later eschatological' fulfilment', and is likely a later insertion.

Lust's second proposed later MT-LXX 'plus' is 32:24b–26, again minus in 𝕲^{967}, commencing the last phrase in v. 24 (after ζωῆς αὐτῶν) (241 letters). Johnson (in Johnson et al., 1938, p. 7) includes these verses in his 𝕲^{967} parablepsis list, saying the 'skip' was "from επι της ζωης to επι της ζωης".[56] However, it appears that v. 26 should read γης not της,

---

[54] Curiously, Block does not mention this as minus in 𝕲^{967}, or the 'provoking' plus in other LXX MSS.

[55] Whilst the Dead Sea Scrolls are outside our focus, Wright (2000, p. 465) mentions the 4Q385 3 fragment wherein Ezekiel appeals to God that the days be hastened or shortened, and he proposes this may be based on 12:21–28. This may support Lust's proposal that this insert called for the vision to be 'historicised' and apply to the present rather than an eschatological future.

[56] Johnson (in Johnson et al., 1938, p. 8) proposes that the parent text had 10 letters to a line, resulting in this pericope occupying 24 lines, yet he admits "it is unlikely that a copyist would have overlooked 24 lines, but if two succeeding columns of narrow width began with the words επι της ζωης it would not be impossible for the scribe to overlook the entire column". However, we have noted previously that there is no textual evidence supporting papyri with 10 words to a line. This undermines Johnson's proposal.

which may question his *parablepsis* theory.[57] Greenberg (1997, p. 659) also sees *parablepsis* here, claiming that "the eye of the copyist of G or its Vorlage skipped from *bwr* 'Pit' at the end of vs. 24 to *bwr* at the end of vs. 25". Lust (2002c, p. 27) notes that "the critical text of LXX is shorter than MT but longer than 𝕲⁹⁶⁷. It is probably an adaptation towards MT, introducing Meshech and Tubal but not Edom". Much of v. 25 is also 'minus' in LXX, which has only the last phrase ('in the midst of the slain'). However, this supports the idea that this also is a pericope in a state of flux, where the first part of v. 25 was a later MT addition not found in LXX MSS.[58] In reference to this, and 𝕲⁹⁶⁷'s greater minus, Lust (2002c, p. 28) states "they are no simple omissions but are part of a different text with its own structure".

This pericope occurs in the section dealing with Assyria (v. 22) and Elam (v. 24), two Gentile nations already in Sheol awaiting Egypt's arrival. The 'inserted' verses add Meshech and Tubal into Sheol's list, and list them with the 'uncircumcised'. However, Lust (2003, p. 88) notes they are not listed with the '*gibborim*'.[59] Lust (2003, p. 89) proposes that the editors of MT sought to lessen the eschatological and apocalyptic content of chapter 32, and they,

> inserted a section on the mythological kingdoms of Meshech and Tubal, aligning them with the historical enemies Assur and Elam, and with Edom which symbolizes Israel's major enemy in their times. In doing so the editors of MT may have tried to suggest that nations, such as Meshech and Tubal, mentioned in the final battle of chs 38–39, are no mysterious apocalyptic entities, but historical agents.

This does appear to be a later editorial attempt to bring Ezekiel's prophetic words into the present, and therefore not the distant future. This was part of their "attempt to bring Ezekiel's visions down to earth" (Lust, 2003, p. 89). That MT has additional material in v. 25 may suggest that they had to again revisit this insert to further historicise it and weave it into the text. While 𝕲⁹⁶⁷ is minus the entire insert, other

---

[57] We should note that 𝕲⁹⁶⁷ and 𝕲ᴬ have της (in vv. 23–24), yet 𝕲ᴮ has γης (followed by Ziegler, witnessing MT's אָרֶץ). Johnson (in Johnson *et al.*, 1938, p. 119) also points out "the final αυτων of Sch. is not found in 𝔐 either in vs. 24 or in vs. 26".

[58] Further evidence of this pericope being in a state of flux may be found with the MT orthographic variants for 'graves': קִבְרֹתֶיהָ (v. 23); קִבְרֹתֶהָ (v. 25); קִבְרוֹתֶיהָ (v. 26) (Tov, 2001, p. 226).

[59] Lust (2003, p. 89) claims that "the dissociation of the נבורים from the mythological giants in Gen. 6:4 seems to confirm" that the MT editors were attempting to historicise Ezekiel's prophecies.

LXX MSS witness the initial insert, but not MT's further revision. The additional wording of v. 25 appears to reflect aspects of the battle with Gog in chapter 38.

Of most significance to us, Lust's view of the third major passage, 36:23c–38, echoes his previous 1981 discussion on this pericope. He repeats his claim that the insertion of this pericope must be considered in conjunction with the change in chapter order found in 𝔊⁹⁶⁷ to the received order. Overall, Lust sees that the received chapter order removes the eschatological and apocalyptic sense of a horrific future battle with Gog, where Israel's slain requires physical resurrection. The received chapter order now allows the dead mentioned in chapter 39 to be Israel's enemies, and not Israel herself. With the received chapter order, and the resulting 'insertion' of this pericope that now 'introduces' chapter 37, Israel is only "morally dead, not physically" (Lust, 2003, p. 90). In the received order, Israel's 'dry bones' resurrection in 37 is a moral and/or spiritual awakening, which is further emphasised by the theology of the 'inserted' pericope. A further result is that the uniting of Israel's divided kingdom and the establishment of a Davidic leader in the second half of chapter 37, now enables the united nation to face Gog, just as they did in times past. Thus, Israel's 'restoration' (36) is now part of her 'resurrection' (37). This again lessens the eschatological and apocalyptical impact found with 𝔊⁹⁶⁷'s chapter order and 'minus'.

Lust's fourth proposed eschatological section covers Ezekiel 7:5b; 6b–7a; 10b; 11c. These are 'minus' in all major LXX MSS, (it is currently unknown whether these are also minus in 𝔊⁹⁶⁷, as this section remains undiscovered). This chapter also has a transposition of verses with vv. 3–6 in LXX located at vv. 6–9 in MT, and vv. 7–9 in LXX are located at vv. 3–5 in MT (Tov, 1999d, pp. 397–399). Lust (2003, p. 91) points out that "all these plusses specify the evil that is coming at the end of the days...whereas LXX emphasizes the punishing role of the Lord and the day of the Lord, MT draws attention to the צפירה, the instrument of the Lord's fury. The day of the Lord is not mentioned explicitly in MT". Lust finds parallels between these verses and Daniel 8 (also 'great evil' in Dan. 9:12–14), and identifies Antiochus IV as the צפירה. Lust believes that these plusses and verse rearrangements also place the eschatological aspect of Ezekiel chapter 7 into the present historical setting (cf. Lust, 1986d).

Lust (2003, p. 84) states that "obviously the [Greek] translator did not 'correct' or 'change' the Hebrew text. Where major differences occur,

these must be due to the Hebrew *Vorlage*, and to the scribes transmitting
and reworking the text". We agree that it is unlikely that the Greek
translator, seeking to accurately transmit the text before him, would
have overlooked such long passages, unless he was extremely incompetent. Lust has demonstrated plausible evidence that it is unlikely that
𝕲⁹⁶⁷ omitted these three pericopes (including 36:23c–38); rather, MT
and later LXX MSS contain them as insertions. It would appear that
these three pericopes are part of the literary development of the text,
born out of early Jewish theological and interpretive reasons. This
can be seen clearly with 32:24b–26. As 𝕲⁹⁶⁷ reflects the Old Greek,
which was written before any other extant text (with the exception of
MasEzek), it is significant that it does not have the plusses of MT and
other LXX MSS.

The main significance for us is that Lust's changing eschatological
proposal provides a plausible theological reason for the chapter reorder, resulting in the creation and insertion of 36:23c–38 in later MSS.
Although his suggestion of concerns over canonical inclusion may be
difficult to prove, we can nevertheless still conclude with Lust that these
pericopes were later additions birthed out of shifting eschatological
theologies.

We may combine Lust's proposal of changing eschatological concerns
that caused the change of chapter order, resulting in the inclusion of
this pericope, with our hypothetical proposal above that this pericope
found its genesis in the liturgical life of the Synagogue. Then we have
an answer for the genesis, and then inclusion for this pericope. Yet, we
do not know who, or which religious party, adjusted the text of Ezekiel
in this way. We will now investigate an early proposal by Lust regarding
a sector of the early Jewish community that may have felt so strongly
about their theology to have interacted with the text, changing the text
to reflect their sifting theology.

7.4.3.1. *Lust's Pharisees Proposal*

Already in his earlier examination of the chapter reorder and 36:23c–38
as an inserted pericope, Lust proposed that theological concerns over a
shift in eschatological and apocalyptic views in early Jewish communities
created the environment for the changes. Lust's (1981a, p. 531) theory
was that the original chapter order and events in the text as found in
𝕲⁹⁶⁷ "probably did not arouse much interest... [and] these chapters
were not read as a continuous story... [but] the situation changed

when apocalyptic tendencies grew stronger". He then proposes that this greater interest in apocalyptic theology, with its varying eschatological sequences, created a polarised environment with one group (the apocalypticists) embracing the events as portrayed in $\mathfrak{G}^{967}$'s chapter order, and another group (the Pharisees) embracing a different order of eschatological events, one that was focused more on their present.

Lust proposes that the Pharisees stood against these rising apocalyptic viewpoints as they were more 'realistic' in their eschatological views. He (1981a, p. 532) claims:

> The Pharisees may be responsible for the restoration of the Book of Ezekiel. According to their view, the restoration of Israel and the coming of the Messiah would precede the final events, all of this belonging to the history of this world. In this perspective, the vision of the dry bones had to follow upon the oracles relating Israel's exile. It referred to the restoration of Israel after its captivity and not to a resurrection strictly speaking.

Lust also examines the idea that the Pharisees were responding to Christian resurrection theology, but he quickly dismisses this as unlikely, with evidence that the addition of 36:23c–38 was pre-Christian.[60] He settles instead with the theory that these textual changes came about because of Pharisee reaction against apocalyptic views of their day.

Yet Lust's Pharisee proposal is not without its critics. Block (1998, p. 339) claims that the Pharisee involvement proposal by Lust is "his own creative interpretation". Significantly, following criticism from Block, Lust (2002c, p. 30) concedes "it must be admitted that my reference to the Pharisees as the party responsible for the restructuring of Ezekiel is highly hypothetical". Yet more significantly, Block questions Lusts' entire proposal that $\mathfrak{G}^{967}$ reflects the Hebrew *Vorlage*, and that the chapter reorder from $\mathfrak{G}^{967}$ to the received text resulted in the need for vv. 23c–38, a detailed matter to which we now turn.

7.4.3.2. *Block's Objections to Lust*
In his 1998 commentary, Block raised seven points of concern over Lust's 1981 article. We will summarise them, and interact in the light of Lust's responses:

---

[60] The discovery of MasEzek (*ca.* 100–50 BCE) undermines any idea that this pericope came about either through Christians, or by any early Jewish reaction against Christian theology.

1. [An] appearance of the recognition formula [וְיָדְעוּ כִּי־אֲנִי יְהוָה] within an oracle rather than at the end is not uncommon in Ezekiel (Block, 1998, p. 340).

Although this is correct, Lust (2002c, p. 29) responds that his point "was not that it [the recognition formula] never occurs in the middle of an oracle, but that 'the recognition formula followed by *ne'um Yhwh* in v. 23b makes a good conclusion'".[61] Even though the declarative formula (נְאֻם אֲדֹנָי יְהוִה) appears commonly at the end of a verse,[62] it also appears in the beginning or middle.[63] The same is true of the recognition formula. However, 36:23b is the only place in Ezekiel where the recognition *and* declarative formulae appear together as 'a string' in the middle of a verse.[64] Having these two formulae together suggests that the recognition formula in v. 23b marked the end of the original chapter, and the declarative formula in v. 23c was part of the editorial weaving of this pericope into the fabric of the text. This can explain why all our representative MSS have the recognition formula, and why the declaration formula is minus in both 𝔊⁹⁶⁷,ᴮ, but present in MT, MasEzek and 𝔊ᴬ. The declaration formula being a later insert also explains 𝔊ᴬ's use of the later Theodotion styled Αδωναι κύριος here (instead of κύριος κύριος). This proposal is again strengthened if we see the declaration formula in v. 32 as an *inclusio* to v. 23c. The 'citation' formula (כֹּה אָמַר אֲדֹנָי יְהוִה) also marks the start of the following two oracles: vv. 33–36 and vv. 37–38 (cf. Block, 1998, pp. 362, 364). The recognition formula is also found at the end of v. 38, as a deliberate overall *inclusio* to the original recognition formula in v. 23b. 36:36 has an expanded form of the recognition formula, and concludes with אֲנִי יְהוָה דִּבַּרְתִּי, which is another Ezekielian phrase used at times to mark

---

[61] 36:38 also ends with the recognition formula of וְיָדְעוּ כִּי־אֲנִי יְהוָה, which is seen as the concluding marker to this oracle and the entire chapter.

[62] Occurrences of the declaration formula at the ending of verses in Ezekiel: 11:8, 21; 12:25, 28: 13:8, 16; 14:11, 14; 15:8; 16:14, 19, 23, 63; 18:9; 20:3, 36, 44; 21:12, 18; 22:12, 31; 23:34; 24:14; 25;14; 26:14; 26:21; 28:10; 29:20; 30:6; 31:18; 32:8, 14, 16, 31, 32; 34:15, 30, 31; 36:14, 15; 39:5, 10, 13, 20, 29; 43:27; 44:15, 27; 45:9, 15; 47:23; 48:29.

[63] Occurrences of the declaration formula at the beginning (often following חַי־אָנִי), or in the middle of a verse in Ezekiel: 14:16, 18, 20; 16:8, 30, 43, 48; 17:16; 18:3, 23, 30, 32; 20:31, 33, 40; 26:5; 32:11; 34:8; 35:6, 11; 36:23, 32; 38:18, 21; 39:8; 43:19; 44:12;

[64] (וְיָדְעוּ [הַגּוֹיִם] כִּי־אֲנִי יְהוָה נְאֻם אֲדֹנָי יְהוִה). Lust (1981, p. 525) compares this string here to the ending of 25:12–14, and uses this as a comparison for an acceptable conclusion to a prophecy.

the end of oracles (cf. 5:17; 17:21, 21:22, 37; 30:12; 37:14). It appears
that this 'inserted' pericope begins with a 'citation/declaration' formula,[65]
as do the intra-oracles (vv. 33, 37), and that the existing recognition
formula in v. 23b finds an overall *inclusio* conclusion in v. 38. We propose that these formulae may have been used deliberately by the scribal
editor in order to 'weave' his inserted text into v. 23c, making it blend
into the Ezekielian standard. As such, נְאֻם אֲדֹנָי יְהוִה in v. 23c can be
seen as an additional 'pause', linking what follows with what precedes.[66]
Whilst this is not 'proof', it does support Lust's proposal.

> 2. The distinctive style in this section may be attributed to the special
> content and need not argue against Ezekielian authorship....[although
> borrowed], the special characteristics...may reflect authorial awareness
> of its significance (Block, 1998, p. 340).

Block is correct in stating that the linguistic and stylistic differences need
not argue against Ezekielian authorship. However, these differences
cause him to defend that it is Ezekielian. It would be extremely unusual
for an editorial scribe to insert a text and not attempt to blend it into
the surrounding text utilising existing formulae. We previously discussed
the proposals of Thackeray, Johnson and Lust that the *hapax legomena*
and stylistic uniqueness in the Hebrew of this pericope suggest later
insertion (cf. 7.4.1). Interestingly, Block does not explain or attempt to
give significant reason for the Hebrew textual uniqueness, yet he (1998,
p. 340) admits that the "diction borrows heavily from previous oracles
and from Jeremiah" [italics mine]. Likewise, Block does not offer a clear
explanation for the 'Theodotion' style in the Greek.[67] His explanation for
unique linguistics is not that this pericope is an editorial insertion, but
that the uniqueness "may reflect authorial awareness of its significance.
A lofty subject deserves an exalted literary style" (Block, 1998, p. 340).
This is a curious explanation for the sudden change of literary styles in
both the Hebrew and Greek. While 'lofty', this pericope is no more so
than other Ezekielian oracles (e.g., 11:17–19; 20:39–44). Yet these other
oracles do not evidence this oracle's literary style. Lust (1981a, p. 519)

---

[65] We propose that this pericope 'begins' with this declaration formula as it is
minus also in 𝔊[B], and may therefore be another later 'stitch' to weave this pericope
into the text.

[66] This appears to be the clause referred to by Zimmerli (1983, p. 248) when he says
"the additional clause in v 23bβ...in which we probably have a later expansion".

[67] Block does not mention or provide explanation for 𝔊[B]'s use of Αδωναι in vv. 33
and 37, avoiding the unique Greek linguistic characteristics of this pericope.

says that this pericope can either been seen as "a culmination of the prophet's theological thinking... [or] a mere summary, borrowing from the surrounding chapters... [and] the gift of a new heart and a new spirit, is almost a literal repetition of Ezek. 11:19". These very differences are given by Lust as evidence for $\mathfrak{G}^{967}$ representing the Hebrew *Vorlage* (Lust, 1981c, p. 45). Block's argument that the linguistic uniqueness of this pericope is due to the 'lofty' subject matter remains weak.

> 3. The LXX evidence is not conclusive. In the first instance, the reliability of Papyrus 967 for reconstruction of the Hebrew *Vorlage* to the Greek translation is not without question.... An accidental loss of a leaf or two seems more likely (Block, 1998, 340).

Block appears to bring up two separate issues in this one point. Firstly, he addresses the issue of scribal practices and the problem of *parablepsis* and/or *homoioteleuton*, and concludes that the omission of 36:23b–38 in this papyrus is due to the 'accidental loss of a leaf or two'. We dismissed this proposal above.

The second issue is the ability to reconstruct the Hebrew *Vorlage* based on $\mathfrak{G}^{967}$. However, $\mathfrak{G}^{967}$ is the oldest extant Greek MSS and therefore the closest in age to a *Vorlage*, and likely witnesses the OG. Its uniqueness is also not without a witness, albeit in the Old Latin.[68] We do not see Lust saying we should 'abandon MT' in favour of $\mathfrak{G}^{967}$, but just that $\mathfrak{G}^{967}$ reflects an earlier Hebrew *Vorlage*. Lust (2002c, p. 30) answers this point, saying that Block

> is right when he holds that a text's antiquity is not necessarily a sign of superiority. He is also right when he does not see the need to abandon MT in favour of a hypothetical 'original' based on P[967]. It is true that MT represents a standardised form making perfect sense. I never defended the view that MT is inferior to LXX as represented by P[967]. I simply suggested that they represent two different stages in the development of the text.

While both of Block's points here are worth examining, we do not find anything that undermines Lust. Both Lust and Block find a 'gap' in the text, but see it from two different stages of the text development: Lust sees that this pericope was originally not in the text and is a later

---

[68] As mentioned previously, Block (1998, p. 340) says that "it is remarkable that it is preserved in only one Greek manuscript and an obscure Latin text". Yet, if the MSS following $\mathfrak{G}^{967}$ were corrected, and the 'gap' filled as Block claims, then we have only a couple of witnesses to what was prior to the correction. We must also question the wording of *W* being an 'obscure' text, as it witnesses the Old Latin.

insertion; Block believes it was there, 'accidentally' lost, and a later 'transmitter' added a Theodotion styled text to fill the 'gap'. But Lust's proposal gives answer to the unique linguistic style in both Hebrew and the Greek. Block only gives answer to the Greek. While we stand with Lust regarding this pericope being a later insertion, and even reflective of the Hebrew *Vorlage*, our textual-comparative methodology is focused on the fact that we have two different textual trajectories, and not which is the 'correct' text.

> 4. Lust's proposal flies in the face of recent form-critical scholarship; he eliminates evidence that runs counter to his theory. V. 23c, 'when through you I vindicate my holiness before their eyes,' is discounted as a secondary correction of 38:16.... Further, deleting 'It is not for your sakes' in v. 32 neutralizes an effective *inclusio* with the same expression in v. 22 (Block, 1998, pp. 340–341).

Block seems to misunderstand Lust here. Nowhere does Lust 'discount' v. 23c; he states that v. 23b "makes a good conclusion... [and] the continuation in v. 23c ff.... is unusual" (Lust, 1981a, p. 525). This clarification can be seen in Lust's (2002c, p. 29) response, "it was not my intention to discard v. 23c. Together with F. Hossfeld, I merely defended the view that 23b presents the conclusion of the section and that its expansion with 23c is secondary". Block (1998, p. 341, n. 20) supplies a long list of examples to show that the recognition formula followed by an infinitive construct with prefixed ב is Ezekielian. The only instances of the declaration formula followed by an infinitive construct with ב are 16:30; 32:14–15. Therefore 36:23 is unique with its use of a recognition formula followed by the declaration formula followed by an infinitive construct with a prefixed ב (Lust, 2002c, p. 29). We agree with Lust that v. 23c is unusual. We have been unable to establish where Lust claims that v. 23c is a "secondary correction of 38:16" (so Block, 1998, p. 341).[69] While Block (1996, p. 341) uses this argument to say that v. 23c is "an expansion of the recognition formula". We respond with the proposal that it is an appropriate editorial expansion (see #1 above).

Block also appears to misunderstand Lust, when he claims Lust deletes 'it is not for your sakes' in v. 32. Lust (2002c, p. 30) responds, saying "in fact I do not delete anything, but simply suggest that the expression in v. 32 belongs to a later insert". Lust (1981a, p. 525) also

---

[69] Interestingly, Lust does not directly address this point in his 2002c article.

points out that "the fact that v. 32 forms an inclusio with v. 22 does not argue in favor of the original unity of vv. 16–32. It rather suggests that the redactor wished to connect his composition (v. 23c ff.) with the foregoing section". We again point out that it would be a very poor redactor who did not seek to weave his insertion into the text, making *inclusio* and employing Ezekielian stylistic features, in particular Ezekiel's typical literary formula markers.

> 5. By itself the section in vv. 16–23bβ appears fragmentary. On the one hand, in contrast to the rest of Ezekiel's restoration oracles, which average twenty-seven verses, deleting 36:23c–38 reduces the present oracle to less than eight verses (Block, 1998, p. 341).

It is true that vv. 16–23bβ forms a short oracle, yet Ezekiel is not without short oracles; 36:13–15 is one such. That one section may appear fragmented on its own to the modern reader, is not evidence that another section is not an insertion. These are two different issues. Block (1998, p. 341) is correct when he says "removing vv. 23c–38 reduces this text [16–23b] to a bland and truncated two-part pronouncement, lacking any explanation of how Yahweh intends to vindicate his holiness". Yet vv. 16–23b, while short, has continuity, fully explaining the dispersion (vv. 16–21), and giving reason for God's future action (vv. 22–23b). In addition, this very blandness may have helped justify the inclusion of vv. 23c–38 into the text.

Block (1998, p. 341) also claims that "since vv. 33–36 and 37–38 each have their own introductory citation and concluding recognition formulae, these look more like *separate oracular fragments* than vv. 23c–38 as a unit" [italics mine]. Curiously, Block admits here that shorter oracle fragments do exist, which appears to undermine his argument. Furthermore, Block (1998, p. 362) asks whether vv. 33–36 is "a fragment of another oracle secondarily added here to fill what the editor considered a gap in the presentation of the restoration". In this Block has admitted the possibility that an oracle was later inserted, even if 'fragmented', for the purposes of filling a 'gap'. This also appears to undermine his argument against Lust regarding short oracles and insertions.[70] It may be that these two fragmentary oracles (vv. 33–36; 37–38) were combined together and inserted as they provide an overall

---

[70] Block (1998, p. 362) is quick to add that "there is no reason to deny the content to the prophet himself", avoiding any thought that a later editor inserted these oracles from other sources.

purpose for God's restorative action for Israel (vv. 23c–32). Block does
not mention or provide explanation for 𝔊ᴮ's use of Ἀδωναι in vv.
33 and 37, avoiding the unique Greek linguistic characteristics of this
pericope. Again, we find that Block's objection does not disprove or
seriously undermine Lust.

> 6. Lust's reconstruction of the history of the LXX is speculative, *lacking
> any objective evidential basis for a Pharisaic reaction* to the sequence of events
> suggested by the arrangement of Papyrus 967 [italics mine] (Block, 1998,
> p. 341).

Of all Block's points, this one holds the most serious challenge to Lust's
proposal, as there is a lack of 'objective evidence' for Lust's Pharisee
involvement.[71] Yet Lust (1981, p. 532) does say that the "Pharisees *may
be* responsible" [italics mine]; he does not make it a definitive assertion.
In his later work Lust (2002c, p. 30) clarifies that his "reference to the
Pharisees as the party responsible for the restructuring of Ezekiel is
highly speculative. I clearly presented it as a hypothetical reconstruction
with its own merits". Regrettably, Lust still does not quote from any
Pharisaic literature, nor does he seek to further support his proposal
from other primary sources. Lust gives little response to Block on this
very important point in his 'Stepbrothers' (2002c) article. Lust's (2003,
p. 90) recent work proposes canonical and eschatological concerns as
reasons for these 'MT plusses', including this pericope, but he does
not provide any suggestion who was responsible. Block (1998, p. 341)
counters Lust, with the following reason for 𝔊⁹⁶⁷'s chapter order:

> the growth of apocalypticism in the late intertestamental period stimu-
> lated the rearrangement of oracles in this text-form, so that the resur-
> rection of the dead is seen as the final eschatological event prior to the
> reestablishment of a spiritual Israel, rather than simply a metaphor for
> the restoration of the nation from exile.

Block's speculation here is similar to Lust's speculative 'Pharisee' proposal. Lust (1981a, pp. 351f.) speculates that any change to the text came
out of their reaction to apocalyptic concerns. Block admits that there has
been a 'rearrangement of oracles' in 𝔊⁹⁶⁷ due to theological concerns.
This raises the point that if 𝔊⁹⁶⁷'s text-form can be rearranged, then

---

[71] These include eschatological and theological concerns with apocalyptic views, or
even "confrontation between Pharisees and Christians" (Lust, 1981a, p. 532).

it may also be possible that the received text is the rearranged text.[72] The primary difference in their proposals is that Lust speculates that it was the Pharisees rearranging the text in reaction to apocalyptic views, with the result being the 'received' text, while Block speculates it was unidentified apocalyptic persons in the late intertestamental period who rearranged the text to give 𝕲⁹⁶⁷'s order. Block's proposal also raises questions of plausibility. Block does not give any explanation why these unidentified 'apocalyptic' exegetes would change the text to 𝕲⁹⁶⁷'s order, which has Israel amongst the slain of chapter 39, making Israel among the corpses defiling the land, requiring a physical resurrection of Israel in the following dry bones epic. A chapter order change from the received text to 𝕲⁹⁶⁷'s order does not make strong theological sense, especially when facing the armies of the Seleucids or Romans. Block (1998, p. 341) explains this by saying "the resurrection of the dead is seen as the final eschatological event prior to the reestablishment of a spiritual Israel". Yet Lust (1981a, p. 351) states that "differing opinions circulated as to the exact sequence of these final events". This means that both the received text and 𝕲⁹⁶⁷ could be representations of early Jewish eschatological views. The arrangement of the 'received' text presents a more positive military view for Israel; a more apocalyptic theology (𝕲⁹⁶⁷) would see the cataclysmic intervention of God in 38–39 destroying the enemies of Israel. Block appears to find himself in unintentional agreement with Lust; that a text form can be rearranged for theological purposes, be that 𝕲⁹⁶⁷ or the received text.

> 7. Lust's understanding of 36:23c–38 as a composition intentionally crafted to serve as a bridge between 36:16–23bβ and ch. 37, after these chapters had been brought together, is not convincing. The evidence of lexical and thematic links cut both ways. The ties between vv. 23c–32 and 16–23bβ argue for unitary treatment (Block, 1998, p. 341).

Block seems to dismiss Lust's insertion proposal with this statement. Block (1998, p. 341) defends his point by stating that "the oracle fragments represented by vv. 33–36 and 37–38 appear authentically Ezekielian, and may have been inserted in the present positions precisely

---

[72] This is based on the methodological argument that if it is possible for one then it is possible for another. Both Block and Lust are being speculative, seeking to find a theological reason for the change of order.

because of their connections with ch. 34 and 36:1–15". Block appears
to be arguing against his own point by admitting that these two smaller
oracles are insertions, even if Ezekielian. Block criticises Lust, but he is
basically presenting a similar argument, albeit on a smaller scale. The
difference is that Block looks 'back' in the book to find reasons for inclusion, whereas Lust primarily looks 'forward' to explain a re-arranged
chapter order that results in this pericope's insertion.

Block (1998, p. 342) also states that "the editors of MT intend
37:1–14 as an explication of 36:27". This is said to counter Lust's proposal that 36:27 was included with the insertion to *prepare* for 37:1–14.
Lust (1981a, p. 523) claims that v. 27 has "the construction, 'I will bring
it about that...' followed by a subordinate clause expressing a purpose
or a consequence [which] is unusual in the Bible and certainly unique in
Ezekiel". Responding to Block, Lust (2002c, p. 30) refers to vv. 26–28,
saying that they serve as a "good example" of a construction to function as a bridge, especially as they "repeat the text of 11,17–19 word
for word". This then opens the way for chapter 37. Ultimately, both
scholars find 36:27 to be an insertion, and both link this to 37:1–14.
Lust (2002c, p. 30) says that "once the editorial character of the section
is admitted, to a large extent on the basis of an objective philological
argumentation, it is perfectly reasonable to recognise a bridge function
in this composition" [of 36:23c–38].

Block (1998, p. 342) claims that these verses connect with their context, saying "37:15–28 not only portrays a reversal of 36:16–23 but
also expands on 34:23–31". While this is correct, it does not disprove
Lust's proposal, as these texts can still refer to each other equally in
$\mathfrak{G}^{967}$'s order as they do with other MSS.

Lust (1981a, p. 523) brings out the uniqueness of the Hebrew in
this pericope, such as in 36:36 where "the combination of verbs 'to
destroy' (*hrs*), 'to build' (*bnh*), and 'to plant' (*nt*) is typical for Jeremiah
and occurs nowhere else in Ezekiel". Lust (1981a, p. 524) also points
out other unusual aspects in the Hebrew for vv. 35 and 37. Yet, Block
(1998, p. 340) does not attempt to answer these points, other than by
referring to the 'exalted literary style' (cf. discussions above).

In summary, Block's criticisms do not undermine Lust's proposal, and
in some cases he unwittingly supports the possibility of textual inserts
(cf. #5 above) and 'oracle rearrangement' (cf. #6 above). Block appears
to imply, without clearly stating it, that $\mathfrak{G}^{967}$ is an innovative text. He
does not give adequate explanation for the unique Hebrew and Greek
linguistic characteristics of 36:23c–38. This is an area of concern, as

this is what causes scholars to view this pericope as an insertion (e.g., Thackeray; Johnson; Lust). Lust has addressed these linguistic issues in his attempt to explain this pericope's genesis and inclusion. Likewise, Block does not adequately address the important issue of the unique chapter order, except to imply that this is a phenomenon for 𝔊⁹⁶⁷ and *W*. Lust does address the chapter order, and proposes it was the chapter reorder that created the need for this pericope to be inserted.

In Block's conclusion (1998, p. 342), he surprisingly concedes that "Papyrus 967 may still represent an old text-form. The text-critical task of retroverting the translated text to a supposed Hebrew *Vorlage* remains an imprecise science". This statement further weakens his own arguments against Lust, and places him in closer agreement with Lust than he may have intended. In his response to Block, Lust (2002c, p. 30) also observes, "somewhat unexpectedly, Block's conclusions are very nuanced and not diametrically opposed to mine". In Block's (1998, p. 365) theological conclusion to this pericope, he states that "perhaps because this literary unit brings together so many strands of Ezekiel's preaching, it is unmatched for its theological intensity and spiritual depth". One is left to wonder why if Block can admit that this pericope is 'unmatched' and combines 'many strands' from Ezekiel, why then does he choose not to deal with the possibility that it may be a later insertion, especially as he appears to suggest that the last two oracles were inserted. One concern from Block's seven points that does require further examination is his sixth point, which criticises Lust for not providing objective evidence that Pharisee eschatological concerns were the possible reason for this redaction. Before we investigate this point, and other theological implications, there is one other area that gives further support to the view that 𝔊⁹⁶⁷ reflects a viable theological trajectory of early Jewish thought.

7.4.4. *External Evidence Supporting* 𝔊⁹⁶⁷

Without seeking to be comprehensive in exploring data outside the text of Ezekiel, we may note some other texts that may lend support to 𝔊⁹⁶⁷'s chapter order and 'minus' of 36:23c–38 being reflective of the Hebrew *Urtext*.

7.4.4.1. *Daniel*
Whereas most LXX MSS have a Theodotion styled text for Daniel that witnesses a similar *Vorlage* to MT, 𝔊⁹⁶⁷ preserves the Old Greek

translation reflecting an earlier pre-revised Hebrew text.[73] Like Ezekiel, $\mathfrak{G}^{967}$ Daniel also has a different chapter order (7–8 come between 4 and 5),[74] and some significant minuses when compared with other MT or LXX MSS. Although a comprehensive discussion of these complex issues is beyond our focus, do note that the OG text for Daniel reflected in $\mathfrak{G}^{967}$ finds 'priority' amongst scholars as "the best witness to the OG text" (McLay, 2005, p. 307). This important papyrus gives further support to the proposal that later LXX MSS have a revised and edited Theodotion-styled text, with later plusses and revised chapter order, replacing the earlier Old Greek style and reflecting MT. If this is the case for Daniel, then it is likely the case for Ezekiel.

Dan. 12:1–3 speaks of a resurrection, which Collins (2000a, p. 126) claims[75] "is the only passage in the Hebrew Bible that clearly predicts resurrection of individuals".[76] Significantly, this resurrection happens *after* the conflict in Dan. 11 that appears to reflect Antiochus Epiphanes' persecution, with the prediction of Antiochus' death in the land of Israel (Dan. 11:45). This order of a major battle followed by a resurrection corresponds to $\mathfrak{G}^{967}$'s order of events in Ezekiel. However, Daniel only talks of a 'king of the north', unlike Revelation which specifically mentions Gog.

7.4.4.2. *Revelation*

Although Revelation is a Christian book, and therefore one step removed from the focus of our investigation, it nevertheless has a significant thematic layout possibly reflecting both $\mathfrak{G}^{967}$ and the received text's chapter order. Lust (1980, p. 180) proposes that John likely utilised Ezekiel when writing Revelation's end time events (Rev. 18–22), while observing a slightly different order of final events in Revelation than in the received text of Ezekiel. Of special interest is Rev. 20:11–15 that

---

[73] The Old Greek of Daniel is also preserved in Codex Chisianus (or Codex 88) which reflects the Hexapla, and in Syro-Hexapla (Lucas, 2002, p. 19).

[74] Daniel $\mathfrak{G}^{967}$'s chapter order reflects a chronological order. It is debated if chronology influenced $\mathfrak{G}^{967}$'s order (McLay, 2005, p. 317).

[75] Dimant (2000, p. 528) also says "an explicit statement of the notion of resurrection is found only in the latest biblical book, the book of *Daniel* (Dan 12:1–2), edited and composed in part around 164 BCE".

[76] Collins (2000a, p. 119) says "the interpretation of the vision is quite explicit, however: 'these bones are the whole house of Israel' (37:11). The resurrection, then, is metaphorical". Collins (2000a, p. 127) also says for Daniel "the hope for resurrection resolves a problem arising from religious persecution... faith in the justice of God would be maintained if the righteous could hope for a reward after death".

has a second resurrection *after* the battle with Gog and Magog (Rev. 20:7–10), therefore matching $\mathfrak{G}^{967}$'s chapter order. It does raise the question of what may have inspired John to write of a second resurrection, if he was using Ezekiel's order of events. Most have focused on the first resurrection in Rev. 20:4–6 before the Gog epic, as that matches Ezekiel's received chapter order. There is nothing, however, in Ezekiel's received order to match John's second resurrection. Significantly, this second resurrection occurs just before the 'new Jerusalem' in Rev. 21. While we may grant John theological licence here, we also suggest that John's writing was in keeping with differing early Jewish eschatological viewpoints, and existing variant textual traditions. Lust (1980, p. 180) questions which textual tradition was before John, suggesting that John knew of both, indicating that "Revelation was made up of two different apocalypses fused into one". Lust proposes that $\mathfrak{G}^{967}$'s order was most likely the tradition influencing John's order of events, and Lust presents a schema supporting his proposal. Curiously, Lust's schema ignores the first resurrection in Rev. 20:4–6. We suggest that John did know of both textual traditions for Ezekiel, and sought to include *both* traditions in Revelation. MasEzek witnesses the received order; therefore the chapter reorder would have been done well before John's time. We modify Lust's (1980, p. 181) schema to reflect the first resurrection; we have changed his numbering[77] and included our clarifying additions in italics:

Revelation	Ezekiel
1. The final battle against the beast: 19, 17–21	1. The final battle against…
2. The first resurrection and Messianic reign: 20, 4–6	2. *The resurrection of 37 in the received text*
3. The final battle against Gog and Magog: 20:7–10	3. Gog of Magog: 38–39
4. The second resurrection: 20:11–15	4. The revival of dry bones: 37 *as in* $\mathfrak{G}^{967}$
5. The descent of the heavenly Jerusalem: 21–22	5. The vision of the New Temple and of the New Israel: 40–48

---

[77] Lust lists the first three events as 1 and 1a (combining our #2 and 3), as he did not put a matching item in Ezekiel's column for the first resurrection.

Therefore, we suggest that Revelation is an implicit witness to the chapter order found in $\mathfrak{G}^{967}$, giving further evidence that $\mathfrak{G}^{967}$ is not a maverick text.

7.4.4.3. *Targum Neofiti and Pseudo-Jonathan Num. 11:26*

We also find implicit support for the different two chapter orders in circulation at some point in the way the various Targumim exegete Num. 11:26. Where MT and LXX state only that Eldad and Medad "prophesied in the camp", Targum Neofiti and Targum Pseudo-Jonathan both include a midrash that they prophesied regarding the end of days and the battle with Gog. Targum Neofiti, along with the Paris BN Fragment, appears to support the received chapter order (McNamara, 1995, p. 74):

> And both of them prophesied together, saying: 'At the very end of the days Gog and Magog ascend on Jerusalem, and they fall at the hands of King Messiah, and for seven years the children of Israel shall kindle fires from their weapons; and they will not have to go out (to) the forest.

That Targum Neofiti has King Messiah ready to defeat Gog and Magog[78] indicates that the chapter order before these scribes has the dry bones and uniting of the nation under a 'Kingly' (even Messianic), military leader coming *before* the Gog epic as in the received text. Significantly, there is no mention of resurrection. The concept of Israel making fires for seven years emphasises the extent of King Messiah's destruction of Gog and Magog.

However, Pseudo-Jonathan's midrash appears to support $\mathfrak{G}^{967}$'s chapter order, and expands on the earlier Neofiti (Clarke, 1992, pp. 220–221):

> But the two prophesied as one and said: 'Behold a king shall rise from the land of Magog at the end of days. He shall gather kings crowned with crowns, and prefects attired in silken clothing, and all the nations shall obey him. They shall prepare for war in the land of Israel against the sons of the exile. However, the Lord is near them at the hour of distress, and all of them will be killed by a burning breath in a consuming fire that comes from beneath the throne of Glory; and their corpses will fall on the mountains of Israel. Then all the wild animals and birds of heaven shall come and consume their bodies. And after this all the dead of Israel shall live [again] and shall delight themselves with the good which was hidden for them from the beginning. Then they shall receive the reward of their labors.

---

[78] Neofiti here treats 'Magog' as a person rather than a place, following LXX.

Pseudo-Jonathan has Magog as a place, yet does not mention Gog by name, stating only that 'a king' will gather other 'kings' and that 'nations will obey him'. In this midrash the LORD appears to lead the battle, destroying Gog and his hosts; there is no mention of any human leader, which matches 𝕲⁹⁶⁷'s order. The use of the pronoun leaves it unclear as to whether the corpses on the ground also include those of Israel. Regardless, Israel is resurrected *after* this battle, which reflects 𝕲⁹⁶⁷'s order. There is also no mention of a human military leader after this resurrection, again reflecting 𝕲⁹⁶⁷'s tradition. Flesher (2000, p. 319) states that "PJ's [Pseudo-Jonathan's] shift away from Proto-PT [Palestinian Targum][79] understanding of resurrection is purposeful, not accidental...he takes steps to eliminate the other view". Flesher (2000, p. 321) also observes that for Pseudo-Jonathan "the resurrection happens in the world we know, but at the end of time. Thus, for PJ, the resurrection of the dead keeps its special character by happening at a special time rather than a special place—Proto-PT's world-to-come".

We refer the reader to Flesher (2000) for a detailed discussion on the various Targumim's treatment of Num. 11:26 and other texts,[80] as we only seek to suggest that Pseudo-Jonathan did not create the order of his midrash out of nowhere; he appears to have known the chapter order tradition found in 𝕲⁹⁶⁷. We can see that both chapter order traditions are reflected in Targum Neofiti and Pseudo-Jonathan's respective midrashic expansions of Num. 11:26.

7.4.5. *Summary of Insertion (and Reorder), not Omission*

Overall, sufficient evidence exists to strongly indicate that 𝕲⁹⁶⁷ is a credible witness of the original Hebrew. Therefore, our received text of Ezekiel has a different chapter order than the original Hebrew and a later inserted plus of 36:23c–38. This does not mean we now abandon MT (or the other LXX MSS); our textual-comparative methodology treats each trajectory as representatives of early Jewish interpretation and theology. We have previously, albeit briefly, covered possible theological reasons and implications for the chapter reorder and resultant inserted pericope, with particular attention given to those proposed by

---

[79] This includes Targum Neofiti, and the Paris fragment.

[80] Targum Ezekiel's expansions reflect only the received order. The one area of interest is 39:16 which contemporises Rome as part of the slain, and therefore identifies Gog with Rome. For Targum Ezekiel see Levey (1987), Ribera (1996), or for Targums in general see McNamara, Cathcart, and Maher (1987).

Lust. However, as noted above, we agree with Block that Lust does not provide sufficient objective evidence to support his 'Pharisee' proposal. Therefore, we now turn to a closer examination of possible theological reasons and hands involved in these textual changes.

7.5. THEOLOGICAL SIGNIFICANCE, TIMEFRAME AND MOTIVATION

With the premise that $\mathfrak{G}^{967}$ is a viable witness to the Hebrew *Urtext* of Ezekiel, we now explore the theological significance of $\mathfrak{G}^{967}$'s chapter order, and the received order. We will seek to identify a possible time-frame and motivation for the change in chapter order and pericope insertion.

7.5.1. *Theological Significance of* $\mathfrak{G}^{967}$

The theological progression found in $\mathfrak{G}^{967}$ shows solid continuity. In 36:1–15 the mountains of Israel are addressed preparing them for the return of Israel, and are assured that they will not miscarry the people again. In the following pericope in $\mathfrak{G}^{967}$, Israel's sin of 'blood' and 'idolatry' is given as the reason for the dispersion (vv. 16–23b), therefore Israel profaned God's holy name amongst the nations (vv. 20–22). It is significant that this section in $\mathfrak{G}^{967}$ finishes chapter 36 with God establishing his holy name (vv. 21–23b), declaring "the nations will know that I am the LORD" (v. 23b).

$\mathfrak{G}^{967}$'s direct progression into chapters 38–39 then provides an immediate answer as to how God will establish his holiness, and let the nations know he is the LORD: he will defeat Gog and his hordes (38: 16, 23; 39:6, 7, 21–24 28). God's name has been profaned amongst the nations, and now the nations despise him thinking he is weak. So God will bring them to his mountains and land to show his power by defeating the nations who oppose him and his people.

'These things' in 36:22 may refer to what precedes. However, in $\mathfrak{G}^{967}$'s order the focus seems to be more on what follows, referring to God's judgment on the nations (38–39), letting the nations know that the exile was not because of God's weakness, but because his holiness demanded that he judge his people (39:21–24). God's people defiled his land and his holy name, so they had to leave his land and God's immediate presence (36:16–23b). God's explanation in 39:21–24 is a reference to 36:16–23b, and can be seen as an *inclusio*, tying these chapters together. God's declaration that he will 'now bring Jacob back from captivity' (39:25–28), sets the scene in 𝕲⁹⁶⁷'s order for the resurrection of the dry bones (37:1–14). In this chapter order, the dry bones appear to include Israel's slain following the battle with Gog. Therefore, LXX's use of θυμός in 39:29, which is likely original,[81] may refer to God's judgment on Israel in battle, which now requires a physical resurrection. This resurrection follows the battle in 𝕲⁹⁶⁷'s order. However, this resurrection need not refer to a physical resurrection; it may be a metaphor for the regathering of Israel from exile (37:11).[82] If so, their 'dryness' may be a reference to their exile, and their 'resurrection' a metaphor for the regathering after being cut off (37:11b). This is significant if we take 39:25–28 into account, which introduces the dry bones epic in 𝕲⁹⁶⁷'s order. This then gives a dual application for the dry bones epic. However, unlike the received order, 𝕲⁹⁶⁷'s order favours a literal reading of the resurrection, as it envisages that there will be actual dead.

Regardless of the metaphor of the received text, or the actual resurrection of 𝕲⁹⁶⁷'s order (which does appear to be the primary reading), in 37:1–14 Israel is raised as a nation and will again be settled in their own land (37:1–14).[83] The 'glory days' of Israel are restored with the nation again a United Kingdom (37:15–23) and 'David' again leading Israel (37:24–28). Significantly, in 𝕲⁹⁶⁷'s order, there is no need for this Davidic ruler to lead Israel into battle, as the LORD has already defeated Gog. The purpose of 𝕲⁹⁶⁷'s Davidic ruler is to shepherd the people peacefully, making sure they are Torah observant (v. 24b), as they live under their 'covenant of peace' (v. 26). His greatest purpose is shepherding the people for the building of God's sanctuary (v. 26b), so God can dwell with his people (v. 27). 𝕲⁹⁶⁷'s Davidic leader is a

---

[81] In our discussion of chapter 39, we proposed θυμός reflected the *Vorlage*, and MT's רוח is a later post-LXX amendment. Our textual-comparative methodology permits both readings to reflect their different theology.

[82] Unfortunately we cannot be sure of its original interpretation within early Jewish communities. We also lack evidence of when a physical resurrection became part of Israel's eschatology. The dry bones epic may be one of the earliest recordings of a physical resurrection, but again, we cannot be sure how this was originally interpreted.

[83] Ezekiel's resurrection is a national one, regardless if 'actual' in 𝕲⁹⁶⁷'s order, or 'moral/spiritual' in the received order. Yet, *Pseudo-Ezekiel* reveals a theology of individual resurrection based on personal purity and righteousness. Therefore, while Dimant (2000, p. 529) points out that "*Pseudo-Ezekiel* furnishes the earliest evidence for a complex and well-developed exegesis linked to the theme of resurrection", its focus on individual resurrection, rather than national, is one step removed from our focus.

peaceful shepherd, rather than the military leader in Israel's history. This theology may find support with LXX's use of ἄρχων rather than βασιλεὺς for MT's מֶלֶךְ (cf. Excursus 4.4.1 in chapter 4).[84] Then God sets his sanctuary in their midst as part of this covenant of peace; ultimate restoration is God in his sanctuary in the midst of his people in his land.

𝕲⁹⁶⁷'s order does not interrupt this everlasting covenant of peace with the Gog epic, but instead flows smoothly into chapters 40–48 where the Temple is built and worship established. The promise of God's sanctuary being set in their midst as part of their everlasting covenant (37:26–28) in 𝕲⁹⁶⁷'s order serves as a natural lead into building the new Temple (40–48). This lead is largely lost in the received order by its interruption of chapters 38–39. With Israel fully restored, Gog and his hordes defeated, and the LORD in his sanctuary, then all nations will finally know that it is the LORD who makes Israel holy (37:28). In the received order a battle follows these promises, a textual flow that suggests the nations do not acknowledge the LORD, but rather rise up against him, delaying his Temple plans. This is not found in 𝕲⁹⁶⁷'s order, where the covenant of peace continues into the building of the new Temple and restablishing of worship.

Therefore, in 𝕲⁹⁶⁷'s order we find continuity in Israel's restoration:

− The mountains are prepared, and assured that they will not miscarry again.
− Israel's sin is established as the result for the dispersion.
− The LORD declares he will establish his holy name.
− Gog and his hordes are defeated, establishing God's holiness.
− Israel is resurrected, united in peace with a 'peaceful shepherd' Davidic leader
− The Temple is built and worship re-established.

𝕲⁹⁶⁷'s order may reflect the eschatology of a writer living in exile. The message is that the land is being prepared for us and will not cast us

---

[84] In that Excursus we proposed that rather than LXX 'softening' the Hebrew, the LXX translator found נָשִׂיא in his *Vorlage*, not מֶלֶךְ (done at the same time as other word changes to support the chapter reorder: cf. 36:23b; הַיִל to קָהָל in 37:10; חֵמָה to רוּחַ to 39:29). This is reflected in LXX's use of ἄρχων, which was continued by the later LXX redactor(s) who aligned the Greek to reflect the changed chapter order and inserted pericope in the Hebrew text.

out again. Our sin caused our exile, but God will defeat his enemies, and our dry bones will be resurrected from the battle and from exile. We will return to a peaceful living with our glory days restored, and will rebuild our Temple.

This is not to say that the returnees ceased their call for further restoration, as everyone had not yet returned. The restoration of the nation continued to be a part of eschatological expectation (cf. Acts 1:6). Evidence also suggests that the call for a new Temple continued even while the post-exilic Temple stood (cf. 11QTemple; Mat. 26:61). In addition, $\mathfrak{G}^{967}$'s order could also be seen to leave the resurrection of Israel's dry bones to a more distant, even eschatological, future; perhaps even seven years after the battle with Gog (cf. 39:9).[85]

$\mathfrak{G}^{967}$'s theology does not appear to reflect the situation of those who at a later period are in the land with an existing Temple, but find themselves surrounded by invading armies (of the Seleucids or Romans), who are threatening their security and perhaps hindering their worship. These inhabitants require a military leader like David who will lead the nation into victory over their enemies. They need this to happen now and not in some more distant eschatological fulfilment; this new theology needs to be now reflected in their texts.

7.5.2. *Theological Significance of the Received Order*

A pressing problem for a later post-exilic time with $\mathfrak{G}^{967}$'s chapter order is that there is no call for Israel to unite and gather against her enemies. While they may have desired another Temple, they had an existing Temple. Their immediate concern was having the freedom to live their daily lives and to worship without oppression from their enemies. In addition, in $\mathfrak{G}^{967}$ the dead on the ground following the battle with Gog appear to include Israel, requiring a physical resurrection; hardly an inspirational call to arms! In $\mathfrak{G}^{967}$'s order, Israel was only united with a peaceful Davidic shepherd *after* the battle with Gog and subsequent resurrection. This order certainly would not have appealed to those facing battle with either the Seleucids or Romans. They now needed to rally the troops against their present enemy. It is therefore suggested that the chapter order was changed from $\mathfrak{G}^{967}$'s

---

[85] Likewise, as we saw with Lust's proposal above (§7.4.3), the events in $\mathfrak{G}^{967}$'s order could be interpreted as happening in the eschatological future.

order to the received order, as part of their attempt to unite all Israel for both spiritual renewal, and to militarily rise against their enemies, even as a call to arms.

The textual flow still has the mountains prepared for Israel's return, and her idolatrous sin and God's holiness are still addressed as in 𝔊⁹⁶⁷'s order. However, the resurrection of Israel's dry bones is now placed immediately after this, and before the Gog epic. In the received order, the battle has not yet occurred to result in these dry bones. The chapter reorder can therefore only mean that the resurrection of the dry bones is a 'moral' and/or 'spiritual' resurrection. It is a nation rising to deal with its present reality, requiring the casting off of an oppressive enemy.

The use of metaphoric language in 37:11 assists this chapter reorder. This does not imply that those responsible for changing the chapter order did not believe in, or had ceased to believe in, physical resurrection, but their primary goal was a call to arms to cast off their oppressors, and talk of death does not often inspire the oppressed to rise up. Thus, while the dry bones epic in the chapter reorder is primarily interpreted metaphorically, it may still have retained its original intent, speaking of a physical resurrection interpretation.[86] The later LXX ἀνθρωπίνων insertion (𝔊ᴮ·ᴬ) may have been the result of this chapter reorder, in an effort to clarify that the dry bones were human. This may indicate that these LXX scribes still interpreted this as both a physical and metaphorical resurrection. As mentioned above, while the dry bones epic in 𝔊⁹⁶⁷'s order clearly portrays a physical resurrection, it may also have allowed a metaphorical interpretation, calling the exiles to return (37:11). If so, then this chapter reorder, which reflects a more metaphorical interpretation, would not be seen as theologically offensive, especially with the call to purity and spiritual renewal found in the inserted pericope. In the received order, the dry bones coming together are clearly the scattered and demoralised Israel being united on their land, and no longer feeling cut off from each other (37:11). The placement of the dry bones chapter does fit its new location before chapter 38, as it continues the restorative theme in 36:1–15, but it *implies* a new military purpose for the Davidic leader.

---

[86] Collins (2000a, pp. 119–120) comments that "the resurrection, then, is metaphorical, although the passage would be interpreted literally in the Dead Sea Scrolls (4Q385) and later tradition". Unfortunately we don't know what textual tradition of Ezekiel was before the Dead Sea community. However, this does demonstrate one clear example of a community that interpreted the dry bones as a literal resurrection.

In the new chapter order the uniting of Israel (37:15–23), and the Davidic leader (37:24–28), appear to take on a new militaristic meaning and purpose that is tied to the 'call to arms'. This new united 'Davidic' kingdom resembles the glory days, when David united Israel into one kingdom, led them to victory against their enemies, and set up his Tabernacle in Jerusalem. Whereas $\mathfrak{G}^{967}$'s Davidic leader is the 'peaceful shepherd', the Davidic leader found in the received chapter order is primarily a 'military' leader. While chapters 38–39 do not explicitly include Israel or David in the battle against Gog, the chapter reorder *implies* that the united Israel under David is involved in defeating Gog.[87] In the reorder, there is no need for a physical resurrection of Israel following the battle as the dead in chapters 38–39 are only Gog and his hordes and their corpses remain buried. This may explain MT's later unique עַמִּי plus in 37:12, clarifying that the 'resurrection' in the renewed order refers only to Israel and not to their enemies. This reinforces the metaphorical 'moral/spiritual' sense of the dry bones resurrection. In the new chapter order, once Israel defeats her enemies under their Davidic leader they build the new Temple (40–48), just as David established his Tabernacle after defeating his enemies. However, in their day it was to reinstate Temple worship, as the Temple already existed.

Unlike the distant eschatological future represented in $\mathfrak{G}^{967}$'s order, the changed chapter order addresses Israel's present reality of oppression, especially during the Hasmonean times. The chapter reorder brings both military and spiritual success to an oppressed people, changing their reality, and bringing future promises into their present, and enabling them to reinstate Temple worship and Jewish lifestyle.

Yet, the change in the text is not complete. Those changing the chapter order now insert 36:23c–38 as support for their chapter reorder. As the chapter reorder appears to be a call to arms, this inserted pericope appears to be a call to purity. It introduces and supports the 'new' moral and/or spiritual resurrection metaphor for the dry bones, and the uniting of the united nation under a military Davidic leader; events that now immediately follow chapter 36.

The insertion of this pericope causes the text to flow from Israel's sin and God's holiness (36:16–23b), to now cover what God will do to purify Israel from their sins and idols (v. 25). Israel will be gathered

---

[87] This interpretation can be seen in Targum Neofiti's use of the Gog epic in Num. 11:26 (cf. above).

(v. 24) and given a new heart and spirit (v. 26), echoing Ezek. 11:19 and Jeremiah (cf. Jer. 31). They will also receive God's Spirit (v. 27; cf. 11:19). They will be resettled and established in the land which would now be like Eden (vv. 33–35), and Israel will once again gather as 'flocks of humanity' in Jerusalem for the festivals (vv. 37–38).

These textual changes result in a new theological flow in Ezekiel 36–39:

– Israel's mountains are prepared, and assured they will not miscarry again.
– Israel's sin is established as the result for the dispersion.
– The LORD declares he will establish his holy name.
– A [new inserted] call to purity declaring what God will do to purify Israel.
– Israel is morally/spiritually resurrected, and united for battle under a military Davidic leader [now as if a call to arms].
– Israel's covenant of peace is interrupted as Gog and his hordes are defeated.
– The Temple built and worship re-established.

The change however does cause a degree of disjointedness within chapters 36–39, where 38–39 now seem out of place, disturbing Israel's covenant of peace (37:26). This has caused a number of scholars to question the legitimacy of 38–39 in Ezekiel. While 39:25–29 still provides an *inclusio* to 36:16–23, it no longer looks forward to fulfilment with the dry bones as it does in 𝕲[967]. Its 'new' distance from chapter 36 causes this *inclusio* to be often overlooked. LXX's θυμός (39:29) also appears to be out of place, with no referent directly following. This may explain MT's change to רוּחַ. 'These things' (36:22) now directly refers to what God will do for his people, not as in 𝕲[967] the establishment of his holy name by defeating his enemies. Also, the inserted pericope does not directly address the way that God will show his holiness among the nations; only how God will purify and renew Israel. The pericope begins (36:23c) by echoing the last phrase in 38:16, but the echo distance is much further away than in the original order.[88]

---

[88] We suggest above that 38:16, which was originally just a few verses away from 36:23b, inspired the use of this phrase in 36:23c.

Finally, it is difficult to establish a reason why the text would have been changed *from* the received chapter order, and its inserted pericope, *to* that found in 𝔊⁹⁶⁷.[89] Any proposal for a change from the received chapter order to 𝔊⁹⁶⁷'s order must cover why the scribe would 'omit' 36:23c–38 (*parablepsis* and other scribal errors were discounted at the beginning of this chapter). The received text makes good moral and spiritual sense, especially with the inserted pericope, yet with 'military' overtones. We propose that these factors led to a wide acceptance of the textual changes, which also resulted in them being added to LXX being at an early stage. The popularity of the changed text in both Hebrew and Greek linguistic circles may explain why we only have one Greek and one Latin extant witness to the original text. It is important to note that although we claim that these changes were made, the basic wording of the surrounding text has remained unchanged, except for a few word changes that likely resulted from the change (e.g., LXX's ἀνθρωπίνων 37:1; MT and LXX 39:29). This reflects a reverence for the original text even though they changed its order. This may also have helped the change to gain acceptance. We are now left with the question of *when* these textual changes may have taken place.

7.5.3. *Possible Timeframe*

Based on previous discussions in our chapter 2, we suggest a broad translational timeframe from the *Urtext* to the Old Greek as reflected in 𝔊⁹⁶⁷ ranging from 230 BCE (Thackeray, Dorival, Siegert) through to 132 BCE (Swete; Jobes and Silva), to 50 BCE (P.D.M. Turner). The exact translational date is for the OG undeterminable, and largely unimportant, whereas a general timeframe for the chapter reorder and pericope insertion does have a measure of importance for our textual-comparative methodology. We examine this timeframe not to establish any textual priority, as we continue to treat 𝔊⁹⁶⁷ and the received text with equal weighting, but to shed light on possible timeframe to determine theological motivations for these changes.

These textual changes fit the time of the Hasmonean uprising in which Antiochus IV could be recognised as Gog from the north (1Macc.1:44–50). While not agreeing with Lust's 'Pharisee' proposal,

---

[89] We briefly discussed this above under Block's (1998, p. 341) sixth objection to Lust's proposal (§7.4.3.2).

Botte and Bogaert (1993) suggest the chapter rearrangement is linked with the Seleucid period as a response to enemy opposition coming after the return to the land.[90] Yet this scenario may also fit a later timeframe as tensions continued with the Seleucids, or possibly in the face of the threat and aftermath of the Roman invasion of 63 BCE, which fanned royal messianic expectation.[91]

Following the evidence of MasEzek dated "the second half of the last century BCE" (Talmon, 1999, p. 60), we suggest the chapter reorder and resulting insertion of 36:23c–38 took place initially in the Hebrew text *after* the OG was translated, but *before* MasEzek *ca.* 50 BCE. This may explain the unique Hebrew in the inserted pericope, as it was penned at a date later than the original surrounding Hebrew. This revised Hebrew text was then taken as the standard for all subsequent Hebrew MSS, leaving us today without an extant Hebrew witness to the *Urtext*. We also suggest that the Hebrew redactor(s) inserted the other 'eschatological' plusses noted by Lust (see above) at the same time that these major textual changes where being made, and for similar theological and shifting eschatological concerns.

All the textual changes in the Hebrew text were then incorporated into LXX by a recensionist at some later date, using the 'proto-Theodotion' style of his time for 36:23c–38. We propose this LXX recension took place in a broad timeframe around 50 BCE (based on MasEzek), through to sometime in the first century CE. As with the Hebrew text, this LXX recension became the standard for subsequent LXX MSS (including 𝕲[B,A]). Today 𝕲[967] remains the only extant Greek witness to the OG, and the Hebrew *Urtext*. While these conclusions are relevant for traditional text-critical concerns, our textual-comparative methodology views both forms of the text with interest for their theological perspectives and so both are objects of study.

---

[90] Botte and Bogaert (1993, p. 643) state that "our feeling is, it is more likely an establishment of the historic fact of the return (37) and the application of chapters 38–39 to Antiochus IV, which have brought about a new sequence where individual purification (36:23b–38 added), and the return and repopulation (37), preceded the events in view (38–39 and 40–48). The original sequence attested by the Septuagint was focused entirely towards the future conflict defeat of Gog and purification of the land (38–39), revival and return (37), New Israel (40–48). In our opinion the literary explanation of J. Lust is worth consideration, not the theological interpretation he offers, with reserve by the way" [translation mine].

[91] It is beyond our scope to pursue this topic, but our finding does provide a further important resource for understanding this period and the responses of pious groups to their crises.

Some have questioned (cf. Thackeray above) how a Theodotion styled text could find its way into LXX Ezekiel when the historical Theodotion lived somewhere around the second century CE.[92] Significantly, scholars now speak of a proto-Theodotion style, placing it as early as the first half of the first century CE (Fernández Marcos, 2000, pp. 148–153).[93] This matches our proposed timeframe for a Greek recension, and provides an answer how the inserted pericope reflects a Theodotion style.

Therefore, we conclude that these textual changes were done in the Hebrew before 50 BCE utilizing the linguistic styles of that time, and then the Greek text was recended late enough to incorporate the 'proto-Theodotion' style (even into the first century CE).

These timeframes, whether for the OG translation, or the Hebrew revisionist, are firmly outside the Christian era. The later LXX recension did not add to the revised Hebrew text, and continued to support the OG LXX variants, which also reflect Jewish hands. We now explore further the motivations during these timeframes that may have generated these textual changes.

7.5.4. *Possible Motivations*

We proposed above two motivating factors for the textual changes: firstly a military call to arms, and secondly, a call to purity or spiritual renewal. While the call to arms may reflect Hasmonean resistance to external threats, there are many groups who could lay claim to the spiritual renewal as defined in the inserted pericope.

The changes occur within a period where there was the rise of a number of different Jewish religio-political parties. Unfortunately, it is very difficult to provide a definitive identification of the many groups of that day, and their theological and eschatological views, even for those supposedly well known to us. Tomasino (2003, p. 162) rightly comments that the three groups mentioned by Josephus (Pharisees, Sadducees, Essenes) should not be taken as the only groups in existence at that time. In fact these groups may represent only a small number of the

---

[92] Fernández Marcos (2000, pp. 142–154) has detailed discussion of the historical Theodotion and the difficulty in dating his existence.

[93] McLay (2005, p. 304) claims that "the term Theodotion is employed for convenience. The Theodotion version of Daniel was known to the New Testament writers, so it could not have been written by a putative second century person known by that name".

Jews living then. Meier (2001, p. 290) points out that "the huge library
we awkwardly dub 'the intertestamental writings' or 'the OT pseudepigrapha' reminds us that there were probably many religious leaders
in Palestine of whom we are largely ignorant". Further, the histories
of many of these groups have been lost forever, and attempts to reconstruct them are often based on speculation from later sources.[94] Even
the traditional view of the Hasidim as the forerunners to the Pharisees
or the Essenes is now a matter of dispute, as Tomasino (2003, p. 162)
states, "evidence for either identification is scant. We know nothing of
what the Hasidim believed or how they worshipped, and little of why
they fought against the Greeks". Meier (2001, p. 292) says that we
can date these groups "only to the period after the Maccabean revolt
in the 2nd century BC, when the Hasmoneans Jonathan, Simon, and
John Hyrcanus were consolidating their power". Scholars today also
distance themselves from the traditional belief that the Pharisees were
the forerunners of Rabbinic Judaism. Likewise they "now understand
that it's really impossible to speak of 'normative' Judaism until well into
the rabbinic era (fourth century AD and beyond)" (Tomasino, 2003,
p. 162).

Modern research has revealed that primary sources for this period
are scant, and often written by those with theological and/or political
bias. Even "the picture presented by Josephus is murky" (Meier, 2001,
p. 294).[95] Most today admit that Josephus wrote with bias. He also
wrote over a century after our proposed timeframe. Even the New
Testament was written over a century after our Hebrew revision timeframe, and was written from the viewpoint of defending the ministry
of Jesus, making it a secondary source. Therefore, it is questionable to
place NT statements on theology and eschatology onto earlier religio-
political group(s).

While we can determine theological motivations behind these textual
changes in Ezekiel, the lack of trustworthy primary sources creates difficulty in clearly establishing *who* believed *what* during that timeframe.
Certainly theologies surrounding the resurrection of the dead have

---

[94] Tomasino (2003, p. 163) points out that even the various Targumim "were
produced centuries after the time when the sects existed and must be used with
caution".

[95] Meier (2001, p. 299) further states that "the sole primary sources for our knowledge
of these groups, sources that were once cited with naïve faith in their total reliability
and with remarkable blindness to their mutual (or even self-) contradictions, are now
viewed with a much more sceptical eye by many scholars".

eschatological and apocalyptic overtones, but we are left with little objective evidence for these various resurrection views prior to 50 BCE. Also, we do not know definitively when the view of physical and/or individual resurrection came into Jewish thought. As pointed out previously, Ezekiel's dry bones may well be the first evidence of physical individual resurrection, especially in $\mathfrak{G}^{967}$'s order. However, we cannot be certain whether this is the case.

In addition, while we do have some evidence of eschatology and resurrection in early writings, we now cannot be sure what party was responsible for them. Prior to discoveries at Qumran it was common to link the OT pseudepigraphic books of *Psalms of Solomon* and *Jubilees* to Pharisees, and so as sources for recreating their views on eschatology and resurrection.[96] Today such authorship "is considered dubious or impossible by many critics" (Meier, 2001, p. 324).

While many have sought to establish a Pharisaic eschatology based on Paul's writings, Meier again cautions that "we must not leap to the conclusion that the eschatology and/or messianic substratum that we may find at the basis of Paul's Christian theology can be attributed to all Pharisees at the time of Paul, to say nothing of all Pharisees from about 150 BC to AD 70". Perhaps for this reason Lust distanced himself in his later writings from his earlier 'Pharisee' proposal, finding himself without empirical evidence.

We can agree with Lust (see §7.4.3.2), that the primary eschatological difference between $\mathfrak{G}^{967}$'s chapter order and the received order, is that the received order places the Gog epic into their immediate time and reality, and not into a more distant eschatological future. We also agree with Lust, that this effort to bring the text and events into their historical present, appears to be reflected in the other inserted texts as noted above (12:26–28; 32:24b–26; ch. 7).

However, we need to concede that the change of chapter order may have been motivated primarily by a call to arms to face their present enemies with a Davidic military leader. The change may be lacking the influence of any major eschatological or apocalyptic theology. Further, any number of religious groups of the period, from those within society (e.g., Pharisees, Sadducees), or those in withdrawn communities (e.g.,

---

[96] Ryle and James' *Psalms of Solomon* (Cambridge, 1891) had the subtitle, *Psalms of the Pharisees, Commonly Called the Psalms of Solomon*; and Charles (1902, p. lxxiii) thought that *Jubilees* was written by "a pharisee of the straitest sect". See Charlesworth, (1985, pp. 44, 46, 51, 639, 642).

Essenes, Qumran), would have embraced the call to purity as found in the inserted pericope.

While we are left without a clear knowledge of who was responsible for these changes, we can with some certainty suggest the Hasmonean times prior to 50 BCE, and that it was a response to a crisis during that period, possibly the time of suppression under Antiochus IV, or the Roman invasion of 63 BCE. Whatever group, or groups, was responsible for the change in the text, these changes were accepted in early Jewish (and later, in Christian) circles for this text to become the dominant text. The result is that there is now only one Greek and Old Latin witness to the OG, and possibly the *Urtext*. However, as we have shown above (cf. Revelation, Targum Numbers), both textual trajectories may well have been in circulation for a period of time.

We cautiously suggest that MasEzek's presence at Masada[97] indicates that the Zealots were one group who supported this chapter reorder, as it reflected their aspirations to unite and rise militarily against the Romans. We also suggest that the surprising[98] find of two *mikva'ot* at Masada revealing their purity concerns as observant Jews, indicates the Zealots' acceptance of the inserted pericope, especially 36:25–28. However, while this may identify one group who found the changes compatible with their aspirations and theology, it does not tell us who was responsible for making the textual changes, although it possibly flowed from comparable concerns.

Again, we cautiously suggest the acceptance of this chapter reorder along with the inserted pericope can be found with its early inclusion in the *haftarot* lectionary readings (cf. Thackeray §7.4.2.). Thackeray (1921, p. 40) emphasises the importance of examining the liturgical use of a passage, saying that it is "a factor in exegesis which has been unduly

---

[97] Tomasino (2003, p. 317) claims that MasEzek was "deliberately buried by Masada's defenders so it could be found by future generations". He (2003, p. 317) proposes various reasons, asking "was it a last act of defiance—a testimony that they were sure their nation would be restored? Or was it a proclamation of faith in the resurrection: that even though they would die, yet they would live again? Or perhaps the text had some significance to them that from our vantage point we can't even begin to guess"? While these may be reasons for MasEzek's burial, this does not give any reason for its presence at Masada. Although we agree it had special significance for those at Masada.

[98] The concept of this find being a 'surprise' comes from Yadin, who concluded that this discovery "illustrates, as do the inscriptions about tithes mentioned earlier, that the defenders of Masada were devout Jews, so that even here, on dry Masada, they had gone to the arduous lengths of building these ritual baths in scrupulous conformity with the injunctions of traditional Jewish laws" (Yadin, 1966, p. 167).

neglected". As above, we again suggest that this inserted pericope *may* have had a liturgical life as part of the early Special Sabbaths, before it was inserted into Ezekiel 36 to assist the flow of the revised chapter order. If so, this liturgical use and the resulting familiarity may have helped the pericope gain acceptance as an inserted text. Difficulty exists however, in determining when a text was set within a lectionary, especially that of the *haftarot*, due to the absence of any original liturgical MSS. We noted above that the exegetical expansions for this pericope in Targum Ezekiel may have been the result of later defence for its inclusion. These expansions link the pericope to the 'Red Cow' (and the *Parah* Special Sabbath reading), the reference to a holy, cleansed people, identifies the festival as the *Passover*, the cities as those in the *land* of Israel, and the people belonging to the *House* of Israel. Again it must be stated that this is conjecture. Yet of all the surrounding pericopes, this pericope has clear Targumic theological expansions.

7.6. SUMMARY OF OBSERVATIONS: PAPYRUS 967

While many scholars have viewed $\mathfrak{G}^{967}$ as a textual anomaly that has omitted a major pericope (Ezek. 36:23c–38), and changed the 'correct' chapter order, we have demonstrated that this is not the case. Rather than being a maverick manuscript, $\mathfrak{G}^{967}$ is in fact a viable witness to the Old Greek, and the Hebrew *Urtext*, and therefore should be heard in its own right along with the received text.

Various proposals for the omission as resulting from 'scribal error' are unlikely, not least because they do not provide any viable reason for $\mathfrak{G}^{967}$'s different chapter order where chapter 37 follows chapter 39. Both the 'missing' pericope and chapter order should be discussed together since discussed in isolation, one may conclude some level of scribal error for each item, or for both. An examination of these two textual issues together results in a satisfactory answer for both, and shows deliberate scribal activity.

Rather than $\mathfrak{G}^{967}$ being minus this pericope and having a 'confused' chapter order, it is the received text that reflects a *changed* chapter order from the *Urtext*, this reorder requiring the *insertion* of 36:23c–38. It seems logical that both these textual changes would have been completed at the same time, and likely for theological reasons.

These reasons include both shifting eschatological concerns, and the post-exilic need for Israel to unite against its surrounding enemies under a military styled Davidic leader as of old, even as a call to arms. The inserted pericope most likely came out of a call to purity, and may have had its genesis in the synagogue liturgy. Both the call to arms and call to purity were designed to encourage an oppressed and discouraged people to rise against their current oppressors.

The witness of MasEzek (*ca.* 50 BCE) indicates the timefame for these changes is pre-Christian, in the Hasmonean times, yet the hands are undeterminable. The changes were made first in the Hebrew text, and at some later unknown date to the Greek with the inserted pericope in a proto-Theodotion style.

This macro application of our textual-comparative methodology has shown we now have two viable extant trajectories for Ezekiel, both of which were in circulation for period. One was lost to us, apart from the witness of the lone Old Latin Codex Wirceburgensis, until the relatively recent discovery of $\mathfrak{G}^{967}$, which we have shown is a viable witness, even of the *Urtext*. The apparent quick and wide acceptance of the received text after its textual changes enables us to accept this as another viable witness of early Jewish exegesis and eschatology. As Tov (1999d, p. 410) correctly states,

> as we are confronted here with different stages in the literary development of the book (preserved in textual witnesses), no reading should be preferred textually to that of another, as is customary among most scholars.

It is difficult to know or establish, but this may have been what Josephus (*Ant.* 10:5:1) referred to when mentioning two books for Ezekiel. We have seen how these two versions influenced the eschatological events in Revelation and in Targums for Numbers 11:26. Our textual-comparative methodology does not seek to replace the received text with a $\mathfrak{G}^{967}$ *Vorlage*, but rather examine both with equal regard to hear the different theologies presented to us from this early Jewish interpretation.

CHAPTER EIGHT

OVERALL CONCLUSIONS

Our purpose was to demonstrate how a textual-comparative methodology can be applied at both micro and macro levels to provide insight into aspects of early Jewish interpretation of the restoration of Israel in Ezekiel 36–39. The methodology was not only able to describe all textual variants, but also enabled us to provide plausible interpretive explanations for variants in Ezekiel 36–39.

There are very few intra-linguistic variants between the three oldest extant Masoretic texts (MT^{C,A,L}) in Ezekiel 36–39. While these are later Hebrew MSS (ranging from 896–1009 CE), very few variants exist between them and the Hebrew fragment from Masada (MasEzek; *ca.* 50 BCE). This reveals that they are all from a similar textual family, and that variants are early Jewish.

However, there are a number of intra-linguistic variants amongst the three oldest extant LXX MSS ($\mathfrak{G}^{967,B,A}$), and many trans-linguistic variants between LXX and MT. These typically reveal implicit interpretive exegesis deliberately done by the translator and subsequent scribes. The variants between the different LXX MSS makes it difficult, if not impossible, to speak now of '*the* LXX Ezekiel'; instead we often need to note which LXX MS we are referring to when discussing variants. If all LXX MSS have the variant, then we may say '*the* LXX'. However, the agreement between MT MSS still permits us to refer to just 'MT Ezekiel' (or the Hebrew text of Ezekiel).

Our textual-comparative methodology permitted these variants to remain as a trajectory witness to some early scribe and/or community. While the aim was not to establish which variant was correct, we did conclude a number of times that one variant was likely original, but this was done only to determine which variants were 'interpretive'. In many cases these variants were produced by deliberate scribal exegetical and theological interaction, rather than some form of scribal error. Interpretation was also found in the various textual plusses in MT as well as in different LXX MSS.

Our application of the textual-comparative methodology on a micro level (chapters 3–6) has shown that the LXX translator(s) understood the Hebrew texts before them, and interpreted whilst they translated, utilising different scribal practices. Some of the ways that LXX interacts with the text before them are: LXX performs trans-lingual wordplays (e.g. 36:2, 8, 12, 17, 30; 37:19, 23; 38:11, 14; 39:11, 28); interprets MT's metaphors (36:13–16; 37:19; 38:4, 12); interprets MT's action (36:3; 37:8; 39:4, 11, 23); clarifies MT (36:3, 8; 37:1; 39:11); adjusts for cultural sensitivities (36:17 'idols' for MT's 'dung-heaps'); interprets countries as people groups, and according to contemporary names (38:5, 13); and LXX's use of the passive implies a feeling of being harshly treated by events that happened to Israel, with the 'dishonour' continuing from current surrounding nations (36:1–15). Both MT and LXX reveal a New Exodus motif (36:3, 8, 30; 37:19, 21, 25); a creation/recreation motif (36:11, 35, 37:5, 9–10); and have echoes of the Book of Numbers (36:3, 8, 13–15, 18, 25; 37:5, 15–19; 39:12). Whilst these are found in MT, LXX frequently clarifies and expands on the points, making the link easier for its readers to follow. In general, LXX interprets the Hebrew text for their community based on their socio-political-theological world view as those now living in the land. MT's later plusses also expand the text with a purity and holiness motif.

The Old Greek (*ca.* 230–135 BCE) is most likely represented in 𝔊⁹⁶⁷, which witnesses the majority of LXX exegetical variants with MT, demonstrating that these variants were done by the original Greek translator, and are therefore early Jewish interpretations. That the later LXX MSS, such as 𝔊ᴮ,ᴬ continued these variants, without correction during different recensions to the Hebrew text, indicate their acceptance of the original translator's exegetical and/or theological interaction with the Hebrew text. These variants therefore have now become an accepted part of early Jewish interpretive tradition, and should be recognised as such today.

At times 𝔊⁹⁶⁷ follows MT more closely in syntax and/or thought than 𝔊ᴮ,ᴬ: 36:3 (insult *of* the people); 36:8 (*hope* to return); 37:17 (ways and sins); 37:1 (bones); 37:25 (David my servant [syntax]); 38:7 (reflects MT's hostility); 38:11 (walls); 38:17 (Gog as vocative beginning v. 17); 38:17 ('hand' follows MT's syntax); 39:7 (syntax); 39:8 (it is coming and will be done). 𝔊⁹⁶⁷ has two longer plusses in 38:20 and 39:4, which reveal a 'holiness' concern, firstly that the LORD will be known among the nations, and secondly, the protection of his name (cf. Unique Plusses, §6.6). That the translator in general sought to follow the Hebrew syntax and thought actually emphasises his deliberate intent to exegete the text before him.

𝔊ᴮ has the major variants seen also in 𝔊⁹⁶⁷ and 𝔊ᴬ, and some that appear elsewhere only in 𝔊⁹⁶⁷ or in 𝔊ᴬ; yet it does not include any of

𝕲ᴬ's plusses. However, it does witness the initial redaction of the chapter reorder and inserted pericope (see more on 𝕲⁹⁶⁷ below). Therefore, 𝕲ᴮ has very few unique plusses or variants, the exceptions being 38:11 (a land); 38:21 (minus 'sword'); 39:27 (minus 'many'). This shows that 𝕲ᴮ's translator did not seek to theologically interpret the text before him (unlike the OG translator, or the later 𝕲ᴬs), but only transmit (or translate) the text before him.

There are a number of times where 𝕲⁹⁶⁷ and 𝕲ᴮ agree together against MT and 𝕲ᴬ: 36:11 (birth people on you); 36:19 (way/sin [singular]); 37:13 (brought up my people from their graves); 37:16 (those added to him); 37:23 (just 'idols' [without MT/𝕲ᴬ's plus]); 38:13 (Carthaginian). There are other times when 𝕲⁹⁶⁷ and 𝕲ᴮ agree with MT against 𝕲ᴬ: 36:9 ('for you ... you be sown'); 36:15 (people); 36:17 (set apart women [cultural sensitivity]); 36:20 (his land); 36:23 (my great name); 37:16 (sons of Israel); 37:28 (*the nations* will know). Yet there are other times when 𝕲ᴮ agrees with 𝕲ᴬ against MT and 𝕲⁹⁶⁷: 36:8 (hope to return); 37:1 (*human* bones); 37:23 (I am the LORD); 38:7 (bring together [without explicit hostile intent]); 38:8 (he will come [plus]); 38:11 (in stillness/quietness [adds to those in rest]); 38:17 (Gog at the end of the introduction formula); 38:17 ('hand' smooths MT's syntax); 39:4 (given to be devoured); 39:8 (it is come and you will know it will be); 39:27 (from the countries of the nations). This indicates that 𝕲ᴮ is a 'middle-of-the-road' manuscript, whereas 𝕲⁹⁶⁷ shows the initial OG interpretive variants, and 𝕲ᴬ later variants and MT plusses; this signifies a text in a state of flux. The variants in the later post-hexaplaric 𝕲ᴬ are also likely early Jewish, as it was Origen's goal to rescind the Greek text to the Hebrew before him. This can be seen where 𝕲ᴬ witnesses many of MT's later plusses (cf. Unique Plusses §6.6). Yet we also found that there are several MT plusses not represented in any LXX MSS, which indicates that recension activity still continued in the Hebrew text past the *Vorlage* for our representative LXX MSS. Interestingly, these unique MT plusses are witnessed, where extant, by Aquila, Symmachus and/or Theodotion. This suggests that the Hebrew text maintained its dominance with the Greek always adjusted towards the Hebrew, until the Hebrew no longer changed.[1]

---

[1] In our chapter 2 we referred to Müller's (1996, p. 102) point that the changes in the Greek text "only gradually came to a standstill once a particular Hebrew text became normative".

While scholars often propose a particular word or phrase to be a plus or gloss, we propose that if all ancient manuscripts witness the word(s), then it is only speculation that it is a plus or gloss. Therefore, caution needs to be exercised making such claims, and should not be used to explain away words or phrases that may not flow with the modern mind.

Our textual-comparative methodology at micro level covered the different sense divisions between manuscripts and showed these should be examined as they give us insights as to how these early communities thematically and exegetically divided their texts. This original paragraphing is often overlooked by the modern reader and commentator. Again, a greater sense of unity was found in MT, and greater diversity in LXX.

The textual-comparative methodology was applied at macro level to $\mathfrak{G}^{967}$, covering its different chapter order than the received text (in $\mathfrak{G}^{967}$, chapter 37 follows chapter 39), and its pericope minus of 36:23c–38 (cf. chapter 7). When both the chapter order and pericope 'minus' are examined together the weakness of separate proposals of scribal error become apparent. This macro observation revealed that rather than scribal error, $\mathfrak{G}^{967}$ likely represents the *Urtext*, leaving the received text with a chapter reorder and inserted pericope. Our textual-comparative methodology enabled us to identify the different theology found in $\mathfrak{G}^{967}$'s chapter order, and that in the received text (along with its inserted pericope). The change in chapter order from $\mathfrak{G}^{967}$ was motivated by a theological desire to unite Israel to rise militarily against the enemies surrounding them as a call to arms. The inserted pericope was motivated by a call to purity, and inserted as support for the chapter reorder. These textual changes were undertaken most likely during the Hasmonean times (*ca.* 165–50 BCE), and in response to the surrounding Seleucids and/or Roman armies. They were also likely motivated by an attempt to bring the text into their historic present rather than some eschatological future. These changes were done first in the Hebrew text, and then incorporated into the Greek in a later recension towards the Hebrew (first in $\mathfrak{G}^{B}$ and then other LXX MSS). However, we were not able to discern a responsible party owing to a lack of objective evidence. Our micro examination showed that MT performed a few word changes after the chapter reorder and pericope insert, perhaps in support of these changes: the declarative formula inserted into 36:23b; the change from קָהָל to חַיִל, in 37:10; and נָשִׂיא to מֶלֶךְ 37:22–24; and חֵמָה to רוּחַ

in 39:29. In these occurrences, LXX can be viewed as original, and again the Hebrew text as being in a state of flux. Yet both variants stand as a witness to the changing traditions.

Overall, both MT and LXX MSS represent theological and exegetical interpretive interaction with their texts, with variants being from early Jewish communities. Variants reveal a text in a state of flux, and often are the result of scribes seeking to meet the theological views of their various representative communities.

Following his examination of variants in 1QpHab, Brooke (1987, p. 100) stated that,

> it could be that in the light of the use of the biblical text in the commentaries at Qumran it is now time for a complete reconsideration to all the additions and omissions, as well as the alterations, in the various recensions so that the exegetical traditions as well as scribal errors can be properly described.

We suggest that Brooke's point can also be applied when researching books in the Tanach, just as we have done here in Ezekiel. Hopefully our textual-comparative methodology can be used alongside the time honoured goals of textual critical methodology, be that for examining an individual verse or pericope, or even when writing commentaries.

We conclude with the realisation that there are many other areas yet to be considered. Our comparative methodology can be applied to the rest of Ezekiel and to other translations of Ezekiel, such as the Old Latin (especially Codex *W* which also witnesses 𝕲^{967}'s chapter order and pericope minus), and the Peshitta. Initial investigation has shown Targum frequently expands on MT, and even LXX. A comparison could be done with Targum Ezekiel, to determine if Müller (1996, p. 43) is correct in regards to Ezekiel, when he says that, "the Targums are dependent on the Septuagint, not the reverse". We observed that 37:23 is represented in 4Q *Florilegium*, yet further research can be done in other Qumranic literature, especially Pseudo-Ezekiel (Dimant, 2000). Speaking of the War Scroll, LaSor (1987, p. 129) says "A reference to Gog (1QM 11:16) suggest that the idea of this great battle was drawn from Ezek. 37–38". Bauckham (1992) also finds reference to 4Q Second Ezekiel in the Apocalypse of Peter; this can be examined further. We agree with Wong (2002, p. 141) who, in reference to grammatical features of 39:27, says "the reason for adopting different translations is not clear. More studies on the translation of grammatical features such as verbal forms are needed to arrive at any conclusion". We also suggest that more studies can be done on punctuation variants found between the Hebrew and Greek texts, along with a more detailed examination of sense divisions. It is tantalising to ask whether it will ever be known what hands changed the chapter order and inserted 36:23c–38.

BIBLIOGRAPHY

Ackroyd, P.R., *Exile and Restoration: A Study of Hebrew Thought of the Sixth Century BC* (London: SCM, 1968).

Aejmelaeus, A., *On the Trail of the Septuagint Translators: Collected Essays* (Kampen: Kok Pharos, 1993).

Ahroni, R., 'The Gog Prophecy and the Book of Ezekiel', *Hebrew Annual Review*, 1 (1977): 1–27.

Alexander, P.S., 'The Targumim and the Rabbinic Rules for the Delivery of the Targum', in J.A. Emerton (ed.), *Congress Volume Salamanca 1983* (Supplements to Vetus Testamentum, 36; Leiden: Brill, 1985), pp. 14–28.

Alexander, R.H., 'A Fresh Look at Ezekiel 38 and 39', *Journal of the Evangelical Theological Society*, 17 (1974): 157–169.

Allen, L.C., 'The Rejected Sceptre in Ezekiel xxi 15b, 18a', *Vetus Testamentum*, 39:1 (1989): 67–71.

———, 'Annotation Clusters in Ezekiel', *Zeitschrift für die Alttestamentliche Wissenschaft*, 102:3 (1990a): 408–413.

———, *Ezekiel 20–48* (Word Biblical Commentary, 29; Dallas: Word, 1990b).

———, 'Structure, Tradition and Redaction in Ezekiel's Death Valley Vision', in P.R. Davies, and D.J.A. Clines (eds), *Among the Prophets: Language, Image and Structure in the Prophetic Writings* (Journal for the Study of the Old Testament Supplement Series, 144; Sheffield: Academic Press, 1993), pp. 127–142.

———, *Ezekiel 1–19* (Word Biblical Commentary, 28; Dallas: Word, 1994).

Aune, D.E., 'Eschatology (Early Christian)', in D.N. Freedman (ed.), *The Anchor Bible Dictionary*, Vol. 2, D–E (New York: Doubleday, 1992), pp. 594–609.

Baer, D.A., *When We All Go Home: Translation and Theology in LXX Isaiah 56–66* (Journal for the Study of the Old Testament Supplement Series, 318; Sheffield: Academic Press, 2001).

Barclay, J.M.G., *Jews in the Mediterranean Diaspora: From Alexander to Trajan (323 BCE–117 CE)* (Edinburgh: T&T Clark, 1996).

Barr, J., *Comparative Philology and the Text of the Old Testament* (Oxford: University Press, 1968).

Barthélemy, D., *Critique Textuelle de l'Ancien Testament: Tome 3. Ézéchiel, Daniel et les 12 prophètes* (Orbis biblicus et orientalis 50/3; Göttingen: Vandenhoeck & Ruprecht, 1992).

Batto, B.F., 'The Covenant of Peace: A Neglected Ancient Near Eastern Motif', *Catholic Biblical Quarterly*, 49:2 (1987): 187–211.

Bauckham, R., 'A Quotation from 4Q Second Ezekiel in the Apocalypse of Peter', *Revue de Qumrân*, 15 (1992): 437–455.

Bauer, W., Arndt, W.F., Gingrich, F.W., and Danker, F.W., *A Greek-English Lexicon of the New Testament and Other Early Christian Literature* [Second Edition] (Chicago: University Press, 1979, Orig. Pub., 1958).

Baumgarten, A.I., 'Bilingual Jews and the Greek Bible', in J.L. Kugel (ed), *Shem in the Tents of Japhet: Essays on the Encounter of Judaism and Hellenism* (Supplements to the Journal for the Study of Judaism, 74; Leiden: Brill, 2002), pp. 13–30.

Beck, J.A., *Translators as Storytellers: A Study in Septuagint Translation Technique* (Studies in Biblical Literature, 25; New York: Peter Lang, 2000).

Becking, B., and Korpel, M.C.A. (eds), *The Crisis of Israelite Religion: Transformation of Religious Tradition in Exilic and Post-Exilic Times* (Oudtestamentische Studiën, 42; Leiden: Brill, 1999).

Beckwith, R., *The Old Testament Canon of the New Testament Church and its Background in Early Judaism* (Grand Rapids: Eerdmans, 1985).

Bedford, P.R., *Temple Restoration in Early Achaemenid Judah* (Supplements to the Journal for the Study of Judaism, 65; Leiden: Brill, 2001).

Begg, C., 'The Non-mention of Ezekiel in the Deuteronomistic History, the Book of Jeremiah and the Chronistic History', in J. Lust (ed.), *Ezekiel and His Book: Textual and Literary Criticism and Their Interrelation* (Bibliotheca Ephemeridum Theologicarum Lovaniensium, 74; Leuven: University Press, 1986), pp. 340–343.

Bewer, J.A., 'Textual and Exegetical Notes on the Book of Ezekiel', *Journal of Biblical Literature*, 72 (1953): 158–169.

Bibliotheca-Vaticana, *Bibliorum SS. Graecorum Codex Vaticanus 1209 [Cod. B] denuo phototypice expressus. I. Testamentum Vetus*, (Milan: Hoepli, 1907).

Bietenhard, H., 'οὐρανός', in C. Brown (ed.), *The New International Dictionary of New Testament Theology*, Vol. 2, G–Pre (Exeter: Paternoster, 1976, German Orig., 1971), pp. 188–196.

Birnbaum, E., *The Place of Judaism in Philo's Thought: Israel, Jews, and Proselytes* (Brown Judaica Series, 290; Studia Philonica Monographs, 2; Atlanta: Scholars, 1996).

Blaiklock, E.M., 'Septuagint', in M.C. Tenney (ed.), *The Zondervan Pictorial Encyclopedia of the Bible*, Vol. 5 (Grand Rapids: Zondervan, 1976), pp. 342–347.

Blenkinsopp, J., *Ezekiel* (Interpretation; Louisville: John Knox, 1990).

Block, D.I., 'Gog and the Pouring Out of the Spirit: Reflections on Ezekiel xxxix 21–9', *Vetus Testamentum*, 37:3 (1987): 257–270.

——, 'Text and Emotion: A Study in the 'Corruptions' in Ezekiel's Inaugural Vision (Ezekiel 1:4–28)', *The Catholic Biblical Quarterly*, 50:3 (1988): 418–442.

——, 'Ezekiel's Boiling Cauldron: A Form-Critical Solution to Ezekiel 24:1–14', *Vetus Testamentum*, 41:1 (1991): 12–37.

——, 'Beyond the Grave: Ezekiel's Vision of Death and Afterlife', *Bulletin for Biblical Research*, 2 (1992a): 113–141.

——, 'Gog in Prophetic Tradition: A New Look at Ezekiel xxxviii 17', *Vetus Testamentum*, 42:2 (1992b): 154–172.

——, 'Bringing Back David: Ezekiel's Messianic Hope', in P.E. Satterthwaite, R.S. Hess and G.J. Wenham (eds), *The Lord's Anointed: Interpretation of Old Testament Messianic Texts* (Carlisle: Paternoster, 1995), pp. 167–188.

——, *The Book of Ezekiel: Chapters 1–24* (The New International Commentary on the Old Testament; Grand Rapids: Eerdmans, 1997a).

——, 'Ezekiel: Theology of', in W.A. VanGemeren (ed.), *New International Dictionary of Old Testament Theology and Exegesis*, Vol. 4 (Grand Rapids: Zondervan, 1997b), pp. 615–628.

——, 'Gog and Magag [sic] in Ezekiel's Eschatological Vision', in K.E. Bower and M.W. Elliott (eds), *The Reader Must Understand: Eschatology in Bible and Theology* (Leicester: Apollos, 1997c), pp. 85–116.

——, *The Book of Ezekiel: Chapters 25–48* (The New International Commentary of the Old Testament; Grand Rapids: Eerdmans, 1998).

——, 'Divine Abandonment: Ezekiel's Adaptation of an Ancient Near Eastern Motif', in M.S. Odell and J.T. Strong (eds), *The Book of Ezekiel: Theological and Anthropological Perspectives* (Society of Biblical Literature Symposium Series, 9; Atlanta: Society of Biblical Literature, 2000), pp. 15–42.

——, 'My Servant David: Ancient Israel's Vision of the Messiah', in R.S. Hess and M.D. Carroll R. (eds), *Israel's Messiah in the Bible and the Dead Sea Scrolls* (Grand Rapids: Baker, 2003), pp. 17–56.

——, 'Shepherds of Israel: The Transformation of Royal Ideology in Ezekiel' (paper presented at the 2007 Annual meeting of SBL; San Diego, 17th November, 2007).

Boadt, D.I., 'Ezekiel, Book of', in D.N. Freedman (ed.), *The Anchor Bible Dictionary*, Vol. 2, D–G (New York: Doubleday, 1992), pp. 711–722.

Boadt, L., 'The Function of Salvation Oracles in Ezekiel 33 to 37', *Hebrew Annual Review*, 12 (1990): 1–21.

Boccaccini, G., *Roots of Rabbinic Judaism: An Intellectual History from Ezekiel to Daniel* (Grand Rapids: Eerdmans, 2002).

Bodi, D., 'Le prophète critique la monarchie: le terme nāśîʾ chez Ézéchiel', in A. Lemaire (ed.), *Prophètes et rois: Bible et Proche-Orient* (Paris: Cerf, 2001), pp. 249–257.

Bodine, W.R. (ed.), *Linguistics and Biblical Hebrew* (Winona Lake: Eisenbrauns, 1992).

Bøe, S., *Gog and Magog: Ezekiel 38–39 as Pre-text for Revelation 19,17–21 and 20,7–10* (Wissenschaftliche Untersuchungen zum Neuen Testament, 2:135; Tübingen: Mohr Siebeck, 2001).

Bogaert, P.M., 'Le témoinage de la Vetus Latina dans l'étude de la tradition des Septante-Ézéchiel et Daniel dans le Papyrus 967', *Biblica*, 59 (1978): 384–395.

Borgen, P., *Early Christianity and Hellenistic Judaism* (Edinburgh: T&T Clark, 1996).

Botte, B., and Bogaert, P.M., 'Septante et versions grecques', *Supplément au Dictionnaire de la Bible* 12 (Supplement, 12; Paris: Letouzey et Ané, 1993), cols. 536–692.

Bowen, N.R., 'The Daughters of Your People: Female Prophets in Ezekiel 13:17–22', *Journal of Biblical Literature*, 118 (1999): 417–433.

Bowker, J., *The Targums and Rabbinic Literature* (Cambridge: University Press, 1969).

Brenton, L.C.L., *The Septuagint with Apocrypha: Greek and English* (Peabody: Hendrickson, 1986, Bagster Orig. Pub., 1851).

Brettler, M.Z., *God is King: Understanding an Israelite Metaphor* (Journal for the Study of the Old Testament Supplement Series, 76; Sheffield: Academic Press, 1989).

Breuer, J., and Hirschler, G., *The Book of Yechezkel: Translation and Commentary* (Nanuet, NY: Feldheim, 1993).

Brewer, D.I., *Techniques and Assumptions in Jewish Exegesis Before 70 CE* (Texte und Studien zum Antiken Judentum, 30; Tübingen: Mohr, 1992).

Brichto, H.C., *Toward a Grammar of Biblical Poetics—Tales of the Prophets* (Oxford: University Press, 1992).

Brock, S.P., 'The Phenomenon of Biblical Translation in Antiquity', in H.M. Orlinsky (ed.), *Studies in the Septuagint: Origins, Recensions, and Interpretations* (Library of Biblical Studies; New York: Ktav, 1974), pp. 541–571.

Brooke, G.J., *Exegesis at Qumran: 4QFlorilegium in its Jewish Context* (Journal for the Study of the Old Testament Supplement Series, 29; Sheffield: Journal for the Study of the Old Testament, 1985).

——, 'The Biblical Texts in the Qumran Commentaries: Scribal Errors or Exegetical Variants?' in C.A. Evans and W.F. Stinespring (eds), *Early Jewish and Christian Exegesis: Studies in Memory of William Hugh Brownlee* (Atlanta: Scholars, 1987), pp. 85–100.

——, 'Ezekiel in Some Qumran and New Testament Texts', in J.T. Barrera and L.V. Montaner (eds), *The Madrid Qumran Congress. Proceedings of the International Congress on the Dead Sea Scrolls, [Madrid 18–21 March, 1991]* (Leiden: Brill, 1992), pp. 317–337.

——, 'Shared Intertextual Interpretations in the Dead Sea Scrolls and the New Testament', in M.E. Stone and E.G. Chazon (eds), *Biblical Perspectives: Early Use and Interpretation of the Bible in Light of the Dead Sea Scrolls* (Studies on the Texts of the Desert of Judah, 28; Leiden: Brill, 1998), pp. 35–58.

Brown, F., Driver, S.R., and Briggs, C.A., *The New Brown-Driver-Briggs-Gesenius Hebrew and English Lexicon* (Peabody: Hendrickson, 1979).

Brownlee, W.H., 'The Scroll of Ezekiel From the Eleventh Qumran Cave', *Revue de Qumrân*, 4 (1963): 11–28.

Bruce, F.F., 'Prophetic Interpretation in the Septuagint', in R.P. Gordon (ed.), *This Place is Too Small for Us: The Israelite Prophets in Recent Scholarship* (Sources for Biblical and Theological Study, 5; Winona Lake: Eisenbrauns, 1995), pp. 539–546 [Reprinted from *Bulletin of the International Organisation for Septuagint and Cognate Studies* 12 (1979): 17–26].

Brueggemann, W., *The Land* (Overtures to Biblical Theology; Philadelphia: Fortress, 1977).

——, *Hopeful Imagination: Prophetic Voices in Exile* (Philadelphia: Fortress, 1986).

——, 'Truth-telling and Peacemaking: A Reflection on Ezekiel', *The Christian Century*, 30 (1988): 1096–1098.

Büchler, A., 'The Reading of the Law and Prophets in a Triennial Cycle', *Jewish Quarterly Review*, 5 (1893): 420–468.

Büchner, D., 'Jewish Commentaries and the Septuagint', *Journal of Jewish Studies*, 48 (1997): 250–261.

Bushell, M.S., and Tan, M.D., *BibleWorks 6.0 CD-ROM* (Norfolk: BibleWorks, LLC, 2003).

Callender, D.E.J., 'The Primal Human in Ezekiel and the Image of God', in M.S. Odell and J.T. Strong (eds), *The Book of Ezekiel: Theological and Anthropological Perspectives* (Society of Biblical Literature Symposium Series, 9; Atlanta: Society of Biblical Literature, 2000), pp. 175–194.

Cathcart, K.J., and Maher M. (eds), *Targumic and Cognate Studies: Essays in Honour of Martin McNamara* (Journal for the Study of the Old Testament Supplement Series, 230; Sheffield: Academic Press, 1996).

Charlesworth, J.H., (ed.), *The OT Pseudepigrapha* Vol. 2 (Garden City: Doubleday, 1985).

——, 'Codex Sinaiticus', in D.N. Freedman (ed.), *The Anchor Bible Dictionary*, Vol. 1, A–C (New York: Doubleday, 1992), p. 1074.

Charlesworth, J.H., Lichtenberger, H., and Oegema, G.S., *Qumran-Messianism* (Studies on the Messianic Expectations in the Dead Sea Scrolls; Tübingen: Mohr-Siebeck, 1998).

Chester, A., 'Resurrection and Transformation', in F. Avemarie and H. Lichtenberger (eds), *Auferstehung—Resurrection: The Fourth Durham-Tübingen Research Symposium, Resurrection, Transfiguration and Exaltation in Old Testament, Ancient Judaism and Early Christianity [Tübingen, September 1999]* (Wissenschaftliche Untersuchungen zum Neuen Testament, 135; Tübingen: Mohr Siebeck, 2001), pp. 47–77.

Chilton, B., and Neusner, J., *Judaism in the New Testament: Practices and Beliefs* (London: Routledge, 1995).

Churgin, P., *Targum Jonathan to the Prophets* (Yale Oriental Series, 14; Princeton: Yale University, 1981).

——, *Studies in Targum Jonathan to the Prophets* (New York: Katv, 1983).

Clarke, E.G., *Targum Pseudo-Jonathan: Numbers; Translated, with Notes* (The Aramaic Bible, 4; Edinburgh: T&T Clark, 1992).

Clines, D.J.A. (ed.), *The Dictionary of Classical Hebrew, Vols. 1–5* (Sheffield: Academic Press, 1993–2001).

Coggins, R.J., 'The Exile: History and Ideology', *The Expository Times*, 110 (1999): 393–398.

Cohen, A., and Neusner, J., *Everyman's Talmud: The Major Teachings of the Rabbinic Sages* (New York: Schocken, 1995).

Cohen, N.G., 'Earliest Evidence of the Haftarah Cycle for the Sabbaths between בתמוז י"ז and סוכות in Philo', *Journal of Jewish Studies*, 48 (1997): 225–249.

Cohen, S.J.D., *From the Maccabees to the Mishnah* (Library of Early Christianity; Philadelphia: Westminister, 1987).

Cohn-Sherbok, D., *The Blackwell Dictionary of Judaica* (Oxford: Blackwell, 1992).

Collette, C.R., 'From Death to Life: Ezekiel 37:1–4', *The AME: Zion Quarterly Review*, 98:1 (1986): 30–32.

Collins, J.J., 'The Afterlife in Apocalyptic Literature', in A.J. Avery-Peck and J. Neusner (eds), *Judaism in Late Antiquity: Part Four. Death, Life-After-Death, Resurrection and the World-to-Come in the Judaisms of Antiquity* (Handbook of Oriental Studies; Leiden: Brill, 2000a), pp. 119–140.

——, *Between Athens and Jerusalem: Jewish Identity in the Hellenistic Diaspora; Second Edition* (The Biblical Resource Series; Grand Rapids: Eerdmans, 2000b).

Collins, N.L., *The Library in Alexandria and the Bible in Greek* (Supplements to Vetus Testamentum, 83; Leiden: Brill, 2000c).

Cook, S.L., *Prophecy and Apocalypticism: The Postexilic Social Setting* (Philadelphia: Fortress, 1995).

——, 'Creation Archetypes and Mythogems in Ezekiel: Significance and Theological Ramifications', *Society of Biblical Literature 1999 Seminar Papers* (Atlanta: Society of Biblical Literature, 1999), pp. 123–146.

Cooke, G.A., *The Book of Ezekiel: A Critical and Exegetical Commentary* (International Critical Commentary; Edinburgh: T&T Clark, 1936).

Cooper, L.E., Sr., *Ezekiel* (The New American Commentary, 17; Nashville: Broadman & Holman, 1994).

Cornill, C.H., *Das Buch des Propheten Ezechiel* (Leipzig: Hinrichs, 1886).

Cowley, A.E. (ed.), *Gesenius' Hebrew Grammar [2nd English Edition: as Edited and Enlarged by the late E. Kautzsch]* (Oxford: Clarendon, 1910, German Orig., 1909).

Cross, F.M., 'A Reconstruction of the Judean Restoration', *Journal of Biblical Literature*, 94:1 (1975): 4–18.

Darr, K.P., 'The Book of Ezekiel: Introduction, Commentary, and Reflections', in L.E. Keck (ed.), *The New Interpreter's Bible*, Vol. 6 (Nashville: Abingdon, 2001), pp. 1073–1607.

Davidson, B., *The Analytical Hebrew and Chaldee Lexicon* (Grand Rapids: Zondervan, 1970, Orig. Pub., 1848).

Davies, E.F., *Swallowing the Scroll: Textuality and the Dynamics of Discourse in Ezekiel's Prophecy* (Journal for the Study of the Old Testament Supplement Series, 78; Sheffield: Almond, 1989).

Davies, P.R., *Second Temple Studies* (Journal for the Study of the Old Testament Supplement Series, 7; Sheffield: Academic Press, 1991).

de Regt, L.J., *Participants in Old Testament Texts and the Translator: Reference Devices and their Rhetorical Impact* (Studia Semitica Neerlandica; Assen: Van Gorcum, 1999).

de Vries, S.J., *From Old Revelation to New: A Traditional-Historical & Redaction-Critical Study of Temporal Transition in Prophetic Prediction* (Grand Rapids: Zondervan, 1995).

Deeley, M.K., 'Ezekiel's Shepherd and John's Jesus: A Case Study in the Appropriation of Biblical Texts', in C.A. Evans and J.A. Sanders (eds), *Early Christian Interpretation of the Scriptures of Israel: Investigations and Proposals* (Journal for the Study of the New Testament Supplement Series, 148; Sheffield: Academic Press, 1997), pp. 252–264.

Dienstag, J.I., *Eschatology in Maimonidean Thought: Messianism, Resurrection, & the World to Come* (New York: Ktav, 1982).

Dijkstra, M., 'The Glosses in Ezekiel Reconsidered: Aspects of Textual Transmission in Ezekiel 10', in J. Lust (ed.), *Ezekiel and His Book: Textual and Literary Criticism and Their Interrelation* (Bibliotheca Ephemeridum Theologicarum Lovaniensium, 74; Leuven: University Press, 1986), pp. 55–77.

——, 'The Valley of Dry Bones: Coping with the Reality of the Exile in the Book of Ezekiel', in B. Becking and M.C.A. Korpel (eds), *The Crisis of Israelite Religion: Transformation of Religious Tradition in Exilic and Post-Exilic Times* (Oudtestamentische Studiën, 42; Leiden: Brill, 1999), pp. 114–133.

Dimant, D., '4Q386 ii–iii. A Prophecy on Hellenistic Kingdoms?' *Revue de Qumrân*, 18:72 (1998): 511–529.

——, 'Resurrection, Restoration, and Time-Curtailing in Qumran, Early Judaism, and Christianity', *Revue de Qumrân*, 76 (2000): 527–548.

——, *Qumrân Cave 4. XXI: Parabiblical Texts, Part 4: Pseudo-Prophetic Texts* (Discoveries in the Judean Desert, 30; Oxford: Clarendon, 2001).

Dirksen, P.B., and Mulder, M.J. (eds), *The Peshitta: Its Early Texts and History* (Leiden: Brill, 1998).

Dorival, G., Harl, M., and Munnich, O., *La Bible Grecque des Septante: du Judaïsme Hellénistique au Christianisme Ancien* (Initiations au Christianisme Ancien; n.c.: C.N.R.S., 1988).

Duguid, I.M., *Ezekiel and the Leaders of Israel* (Supplements to Vetus Testamentum, 56; Leiden: Brill, 1994).

Dumbrell, W.J., *The Faith of Israel: A Theological Survey of the Old Testament*, 2nd Edition (Grand Rapids: Baker, 2002).

Eichrodt, W., *Ezekiel: A Commentary* (Old Testament Library; London: SCM, 1970, German Orig. 1965).

Eisemann, M., *Ezekiel, Yechezkel: A New Translation with a Commentary Anthologized from Talmudic, Midrashic, and Rabbinic Sources* (Artscroll Tanach Series; Brooklyn: Mesorah, 1994, Orig. Pub., 1988).

Ellinger, K., and Rudolph, W. (eds), *Biblia Hebraica Stuttgartensia* (Stuttgart: Deutsche Bibelstiftung, 1977).

Ellinger, L., 'Ezekiel 20 and the Metaphor of Historical Teleology: Concepts of Biblical History', *Journal for the Study of the Old Testament*, 81 (1998): 93–125.

Elliott, M.A., *The Survivors of Israel: A Reconsideration of the Theology of Pre-Christian Judaism* (Grand Rapids: Eerdmans, 2000).

Ellis, E.E., 'The Old Testament Canon in the Early Church', in M.J. Mulder (ed.), *Mikra: Text, Translation, Reading and Interpretation of the Hebrew Bible in Ancient Judaism and Early Christianity* (Compendia Rerum Iudaicarum Ad Novum Testamentum; Assen: Van Gorgum, 1988), pp. 653–690.

Eslinger, L., 'Ezekiel 20 and the Metaphor of Historical Theology: Concepts of Biblical History', *Journal for the Study of the Old Testament*, 81 (1998): 98–103.

Evans, C.A., and Flint, P.W. (eds), *Eschatology, Messianism, and the Dead Sea Scrolls* (Studies in the Dead Sea Scrolls and Related Literature; Grand Rapids: Eerdmans, 1997).

Exum, J.C., and Clines, D.J.A. (eds), *The New Literary Criticism and the Hebrew Bible* (Journal for the Study of the Old Testament Supplement Series, 143; Sheffield: Academic Press, 1993).

Fairbairn, P., *An Exposition of Ezekiel* (n.c.: National Foundation of Christian Education, 1969).

——, *Commentary on Ezekiel* (Grand Rapids: Zondervan, 1989).

Feldman, L.H., 'Use, Authority and Exegesis of Mikra in the Writings of Josephus', in M.J. Mulder (ed.), *Mikra: Text, Translation, Reading and Interpretation of the Hebrew Bible in Ancient Judaism and Early Christianity* (Compendia Rerum Iudaicarum ad Novum Testamentum; Assen: Van Gorcum, 1988), pp. 455–518.

Fensham, F.C., 'The Curse of the Dry Bones in Ezekiel 37:1–14 Changed to a Blessing of Resurrection', *The Journal of Northwest Semitic Languages*, 13 (1987): 59–60.

Ferguson, E., *Backgrounds of Early Christianity*: Second Edition (Grand Rapids: Eerdmans, 1993).

Fernández Galiano, M., 'Notes on the Madrid Ezekiel Papyrus', in D.H. Samuel (ed.), *Proceedings of the Twelfth International Congress of Papyrology* (American Studies in Papyrology, 7; Toronto: Hakkert, 1970), pp. 133–138.

——, 'Nuevas Paginás del Códice 967 del A.T. Griego (Ez 28,19–43,9) (P Matr. bibl. 1)', *Studia Papyrologica*, 10:1 (1971): 9–76.

Fernández Marcos, N., *The Septuagint in Context: An Introduction to the Greek Versions of the Bible* (Leiden: Brill, 2000).

Field, F., *Origenis Hexapla II: Jobus—Malachias* (Hildesheim: George Olms, 1964, Clarendon Orig., 1875).

Filson, F.V., 'The Omission of Ezek. 12, 26–28 and 36, 23b–38 in Codex 967', *Journal of Biblical Literature*, 62 (1943): 27–32.

Finley, T.J. (ed.), *Bilingual Concordance to the Targum of the Prophets: Ezekiel 1–3* (Leiden: Brill, 1999).

Fisch, M.A., *Ezekiel: Hebrew Text & English Translation with an Introduction and Commentary* (Soncino Books of the Bible; London: Soncino, 1985, Orig. Pub., 1950).

Fishbane, M., 'Sin and Judgement in the Prophecies of Ezekiel', *Interpretation*, 38:2 (1984): 131–150.

——, *Biblical Interpretation in Ancient Israel* (Oxford: Clarendon, 1985).

Fitzpatrick, P.E., *The Disarmament of God: Ezekiel 38–39 in Its Mythic Context* (The Catholic Biblical Quarterly Monograph Series, 37; Washington, DC: Catholic Biblical Association of America, 2004).

Flesher, P.V.M., 'The Resurrection of the Dead and the Sources of the Palestinian Targums to the Pentateuch', in A.J. Avery-Peck and J. Neusner (eds), *Judaism in Late Antiquity: Part Four. Death, Life-After-Death, Resurrection and the Word-to-Come in the Judaisms of Antiquity* (Handbook of Oriental Studies; Leiden: Brill, 2000), pp. 311–331.

——, (ed.), *Targum Studies*, [2 Vols.] (Tampa: University of South Florida, 1998).

Fohrer, G., 'Die Glossen im Buche Ezechiel', *Zeitschrift für die Alttestamentliche Wissenschaft*, 63 (1951): 33–53.

Fox, M., 'The Rhetoric of Ezekiel's Vision of the Valley of the Bones', in R.P. Gordon (ed.), *The Place is Too Small for Us: The Israelite Prophets in Recent Scholarship* (Sources for Biblical and Theological Study, 5; Winona Lake: Eisenbrauns, 1995), pp. 176–190 (Reprint from *Hebrew Union College Annual* 51 (1980): 1–15.

Fredericks, D.C., 'שׁאף', in W.A. VanGemeren (ed.), *New International Dictionary of Old Testament Theology and Exegesis*, Vol. 4 (Grand Rapids: Zondervan, 1997), p. 11.

Freedman, D.N. (ed.), *The Leningrad Codex: A Facsimile Edition* (Winona Lake: Eisenbrauns, 1998).

Freedy, K.S., 'The Glosses in Ezekiel 1–40', *Vetus Testamentum*, 20 (1970): 129–152.

Friebel, K., *Jeremiah's Ezekiel's Sign-Acts: Rhetorical and Nonverbal Communication* (Journal for the Study of the Old Testament Supplement Series, 283; Sheffield: Academic Press, 1999).

Galambush, J., *Jerusalem in the Book of Ezekiel: The City as Yahweh's Wife* (Society of Biblical Literature Dissertation Series, 130; Atlanta: Scholars, 1992).

——, 'Castles in the Air: Creation as Property in Ezekiel', *Society of Biblical Literature 1999 Seminar Papers* (Atlanta: Society of Biblical Literature, 1999), pp. 147–172.

García Martínez, F., *The Dead Sea Scrolls Translated: The Qumran Texts in English* (Leiden: Brill, 1994, Spanish Orig. 1992).

——, (and Tigchelaar, E.J.C.) *The Dead Sea Scrolls Study Edition*, [2 Volumes], (Leiden: Brill, 1997, 1998).

Gehman, H.S., 'Observationes Criticae', in A.C. Johnson, H.S. Gehman and E.H. Kase, Jr. (eds), *The John H. Scheide Biblical Papyri Ezekiel* (Princeton University Studies in Papyrology, 3; Princeton: University Press, 1938).

Gibson, J.C.L., *Davidson's Introductory Hebrew Grammar ~ Syntax* (Edinburgh: T&T Clark, 1994, 4th edit.).

Glatt-Gilad, D.A., 'Yahweh's Honor at Stake: A Divine Conundrum', *Journal for the Study of the Old Testament*, 98 (2002): 63–74.

Goldingay, J.E., *Daniel* (Word Biblical Commentary, 30; Dallas: Word, 1989).

Goshen-Gottstein, M.H., 'Hebrew Biblical MSS: Their History and their Place in the HUBP Edition', *Biblica*, (1967): 243–290.

——, *The Aleppo Codex* (The Hebrew University Bible Project; Jerusalem: Hebrew University, 1976).

Gowan, D.E., *Bridge Between the Testaments: A Reappraisal of Judaism from the Exile to the Birth of Christianity*; [Second Edition, Revised] (Pittsburgh: Pickwick, 1980, Orig. Pub., 1976).

——, *Theology of the Prophetic Books: The Death and Resurrection of Israel* (Louisville: John Knox, 1998).

Grabbe, L.L., 'Eschatology in Philo and Josephus', in A.J. Avery-Peck and J. Neusner (eds), *Judaism in Late Antiquity: Part Four. Death, Life-After-Death, Resurrection and the World-to-Come in the Judaisms of Antiquity* (Handbook of Oriental Studies; Leiden: Brill, 2000a), pp. 163–188.

——, *Judaic Religion in the Second Temple Period: Belief and Practice from the Exile to Yavneh* (London: Routledge, 2000b).

Grassi, J., 'Ezekiel xxxvii. 1–14 and the New Testament', *New Testament Studies*, 11:2 (1965): 162–164.

Greenberg, M., *Ezekiel 1–20* (The Anchor Bible, 22; New York: Doubleday, 1983).

——, 'The Design and Themes of Ezekiel's Program of Restoration', *Interpretation*, 38:2 (1984): 181–208.

——, 'What are the Valid Criteria for Determining Inauthentic Matter in Ezekiel', in J. Lust (ed.), *Ezekiel and His Book: Textual and Literary Criticism and Their Interrelation* (Bibliotheca Ephemeridum Theologicarum Lovaniensium, 74; Leuven: University Press, 1986), pp. 123–135.

——, *Ezekiel 21–37: A New Translation with Introduction and Commentary* (The Anchor Bible, 22A; New York: Doubleday, 1997).

Greenspoon, L.J., 'The Origin of the Idea of Resurrection', in B. Halpern and J.D. Levenson (eds), *Traditions in Transformation: Turning Points in Biblical Faith* (Winona Lake: Eisenbrauns, 1981), pp. 247–322.

——, 'Aquila's Version', in D.N. Freedman (ed.), *The Anchor Bible Dictionary*, Vol. 1, A–C (New York: Doubleday, 1992a), pp. 320–321.

——, 'Symmachus' Version', in D.N. Freedman (ed.), *The Anchor Bible Dictionary*, Vol. 6, Si–Z (New York: Doubleday, 1992b), p. 251.

——, 'Theodotion, Theodotion's Version', in D.N. Freedman (ed.), *The Anchor Bible Dictionary*, Vol. 6, Si–Z (New York: Doubleday, 1992c), pp. 51–52.

Gross, G.D., 'Ezekiel & Solomon's Temple', *The Bible Translator*, 50 (1999): 207–214.

Gruen, E.S., *Heritage and Hellenism: The Reinvention of Jewish Tradition* (Berkeley: University Press, 1998).

Habel, N., 'The Silence of the Lands: The Ecojustice Implications of Ezekiel's Judgement Oracles', *Society of Biblical Literature 2001 Seminar Papers* (Society of Biblical Literature Seminar Paper Series, 40; Atlanta: Society of Biblical Literature, 2001), pp. 305–320.

Hagner, D.A., 'Pharisees', in M.C. Tenney (ed.), *The Zondervan Pictorial Encyclopedia of the Bible*, Vol. 4, M–P (Grand Rapids: Zondervan, 1976), pp. 745–752.

Hahn, S.W., and Bergsma, J.S., 'What Laws Were 'Not Good'? A Canonical Approach to the Theological Problem of Ezekiel 20:25–26', *Journal of Biblical Literature*, 123:2 (2004): 201–218.

Halperin, D.J., *Faces of the Chariot: Development of Rabbinic Exegesis of Ezekiel* (Texts and Studies in Ancient Judaism, 16; Tuebingen: Mohr Siebeck, 1988).

Halpern, B., and Levenson, J.D. (eds), *Traditions in Transformation: Turning Points in Biblical Faith* (Winona Lake: Eisenbrauns, 1981).

Hals, R.M., *Ezekiel* (The Forms of the Old Testament Literature, 19; Grand Rapids: Eerdmans, 1989).

Hamilton, V.P., 'שָׂכַל', in R.L. Harris, G.L. Archer and B.K. Waltke (eds), *Theological Wordbook of the Old Testament*, Vol. 2 (Chicago: Moody, 1980), p. 923.

——, 'שָׂכַל', in W.A. VanGemeren (ed.), *New International Dictionary of Old Testament Theology and Exegesis*, Vol. 4 (Grand Rapids: Zondervan, 1997), pp. 105–107.

Harl, M., 'Le renouvellement du lexique des 'Septante' d'après le témoignage des recensions, révisions et commentaires grecs anciens', in C.E. Cox (ed.), *LXX: VII Congress of the International Organization for Septuagint and Cognate Studies Leuven 1989*, (Septuagint and Cognate Studies, 31; Atlanta: Scholars, 1991), pp. 239–259.

Harland, P.J., 'A Land Full of Violence: The Value of Human Life in the Book of the Prophet Ezekiel', in P.J. Harland and C.T.R. Hayward (eds), *Hew Heaven and New Earth: Prophecy and the Millennium* (Leiden: Brill, 1999), pp. 113–127.

Harrington, D.J., *Invitation to the Apocrypha* (Grand Rapids: Eerdmans, 1999).

Harris, R.L., Archer, G.L., and Waltke, B.K. (eds), *Theological Wordbook of the Old Testament* [2 Vols.] (Chicago: Moody, 1980).

Hauspie, K., 'πίπτω ἐπὶ πρόσωπόν μου: A Set Phrase in Ezekiel?' in B.A. Taylor (ed.), *LXX: X Congress of the International Organization for Septuagint and Cognate Studies; Oslo, 1998* (Septuagint and Cognate Studies, 51; Atlanta: Scholars, 1998), pp. 513–530.

Hayward, R., *Divine Name and Presence: The Memra* (Totowa, NJ: Rowman & Littlefield, 1981).

Hengel, M., *The Septuagint as Christian Scripture: Its Prehistory and the Problem of its Canon* (Old Testament Studies; Edinburgh: T&T Clark, 2002).

Herbert, E.D., '11QEzekiel', in F. García Martínez, E.J.C. Tigchelaar and A.S. Van Der Woude (eds), *Qumran Cave 11 II: 11Q2–19, 11Q20–31* (Discoveries in the Judaean Desert, 23; Oxford: Clarendon, 1998), pp. 15–28.

Hertz, J.H. (ed.), *Pentateuch and Haftorahs: Hebrew Text, English Translation and Commentary* (London: Soncino, 1960, Orig. Pub., 1937).

Hess, R.S., and Wenham, G.J. (eds), *Zion, City of Our God* (Grand Rapids: Eerdmans, 1999).

Holladay, W.L., *A Concise Hebrew and Aramaic Lexicon of the Old Testament* (Grand Rapids: Eerdmans, 1988).

Howie, C.G., *The Date and Composition of Ezekiel* (Journal of Biblical Literature Monograph Series, 6; Philadelphia: Society of Biblical Literature, 1950).

Hulst, A.R., *Old Testament Translation Problems* (Helps for Translators, 1; Leiden: Brill, 1960).

Irwin, B.P., 'Molek Imagery and the Slaughter of Gog in Ezekiel 38 and 39', *Journal for the Study of the Old Testament*, 65 (1995): 93–112.

Irwin, W.A., *The Problem of Ezekiel: An Inductive Study* (Chicago: University of Chicago, 1943).

Isaacs, M.E., *The Concept of Spirit: A Study of Pneuma in Hellenistic Judaism and its Bearing on the New Testament* (Heythrop Monographs 1; London: Heythrop, 1976).

Jacob, L., 'Torah, Reading of, History', *Encyclopedia Judaica*, Vol. 15, Sm–Un (Jerusalem: Keter, 1972), pp. 1246–1255.

Jahn, L.G., *Der Griechische Text des Buches Ezechiel nach dem Kölner Teil des Papyrus 967* (Papyrologische Texte und Abhandlungen, 15; Bonn: Habelt, 1972).

Jellicoe, S., *The Septuagint and Modern Study* (Oxford: Clarendon, 1968).

Job, J.B., 'Ezekiel: Theology of', in W.A. VanGemeren (ed.), *New International Dictionary of Old Testament Theology and Exegesis*, Vol. 4 (Grand Rapids: Zondervan, 1997), pp. 628–634.

Jobes, K.H., and Silva, M., *Invitation to the Septuagint* (Grand Rapids: Baker, 2000).

Johnson, A.C., Gehman, H.S., and Kase, J.E.H. (eds), *The John H. Scheide Biblical Papyri: Ezekiel* (Princeton University Studies in Papyrology, 3; Princeton: University Press, 1938).

Jones, S., and Pearce, S. (eds), *Jewish Local Patriotism and Self-Identification in the Graeco-Roman Period* (Journal for the Study of the Pseudepigrapha Supplement Series, 31; Sheffield: Academic Press, 1998).

Jonker, L., 'רעה', in W.A. VanGemeren (ed.), *New International Dictionary of Old Testament Theology and Exegesis*, Vol. 3 (Grand Rapids: Zondervan, 1997), pp. 1138–1143.

Joosten, J., 'On the LXX Translator's Knowledge of Hebrew', in Taylor, B.A. (ed.), *LXX: X Congress of the International Organization for Septuagint and Cognate Studies; Oslo, 1998* (Septuagint and Cognate Studies, 51; Atlanta: Scholars, 1998), pp. 165–180.

Joüon, P., and Muraoka, T., *A Grammar of Biblical Hebrew*, [2 Vols.] (Rome: Editrice Pontificio Istituto Biblico, 1991).

Joyce, P.M., *Divine Initiative and Human Response in Ezekiel* (Journal for the Study of the Old Testament Supplement Series, 51; Sheffield: Academic Press, 1989).

——, 'King and Messiah in Ezekiel', in J. Day (ed.), *King and Messiah in Israel and the Ancient Near East: Proceedings of the Oxford Old Testament Seminar* (Sheffield: Academic Press, 1998), pp. 323–337.

Kahle, P., *Der Hebräische Bibeltext seit Franz Delitzch* (Stuttgart: Hildesheim, 1961).

Kalimi, I., *Early Jewish Exegesis and Theological Controversy: Studies in Scriptures in the Shadow of Internal and External Controversies* (Jewish and Christian Heritage Series, 2; Assen: Van Gorcum, 2002).

Kaplan, A., *The Living Torah: The Five Books of Moses* (New York: Maznaim, 1981).

Kaufman, S.A., and Sokoloff, M., *A Key-Word-in-Context Concordance to Targum Neofiti: A Guide to the Complete Palestinian Aramaic Text of the Torah* (The Journal of the American Oriental Society; Baltimore: John Hopkins, 1993).

Kelley, P.H., Mynatt, D.S., and Crawford, T.G., *The Masorah of Biblia Hebraica Stuttgartensia: Introduction and Annotated Glossary* (Grand Rapids: Eerdmans, 1998).

Kenyon, F.G., *The Chester Beatty Biblical Papyri Descriptions and Texts of Twelve Manuscripts on Papyrus of the Greek Bible. Fasc. 7: Ezekiel, Daniel, Esther [Text]* (London: Emery Walker, 1937).

——, *The Chester Beatty Biblical Papyri Descriptions and Texts of Twelve Manuscripts on Papyrus of the Greek Bible. Fasc. 7: Ezekiel, Daniel, Esther [Plates]* (London: Emery Walker, 1938).

Kline, M.G., 'Har Magedon: The End of the Millennium', *Journal of the Evangelical Theological Society,* 39:2 (1996): 207–222.

Kohn, R.L., 'Ezekiel, the Exile and the Torah', *Society of Biblical Literature 1999 Seminar Papers* (Atlanta: Society of Biblical Literature, 1999), pp. 501–526.

Korpel, M., and Oesch, J. (eds), *Delimitation Criticism: A New Tool in Biblical Scholarship* (Pericope, 1; Assen: Van Gorcum, 2000).

Korpel, M.C.A., and de Moor, J.C., *The Structure of Classical Hebrew Poetry: Isaiah 40–55* (Leiden: Brill, 1998).

Kotlar, D., 'Mikveh', *Encyclopaedia Judaica*, Vol. 11, LEK–MIL (Jerusalem: Keter, 1972), pp. 1534–1544.

Kraft, R.A., 'Reassessing the Impact of Barthelémy's *Devanciers*, Forty Years Later', *Bulletin of the International Organization of Septuagint and Cognate Studies*, 37 (2004): 1–28.

Kutsko, J.F., *Between Heaven and Earth: Divine Presence and Absence in the Book of Ezekiel* (Biblical and Judaic Studies, 7; Winona Lake: Eisenbrauns, 2000a).

——, 'Ezekiel's Anthropology and Its Ethical Implications', in M.S. Odell and J.T. Strong (eds), *The Book of Ezekiel: Theological and Anthropological Perspectives* (Society of Biblical Literature Symposium Series, 9; Atlanta: Society of Biblical Literature, 2000b), pp. 119–142.

Lake, H., (ed), *Codex Sinaiticus* [facsimile] (Oxford: Clarendon, 1922).

Lang, B., 'Street Theater, Raising the Dead, and the Zoroastrian Connection in Ezekiel's Prophecy', in J. Lust (ed.), *Ezekiel and His Book: Textual and Literary Criticism and Their Interrelation* (Bibliotheca Ephemeridum Theologicarum Lovaniensium, 74; Leuven: University Press, 1986), pp. 297–316.

Lapsley, J.E., 'Shame and Self-Knowledge: The Positive Role of Shame in Ezekiel's View of the Moral Self', in M.S. Odell and J.T. Strong (eds), *The Book of Ezekiel: Theological and Anthropological Perspectives* (Society of Biblical Literature Symposium Series, 9; Atlanta: Society of Biblical Literature, 2000), pp. 143–174.

Lasine, S., 'Manasseh as Villain and Scapegoat', in J.C. Exum and D.J.A. Clines (eds), *The New Literary Criticism and the Hebrew Bible* (Journal for the Study of the Old Testament Supplement Series, 143; Sheffield: Academic Press, 1993), pp. 163–183.

LaSor, W.S., 'Interpretation and Infallibility: Lessons from the Dead Sea Scrolls', in C.A. Evans and W.F. Stinespring (eds), *Early Jewish and Christian Exegesis: Studies in Memory of William Hugh Brownlee* (Atlanta: Scholars, 1987), pp. 123–138.

Leene, H., 'Ezekiel and Jeremiah: Promises of Inner Renewal in Diachronic Perspective', in J.C. de Moor and H.F. van Rooy (eds), *Past, Present, Future: The Deuteronomistic History and the Prophets* (Oudtestamentische Studien; Leiden: Brill, 2000), pp. 150–175.

Lemke, W.E., 'Life in the Present and Hope for the Future', *Interpretation*, 38:2 (1984): 165–180.

Levenson, J.D., 'Ezekiel in the Perspective of Two Commentators', *Interpretation,* 38:2 (1984): 210–217.

——, *Theology of the Program of Restoration of Ezekiel 40–48* (Harvard Semitic Monographs, 10; Atlanta: Scholars, 1986).

——, *The Hebrew Bible, The Old Testament, and Historical Criticism* (Jews and Christians in Biblical Studies; Louisville: John Knox, 1993).

Levey, S.H., *The Messiah: An Aramaic Interpretation. The Messianic Exegesis of The Targum* (Monograph of the Hebrew Union College, 2; Cincinnati: Hebrew Union College, 1974).

——, *The Targum of Ezekiel: Translated, with a Critical Introduction, Apparatus, and Notes* (The Aramaic Bible, 13; Edinburgh: T&T Clark, 1987).

Liddell, H.G., Scott, R., and Jones, H.S., *A Greek-English Lexicon, 9th Edition (1948), with Supplement* (Oxford: Clarendon, 1968).

Lieb, M., *Children of Ezekiel: Aliens, UFO's, the Crisis of Race and the Advent of End Times* (1998).

Lipman, E.J., *The Mishnah: Oral Traditions of Judaism* (New York: Shocken, 1974).

Litwak, K.D., 'Echoes of Scripture? A Critical Survey of Recent Works on Paul's Use of the Old Testament', *Currents in Research: Biblical Studies*, 6 (1998).

Lowinger, D.S. (ed.), *Codex Cairo of the Bible from the Karaite Synagoge at Abbasiya* (Jerusalem: Makor, 1971).

Lucas, E.C., *Daniel* (Apollos Old Testament Commentary, 20; Leicester: Apollos, 2002).

Lust, J., 'The Order of the Final Events in Revelation and in Ezekiel', in J. Lambrecht (ed.), *L'Apocalypse johannique et l'Apocalyptique dans le Nouveau Testament* (Bibliotheca Ephemeridum Theologicarum Lovaniensium, 53; Leuven: University Press, 1980), pp. 179–183.

——, 'Ezekiel 36–40 in the Oldest Greek Manuscript'', *Catholic Biblical Quarterly*, 43 (1981a): 517–533.

——, '"Gathering and Return" in Jeremiah and Ezekiel', in P.M. Bogaert (ed.), *Le Livre de Jérémie* (Bibliotheca Ephemeridum Theologicarum Lovaniensium, 54; Leuven: University Press, 1981b), pp. 119–142.

——, 'The Sequence of Ez 36–40 and the Omission of Ez 36,23c–38 in Pap. 967 and in Codex Wirceburgensis', *Bulletin of the International Organization of Septuagint and Cognate Studies*, 14 (1981c): 45–46.

——, 'Messianism and Septuagint: Ezek. 21:30–32', in J.A. Emerton (ed.), *Congress Volume Salamanca 1983* (Supplements to Vetus Testamentum, 36; Leiden: Brill, 1985), pp. 174–191.

——, 'Exegesis and Theology in the Septuagint of Ezekiel: The Longer 'Pluses' and Ezek 43:1–9', in C.E. Cox (ed.), *LXX: VI Congress of the International Organization For Septuagint and Cognate Studies; Jerusalem 1986* (Septuagint and Cognate Studies, 23; Atlanta: Scholars, 1986a), pp. 201–232.

——, 'Ezekiel Manuscripts in Qumran. Preliminary Edition of 4Q Ez a and b', in J. Lust (ed.), *Ezekiel and His Book: Textual and Literary Criticism and Their Interrelation* (Bibliotheca Ephemeridum Theologicarum Lovaniensium, 74; Leuven: University Press, 1986b), pp. 90–100.

——, 'The Final Text and Textual Criticism. Ez 39,28', in J. Lust (ed.), *Ezekiel and His Book: Textual and Literary Criticism and Their Interrelation* (Bibliotheca Ephemeridum Theologicarum Lovaniensium, 74; Leuven: University Press, 1986c), pp. 48–54.

——, 'The Use of Textual Witnesses for the Establishment of the Text. The Shorter and Longer Texts of Ezekiel. An Example: Ez 7', in J. Lust (ed.), *Ezekiel and His Book: Textual and Literary Criticism and Their Interrelation* (Bibliotheca Ephemeridum Theologicarum Lovaniensium, 74; Leuven: University Press, 1986d), pp. 7–20.

——, 'And I Shall Hang Him on a Lofty Mountain: Ezek. 17:22–24 and Messianism in the Septuagint', in B.A. Taylor (ed.), *LXX: IX Congress of the International Organization for Septuagint and Cognate Studies; Cambridge, 1995* (Septuagint and Cognate Studies, 45; Atlanta: Scholars, 1995a), pp. 231–250.

——, 'Gog', in K. van der Toorn, B. Becking and P.W. van der Horst (eds), *Dictionary of Deities and Demons in the Bible (DDD)* (Leiden: Brill, 1995b), pp. 708–712.

——, 'Magog', in K. van der Toorn, B. Becking, and P.W. van der Horst (eds), *Dictionary of Deities and Demons in the Bible (DDD)* (Leiden: Brill, 1995c), pp. 999–1002.

——, 'אדני יהוה in Ezekiel and its Counterpart in the Old Greek', *Ephemerides Theologicae Lovanienses*, 72 (1996a): 138–145.

——, 'The Septuagint of Ezekiel According to Papyrus 967 and the Pentateuch', *Ephemerides Theologicae Lovanienses*, 72 (1996b): 131–137.

——, 'The Vocabulary of LXX Ezekiel and Its Dependence Upon the Pentateuch', in M. Vervenne and J. Lust (eds), *Deuteronomy and Deuteronomic Literature* (Bibliotheca Ephemeridum Theologicarum Lovaniensium; Leuven: University Press, 1997), pp. 529–546.

——, 'The Delight of Ezekiel's Eyes: Ez 24:15–24 in Hebrew and in Greek', in B.A. Taylor (ed.), *LXX: X Congress of the International Organization for Septuagint and Cognate Studies; Oslo, 1998* (Septuagint and Cognate Studies, 51; Atlanta: Scholars, 1998), pp. 1–25.

——, 'Exile and Diaspora. Gathering from Dispersion in Ezekiel', in J.M. Auwers and A. Wénin (eds), *Lecures et Relectures de la Bible: Festschrift P.M. Bogaert* (Bibliotheca Ephemeridum Theologicarum Lovaniensium, 144; Leuven: University Press, 1999), pp. 99–122.

——, 'Syntax and Translation Greek', *Ephemerides Theologicae Lovanienses*, 77:4 (2001): 395–401.

——, 'The 'Rekenaar' and the Septuagint-LXX Ezekiel: A Case Study', in J. Cooke (ed.), *Bible and Computer: The Stellenbosch AIBI-6 Conference: Proceedings of the Association Internationale Bible et Informatique "From Alpha to Byte," University of Stellenbosch 17–21 July 2000* (Leiden: Brill, 2002a), pp. 365–393.

——, 'The Spirit of the Lord, or the Wrath of the Lord? Ez 39,29', *Ephemerides Theologicae Lovanienses*, 78:1 (2002b): 148–155.

——, 'Textual Criticism of the Old and New Testaments: Stepbrothers?' in A. Denaux (ed.), *New Testament Textual Criticism and Exegesis* (Leuven: University Press, 2002c), pp. 15–31.

——, 'Major Divergences Between LXX and MT in Ezekiel', in A. Schenker (ed.), *The Earliest Text of the Hebrew Bible: The Relationship between the Masoretic Text and the Hebrew Base of the Septuagint Reconsidered* (Septuagint and Cognate Studies, 52; Atlanta: Society of Biblical Literature, 2003), pp. 83–92.

——, 'Messianism in LXX-Ezekiel: Towards a Synthesis' in M.A. Knibb (ed.) *The Septuagint and Messianism* (Bibliotheca Ephemeridum Theologicarum Lovaniensum 195; Leuven: University Press, 2006), pp. 417–430.

Lust, J. (ed.), *Ezekiel and His Book: Textual and Literal Criticism and Their Interrelation* (Leuven: University Press, 1986e).

Lust, J., Eynikel, E., and Hauspie, K., *Greek-English Lexicon of the Septuagint; Revised Edition* (Stuttgart: Deutsche Bibelgesellschaft, 2003).

Maori, I., 'The Tradition of Pisqa'ot in Ancient Hebrew Mss: The Isaiah Text and Commentaries from Qumran', *Textus*, 10 (1982): 1–50.

Marquis, G., 'Consistency of Lexical Equivalents as a Criterion For the Evaluation of Translational Technique As Exemplified in the LXX of Ezekiel', in C.E. Cox (ed.), *LXX: VI Congress of the International Organisation For Septuagint and Cognate Studies; Jerusalem 1986* (Septuagint and Cognate Studies Series, 23; Atlanta: Scholars, 1986a), pp. 405–424.

——, 'Word Order as a Criterion for the Evaluation of Translation Technique in the LXX and the Evaluation of Word-Order Variants as Exemplified in LXX-Ezekiel', *Textus*, 13 (1986b): 59–84.

——, 'McGregor, The Greek Text of Ezekiel [Book Review]', *The Jewish Quarterly Review*, 83:3–4 (Jan.–Apr. 1993): 440–444.

McConville, J.G., 'Priests and Levites in Ezekiel: A Crux in the Interpretation of Israel's History', *Tyndale Bulletin*, 34 (1983): 3–31.

McGregor, L.J., *Greek Text of Ezekiel: An Examination of Its Homogeneity* (Septuagint and Cognate Studies, 18; Atlanta: Scholars, 1985).

McKay, H.A., *Sabbath and Synagogue: The Question of Sabbath Worship in Ancient Judaism* (Boston: Brill, 2001).

McKeating, H., *Ezekiel* (Old Testament Guides; Sheffield: Academic Press, 1993).

——, 'Ezekiel the 'Prophet Like Moses'?' *Journal for the Study of the Old Testament*, 61 (1994): 97–109.

McLay, R.T., 'The Old Greek Translation of Daniel IV–VI and the Formation of the Book of Daniel', *Vetus Testamentum*, 55:3 (2005): 304–323.

McNamara, M., *The New Testament and the Palestinian Targum to the Pentateuch* (Rome: Pontifical Biblical Institute, 1966).

——, *Targum and Testament, Aramaic Paraphrases of the Hebrew Bible: A Light on the New Testament* (Shannon: Irish University Press, 1972).

——, *Palestinian Judaism and the New Testament* (Wilmington: Michael Glazier, 1983).

——, *Targum Neofiti 1: Numbers; Translated, with Apparatus and Notes* (The Aramaic Bible, 4; Edinburgh: T&T Clark, 1995).

McNamara, M., Cathcart, K.J., and Maher, M., *The Aramaic Bible: the Targums* (Wilmington: Michael Glazier, 1987).

Meier, J.P., *A Marginal Jew: Rethinking the Historical Jesus; Volume III Companions and Competitors* (The Anchor Bible Reference Library; New York: Doubleday, 2001).

Metzger, B.M., *Manuscripts of the Greek Bible: An Introduction to Greek Palaeography* (New York: Oxford University Press, 1981).

Milne, H.J.M., and Skeat, T.C., *Scribes and Correctors of the Codex Sinaiticus* (Oxford: British Museum, 1938).

Morrow, W.S., 'Ketibh and Qere', in D.N. Freedman (ed.), *The Anchor Bible Dictionary*, Vol. 4, K–N (New York: Doubleday, 1992), pp. 24–30.

Mueller, J.M., 'Ezekiel, Apocryphon of', in D.N. Freedman (ed.), *The Anchor Bible Dictionary*, Vol. 2, D–G (New York: Doubleday, 1992), pp. 709–711.

Müller, M., *The First Bible of the Church: A Plea for the Septuagint* (Journal for the Study of the Old Testament Supplement Series, 206; Sheffield: Academic Press, 1996).

Muraoka, T., *A Greek-English Lexicon of the Septuagint (Twelve Prophets)* (Louvain: Peeters, 1993)

Neusner, J., *A Life of Rabban Yohanan ben Zakkai* (Leiden: Brill, 1970).

——, *Self Fulfilling Prophecy: Exile and Return in the History of Judaism* (South Florida Studies in the History of Judaism, 2; Atlanta: Scholars, 1987).

Newsom, C.A., 'A Maker of Metaphors: Ezekiel's Oracle Against Tyre', in R.P. Gordon (ed.), *The Place is Too Small for Us: The Israelite Prophets in Recent Scholarship* (Sources for Biblical and Theological Study, 5; Winona Lake: Eisenbrauns, 1995), 191–204 [Reprinted from *Interpretation* 38:4 (1984): 151–164].

Nickelsburg, G.W.E., 'Eschatology (Early Jewish)', in D.N. Freedman (ed.), *The Anchor Bible Dictionary*, Vol. 2, D–G (New York: Doubleday, 1992), pp. 579–594.

Odell, M.S., 'The City of Hamonah in Ezekiel 39:11–16: The Tumultuous City of Jerusalem', *Catholic Biblical Quarterly*, 56:3 (1994): 479–489.

——, 'You Are What You Eat: Ezekiel and the Scroll', *Journal of Biblical Literature*, 117:2 (1998): 229–248.

——, *Ezekiel* (Smyth & Helwys Bible Commentary; Macon: Smyth & Helwys, 2005).

Odell, M.S., and Strong, J.T. (eds), *The Book of Ezekiel: Theological and Anthropological Perspectives* (Society of Biblical Literature Symposium Series, 9; Atlanta: Society of Biblical Literature, 2000).

Oegema, G.S., *The Anointed and his People: Messianic Expectations from the Maccabees to Bar Kochba* (Journal for the Study of the Pseudepigrapha Supplement Series, 27; Sheffield: Academic Press, 1998).

Oesch, J.M., *Petucha und Setuma: Untersuchungen zu einer überlieferten Gliederung im hebräischen Text des Alten Testaments* (OBO 27; Göttingen: Vandenhoeck and Ruprecht, 1979).

Olley, J.W., '"Hear the Word of YHWH": The Structure of the Book of Isaiah in 1QIsaᵃ', *Vetus Testamentum*, 43:1 (1993): 19–49.

——, 'Texts Have Paragraphs Too—A Plea For Inclusion In Critical Editions', *Textus*, 19 (1998): 111–125.

——, 'Paragraphing in the Greek Text of Ezekiel in P⁹⁶⁷, With Particular Reference to the Cologne Portion', in M. Korpel and J. Oesch (eds), *Studies on Scriptural Unit Division* (Pericope, 3; Assen: Van Gorcum, 2002), pp. 202–225.

——, 'Trajectories in Paragraphing of the Book of Ezekiel', in M. Korpel and J. Oesch (eds), *Unit Delimitation in Biblical Hebrew and Northwest Semitic Literature* (Pericope, 4; Assen: Van Gorcum, 2003), pp. 204–231.

——, 'Divine Name and Paragraphing in Ezekiel: Highlighting Divine Speech in an Expanding Tradition', *Bulletin of the International Organization of Septuagint and Cognate Studies*, 37 (2004): 87–105.

Olofsson, S., *God is My Rock: A Study of Translation Technique and Theological Exegesis in the Septuagint* (Coniectanea Biblica Old Testament Series, 31; Stockholm: Almqvist & Wiksell, 1990a).

——, *The LXX Version: A Guide to the Translation Technique of the Septuagint* (Coniectanea Biblica Old Testament Series, 30; Stockholm: Almqvist & Wiksell, 1990b).

Olyan, S.M., '"We Are Utterly Cut Off": Some Possible Nuances of נגזרנו לנו in Ezek 37:11', *Catholic Biblical Quarterly*, 65:1 (2003): 43–51.

Orlinsky, H.M., (ed.), *Studies in the Septuagint: Origins, Recensions and Interpretations* (Library of Biblical Studies; New York: Katav, 1974).

Parker, D.C., 'Codex Vaticanus', in D.N. Freedman (ed.), *The Anchor Bible Dictionary*, Vol. 1, A–C (New York: Doubleday, 1992a), pp. 1074–1075.

——, 'Hexapla of Origen, The', in D.N. Freedman (ed.), *The Anchor Bible Dictionary*, Vol. 3, H–J (New York: Doubleday, 1992b), pp. 188–189.

Patmore, H.M., 'The Shorter and Longer Texts of Ezekiel: The Implications of the Manuscript Finds from Masada and Qumran', *Journal For the Study of the Old Testament*, 32:2 (2007): 231–241.

Patton, C., 'I Myself Gave Them Laws That Were Not Good: Ezekiel 20 and the Exodus Traditions', *Journal for the Study of the Old Testament*, 69 (1996): 73–90.

——, 'Priest, Prophet, and Exile: Ezekiel as a Literary Construct', *Society of Biblical Literature 2000 Seminar Papers* (Society of Biblical Literature Seminar Paper Series, 39; Atlanta: Society of Biblical Literature, 2000), pp. 700–727.

Payne, J.B., 'The Relationship of the Chester Beatty Papyri of Ezekiel to Codex Vaticanus', *Journal of Biblical Literature*, 69 (1949): 251–265.

Penkower, J.S., 'The Chapter Divisions in the 1525 Rabbinic Bible', *Vetus Testamentum*, 48 (1998): 350–174.

Perrot, C., 'Petuhot et setumot: Étude sur les alineas du Pentateuque', *Revue Biblique*, 76 (1969): 50–91.

Peters, M.K.H., 'Septuagint', in D.N. Freedman (ed.), *The Anchor Bible Dictionary*, Vol. 5, O–Sh (New York: Doubleday, 1992), pp. 1093–1104.

Petersen, D.L., 'Eschatology (OT)', in D.N. Freedman (ed.), *The Anchor Bible Dictionary*, Vol. 2, D–G (New York: Doubleday, 1992), pp. 575–579.

——, 'Creation in Ezekiel: Methodological Perspectives and Theological Prospects', *Society of Biblical Literature 1999 Seminar Papers* (Atlanta: Society of Biblical Literature, 1999), pp. 490–500.

Pietersma, A., 'Chester Beatty Papyri', in D.N. Freedman (ed.), *The Anchor Bible Dictionary*, Vol. 1, A–C (New York: Doubleday, 1992), pp. 901–903.

Polak, F.H., 'The Interpretation of כָּלָה כָּלֹה in the LXX: Ambiguity and Intuitive Comprehension', *Textus*, 17 (1994): 57–77.

Propp, W.H., Halpern, B., and D.N. Freedman (eds), *The Hebrew Bible and Its Interpreters* (Biblical and Judaic Studies, 1; Winona Lake: Eisenbrauns, 1990).

Rabinowitz, L.I., 'Haftarah', *Encyclopedia Judaica*, Vol. 16, Ur–Z (Jerusalem: Keter, 1972), pp. 1342–1345.

Railton, N.M., 'Gog and Magog: the History of a Symbol', *Evangelical Quarterly*, 75:1 (2003): 23–44.

Raurell, F., 'The Polemical Role of the ΑΡΧΟΝΤΕΣ and ΑΦΗΓΟΥΜΕΝΟΙ in Ez LXX', in J. Lust (ed.), *Ezekiel And His Book: Textual and Literary Criticism and Their Interrelation* (Bibliotheca Ephemeridum Theologicarum Lovaniensium, 74; Leuven: University Press, 1986), pp. 85–89.

Reif, S.C., *A Jewish Archive From Old Cairo: The History of Cambridge University's Genizah Collection* (Richmond: Curzon, 2000).

Renz, T., *The Rhetorical Function of the Book of Ezekiel* (Leiden: Brill, 1999).

Revell, E.J., 'Biblical Punctuation and Chant in the Second Temple Period', *Journal for the Study of Judaism*, 7 (1976a): 181–198.

——, 'A Note on Papyrus 967', *Studia Papyrologica*, 15 (1976b): 131–136.

——, 'Masorah', in D.N. Freedman (ed.), *The Anchor Bible Dictionary*, Vol. 4, K–N (New York: Doubleday, 1992a), pp. 592–593.

——, 'Masoretes', in D.N. Freedman (ed.), *The Anchor Bible Dictionary*, Vol. 4, K–N (New York: Doubleday, 1992b), pp. 593–594.

——, 'Masoretic Accents', in D.N. Freedman (ed.), *The Anchor Bible Dictionary*, Vol. 4, K–N (New York: Doubleday, 1992c), pp. 594–596.

——, 'Masoretic Studies', in D.N. Freedman (ed.), *The Anchor Bible Dictionary*, Vol. 4, K–N (New York: Doubleday, 1992d), pp. 596–597.

——, 'Masoretic Text', in D.N. Freedman (ed.), *The Anchor Bible Dictionary*, Vol. 4, K–N (New York: Doubleday, 1992e), pp. 597–599.

Ribera, J., 'The Image of Israel According to the Targum of Ezekiel', in K.J. Cathcart and M. Maher (eds), *Targumic and Cognate Studies: Essays in Honour of Martin McNamara* (Journal for the Study of the Old Testament Supplement Series, 230; Sheffield: Academic Press, 1996).

Ribera-Florit, J., 'The Use of the Derash Method in the Targum of Ezekiel', in C.A. Evans (ed.), *The Interpretation of Scripture in Early Judaism and Christianity: Studies in Language and Tradition* (Journal for the Study of the Pseudepigrapha Supplement Series, 33; Sheffield: Academic Press, 2000), pp. 406–422.

Robinson, H.W., *Two Hebrew Prophets: Studies in Hosea and Ezekiel* (London: Lutterworth, 1948).

Rofé, A., 'Qumranic Paraphrases, The Greek Deuteronomy and the Late History of the Biblical נשיא', *Textus*, 14 (1988): 164–174.

Rooker, M.F., *Biblical Hebrew in Transition: The Language of the Book of Ezekiel* (Journal for the Study of the Old Testament Supplement Series, 90; Sheffield: Academic Press, 1990).

Rosenberg, A.J. (ed), *Ezekiel, Vol. 1 & II—Complete Mikraoth Gedoloth with English Translation and Commentary* (New York: Judaica, 1998).

——, (ed.), *Ezekiel: A New English Translation: Rashi and Commentary* [2 Vols.] (New York: Judaica, 1991).

Rowley, H.H., *Worship in Ancient Israel: Its Forms and Meaning* (London: Society for Promoting Christian Knowledge, 1967).

Russell, L.M., Farley, M.A., and Jones, S. (eds), *Liberating Eschatology: Essays in Honor of Letty M. Russell* (Louisville: John Knox, 1999).

Saldarini, A.J., 'Pharisees', in D.N. Freedman (ed.), *The Anchor Bible Dictionary*, Vol. 5, O-Sh (New York: Doubleday, 1992), pp. 289–599.

——, *Pharisees, Scribes and Sadducees in Palestinian Society: A Sociological Approach* (The Biblical Resource Series; Grand Rapids: Eerdmans, 2001).

Sanderson, J.E., 'Ezekiel', in E. Ulrich (ed.), *Qumran Cave 4: X, The Prophets* (Discoveries in the Judaean Desert 15; Oxford: Clarendon, 1997), pp. 209–220.

Satterthwaite, P.E., Hess, R.S., and Wenham, G.J. (eds), *The Lord's Anointed: Interpretation of Old Testament Messianic Texts* (Carlisle: Paternoster, 1995).

Schultz, A.C., 'Ezekiel, Book of', in M.C. Tenney (ed.), *The Zondervan Pictorial Encyclopedia of the Bible*, Vol. 2 (Grand Rapids: Zondervan, 1976), pp. 455–468.

Schwartz, B.J., 'Ezekiel's Dim View of Israel's Restoration', in M.S. Odell and J.T. Strong (eds), *The Book of Ezekiel: Theological and Anthropological Perspectives* (Society of

Biblical Literature Symposium Series, 9; Atlanta: Society of Biblical Literature, 2000), pp. 43–67.

Scott, J.J., *Jewish Backgrounds of the New Testament* (Grand Rapids: Baker, 2000).

Scott, J.M. (ed.), *Restoration: Old Testament, Jewish and Christian Perspectives* (Supplements to the Journal for the Study of Judaism, 72; Leiden: Brill, 2001).

Scott, W.R., *A Simplified Guide to BHS: Critical Apparatus, Masora, Accents, Unusual Letters & Other Markings* (Berkeley: Bibal, 1987).

Seeligman, I.L., *The Septuagint Version of Isaiah: A Discussion of Its Problems* (Leiden: Brill, 1948).

——, 'Problems and Perspectives in Modern Septuagint Research', *Textus*, 15 (1990): 169–232.

Seitz, C.R., 'Expository Articles: Ezekiel 37:1–14', *Interpretation*, 46:1 (1992): 53–56.

Shutt, R.J.H., 'Letter of Aristeas: A New Translation and Introduction', in J.H. Charlesworth (ed.), *The Old Testament Pseudepigrapha*, 2 (Garden City: Doubleday, 1985).

Siegert, F., *Zwischen Hebräischer Bibel und Altem Testament: Eine Einführung in die Septuaginta* (Institutem Judaicum Delitzschianum, Münsteraner Judaistische Studien, 9; Münster: Lit Verlag, 2001).

Slayton, J.C., 'Codex Alexandrinus', in D.N. Freedman (ed.), *The Anchor Bible Dictionary*, Vol. 1, A–C (New York: Doubleday, 1992), p. 1069.

Sloan, I.B., 'Ezekiel and the Covenant of Friendship', *Biblical Theology Bulletin*, 22:4 (1992): 149–154.

Sonderlund, S.K., 'Septuagint', in G.W. Bromiley (ed.), *The International Standard Bible Encyclopedia*, Vol. 4 (Grand Rapids: Eerdmans, 1988), pp. 400–409.

Speiser, E.A., 'Background and Function of the Biblical Nāśî', *Catholic Biblical Quarterly*, 25:1 (1963): 111–117.

Sperber, A., *The Prophets According to the Codex Reuchlinianus [in a Critical Analysis]* (Leiden: Brill, 1969).

Spottorno y Díaz-Caro, V.M., 'The Divine Name in Ezekiel Papyrus 967', in N. Fernández Marcos (ed.), *La Septuaginta en la Investigacion Contemporanea [V Congreso de la IOSCS]* (Consejo Superior De Investigaciones Cientificas; Madrid: Instituto Arias Montano, 1985), pp. 213–218.

Sterling, G.E., 'Thus are Israel: Jewish Self-Definition in Alexandria', *The Studia Philonica Annual*, 7 (1995): 1–18.

Stevenson, K.R., 'The Land is Yours: Ezekiel's Outrageous Land Claim', *Society of Biblical Literature 2001 Seminar Papers* (Society of Biblical Literature Seminar Paper Series, 40; Atlanta: Society of Biblical Literature, 2001), pp. 175–196.

Stevenson, W.B., *Grammar of Palestinian Jewish Aramaic: Second Edition with an Appendix on the Numerals by J.A. Emerton* (Oxford: Clarendon, 1924, 2nd Edition, 1962).

Stone, M.E. (ed.), *Jewish Writings of the Second Temple Period: Apocrypha, Pseudepigrapha, Qumran Sectarian Writings, Philo, Josephus* (Literature of Jewish People in Period of Second Temple & Talmud; Philadelphia: Fortress, 1994).

Stromberg, J., 'Observations on Inner-Scriptural Scribal Expansion in MT Ezekiel' *Vetus Testamentum* 58:1 (2008): 68–86.

Suh, R.H., 'The Use of Ezekiel 37 in Ephesians 2' *Journal of the Evangelical Theological Society* 50:4 (2007): 715–734.

Sweeney, M.A., 'Ezekiel: Zadokite Priest and Visionary Prophet of the Exile', *Society of Biblical Literature 2000 Seminar Papers* (Society of Biblical Literature Seminar Papers Series, 39; Atlanta: Society of Biblical Literature, 2000), pp. 729–751.

Swete, H.B., *Introduction to the Old Testament in Greek* (Peabody: Hendrickson, 1989, Cambridge Orig., 1914).

Talmon, S., 'Fragments of an Ezekiel Scroll from Masada 1043–2220 (Ezekiel 35:11–38:14)', in M. Cogan, B.L. Eichler and J.H. Tigay (eds), *Tehilla le-Moshe: Biblical and Judaic Studies in Honor of Moshe Greenberg* (Winona Lake: Eisenbrauns, 1997), p. 318.

——, *Masada VI: Yigael Yadin Excavations 1963–1965 Final Reports. Hebrew Fragments from Masada* (Jerusalem: Hebrew University, 1999).

Tanner, P.J., 'Rethinking Ezekiel's Invasion by Gog', *Journal of the Evangelical Theological Society*, 39:1 (1996): 29–46.

Taylor, J.B., *Ezekiel* (Tyndale Old Testament Commentaries; Leicester: Inter Varsity Press, 1969).

Teichtal, Y.S., *Restoration As a Response to the Holocaust* (New York: Ktav, 1995).

Thackeray, H.St.J., 'The Greek Translators of Ezekiel', *The Journal of Theological Studies*, 4 (1903a): 398–411.

——, 'The Greek Translators of the Prophetical Books', *The Journal of Theological Studies*, 4 (1903b): 578–585.

——, *A Grammar of the Old Testament in Greek According to the Septuagint* (Cambridge: University Press, 1909).

——, *The Septuagint and Jewish Worship: A Study in Origins* (The Schweich Lectures, 1920; London: Oxford, 1921).

Thayer, J.H., *The New Thayer's Greek-English Lexicon of the New Testament* (Lafayette: Apsa, 1979, Orig. Pub., 1889).

Thompson, E.M. (ed.), *Facsimile of the Codex Alexandrinus: Old Testament, Vol. 2: Hosea-4 Maccabees* (London: British Museum, 1883).

Tomasino, A.J., *Judaism Before Jesus: The Events and Ideas that Shaped the New Testament World* (Downers Grove: InterVarsity Press, 2003).

Tov, E., 'Recensional Differences between the MT and the LXX of Ezekiel', *Ephemerides Theologicae Lovanienses*, 62 (1986): 89–101.

——, 'The Septuagint', in M.J. Mulder (ed.), *Mikra: Text, Translation, Reading and Interpretation of the Hebrew Bible in Ancient Judaism and Early Christianity* (Compendia Rerum Iudaicarum ad Novem Testamentum; Assen: Van Gorcum, 1988), pp. 161–188.

——, 'Interchanges of Consonants between the Masoretic Text and the *Vorlage* of the Septuagint', in M. Fishbane and E. Tov (eds), *Sha'arei Talmon: Studies in the Bible, Qumran, and the Ancient Near East; Presented Shemaryahu Talmon* (Winona Lake: Eisenbrauns, 1992a), pp. 255–266.

——, 'Textual Criticism: Old Testament', in D.N. Freedman (ed.), *The Anchor Bible Dictionary*, Vol. 6, Si–Z (New York: Doubleday, 1992b), pp. 393–412.

——, *The Text-Critical Use of the Septuagint in Biblical Research: Revised and Enlarged Second Edition* (Jerusalem Biblical Studies, 8; Jerusalem: Simor, 1997).

——, 'Sense Divisions In the Qumran Texts, The Masoretic Texts, and Ancient Translations of the Bible', in J. Krasovec (ed.), *The Interpretation of the Bible: The International Symposium in Slovenia* (Journal for the Study of the Old Testament Supplement Series, 289; Sheffield: Academic Press, 1998), pp. 121–145.

——, 'Did the Septuagint Translators Always Understand Their Hebrew Text?' in E. Tov (ed.), *The Hebrew and Greek Bible: Collected Essays on the Septuagint* (Supplements to Vetus Testamentum, 72; Leiden: Brill, 1999a), pp. 203–218 [Reprint from A. Pietersma and C.E. Cox (eds), *De Septuaginta* (Mississauga, Ont: Benben, 1984), pp. 53–70].

——, 'Glosses, Interpolations, and Other Types of Scribal Additions in the Text of the Hebrew Bible', in E. Tov (ed.), *The Hebrew and Greek Bible: Collected Essays on the Septuagint* (Supplements to Vetus Testamentum, 72; Leiden: Brill, 1999b), pp. 53–74 [Reprint from S.E. Balentine and J. Barton (eds), *Language, Theology and the Bible* (Oxford: University Press, 1994), pp. 40–66].

——, *The Greek and Hebrew Bible: Collected Essays on the Septuagint* (Supplements to Vetus Testamentum, 72; Leiden: Brill, 1999c).

——, 'Recensional Differences between the Masoretic Text and the Septuagint of Ezekiel', in E. Tov (ed.), *The Hebrew & Greek Bible: Collected Essays on the Septuagint* (Supplements to Vetus Testamentum, 72; Leiden: Brill, 1999d), pp. 397–410 [Reprint from *Ephemerides Theologicae Lovanienses* 62 (1986): 89–101].

——, 'Theologically Motivated Exegesis Embedded in the Septuagint', in E. Tov (ed.), *The Hebrew and Greek Bible: Collected Essays on the Septuagint* (Supplements to Vetus Testamentum, 72; Leiden: Brill, 1999e), pp. 257–269 [Reprint from *Proceedings of a Conference at the Annenberg Research Institute May 15–16, 1989* (Philadelphia, 1990), pp. 215–233].

———, 'Three Dimensions of Words in the Septuagint', in E. Tov (ed.), *The Hebrew and Greek Bible: Collected Essays on the Septuagint* (Supplements to Vetus Testamentum, 72; Leiden: Brill, 1999f), pp. 85–94 [Reprint from *Revue Biblique* 83 (1976): 529–544].

———, 'The Background of the Sense Divisions in the Biblical Texts', in M. Korpel and J. Oesch (eds), *Delimitation Criticism* (Pericope, 1; Assen: Van Gorcum, 2000), pp. 312–350.

———, *Textual Criticism of the Hebrew Bible* [Second Revised Edition] (Minneapolis: Fortress, 2001).

———, 'The Indication of Small Sense Units (Verses) in Biblical Manuscripts', in M.F.J. Baasten and W.T. van Peursen (eds), *Hamlet on a Hill: Semitic and Greek Studies Presented to Professor T. Muraoka on the Occasion of his Sixty-Fifth Birthday* (Orientalia Lovaniensia Analecta 118; Leuven: Peeters, 2003), pp. 473–486.

Tuell, S.S., 'Divine Presence and Absence in Ezekiel's Prophecy', in M.S. Odell and J.T. Strong (eds), *The Book of Ezekiel: Theological and Anthropological Perspectives* (Society of Biblical Literature Symposium Series, 9; Atlanta: Society of Biblical Literature, 2000a), pp. 97–118.

———, 'Haggai-Zechariah: Prophecy after the Manner of Ezekiel', *Society of Biblical Literature 2000 Seminar Papers* (Atlanta: Society of Biblical Literature, 2000b), pp. 263–286.

Turner, N., 'The Greek Translators of Ezekiel', *Journal of Theological Studies*, 7 (1956): 12–24.

Turner, P.D.M., 'The Translator(s) of Ezekiel Revisited: Idiosyncratic LXX Renderings as a Clue to Inner History', in R. Sollamo and S. Sipilä (eds), *Helsinki Perspectives on the Translation Technique of the Septuagint* (The Finnish Exegetical Society in Helsinki; Göttingen: Vandenhoeck & Ruprecht, 2001), pp. 279–307.

van der Kooij, A., 'Accident or Method? On 'Analogical' Interpretation in the Old Greek of Isaiah and in 1QIsaa', *Bibliotheca Orientalis*, 43 (1986): 366–375.

van der Merwe, C.H.J., Naude, J.A., and Kroeze, J.H., *A Biblical Hebrew Reference Grammar* (Sheffield: Academic Press, 1999).

van Seters, J., 'The Creation of Man and the Creation of the King', *Zeitschrift für die Alttestamentliche Wissenschaft*, 101:3 (1989): 333–342.

VanderKam, J.C., *An Introduction to Early Judaism* (Grand Rapids: Eerdmans, 2001).

Vawter, B., and Hoppe, L.J., *A New Heart: A Commentary on the Book of Ezekiel* (International Theological Commentary; Grand Rapids: Eerdmans, 1991).

Vermes, G., *The Dead Sea Scrolls in English* [3rd Edition] (Sheffield: Journal for the Study of the Old Testament, 1987, Orig. Pub., 1962).

Wacholder, B.Z., 'Ezekiel and Ezekielianism as Progenitors of Essenianism', in D. Dimant and U. Rappaport (eds), *In The Dead Sea Scrolls. Forty Years of Research* (Studies on the Texts of the Desert of Judah, 10; Leiden: Brill, 1992), pp. 186–196.

———, 'Deutero Ezekiel and Jeremiah (4Q384–4Q391): Identifying the Dry Bones of Ezekiel 37 as the Essenes', in L.H. Schiffman, E. Tov and J.C. VanderKam (eds), *The Dead Sea Scrolls: Fifty Years After Their Discovery. Proceedings of the Jerusalem Congress, July 20–25, 1997* (Jerusalem: Israel Exploration Society, 2000), pp. 445–461.

Waltke, B.K., and O'Connor, M., *An Introduction to Biblical Hebrew Syntax* (Winona Lake: Eisenbrauns, 1990).

Wegner, P.D., *The Journey from Texts to Translations: The Origin and Development of the Bible* (Grand Rapids: Baker, 1999).

Weissert, D., 'Qal versus Nif'al in Ezekiel 37:8', *Textus*, 21 (2002): 129–138.

Wevers, J.W., 'Evidence of the Text of the John H. Scheide Papyri for the Translation of the Status Constructus in Ezekiel', *Journal of Biblical Literature*, 70 (1951): 211–216.

———, *Ezekiel* (The Century Bible; London: Nelson, 1969); reprinted (Grand Rapids: Eerdmans, 1982).

Whybray, R.N., *The Making of the Pentateuch: A Methodological Study* (Journal for the Study of the Old Testament Supplement Series, 53; Sheffield: Academic Press, 1994, Orig. Pub., 1987).

Williams, T.F., 'שמם', in W.A. VanGemeren (ed.), *New International Dictionary of Old Testament Theology and Exegesis*, Vol. 4 (Grand Rapids: Zondervan, 1997), pp. 167–171.

Williamson, R., *Jews in the Hellenistic World: Philo* (Cambridge Commentaries on Writings of the Jewish and Christian World 200 BC to AD 200, Vol. 1, Part 2; Cambridge: University Press, 1989).

Wilson, R.R., 'Prophecy in Crisis: The Call of Ezekiel', *Interpretation*, 38:2 (1984): 117–130.

Wong, K.L., *The Idea of Retribution in the Book of Ezekiel* (Supplements to Vetus Testamentum, 87; Leiden: Brill, 2001).

——, 'The Masoretic and Septuagint Texts of Ezekiel 39,21–29', *Ephemerides Theologicae Lovanienses*, 78:1 (2002): 130–147.

——, 'Profanation/Sanctification and the Past, Present and Future of Israel in the Book of Ezekiel', *Journal for the Study of the Old Testament*, 28:2 (2003): 210–239.

Wright, B.G., 'The Apocryphon of Ezekiel and 4QPseudo-Ezekiel', in L.H. Schiffman, E. Tov and J.C. VanderKam (eds), *The Dead Sea Scrolls: Fifty Years After Their Discovery. Proceedings of the Jerusalem Congress, July 20–25, 1997* (Jerusalem: Israel Exploration Society, 2000), pp. 463–480.

Wright, B.G., Satran, D., and Stone, M.E., *The Apocryphal Ezekiel* (Atlanta: Society of Biblical Literature, 2000).

Wright, C.J.H., *The Message of Ezekiel: A New Heart and a New Spirit* (The Bible Speaks Today; Leicester: IVP, 2001).

Yadin, Y., *Masada: Herod's Fortress and the Zealots' Last Stand* (Jerusalem: Steimatzky's, 1966).

Yeivin, I., *Introduction to the Tiberian Masorah* [translated and edited by E.J. Revell] (Society for Biblical Literature; Missoula, MT: Scholars, 1980).

Ziegler, J., 'Die Bedeutung des Chester-Beatty-Scheide 967 für die Textüberlieferung der Ezechiel-LXX', *Zeitschrift für die Alttestamentliche Wissenschaft*, 20 (1945–1948): 76–94.

——, *Septuaginta Vetus Testamentum Graecum: Ezechiel [2nd Edition]* (Septuaginta 16/1; Göttingen: Vandenhoeck & Ruprecht, 1977).

Zimmerli, W., *Ezekiel: A Commentary on the Book of the Prophet Ezekiel, Chapters 1–24* (Hermeneia; Philadelphia: Fortress, 1979).

——, *I am Yahweh* ([edited by W. Brueggemann,]; Atlanta: John Knox, 1982).

——, *Ezekiel 2: A Commentary on the Book of the Prophet Ezekiel, Chapters 25–48* (Hermeneia; Philadelphia: Fortress, 1983).

TEXTUAL INDEX

AUTHOR INDEX

SUBJECT INDEX

SUPPLEMENTS TO VETUS TESTAMENTUM

84. COHEN, C.H.R. *Contextual Priority in Biblical Hebrew Philology*. An Application of the Held Method for Comparative Semitic Philology. 2001. ISBN 90 04 11670 2 (In preparation).
85. WAGENAAR, J.A. *Judgement and Salvation*. The Composition and Redaction of Micah 2-5. 2001. ISBN 90 04 11936 1
86. MCLAUGHLIN, J.L. *The Marzēaḥ in sthe Prophetic Literature*. References and Allusions in Light of the Extra-Biblical Evidence. 2001. ISBN 90 04 12006 8
87. WONG, K.L. *The Idea of Retribution in the Book of Ezekiel* 2001. ISBN 90 04 12256 7
88. BARRICK, W. Boyd. *The King and the Cemeteries*. Toward a New Understanding of Josiah's Reform. 2002. ISBN 90 04 12171 4
89. FRANKEL, D. *The Murmuring Stories of the Priestly School*. A Retrieval of Ancient Sacerdotal Lore. 2002. ISBN 90 04 12368 7
90. FRYDRYCH, T. *Living under the Sun*. Examination of Proverbs and Qoheleth. 2002. ISBN 90 04 12315 6
91. KESSEL, J. *The Book of Haggai*. Prophecy and Society in Early Persian Yehud. 2002. ISBN 90 04 12368 7
92. LEMAIRE, A. (ed.). *Congress Volume, Basel 2001*. 2002. ISBN 90 04 12680 5
93. RENDTORFF, R. and R.A. KUGLER (eds.). *The Book of Leviticus*. Composition and Reception. 2003. ISBN 90 04 12634 1
94. PAUL, S.M., R.A. KRAFT, L.H. SCHIFFMAN and W.W. FIELDS (eds.). *Emanuel*. Studies in Hebrew Bible, Septuagint, and Dead Sea Scrolls in Honor of Emanuel Tov. 2003. ISBN 90 04 13007 1
95. VOS, J.C. DE. *Das Los Judas*. Über Entstehung und Ziele der Landbeschreibung in Josua 15. ISBN 90 04 12953 7
96. LEHNART, B. *Prophet und König im Nordreich Israel*. Studien zur sogenannten vorklassischen Prophetie im Nordreich Israel anhand der Samuel-, Elija- und Elischa-Überlieferungen. 2003. ISBN 90 04 13237 6
97. LO, A. *Job 28 as Rhetoric*. An Analysis of Job 28 in the Context of Job 22-31. 2003. ISBN 90 04 13320 8
98. TRUDINGER, P.L. *The Psalms of the Tamid Service*. A Liturgical Text from the Second Temple. 2004. ISBN 90 04 12968 5
99. FLINT, P.W. and P.D. MILLER, JR. (eds.) with the assistance of A. Brunell. *The Book of Psalms*. Composition and Reception. 2004. ISBN 90 04 13842 8
100. WEINFELD, M. *The Place of the Law in the Religion of Ancient Israel*. 2004. ISBN 90 04 13749 1
101. FLINT, P.W., J.C. VANDERKAM and E. TOV. (eds.) *Studies in the Hebrew Bible, Qumran, and the Septuagint*. Essays Presented to Eugene Ulrich on the Occasion of his Sixty-Fifth Birthday. 2004. ISBN 90 04 13738 6
102. MEER, M.N. VAN DER. *Formation and Reformulation*. The Redaction of the Book of Joshua in the Light of the Oldest Textual Witnesses. 2004. ISBN 90 04 13125 6
103. BERMAN, J.A. *Narrative Analogy in the Hebrew Bible*. Battle Stories and Their Equivalent Non-battle Narratives. 2004. ISBN 90 04 13119 1
104. KEULEN, P.S.F. VAN. *Two Versions of the Solomon Narrative*. An Inquiry into the Relationship between MT 1 Kgs. 2-11 and LXX 3 Reg. 2-11. 2004. ISBN 90 04 13895 1
105. MARX, A. *Les systèmes sacrificiels de l'Ancien Testament*. Forms et fonctions du culte sacrificiel à Yhwh. 2005. ISBN 90 04 14286 X
106. ASSIS, E. *Self-Interest or Communal Interest*. An Ideology of Leadership in the Gideon, Abimelech and Jephthah Narritives (Judg 6-12). 2005. ISBN 90 04 14354 8

107. WEISS, A.L. *Figurative Language in Biblical Prose Narrative*. Metaphor in the Book of Samuel. 2006. ISBN 90 04 14837 X

108. WAGNER, T. *Gottes Herrschaft*. Eine Analyse der Denkschrift (Jes 6, 1-9,6). 2006. ISBN 90 04 14912 0

109. LEMAIRE, A. (ed.). *Congress Volume Leiden 2004*. 2006. ISBN 90 04 14913 9

110. GOLDMAN, Y.A.P., A. van der Kooij and R.D. Weis (eds.). *Sôfer Mahîr*. Essays in Honour of Adrian Schenker Offered by Editors of *Biblia Hebraica Quinta*. 2006. ISBN 90 04 15016 1

111. WONG, G.T.K. *Compositional Strategy of the Book of Judges*. An Inductive, Rhetorical Study. 2006. ISBN 90 04 15086 2

112. HØYLAND LAVIK, M. *A People Tall and Smooth-Skinned*. The Rhetoric of Isaiah 18. 2006. ISBN 90 04 15434 5

113. REZETKO, R., T.H. LIM and W.B. AUCKER (eds.). *Reflection and Refraction*. Studies in Biblical Historiography in Honour of A. Graeme Auld. 2006. ISBN 90 04 14512 5

115. BERGSMA, J.S. *The Jubilee from Leviticus to Qumran*. A History of Interpretation. 2006. ISBN-13 978 90 04 15299 1. ISBN-10 90 04 15299 7

116. GOFF, M.J. *Discerning Wisdom*. The Sapiential Literature of the Dead Sea Scrolls. 2006. ISBN-13 978 90 04 14749 2. ISBN-10 90 04 14749 7

117. DE JONG, M.J. *Isaiah among the Ancient Near Eastern Prophets*. A Comparative Study of the Earliest Stages of the Isaiah Tradition and the Neo-Assyrian Prophecies. 2007. ISBN 978 90 04 16161 0

118. FORTI, T.L. *Animal Imagery in the Book of Proverbs*. 2007. ISBN 978 90 04 16287 7

119. PINÇON, B. *L'énigme du bonheur*. Étude sur le sujet du bien dans le livre de Qohélet. 2008. ISBN 978 90 04 16717 9

120. ZIEGLER, Y. *Promises to Keep*. The Oath in Biblical Narrative. 2008. ISBN 978 90 04 16843 5

121. VILLANUEVA, F.G. *The 'Uncertainty of a Hearing'*. A Study of the Sudden Change of Mood in the Psalms of Lament. 2008. ISBN 978 90 04 16847 3

122. CRANE, A.S. *Israel's Restoration*. A Textual-Comparative Exploration of Ezekiel 36–39. 2008. ISBN 978 90 04 16962 3